PMO
to
Delhi Secretariat

RTIs Expose Common-Wealth Scam

Attention Authors

'We Convert Fighters into Writers.' That's the motto of Manas Publications since more than four decades. Our message to the world is that India can win the battle not only by the bullet but also by the pen. There is no dearth of intellectuals in our country, but their knowledge is confined to them only. No sincere effort has been made by any other publisher to channelise their knowledge in national interest. That is why the talent of a large number of intellectuals remains latent. An author transforms his knowledge into a manuscript, and it is our job to spread his/her knowledge by converting it into a beautiful book. For over four decades, Manas has been motivating the intellectuals by publishing their manuscripts and would like to publish your manuscript too. So if you or your colleagues have any manuscript ready for publication or are working on it, kindly contact us with detailed synopsis and list of contents. We will transform your work into a valuable publication. If you wish, we can also suggest you the suitable subjects for writing the books related to your area of expertise. Manas is known for its publishing quality and commitments. We take utmost care in production and give wide publicity to the book as well as its author through our national and international distribution network.

PMO
to
Delhi Secretariat

RTIs Expose Common-Wealth Scam

Vivek Garg
Advocate & RTI Activist

Manas Publications
(We Convert Fighters into Writers)
New Delhi-110002 (INDIA)

MANAS PUBLICATIONS
(We Convert Fighters into Writers)
(Publishers, Library Suppliers, Importers & Exporters)
4402/5-A, Ansari Road (Opp. HDFC Bank)
Darya Ganj, New Delhi-110 002 (India)
Off. (23260783, 23265523, Fax: 011-23272766
E-mail: manaspublications@vsnl.com
manaspublications@gmail.com

We have tried our level best to print the best possible quality of the documents, received from the PMO/ Ministries in photostat mode

ISBN 978-81-7049-436-2
₹ 995/-

Designed at
Manas Publications

Printed in India at
HS Offsets, Delhi
and published by Mrs Suman Lata for
Manas Publications, 4402/5-A,
Ansari Road, (Opp. HDFC Bank),
Darya Ganj, New Delhi-110 002 (INDIA)

Preface

In any government or administration prone to corruption, the seeds of corruption are watered by the people sitting at the top. In other words, without the blessings of the top brass, the corrupt just can't put their nefarious plans in operation. We can draw a long list of huge scams blessed by the powers that be. But to name just a few – Commonwealth Games (CWG) scam, 2G spectrum scam, NHRM scam, MNREGA scam, toll plaza scam, fodder scam and hawala scam. These scams cost India lakhs of crores of rupees. The amount involved in the CWG scam is so huge that one cannot imagine this scam materializing without the involvement of the top politicians. Here an obvious poser is: How the then Sports Minister Suresh Kalmadi could indulge in this huge swindling on his own without the knowledge of the Prime Minister, the Delhi Chief Minister, the Ministry of Finance and others?

While trying to get answer to this question, the CWG scam became yet another cause for me to expose corruption at high places. Over the past few months, I have been seeking information from different government departments (including the PMO) to get to the bottom of the CWG scam and other scams involving gross misuse of precious public funds.

Regarding the CWG scam, I filed a series of applications under the RTI Act in the PMO, the Ministry of Sports and Youth Affairs, the Ministry of Finance, the Ministry of Home Affairs, the CWG Organising Committee and the office of Delhi Chief Minister. From these offices, I have not yet got all the documents sought under the RTI Act, as they have tried their best to hide the information unpalatable for them. They provided me the documents on pick-and-choose basis. But still I succeeded in laying my hands on many documents connected with the CWG scam sent by PMO and other departments. Maybe, the involvement of some big fish in the CWG scam is the main reason for all the desired documents not reaching me.

While going through a bunch of documents sent by the PMO, I found many controversial and eye-opening details which prima facie indicate the role of many top politicians in the CWG scam. Some of these documents, I gave to the media to bring the truth in the public domain. Because of the hue and cry raised by these important documents in the political circles and among people, I thought it proper to bring them in the book form to make public many startling revelations related to the CWG scam, which have still not come in the public domain.

In fact, few people know that the RTI Act was first prepared as the Freedom of Information Act 2002 and the present RTI Act is a polished version of the same. To curb scams and corruption at all levels, the Right to Information (RTI) Act, 2005 has the great potential of proving a highly effective tool. In fact, the RTI Act has transformed the whole of India into people's real parliament by empowering the masses to elicit information from the government on any issue. Now, a common man, like an elected Member of Parliament (MP), is empowered to make government accountable by inquiring about the implementation (wrong or right) of its policies and its budgetary expenditures.

Today, infrastructure development should be the utmost priority of the government. Many ambitious schemes for development have been launched by the government, but their full benefits could not be realized because of poor infrastructure, corruption and technological inadequacies, thus wasting precious public resources. Needless to say, our country today is in the clutches of many self-centred leaders, lacking a pragmatic vision. Political corruption has badly damaged the trust and strength of the nation. Cobbling together of various political parties to usurp power has further damaged the prospect of expressing a strong national will to address serious concerns besetting India on priority. Crafty and corrupt among politicians are always engaged in queering the pitch against their political opponents. They are the major roadblocks on the way to building a national consensus on resolving important issues that have been lingering for decades. Our leaders of diverse political hues inflame the fragile emotions and passions of the masses, provoking them into flagrant violation of law.

Unfortunately, our leaders have drawn no lessons from the exposure of alarmingly rising corruption cases. People at the helm are still busy bestowing benefits and bounties on their henchmen and cronies without any regard for the rule of law, justice and equality. In 2010, Transparency International (TI) ranked India 87th on its corruption index of 178 countries. Here an interesting fact is that China is at the 78th position in this index. It implies that we are nine places ahead of China in corruption as per the TI index.

Computerization of government services, e-banking, economic reforms and the RTI Act have helped little in tackling the corruption and making the system more transparent. The economic reforms of 1991 have reduced the red tape, bureaucratic hurdles and the Licence-Permit Raj to a great extent. But, corruption can be removed only if it is rooted out first at the top. Then as a cascading effect everything else down the line will become corruption-free. The big fish must be caught first and penalized properly. Unless the law is used in letter and spirit to punish the corrupt whose deeds are no less dangerous than those of the terrorists, the helpless common man will continue to swallow the venom of corruption which is fast eating into the fabric of our motherland.

Vivek Garg
Advocate & RTI Activist

PMO to Delhi Secretariat

Speed Post A.D.
Right to Information

PRIME MINISTER'S OFFICE

South Block
New Delhi – 110 101

No. RTI/3213/2011-PMR

Dated: 20 September, 2011

To:
Shri Vivek Garg
18/1, Ground Floor
Shakti Nagar
Delhi - 110 002

Subject: Application under Right to Information Act, 2005.

Sir,

Please refer to this office's interim reply of even number dated 7.9.2011 and memorandum of even number dated 12.8.2011, transferring your application dated 7.8.2011, received on 8.8.2011, to the Department of Sports regarding relevant portion of points 6, 7 and 12, for action as appropriate. The matter was also referred to the office for providing input in respect of this office. Information provided by the office, is enclosed (3 pages). Copy of documents referred to in the enclosure, is enclosed (1044 pages).

2. For the purpose of section 19 of the Right to Information Act, 2005, Shri Amit Agrawal, Director, is the appellate authority in respect of this office.

Yours faithfully,

(Sanjukta Ray)
Deputy Secretary and
Central Public Information Officer
☎ : 2307 4072

Encl: As above

सत्यमेव जयते

SHEILA DIKSHIT
CHIEF MINISTER

GOVT. OF NATIONAL CAPITAL TERRITORY OF DELHI
DELHI SECRETARIAT, I.P. ESTATE, NEW DELHI-110113
PHONE : 23392020, 23392030 FAX : 23392111

D.O.NO.: CMO/VS/2011/152
Dated : 28/03/2011

Respected Prime Minister,

What does one make of a report which begins by stating that "even though, city infrastructure was 'adequate' for hosting the Commonwealth Games 2010 even in 2003, Delhi government embarked on an ambitious programme to upgrade city infrastructure at a considerable cost" thereby suggesting that there was a malafide design to undertake city infrastructure projects.

I feel constrained but compelled to point out that the HLC report is not just full of contradiction and anomalies but has caused damage to the image of my Government & myself personally. This is not acceptable.

The HLC report on city infrastructure seems to be the product of a paranoia, suspecting every action, every individual and assumes that every policy bespoke for a 'grand construct of corruption'. The report has been placed on the net making it available for public consumption without giving any opportunity to the senior officers and political executives of GNCT of Delhi concerned, to rebut HLC's observations which are speculative and presumptuous. The intent to slander with which the report constructs to tarnish the endeavour of GNCT of Delhi is apparent with the choice of phrases like "how stage was set for restricted tender", "subterfuge to share the spoils", "Method in madness" and "unusual interests" - all assumptions.

The report insinuates at a grand machination conspiring to achieve illegal gains in which all and sundry acted in tandem. The details of the report go on to justify this figment of "conspiracy theory" by deliberately choosing to adopt a logic of convenience indicative of palpable corruption in every policy, every design, every tender and every execution.

With this assumption of ubiquitous corruption in every intent and action, this "conspiracy theory" of HLC report states that the delay in the execution of the projects was deliberately done in order to inflate the cost in the remaining compressed time limit and this scheme started way back in the year 2002-03.

It is important to understand that this grand conspiracy which started 6 years in advance should have a set of conspirators who are certain of getting these spoils after the lapse of 8 years by virtue of the delay. Who are the conspirators? Is it the elected Government, which faced an election in 2008. Considering that election is always an unpredictable phenomenon for any elected Government without any certainty of resumption of power. If the re-election of the ruling party was not certain, then was the delay done to benefit another government – possibly to the Opposition?

Was it AGMU cadre senior officers who are liable to be transferred every 3-4 years out of Delhi? Or the senior engineers coming from CPWD on deputation to Government of NCT of Delhi who goes back to their parent cadre after 5 years. I wonder whether any senior officer or any senior engineer working in 2002-03 could hope to be present in Delhi during 2008-10. It skips comprehension as to who would be the probable conspirator of this delay certain of "sharing the booty" after a lapse of 8 years.

The report mentions the chronology in which No Objection Certificates were given by different authorities outside the purview of Government of NCT of Delhi, e.g. DUAC, DDA, UTTIPEC, MCD for various projects. In certain cases the time difference between the initial application for a No Objection Certificate and the final clearance from the authority is almost two years. If the report is to be believed then all the statutory authorities in-charge of giving clearances to the projects of Delhi are complicit in this purported act of delay. It is shocking to learn that the report blames the GNCT of Delhi for the delay in the commencement of all city improvement projects and goes on to state on page-4 para-5 of Executive Summary that there was a three year period of inactivity (end 2003 to end 2006) except two projects (Geeta Colony fly over and Munak canal) which had been on the anvil for some time. This delay compromised every subsequent stage of planning and execution. The report has totally failed to appreciate the efforts made by the Government of NCT of Delhi during this period.

I had drawn the attention of the Union Finance Minister towards the need for infusion of funds to enable the development of the city commensurate with standards set worldwide vide my letter dated 28.6.2004. After giving the detailed account of the efforts of the NCT to raise its own resources along with the status of committed liabilities for maintaining the city infrastructure and implementing the reform measures, the need for a separate budget for the infrastructure development of the city was highlighted. I pointed out that most of the countries that hosted the Commonwealth Games started preparations at least 5 to 6 years in advance. I further stated that major projects, like expressway, elevated roads, flyovers, sub-ways take upto 3 to 4 years to complete. The request was made to the Finance Minister to consider this letter as an effort to highlight Delhi's situation and an expression of our need for a specific allocation of funds to fulfill the responsibilitie of the city government. I even requested for convening a meeting where some thought can be given to the manner in which this can now be brought on the drawing broad and where there is clarity about the subsequent steps to be taken by all the stakeholders.

I followed up with another letter to the Union Minister, Sports & Youth Affairs informing about my request for funding and suggesting that an Apex level steering committee for the Commonwealth Games be constituted to coordinate the activities of various Union Ministries and inputs from Delhi Government. I further suggested that a local level Coordination and Implementation Committee should be formed.

A letter was sent on May 17, 2005 to the Union Secretary, M/O Sports & Youth Affairs by the Chief Secretary of Delhi indicating the requirement of additional funds to the tune of ₹ 1314 crores. This was followed up by a letter from the Finance Minister of Delhi Government dated May 22, 2005 to the Dy. Chairman, Planning Commission about the requirement for providing plan funds amounting to ₹ 1314 crores wherein the justification were highlighted. The letter also explained the financial position of the Govt. of NCT of Delhi which had been drawing funds from the Small Savings Fund (NSSF) to meet its plan and non-plan liabilities. The Finance Minister GNCTD clearly stated "it will be difficult for the Government to prepare for the Commonwealth Games unless additional budget provision is set aside to cater to specific requirements".

In the 9th meeting of Core Group of Ministers on 18.1.2006, a decision was taken to the effect that the GNCT of Delhi shall include all its requirements covering civic infrastructure and venue infrastructure in its proposal being submitted to the Planning Commission. As a follow up, the Committee of Secretaries (CoS) in its meeting dated 5.5.2006 recommended setting up of a committee under Member Secretary, Planning commission for development of infrastructure of Delhi. It further recommended that the committee would identify comprehensively various infrastructural projects and facilities required by Delhi for the smooth conduct of the Commonwealth Games and would submit their report within a fortnight. The planning commission gave in principle approval for allocating ₹ 770 crore for development of Delhi's infrastructure, however the actual flow of plan fund for CWG infrastructure projects commenced from 2007-08.

The HLC has failed to appreciate the budgetary constraints faced by the GNCTD for commencing infrastructure works. It has also failed to appreciate the need for consultations with the Organizing Committee, which was only constituted in February 2005 and the Planning Commission. Finally, it has overlooked the efforts made by the GNCTD which in spite of budgetary constraints started formulation of project proposals and finalized 13 of the 24 flyover projects and submitted the same to the statutory authorities by 2005.

In the series of indictment against city government the report cites the bifurcation of EFC wherein instead of one EFC for projects ranging from ₹ 5 to 100 crores under the Finance Minister was replaced by two EFCs of which one EFC dealing with projects from ₹ 5 to 50 crores continue to be headed by the Finance Minister while the second EFC was set up under the Chairmanship of the Chief Minister for considering projects costing between ₹ 50 to 100 crores and for all Commonwealth Games related projects. The HLC did not care to consult the Chief Minister or Finance Minister, any other Ministries or officials of the Finance department to ascertain the reason for bifurcating the EFC. This was adopted to expedite decisions involving all stake-holders on the spot.

While monitoring the projects and progress of work of various projects, the Chief Minister was faced with conflicting versions by the subject Ministers and the Finance Minister. While the Finance Ministry felt that the projects placed before the EFC needed further clarification and higher level of deliberations, the project implementing Ministries complained of delays in getting the financial clearances. As a first step to improve better coordination and communication, it was directed that the meetings of the EFC will be attended by the concerned Minister. When it was found that even this mechanism was not functioning properly, I reluctantly took the initiative (despite being already very overburdened) of heading the EFC for timely clearance of a limited number of CWG projects and for the clearance of projects between ₹ 50 to 100 crores. Moreover, all projects above 100 crores are cleared by the Cabinet. In these EFC meetings both the Finance Minister and concerned Minister were present. The report has failed to appreciate the need for bifurcating the EFC and ascertaining the reason for speedy clearances of Commonwealth Games related projects through this bifurcation.

In its observation the report suggests the total absence of coordination mechanism and planning for review intervention and course correction. At the same time it refers to the "Empowered

Committee", the "committee under cabinet secretary" and "Group of Ministers" for interagency coordination contradicting its own surmise. The HLC has failed to appreciate the fact that the various statutory authorities in Delhi that do not come under GNCT of Delhi and the act of reconciliation of varying demands of these statutory authorities could not have been possible without the existence of the Empowered Committee set up by the Cabinet Secretariat on the request of GNCT of Delhi. The report has also ignored the fact that the Group of Ministers and the monitoring committee under Cabinet Secretary were in existence precisely for the monitoring and resolution of all CWG related issues on a regular basis. There are many instances when the matter of non-clearance of projects by DUAC/ASI and other authorities was taken up in the CoS and even in the GoM. The failure of HLC to highlight the role of DUAC/ASI and other statutory agencies in delaying the implementation of the projects and the consequential cost escalation is in-explicable.

A comprehensive city development plan was prepared after several rounds of deliberations and presentations before the CoS and the Planning Commission. Surprisingly, the report states that there was no comprehensive plan for the Games and all decisions were taken by the Government of NCT of Delhi in an adhoc manner. The report also fails to acknowledge that the city improvement strategy having 76 major projects cannot be planned overnight and improvisations are inevitable to adjust with the requirements and stipulations insisted by other agencies. Inclusion of new projects therefore became necessary for the conduct of the games. All the departments working for the city development were entrusted with the task to execute the projects required for the city improvement and conduct of the games. Without going into the plans of these departments, the report jumps to the conclusion that there was a lack of comprehensive planning process.

The rampant contradictions in the report are apparent as at one place it suggests one policy guideline while elsewhere, a completely opposite policy guideline is suggested. It goes on to suggest in Chapter 15 that the executing agencies should have project specific prequalification but when the same agency adopted such a method for streetlight up-gradation, the report decries the policy suggesting that it pre-empted a wider participation in tender. The report carelessly alludes to cartelization in almost all the projects without giving any tangible evidence.

Shockingly the report sets out to seek probable connivance by calculating the project cost and the contractors who secured these works. It reaches to a perverse conclusion that few contractors bagged the major contracts with the complicity of officers. It goes to the ridiculous extent of suggesting that in different time periods different contractors were favoured suggesting a favourable season for these contractors. The report blatantly hints that few big contractors like M/s. Gammon India Ltd, M/s. Larson & Turbo Ltd and M/s. Hindustan Construction Company were kept at bay in the projects floated by PWD by dividing them into smaller packages. It is an established principle that the projects are awarded only to the lowest bidder. In light of faith shown by the HLC in these three big companies, may I suggest that a government directive be issued across the country to ensure the participation of these companies on their terms and conditions! One wonders whether the HLC has any conclusive evidence that

8

these three companies are the most straight forward and efficient companies in India.

In fact I am informed that Gammon India put in its bids for at least 8 projects and L&T for 1 project in PWD. They did not secure the contracts because they were not the L-1. Therefore, it is completely erroneous for HLC to allege that these big companies did not participate in the tender process only because the works in few projects were split to match the timelines.

The intent of the report is apparent from the fact that it makes an appalling suggestion to debunk the CPWD Works Manual itself, after finding that all justification of rates prepared by the department fall within the guidelines of the Manual. The CPWD Works Manual is the holy touch-stone for all engineering works in India. It is horrifying to note that the basic principles enunciated in the manual itself are vilified by the report. Though the report claims that it has interviewed some officers but it is apparent it has not bothered to understand the logic behind the splitting of works from the officers concerned. As the games drew closer and delay in No Objection Certificates from various statutory authorities put the projects against a tight schedule, it was prudent to have works executed in smaller packages to ensure more commitment of resources from all available contractors.

The report states that few projects like; Barapullah Nallah elevated corridor. Suneheri Nallah project have limited legacy value and millennium park depot is temporary in nature. It does not need additional evidence to show that all these projects are serving the city to their full potential. I am informed that the Barapulla elevated Road is already drawing peak hour traffic of

9

more than 5000 PCUs. The utility of all these projects cannot be slighted only on unverified conjectures.

The report talks about the dedicated lanes as an alternative to these infrastructure projects specially the Barapullah Nallah Elevated Road and Salimgarh Fort Road. The report totally undermines the fact that the additional infrastructure option in terms of Barapullah Nallah elevated road was mooted only because of the existing chicken neck at Bhairo Marg, which can't be made wider because of the heritage monument Purana Quila. The report has also glossed over the fact that the dedicated lanes during the games were successful only because a huge load from these lanes could be shifted onto Barapullah elevated corridor throughout the day. The traffic snarls without these elevated corridors would have been immense if the games related vehicles load was not taken off from the usual roads. Besides, the presumptive conclusion of the report regarding the sufficiency of dedicated lane for ferrying the athletes is without any concrete technical understanding.

Today after six months of the games, the streets where street-scaping had been carried out provide a pleasant driving experience for all categories of commuters. All necessary arrangements for plantation work were undertaken in advance. The conclusion of the report regarding high mortality of the plants is conjectural and totally contrary to the existing ground realities.

The direct insinuations against the undersigned are deliberate mischievous, defamatory and totally out of context. The report suggests that active interest of the undersigned was observed in the entire decision making process of up-gradation of streetlights hinting obliquely that there was a hidden motive. It goes on to

10

state that "unusual interest was displayed by the Chief Minister in this project. This is demonstrated by the fact that meetings were held at her residence, imported luminaries were approved by her and competition was restricted to only three parties at her instructions". This insidious argument hints that the Chief Minister cannot and should not hold any meeting at her official residence which is a common practice in the executive functioning of our country. In fact, even the senior officers have a camp office facility at their residences.

The report itself mentions that all kinds of luminaries were tested on the poles and were examined by the Group of Ministers and officers. Again it is mentioned that at a different place the lux level of luminaries were tested and found that imported luminaries are showing higher results. The report never questions the findings of these two tests but jumps to a conclusion that the decision to affix imported luminaries was wrong & motivated. This conclusion that the undersigned ordered to use imported luminaries is erroneously arrived at by the HLC by selecting limited phrases from the unofficial note of the Engineer-in-Chief. Though my approval on this note was never sought, it is extremely pertinent to mention here that even this note does not talk about my direct orders to use only imported luminaries. In fact, a detailed reply on the same subject has been earlier sent by the Chief Secretary to the HLC in which it was clearly mentioned that the use of imported luminaries on the category-A roads of PWD was the well considered decision, based on technical inputs and after lots of deliberations at various levels of departments with the objective of upgrading the street lights of Delhi to international standards in the run up to Commonwealth Games - 2010 and

11

beyond. The remarks of HLC stating that decisions in this regard was taken in one of the meetings at Hon'ble Chief Minister's residence are not based on full facts. I am informed that at one stage 29 options of the illumination level were worked out by PWD and presentations were made before the Hon'ble Minister of Finance, Planning, UD and PWD in the month of May, 2007 and the preferred options were identified to meet the international standard of uniformity, Zebra effect and luminance. My concern throughout was limited to selection of aesthetically suitable luminary designs, poles and fittings as these impact the urban scape of the city.

I am informed that the PWD floated expression of interests on global basis without any restriction on the participation of indigenous firms. The final decision for using imported luminaries on A-category wider city roads was based on the recommendation of PWD and was approved by the Cabinet. The HLC in its report has failed to appreciate the reply sent by the Chief Secretary and has gone to the extent of levelling a baseless allegation.

While I note that the HLC report talks about a letter written by Engineer-in-chief in which he mentions that only four companies are suitable for the up-gradation of street lighting to bring it at par with the international standards, the HLC alleges that the decision to include these international companies was that of the undersigned. If the intent was to favour the imported manufactured goods then there would not have been a decision to install these imported fixtures on a few selected wider roads. The prequalification by the clause of having in-house R&D facility for the firms was to ensure that no substandard firm gets the contract.

12

In fact, the report itself suggests prequalification of firms for a major project in Chapter 15.

The phrase used in the report "Unusual interest in the project" hinting at a hidden motive, is fallacious and with malicious intent. I have been highlighting the need for professional landscaping, up-gradation of street lighting and street furniture to international standards right from June 2004. Even after the completion of the games I continue to hold meetings almost on monthly basis to review the functioning of street lights. I have instituted a system whereby daily reports on the efficiency of new street lights are received in my office. In my review meetings, I have been extremely harsh with top executives of the firms which have installed the street lights and warned them that there will be no tolerance in respect of ensuring complete efficiency and functionality of the lights.

In a similar vein it is written in the report that "after the Dubai visit of the Chief Minister the up-gradation of street signages was undertaken". The improprietary of the words used here are highly objectionable and can be construed in a negative manner.

You would agree that it is the bounden duty of any Chief Executive to encourage its team to adopt the best practices of world class cities. The signages of the city of Dubai were found to be of good standard during my visit which was worth emulating. (I may add that my visit to Dubai was not in anyway connected with the CWG) I was impressed with the signages and cited it as an example which our city could follow. The reference of this visit has been put in such a manner that the positive outcome of adoption of best signage standard is eclipsed by a patently negative understanding.

I wish to emphasize that all the up-gradation work done was not with the intent for only 10 days of the Games but also a legacy value for the Capital city of Delhi. Commonwealth Games were taken as an opportunity as the Asiad Games were in 1982. I reiterate that Government allocations are not as per personal fancy but are policy based, need based, project size based, time constrained based and also legacy based.

As the head of the executive, one has to rise to the occasion in every respect when the prestige of the nation is at stake. I fear that the hurdles and predicaments faced during the execution of the project have been forgotten in an effort to find only faults in the process. Post-mortem of an event is easy when the efforts and circumstance are overlooked. The most disheartening aspect of the report is that it has only tried to castigate each and every endeavor and malign all officers and political executives who worked selflessly for the prestige of the Nation and for hosting an International Games event – the largest ever by our nation. I wish to recall Mike Fennels words "The best ever Commonwealth Games........"

I am deeply disappointed and anguished with the HLC report. My government believed that this committee would throw light on improving governance structures in the city and suggest organizational reforms and also identity lapses and misdemeanor, if any, in a fair and impartial manner without prejudice or favour. Instead it turned out to be a report in which conclusions are pre-decided, false averments and statements are written continuously and wrong surmises and conjectures are made.

It is unfortunate that officers and engineers who have toiled unceasingly to meet national goals should be indicted by HLC without being given any opportunity of hearing.

These are my preliminary remarks based on the report downloaded from the web and in the absence of any official communication. A detailed and comprehensive reply would be furnished shortly.

With regards,

Yours sincerely,

(SHEILA DIKSHIT)

Dr.Manmohan Singh,
Hon'ble Prime Minister of India,
South Block,
New Delhi.

सत्यमेव जयते

प्रधान मंत्री

Prime Minister

New Delhi
February 1, 2005

Dear Shri Arjun Singh ji,

I have received your letter of January 26, 2005 regarding Commonwealth Games 2010 at New Delhi.

With warm regards,

Yours sincerely,

(Manmohan Singh)

Shri Arjun Singh
Minister of Human Resource Development
New Delhi

SECRET

अर्जुन सिंह
ARJUN SINGH

सत्यमेव जयते

मानव संसाधन विकास मंत्री
भारत
नई दिल्ली-११० ००१
MINISTER OF
HUMAN RESOURCE DEVELOPMENT
INDIA
NEW DELHI-110 001

Respected Prime Minister,

26th January, 2005.

Under the overall guidance given by you, I am happy to report that all the issues concerning with the Commonwealth Games in India in 2010, that had surfaced recently, have been settled to the satisfaction of all concerned.

I am sending herewith a copy of the issues on which the consensus was reached in the presence of the Hon'ble Congress President, Smt Sonia Gandhi Ji.

With kind regards,

Yours faithfully,

(ARJUN SINGH)

Dr. Manmohan Singh,
Hon'ble Prime Minister of India,
7, Race Course Road,
New Delhi.

DRAFT

DECISION OF THE GROUP OF MINISTERS

At the last meeting of the Group of Ministers (GOM), the communication, PMO ID No. 570/50/C/1/04-ES.II, dated 6.12.2004 was given to all the Members. All the issues concerning the various aspects of conducting the Commonwealth Games of 2010 at New Delhi were discussed and each Member of the GOM expressed his views in the matter. It was further suggested that I should have further discussions with the Minister of Sports, Shri Sunil Dutt and the Chairman of the Indian Olympic Association, Shri Suresh Kalmadi.

After a series of discussions the consensus arrived at was that:

(a) there shall be an Empowered Committee headed by the Minister of Sports, Shri Sunil Dutt which will have the overriding power and responsibility for overseeing and coordinating the Commonwealth Games. The Minutes of the other Committees mentioned in this paper below shall be submitted to the Empowered Committee periodically for its information and such guidance that it may deem fit to give.

(b) as is customary, the Indian Olympic Association will organize the Commonwealth Games and its Chairman will head the Organizing Committee. The Organising Committee will deal with the Government of India through the Ministry of Youth Affairs and Sports and with the Delhi Government. The Organising Committee will have 13 Members, who will be appointed by the Chairman in consultation with GOM.

(c) A three-member Sub-committee of the GOM, headed by Finance Minister, Shri P. Chidambaram will supervise and deal with all financial matters. The other members of the sub-Committee will be decided by GOM.

(d) A Committee headed by Lt. Governor of Delhi and Chief Minister of Delhi as its Vice Chairman will look after the construction of stadium and other infrastructure facilities required for the Games. The other Members of the Committee will be appointed by GOM.

(e) A Committee of Secretaries (COS) headed by the Cabinet Secretary will be responsible for the implementation of the decisions of the GOM regarding the Commonwealth games. The Sports Department through its Secretary will service this Committee.

MINISTER FOR HUMAN RESOURCE DEVELOPMENT

A copy of the decisions taken by the Group of Ministers constituted for overseeing the organization and conducting of Commonwealth Games – 2010 in its meeting held on 29 January 2005 is enclosed herewith for your kind perusal.

(ARJUN SINGH)
01 February 2005

Hon'ble Prime Minister

COMMONWEALTH GAMES 2010 : DECISIONS OF THE GROUP OF MINISTERS (GOM)

The Group of Ministers constituted for overseeing the organization and conduct of Commonwealth Games of 2010 met on 29th January 2005 at Shastri Bhavan, New Delhi and took the following decisions:

(a) An Apex Committee headed by the Minister of Sports, Shri Sunil Dutt shall be constituted which will have the over-riding power and responsibility for overseeing and coordinating the Commonwealth Games. The Minutes of all the other Committees related to the conduct of Commonwealth Games 2010 shall be submitted to the Apex Committee periodically for its information. The Chairman of the Apex Committee can also call for such information, which he deems fit and can give such guidance that may be required. The Chairman of the Apex Committee may be kept informed by all the other Committees whenever any major decision is taken.

(b) The organizing Committee shall be headed by the President of the Indian Olympic Association, Shri Suresh Kalmadi and this Committee will conduct the Commonwealth Games

2010. The Organizing Committee will deal with the Government of India through the Ministry of Youth Affairs and Sports and with the Delhi Government. The Executive Board of the Organising Committee will have 15 Members including the Chairman and the Vice Chairman. The members of the Committee will be appointed by the Chairman in consultation with GOM.

(c) A three-member Sub-committee of the GOM, headed by Finance Minister, Shri P. Chidambaram will supervise and deal with all financial matters.

(d) The Lt. Governor of Delhi will have the overall responsibility regarding the games with specific reference to security, law & order and matters coming under DDA.

(e) There will a Sub-Committee headed by CM of Delhi which will look after all other issues that come under the jurisdiction of the Govt. of NCT of Delhi, as per the Constitution.

(f) A Committee of Secretaries (COS) headed by the Cabinet Secretary will be responsible for the implementation of the decisions of the GOM regarding the Commonwealth games. The Sports Department through its Secretary will service this Committee.

(g) All the arrangements worked out above shall apply only to the Commonwealth Games-2010.

सत्यमेव जयते

प्रधान मंत्री

Prime Minister

New Delhi
24 August, 2010

Dear Shri Pal,

I have received your letter of 11 August, 2010 regarding Shri V.K. Verma, Director General, Commonwealth Games, 2010.

With regards,

Yours sincerely,

(Manmohan Singh)

Shri Jagdambika Pal, MP
12, Teen Murti Marg
New Delhi

जगदम्बिका पाल
संसद सदस्य (लोकसभा)
पूर्व मुख्यमंत्री, उ.प्र.

सत्यमेव जयते

फोन / फैक्स: 0522-4000917

दिनांक ....

11-08 2010

Subject:- **Misdeeds and Corrupt Practices of Mr. V.K. Verma, Director General, Commonwealth Games 2010.**

Hon'ble Sir,

With reference to the above subject, it is my prime duty in the national interest to bring the following facts to your knowledge:-

(1) Mr. V.K. Verma was working as Director (Commercial) in Air India. A CBI inquiry was instituted against him for his misdeeds in Air India. The inquiry is still pending and because of that, he was not given any re-employment in the government in spite of his best efforts and he retired at the age of 58 years only.

Here, the important question is that how such a corrupt person has been made Director General (DG) of the prestigious Commonwealth Games which involve huge financial decisions/ transactions/ expenditure?

(2) As DG, VK Verma is getting a whopping Salary + perks of Rs.3 Lacs per month which is an illegal payment because he is also the Associate Vice President of Indian Olympic Association (IOA) and the President of Badminton Association of India (BAI). Both these organizations have got tax exemption from Income Tax Dept. As per rules, any office bearer of IOA or its affiliate bodies like BAI cannot take any salary or perks otherwise income tax exemption can be revoked. Commonwealth Games Organizing Committee (CGOC) is a subsidiary constituted and registered by IOA and, hence, the appointment of V.K.Verma on salary & perks is unlawful and his services are liable to be terminated immediately and salary paid to him needs to be recovered from him.

<u>Some of the corrupt practices and financial irregularities committed by Mr. VK Verma as DG, CGOC</u>:

1) Mr. V.K.Verma, till December, 2009 was the Chairman of Finance Committee of the CGOC which processed all the tenders and stipulated conditions of the tenders for awarding contracts to the tenderers.

2) The majority of tenders, their process and the conditions stipulated therein have been manipulated and exploited by VK Verma and his associates so that the work could be given as per their own choice for their personal gains. Here, it is specifically pointed out that conditions of a large number of tender documents were tailor-made, specially made with connivance of the particular tenderers who were finalized before hand.

3) Even after December'09, VK Verma is involved in each & every financial decision and all the files in respect to the tenders move through him only. Given hereunder are some specific cases of tendering in which he has taken huge commission and shared it with his bosses and colleagues:

रा: उसका रोड सिद्धार्थ नगर, 11, अशोक मार्ग, लखनऊ, फोन : 0522-4000917 9415037381

जगदम्बिका पाल
सांसद सदस्य (लोकसभा)
पूर्व मुख्यमंत्री, उ.प्र.

फोन / फैक्स: 0522-40... ...7

दिनांक ....

11-08 2010

(a) **Queen's Baton Relay**: Both in and outside India, this arrangement was finalized by VK Verma and TS Darbari who is Joint DG, CGOC and is related to Mr. Verma and working under him. VK Verma, DG had personally visited UK in the month of June 2010 and is believed to have taken the settled commission with the officials of AM Films, UK Ltd, flouting all norms of Money Laundering Act, 2002.

(b) **Tender for Overlays**: (like Tents and other temporary setup for the Games)
Rs. 687 Crore.
(Under Process)
It is reported that altogether a commission of more than Rs. 300 Crore has been settled out of this tender alone.

(c) **TSR** (Time, Scoring & Results). Tender has been given to "**Swiss Timing**" (Omega/Longines) for Rs.109 Crore.

It is reported that the total cost of this work as per the international market is not more than Rs. 30 Crore. VK Verma and his colleagues are said to have taken more than Rs.40 Crore commission out of this tender. In addition to this, within the tender, a fraud has been played pertaining to the "**Legacy Equipments**".

(d) Similarly, tendering for **Cleaning & Waste Management** is being handled by VK Verma, DG. This work alone has been awarded for Rs.60 Crore whereas this could entirely be done within Rs.10 - 15 Crore. Obviously, Verma has extracted huge commission out of this.

(e) **Image & Look**: This job is also being looked after by VK Verma alongwith Additional DG Ms. Sangeeta Valinkar. This work has been estimated around Rs.30 Crore whereas this could be done for hardly Rs.10 Crore. The remaining Rs.20 Crore are being shared by VK Verma & others.

(f) **Catering**: The work of catering is also a grey area where VK Verma is involved in heavy irregularities.

(g) Mr. Verma has purchased 26 synthetic **hova courts** from Yonex. These have been purchased @ Rs.6 Lac each costing Rs.156 Lac whereas these could be bought for hardly Rs.26 Lac. Thus, straightaway an excess of Rs.1.30 Crore have been given to Yonex. It is reported that VK Verma has taken a bribe of Rs.75 Lac which has been paid to him in Kuala Lumpur (Malaysia) and London where he is having personal accounts.

(h) The most interesting part in the purchase of hova courts is that VK Verma wrongly and fraudulently manipulated this order for Yonex by saying on record that Yonex is the only approved supplier of hova courts as per World Badminton Federation (WBF) and, hence, no tendering was required. Whereas on the website of WBF, there is a list of 18 potential

आ: उसका रोड सिद्धार्थ नगर, 11, अशोक मार्ग, लखनऊ, फोन : 0522-4000917 9415037381

जगदम्बिका पाल
संसद सदस्य (लोकसभा)
पूर्व मुख्यमंत्री, उ.प्र.

फोन / फैक्स: 0522-4... 17

दिनाक ....

11-08-2010

suppliers who are far better than Yonex. That is why no tender was called which clearly tells the corrupt story of VK Verma.

(i) VK Verma is the key man and right hand of Mr. Suresh Kalmadi, Chairman, CGOC and both are hand in gloves. Mr. Nambiar, Mr. Jaichandran, TS Darbari, VK Verma, Mr. Mahendru and Mr. Kalmadi put together make a single chain and they are involved in all wrongful activities and misdeeds for their personal gains.

(j) Recently, Mr. Verma, as President BAI, has been issued a show-cause notice by the Govt. of India. In this show cause notice dated 4th August'10, in para 9, the GoI has written "***And Whereas President, BAI, vide his letter dated 2nd June 2010, wrote in derogatory terms against Government of India by stating that International Olympic Committee had issued a show cause notice to the Government of India***".

(k) The Hon'ble Prime Minister of India has constituted a High Power Committee under the Cabinet Secretary. I am sure the affairs of the Common Wealth Games would be in right hands now, but I would like to mention here specifically that since Mr. V.K.Verma was instrumental in making the conditions of all the tendered documents, the real manipulation has already been done so that the awards will only be given to the favoured ones of Mr. Verma and Mr. Kalmadi. Hence, the High Power Committee by Cabinet Secretary has to be very careful.

In view of the above findings, I would request you to issue necessary instructions to the concerned authorities for initiating an enquiry in the matter so that dishonest and corrupt persons like V.K. Verma & his said associates are punished appropriately for misusing the public money and destroying the country's image. An urgent action for removing Mr. Verma from the post of DG, CGOC and President, BAI, is unavoidable now as any delay will give him ample time to raze the evidences and prepare him to cover up his other wrong doings and exploit the situation.

Thanking you,

Yours sincerely,

Jagdambika Pal

Dr. Manmohan Singh,
Hon'ble Prime Minister,
Government of India,
New Delhi.

रा: उसका रोड सिद्धार्थ नगर, 11, अशोक मार्ग, लखनऊ, फोन : 0522-4000917 9415037381

उपराज्यपाल
दिल्ली
LIEUTENANT GOVERNOR
DELHI

सत्यमेव जयते

राज निवास
दिल्ली-११००५४
RAJ NIWAS
DELHI-110054

7 October 2010

D.O.No.5(11)/RN/2010/RM/GV/2846

Respected Prime Minister,

The Commonwealth Games Village which was visited last Sunday by Prince Charles and a few days earlier by the Australian Sports Minister has been uniformly receiving very favourable reports from over 6,500 athletes and officials staying at the Village. Apart from the temporary overlay facilities like the kitchen and dining area, set up under contracts awarded by the Organising Committee, the remaining permanent structures including 34 towers having 1,168 flats, an Olympic size swimming pool, two leisure pools, one athletic track, fully equipped gymnasium and weightlifting and wrestling training halls have been constructed under DDA's supervision over the past 2 ½ years. There is great appreciation of the comprehensive nature of facilities provided at the Games Village and the overall pleasant ambience. The other two sports venues built by DDA, viz. Siri Fort Badminton & Squash Complex and the Yamuna Sports Archery & Table Tennis Complex have also elicited commendations for the excellent playing and training facilities. Prince Albert of Monaco who visited the Siri Fort Complex on 4th October also voiced his great appreciation of the world class facilities there.

2. A fortnight earlier the same Games Village had unfortunately received highly exaggerated adverse media coverage focussing on some house-keeping and maintenance issues. These were set right within a few days with the concerted efforts of various agencies. To fairly record the work actually done by each of the agencies, a chart showing the factual position is enclosed for your kind information. The projection given in a certain section of the media that a "turnaround miracle" was achieved within a few days by one single agency after "taking over the management of the Commonwealth Games Village" is, in my perception, unfair, factually incorrect and demoralizing for personnel of all the other agencies who have been working earnestly as a team to expeditiously bridge the gaps that were noticed.

3. As you are well aware, construction of the Village could only be taken up after overcoming a number of hurdles including opposition by Akshardham

सत्यमेव जयते

authorities regarding siting of the Village between the temple and the river, opposition by environmentalists for location of the Village on the Yamuna flood plain and need for several statutory clearances. Construction activity could only commence after approvals, in late 2007. In February-March 2009, serious financial problems were faced by the Developers because of the reluctance of private investors to book flats in the complex. In that situation an out-of-box decision was taken by DDA with the participation of the Union Secretary for Urban Development, Dr. Ramachandran, to purchase 330 flats out of Developer's share and release necessary funds to the Developer in a staggered manner to ensure completion of this prestigious and critical project in time.

4. The first towers were handed over by the Developer to the DDA in mid-June and were immediately passed on to the India Tourism Development Corporation for furnishing. Furnishing work was started by ITDC on 20th June 2010. After furnishing by ITDC, the flats were handed over to the Organising Committee (OC) in a phased manner : 9 Towers being handed over on 07 August 2010, 8 more on 19 August 2010 and the remaining 17 on 30 August 2010. It has to be admitted that when the labour engaged by ITDC for furnishing the flats were laying the items of furniture (nearly 43,000 pieces) in the rooms there was no supervisory control of the operation and the state of cleanliness in the rooms and particularly the wash rooms was adversely impacted.

5. Despite the handing over of furnished flats in stages during August 2010, the Organising Committee did not take proper custodial responsibility thereof.

6. I had visited the Village along with other project sites of the DDA on 29 August 2010 for over four hours and sent a detailed communication on 31 August 2010 to the Hon'ble Union Urban Development Minister, Shri Jaipal Reddy, enclosing my observations and also actions required to be taken by various agencies. This was also copied to the Cabinet Secretary and Sports Secretary. A copy of the communication is enclosed for information (Annexure I).

7. The very first item in my note related to the need for O.C. to establish its custodial control over all flats and deployment of at least 400 persons for

सत्यमेव जयते

house-keeping functions. This note was circulated by the Sports Secretary in the meeting of the Group of Ministers on the 1st of September and thus came to the notice of Chairman, O.C. and C.E.O., Shri Jarnait Singh also. During that visit when Lieutenant General Ashok Kapoor of O.C., in charge of the Games Village had mentioned to me that he did not have proper staff to take charge of the keys of the flats in different towers, I immediately arranged 70 Junior Commissioned officers who had been selected by Raj Niwas from the Delhi Rajya Sainik Board for duty in the parking lots of Municipal Corporation of Delhi to be deployed two per tower in the Games Village, under O.C.'s supervision. They were put in position the next day itself and have been working since. Surprisingly, the Organising Committee deployed their outsourced house-keeping staff only w.e.f. 15 September 2010 through two agencies, namely, I.S.S. and Kalpataru and did not take any corrective action earlier to improve the condition of cleanliness in the flats.

8. When the issue of cleanliness was brought up by some members of the advance teams on 17 September, Shri Sudhir Mittal, Additional Secretary, who is presently posted as Special Director-General in the Organising Committee in charge of the Commonwealth Games Village sought the help of Raj Niwas to deploy some reliable agencies to undertake the requisite cleaning operation in the flats. Raj Niwas immediately responded by asking the Delhi-based Metro Waste Handling Agency and the Global-Excellence-Lions Group (an Indo-U.K. joint venture), the latter of which have been deployed for cleaning operations in the new Delhi International Airport, to send trained personnel to the Village for undertaking cleaning of wash rooms, etc. in the flats. The professional work done by these agencies was fully appreciated by the advance teams and within the space of a little over a week, the inner cleaning issues could be sorted out by these agencies. In case of the towers occupied by New Zealand, Australia and England, the firm, Crest Services provided by the New Zealand High commission undertook the same work to the satisfaction of the respective advance teams.

9. Raj Niwas's efforts to always provide prompt and practical support for Commonwealth Games related projects can further be illustrated by the fact that all co-ordination meetings and decisions in respect of entrusting the electronic surveillance, security and technical support services to Electronic Corporation of India Limited, providing a secure, encrypted communication

सत्यमेव जयते

network, TETRA, for proper communication networking among concerned agencies for the conduct of the Games and drawing up of detailed transportation, parking and traffic plans in respect of all venues and various categories of persons (officials/visitors) were worked out under the close supervision of the Lieutenant Governor. Monitoring of arrangements at the Games Village and other venues and assistance to resolve issues has been continuing on on-going basis, from Raj Niwas.

10. Just a fortnight ago when a foot over-bridge being constructed by Delhi PWD meant for spectators to access Jawahar Lal Nehru Stadium collapsed, the proposal to get it quickly replaced by a temporary bailey bridge with Army's help was mooted at the Law & Order review meeting at Raj Niwas on 23rd September and thereafter acted upon by the Chief Secretary.

11. At the meeting chaired by me at the Games Village on the morning of Monday, the 20th September 2010, which was attended by Cabinet Secretary, Principal Secretary to Prime Minister, Chief Secretary, Delhi, Vice-Chairman, DDA, etc. and other officials, it was decided at the suggestion of the Chief Secretary that instead of an engineer from the DDA an officer from the Delhi State Administration Cadre (DANICS) should be posted in each of the 34 towers for effective liaison between the accompanying officials of the incoming delegations and the agencies responsible for day-to-day maintenance, house-keeping, etc. Seven senior retired Air Force officers working in the DDA had already been assigned responsibility to support the 24 x 7 rectification and maintenance activities in the towers since 23.08.2010. Personnel from the Engineering staff of DDA who had also been on duty at the Village were also placed at the disposal of the DANICS officers. For dealing with problem of water seepage, etc. in the basements and lift wells on account of high flood levels in the Yamuna rivers, dewatering operations were undertaken with the additional deployment of pumps provided by MCD and the Flood Control Department of Delhi Government as well as the dewatering pumps available with the Developer. The Chief engineer (Electrical), DDA was directed to personally supervise the dewatering and drying of affected lift wells and restoration of the 16 lifts out of 73, which had to be temporarily shut down due to the water accumulation in the wells of the shafts. With the return of sunshine and ending of the spell of rain from September 24, within the next five days, i.e., by September 29 all dewatering had been completed and lifts

सत्यमेव जयते

fully restored in all towers. The situation has remained stable without any recurrence of the problem, since then.

12. The additional staff provided under C.M.'s directions by MCD and NDMC have been basically deployed for outside cleaning of the landscape area in the residential zone of the Village and for some cleaning by the NDMC staff in the common areas of towers, like lifts and staircases. None of them have, however, been involved in the deep cleaning of the wash rooms, etc. which had been the main grouse of the advance team officials.

13. The keen, timely and focussed attention devoted by the Cabinet Secretary in monitoring affairs at the Games Village and pointing out areas of concern to concerned agencies as well as tracking the subsequent actions taken to rectify the deficiencies through spot visits have been very valuable.

14. I have thought it fit to bring the above facts to your kind notice by way of the background of what has actually happened.

With Kind Regards,

Yours sincerely,

TKhanna

(Tejendra Khanna)

Encl:As above.

Dr. Manmohan Singh,
Hon'ble Prime Minister of India,
Prime Minister's Office,
South Block,
New Delhi - 110 011

OFFICE OF THE CHIEF MINISTER
GOVERNMENT OF N. C. T. OF DELHI

Subject: Commonwealth Games to be held in Delhi in 2010

This is in continuation of our discussion on the above subject when I had called on you on August 5, 2004.

2. The broad financial requirements relating to the planning for the Commonwealth Games had been indicated by the Government of NCT of Delhi to the Union Finance Ministry and they have intimated that: -

- ***An anticipated expenditure of Rs.400 crores is involved.***
- ***They have advised the Ministry of Youth Affairs & Sports for the effective mobilisation of resources and the sharing of revenues and expenditures with the stakeholders.***

3. The Union Minister for Youth Affairs & Sports has been requested by the Government of NCT of Delhi to set up: -

- ***An apex level committee under the Ministry of Youth Affairs & Sports to coordinate the activities of various Ministries and the Delhi Government.***

4. We have to create new infrastructure, upscale the existing infrastructure and other facilities. This would require the coordinated efforts and work of many Ministries and their departments. It will need a special organisation in the form of a **Core Planning Committee** to plan and design the required infrastructure and to speed up decisions for implementation. The group should be headed by a fairly senior person with adequate power and seniority to cut across the multiplicity of organisations / agencies, tide over inter-ministerial issues and delays and facilitate consultations. The composition of the committee could include: -

- ***Union Ministers for Youth Affairs & Sports; Urban Development; Finance; and Home***
- ***A representative from the Prime Minister's Office.***
- ***Government of NCT of Delhi represented by the Lt. Governor/Chief Minister***
- ***A representative of the Indian Olympic Association [which has bid for the 2016 Olympic Games]***

5. At the local level we will set up the necessary coordination and implementation groups to take forward all decisions taken by the Core Planning Committee.

6. The matter has been discussed with the Lt. Governor also.

Sheila Dikshit

[Sheila Dikshit]
Chief Minister, Delhi
06-08-2004

Hon'ble Prime Minister of India

Enclosures:

1. *Letter dated 28-06-2004 addressed to Union Finance Minister*
2. *Letter dated 29-06-2004 addressed to Union Minister for Youth Affairs & Sports*
3. *Letter dated 29-06-2004 addressed to the Lt. Governor, Delhi*
4. *Letter dated 02-08-2004 received from the Union Finance Minister.*

प्रधान मंत्री

Prime Minister

New Delhi
May 4, 2006

Dear Shiela ji,

Taking note of the concerns you expressed about the preparations for the Commonwealth Games 2010, I had asked my Principal Secretary to meet you along with the Secretary, Ministry of Youth Affairs and Sports.

Now I have been informed that based on your discussions with them, a meeting of the Committee of Secretaries, which is responsible for the implementation of the decisions of the Group of Ministers regarding the Commonwealth Games is scheduled to be held on the 5th May. The next meeting of the Group of Ministers is also scheduled on the 10th May 2006. Let us hope that decisions taken at these two meetings will clear the way for putting the preparations for the Games on the fast track.

I am also asking my office to keep me informed of the progress in the preparations for the Games.

Yours sincerely,

Manmohan Singh
(Manmohan Singh)

Smt. Shiela Dikshit
Chief Minister
Government of NCT of Delhi
Delhi

SHEILA DIKSHIT
CHIEF MINISTER

GOVT. OF NATIONAL CAPITAL TERRITORY OF DELHI
DELHI SECRETARIAT, I.P. ESTATE, NEW DELHI-110002

D.O.NO.: Spl-Secy CM/1221
Dated : 31/08/2006

Respected Dr Manmohan Singh,

I am enclosing draft of a possible mechanism to ensure expeditious clearances of the projects relating to the Commonwealth Games 2010 so that they can be completed well in time.

As of today, a plethora of meetings are being held but implementation is yet to begin. In the present framework, at least **seventeen** clearances are required before any project starts on the ground and in the normal course it take months to obtain each clearance at every step. Unless a fast track mechanism is put into place to grant the necessary clearances and coordinate between numerous project-implementing agencies specifically for the Commonwealth Games, it may not be possible to complete the projects in time.

I would like to submit that the mechanism suggested in the enclosed note is only a draft and may be suitably modified to make it effective.

With warm regards,

Yours sincerely,

Sheila Dikshit

(Sheila Dikshit)

Dr. Manmohan Singh,
Hon'ble Prime Minister of India,
South Block, New Delhi.

PHONE : OFF. 23392020, 23392030 • FAX : 23392111

GOVERNMENT OF N.C.T OF DELHI
OFFICE OF THE CHIEF MINISTER
I.P.ESTATE, NEW DELHI

Delhi won the bid to host the 2010 Commonwealth Games in November 2003, becoming only the 2nd city in Asia after Kuala Lumpur to get these games. Not only we have to put in place the stadia, games village and other games related infrastructure but the entire city needs to be given a facelift through better roads, flyovers, multimodal public transport system, renovation of airport and railway stations, greening and so on. But even after three years of winning the bid, the work is yet to pick up the desired pace, which is a matter of great concern as we have just four more years to go. Since the projects must be completed atleast 4 months prior to the commencement of the games, the actual time available with us is even less. In addition, before2010 there will be two major elections i.e. Delhi Legislative Assembly elections in 2008 and Lok Sabha elections in 2009.

2. You are very well acquainted with the multiplicity of agencies in Delhi. Due to the prevalent political and administrative structure there is complete absence of unity of command and control. Consequently, for the Commonwealth Games related projects, there are several executing agencies viz. the Sports Authority of India under the Ministry of Youth Affairs & Sports, DDA under Ministry of Urban Development, Municipal Corporation of Delhi partly under Ministry of Home Affairs and partly under Ministry of Urban Development, NDMC and various departments of the Government of NCT of Delhi. This multiplicity is perhaps unavoidable at the moment but it may be possible to bring about some semblance of improved coordination between them, if the Chief Secretary, GNCT of Delhi, the host city of the games, is vested with over-riding responsibility with corresponding powers in the games related matters.

3. TThe projects to be executed by the Sports Authority of India and DDA would necessarily require EFC clearance and other approvals from the Central Government and the schemes to be executed by the MCD and NDMC would require clearance of the Standing Committee and the Council respectively. Also the Ministry of Youth Affairs and Sports and Ministry of Urban Development would administratively be responsible for the speedy execution of games related projects with SAI and DDA respectively. But a great deal of coordination and integration in all matters is essential for organising the games successfully. This is wholly absent at present. For this I would request setting up of the following mechanisms :

a. The Chief Secretary, Delhi in addition to exercising full supervisory control over the Departments of the Government of NCT of Delhi should also be given over riding responsibility to supervise the execution of Commonwealth Games related projects of both the local bodies i.e. MCD and NDMC, including creation of related infrastructure and all measures necessary for beautification of the city. These bodies are presently not directly under the control of the elected Government of the NCT of Delhi.

b. For expeditious / fast track clearances, the Chief Secretary, Delhi should be authorised to head an **Empowered Committee** comprising of the following :

   i. Heads of the Departments directly under the Government of NCT of Delhi.

   ii. Heads of the Departments of various Ministries of the Government of India directly involved in creation of infrastructure/facilities for the Commonwealth Games.

   iii. Heads of other departments of Government of India associated with Commonwealth Games.

The draft composition of the empowered committee is enclosed at **Annexure 'A'**.

This committee will ensure that various clearances required for games related projects are granted expeditiously. Such clearances inter-alia include layout/building plan clearance, DDA's technical committee clearance, fire clearance, tree cutting clearance, traffic police clearance, clearance by defence authorities (particularly in respect of roads etc in the vicinity of the cantonment and the airport), clearance from ASI etc in respect of various projects being executed by the Delhi Government. The empowered committee would also expedite clearances in the local body/local government sector in respect of projects being executed by the Central government organisations like SAI and DDA.

c. A separate **Coordination Committee** should also be formed under the Chief Secretary, Delhi to coordinate and integrate connectivity with various games venues including the airport. Draft composition of the committee is enclosed at **Annexure 'B'**.

d. Similarly, it would perhaps be essential to constitute an empowered committee under the Secretary, Union Ministry of Youth Affiars and Sports to deal with various clearances in the central sectors such as custom clearances for imported games related equipments, Environment Minstry clearances including EIA, games related security matters and so on.

e. We also feel that one post of the level of the Joint Secretary to the Government of India should be created specially for conduct of the games including implementation of projects directly under the Chief Secretary, Delhi and the officer posted must continue till the games are concluded. Similarly, we may also need that officers of the Delhi government posted in some other critical areas like power, water etc are not transferred out of Delhi by the Ministry of Home Affairs till conclusion of the games.

4. I shall be grateful if setting up of such enabling mechanisms is ordered with further inputs and details to facilitate coordination and integration. This would, of course, be without prejudice to the coordination meetings being held by the Cabinet Secretary at the apex level, which would in any case be essential to ensure expeditious all round facilitation of games related matters.

(SHEILA DIKSHIT)
Chief Minister ; Delhi
August 31, 2006

OFFICE OF THE CHIEF MINISTER : GNCT OF DELHI
DELHI SECRETARIAT : I.P.ESTATE : NEW DELHI

Please find enclosed a note titled "Urgent need to accelerate pace of works related to Commonwealth Games 2010". This note has been prepared as per directions of Hon'ble Chief Minister, Government of NCT of Delhi who has directed me to forward the same to you for taking appropriate action in the matter.

(P.K.TRIPATHI)
Principal Secretary to CM
June 26, 2007

Sh.T.K.A.Nair,
Principal Secretary to Hon'ble Prime Minister of India,
South Block,
New Delhi.

NOTE

SUBJECT: URGENT NEED TO ACCELERATE PACE OF WORKS RELATED TO COMMONWEALTH GAMES 2010

Delhi will host the Commonwealth Games in October 2010. Considering the high standards set by Melbourne and other host cities in the past, we have to work really hard to put in place world class sporting facilities and infrastructure to present a good image of Delhi as well as our country. As the facilities should be ready at least 6 months before the games, we do not have much time left for making the arrangements. As most of the projects are yet to take off on the ground, there is need to accelerate the pace quickly.

The Cabinet Secretary may be requested to review the progress of works related to the games every month with Chief Secretary, Delhi; Secretary (Sports), Government of India; VC, DDA; Chairperson NDMC; Commissioner MCD and other concerned officers. All the agencies may be directed to give definite time lines supported by PERT charts to complete their projects well before the games.

The following agencies are playing critical role in preparing the National Capital to host the games in a befitting manner and are responsible for various works related to the games :

1. DDA

- Construction of Games village.
- Improvement of sports venues like Siri Fort Stadium, Yamuna Sports Complex, Saket Sports Complex
- Making available suitable plots of land for hotels and other facilities.
- Improvement of DDA roads, greening and face lifting of DDA parks and sprucing up its various shopping and housing complexes.
- River front development.
- Convention Centre at Dwarka
- Parking facilities
- Allotment of land for setting up power plant in Bamnouli

2. Ministry of Sports, Government of India

- Renovation of Jawahar Lal Nehru stadium, Indira Gandhi Indoor stadium, Maj.Dhyan Chand Stadium (National Stadium), Dr. Karni Singh Shooting

Range, Dr.S.P.M. Aquatic complex, Yamuna Velodrome etc. (to be undertaken by the Sports Authority of India).

3. Ministry of Civil Aviation

- Commissioning of 4 runways at IGI airport.
- Construction of new terminal for both domestic and international traffic at airports.
- In cooperation with NHAI and PWD to make the road/flyovers etc to the city not just ready but with aesthetic lights, landscaping etc.

4. Ministry of Railways

- Upgradation of Delhi, New Delhi, Nizamuddin and Sarai Rohilla Railway stations as state-of-art modern railway stations.
- Completion of Anand Vihar railway station.
- Construction of ROB/RUBs to replace level crossings.
- MCD to ensure that the approaches to the stations are well and cleanly planned

5. Ministry of Health & Family Welfare

- Review by the Secretary, Ministry of Health/DGHS of all health related arrangements connected with the games, as many central government hospitals would also need to be sensitised.

6. Delhi University

- Preparation for Rugby 7s competition venue in North Campus and training venues for the event in various colleges.

7. Delhi Police

- Security
- Traffic and Parking Management.

8. Government of NCT of Delhi

a. Games Venues

- Improvement of Chhatarsal Stadium and remodelling of Tyagaraja Sports complex.

b. Transport

- Procurement of 1100 low floor AC and deluxe buses for movement of athletes and officials and shuttle services for spectators.
- Completion of Phase-II of Delhi Metro including connectivity to JLN stadium and other games venues and High-speed link from Airport to Cannaught Place.
- Operationalisation of High Capacity Bus System corridors.
- Efficient and modern taxi phone in service.

c. Connectivity (PWD)

- Completion of 24 flyovers/bridges, widening and beautification of roads.
- Completion of Mahipalpur - Massoodpur byepass (pending with DDA for clearance)
- Completion of tunnel road connecting NH24 to Lodhi Road (pending with DUAC for clearance)
- Completion of Shantivan to Geeta colony bridge across river Yamuna.
- Construction of Salimgarh Fort road (pending with ASI).
- Improved streetlights, road signage, street furniture and public conveniences.
- Coordinate beautification of roundabouts etc with MCD/DDA/NDMC

d. Power

- Augmenting power generation capacity and making arrangements for procurement of sufficient power to ensure uninterrupted power supply to games village, competition venues and training venues.

e. Water

- Augmenting drinking water availability in the city to ensure water supply at adequate pressure across the city. For this early clearance/completion of following projects is very crucial

    i. Completion of Munak Hyderpur Canal by the Irrigation Department of Haryana. The project will save 80 MGD water, which is presently wasted due to seepage.

    ii. Environmental clearance of Renuka Dam project for Himachal Pradesh.

iii. Release of 20 MGD of water by Government of Haryana for Nangloi water treatment plant, which is ready for commissioning.

iv. Finalisation of MoU for supply of 140 MGD of water by Uttar Pradesh for Sonia Vihar water treatment plant.

- Up gradation of water supply at games venues including new 1 MGD water treatment plant on Eastern side of River Yamuna for the games village.

- Upgradation of Sewerage facilities including one new STP at games village for population of 10,000 persons

f. Department of Health & Family Welfare:

- Setting up 12 Health Posts (one at each venue), a polyclinic at Commonwealth Games Village and strengthening of Ambulance Services. Also designating both primary and secondary hospitals with particular games venues.

g. NDMC

- Renovation of Talkatora Stadium and Shivaji Stadium.
- Improvement of major roads around stadiums, upgradation of central vista, Cannaught place and its environment.

h. MCD

- Procurement of 50 mechanical sweepers, other sanitation equipments and dustbins.
- Improvement of major MCD roads and construction of flyovers.
- Construction of ROB/RUBs to replace level crossings in the city.
- Face-lifting and greening of parks and public areas in the jurisdiction of MCD.
- Improvement of streetlights.
- Identification of adequate parking sites across the city and development of multilevel parking.

Apart from above:

a. The Siri Fort Auditorium needs complete overhauling urgently (L&D)/Ministry of Culture/Ministry of Information and Broadcasing)

b. The Bharat Scouts and Guides Complex at Nizamuddin, which is a property of L&DO, needs complete overhauling and up gradation. It can be used to house students, athletes etc.

D.O. No. 550 Min. (YAS)/C

मंत्री
युवा कार्यक्रम एवं खेल
भारत सरकार
नई दिल्ली-110 001

Minister
Youth Affairs and Sports
Government of India
New Delhi-110 001

सुनील दत्त
SUNIL DUTT

October 7, 2004.

Dear DR. ManMohan Singh Ji.

At the outset, I am extremely thankful to you for taking initiative to constitute the GOM for coordinating the work related to the organisation of the Commonwealth Games to be held in Delhi in 2010.

Successful organisation of a mega international event like Commonwealth Games demands convergence of vast resources and multiple synergies of various stakeholders from within as well as outside the government. The initiative by you is the first positive step in this direction. I am encouraged by your decision to chair the first GOM meeting which will go a long way in articulation of the vision and preparation of future roadmap for making this event a grand show.

I have had preliminary discussion on the subject with Shri B.L.Joshi, Lt.Governor of Delhi, Smt.Sheila Dixit, CM of Delhi, Shri Suresh Kalmadi, President of Indian Olympic Association and officials of Sports Ministry, Delhi Government and DDA before the Athens Olympics. Accordingly, a copy of the note for the GOM containing important issues to be discussed in the first meeting to be chaired by you has been prepared and enclosed with this letter for your kind perusal.

I take this opportunity to request you to give the date for the first meeting as per your convenience.

with Regards.

(SUNIL DUTT)

Dr.Manmohan Singh,
Prime Minister of India,
New Delhi.

224

मंत्री
युवा कार्यक्रम एवं खेल
भारत सरकार
नई दिल्ली-110 001

Minister
Youth Affairs and Sports
Government of India
New Delhi-110 001

सुनील दत्त
SUNIL DUTT

CONFIDENTIAL
14th November, 2004

Dear Dr. Man Mohan Singh Ji

This is to acknowledge with thanks your gracious gesture in permitting me to go to USA and Canada on a mission to support the cause of cancer. You will be happy to know that I have been able to collect large voluntary donations. Meanwhile, I have been closely following your success in the international fora in projecting our case against terrorism as well as in handling domestic issues.

I take this opportunity to refer to the Group of Ministers (GOM) meeting chaired by you on 25th October, 2004 which discussed the plan of action related to allotment and hosting of Commonwealth Games 2010 in New Delhi. After the meeting, the media persons were also briefed about the gist of discussions and decisions taken under your able leadership and Government's strategy for a successful conduct of the Games was highlighted. Thereafter, I went abroad. During my stay abroad, I was surprised to see newspaper reports about a resolution passed by Indian Olympic Association (IOA) regarding appointment of President, IOA as Chairman of the Organising Committee which is at variance with the decisions taken in the GOM meeting. The letter of President, IOA dated 28th October, 2004 addressed to you (a copy of which has been received in my office from PMO) clearly shows that President, IOA was aware of the decision of the GOM appointing Minister, Youth Affairs & Sports as Chairman of the Organising Committee for preparation and conduct of Commonwealth Games, 2010. Notwithstanding a serious sense of disquiet, I waited for the formal minutes of the GOM meeting which reached my office on 10th November, 2004. The minutes, as issued by the Cabinet Secretariat, do not reflect the decisions taken in the meeting of 25th October,2004 regarding various aspects of composition of Organising Committee. It seems the word 'Apex', instead of the word 'Organising has been used inadvertantly in para

8(ii) of the minutes. Moreover, the decision regarding constitution of Executive Board under my Chairmanship has not been recorded. I may add that 'Empowered Committee on Infrastructure' under the Chairmanship of LG, Delhi was also to report to the Organising Committee as per the decision taken in the GOM. You may kindly consider issuing directions to amend the minutes accordingly.

In view of the above facts, I seek your indulgence for withholding the circulation of the minutes of the GOM meeting of 25th October, 2004 till a final view is taken by you on the above issues.

I request you to grant me an early audience so as to enable me to brief you on the facts and recent developments on the issue of hosting of Commonwealth Games, 2010.

With kind regards And happy Diwali and EED MUBARAK.

Yours Sincerely,

Sunil Dutt

(Sunil Dutt)

To,
Dr. Manmohan Singh,
Hon'ble Prime Minister of India,
South Block,
New Delhi

No. 1(11)/MWR/04/754

OFFICE OF UNION MINISTER OF WATER RESOURCES

Attn.: Hon'ble Prime Minister, Dr. Manmohan Singh.

The Cabinet Committee on Commonwealth Games composition has been circulated to us. Indeed it is a great attempt to plan, in detail, these games, which will enhance and justify India's administrative credibility and credentials in the globe, particularly, among the Commonwealth nations. In the composition of the Committee, Prime Minister's decision is final. This is just to inform the Hon'ble Prime Minister that in the present Cabinet, there are two other Cabinet Ministers who had been with the sports and international activities of sports. One is the present Agriculture Minister, Shri Sharad Pawar and the other is myself. I myself had been to 9th Asian Games Organizing Committee, New Delhi and I was the Official Delegate to make the presentation in the Commonwealth Federation from the Olympic Committee in Athens, recently. I have been Official Designated in the World Football Body in three World Cups. I am also the Vice-President of Indian Olympic Committee, who is inside the Cabinet and the Games will be basically looked after by the Indian Committee and the Government.

Hence, Hon'ble Prime Minister may consider to include me and Shri Sharad Pawar in the Cabinet Committee on Olympic Games if Prime Minister feels it proper.

(P.R. DASMUNSI)
Minister of Water Resources
15.10.2004

Hon'ble Prime Minister of India.

ov 03 11:18 Political Wing 020 7 240 7151 p.2
03 17:09 FAX +44 20 7747 6117 OSG 001

COMMONWEALTH
SECRETARY-GENERAL

H E Rt Hon Donald C McKinnon

14 November 2003

Dear Prime Minister

I was delighted to learn that India will host the 2010 Commonwealth Games in New Delhi. Please accept my warmest congratulations on India's successful bid. I am confident that India will prove to be an excellent and hospitable host and that the 2010 Games will be a big success. This is an opportunity for India not only to display its own sporting prowess but also to showcase itself to the Commonwealth and the world at large.

I wish the organisers of the Games the very best as they embark on the preparations.

Sincerely

Don McKinnon

The Hon Atal Bihari Vajpayee
Prime Minister of India
Prime Minister's Office
South Block
New Delhi
India

Marlborough House Pall Mall London SW1Y 5HX United Kingdom
Tel: *Switchboard* +44 (0)20 7747 6500 *Direct Line* +44 (0)20 7747 6103 Fax: +44 (0)20 7930 2299
e-mail: secretary-general@commonwealth.int Web site: www.thecommonwealth.org

Randhir Singh
Vice President

Shanti Farm, Village Chandan Hula,
Mehrauli, New Delhi - 110030 India
Tel.: 91-11-6653353 Fax : 91-11-6653181

Commonwealth Games Federation

January 19, 2005

Dear Prime Minister,

I would like to bring to your kind knowledge that the formation of the Delhi 2010 Commonwealth Games Organizing Committee is unnecessarily being delayed by the Sports Ministry by not sending the names of the two nominees.

The Host City Contract signed by the Ministry of Sports, Commonwealth Games Federation and the Indian Olympic Association jointly specifies the details of the formation of the Organizing Committee under the Chairmanship of the President, Indian Olympic Association.

My colleague, the President of Commonwealth Games Federation, Mr. Michael Fennell is visiting New Delhi from the 3rd of February to till the 8th February, 2005 to oversee the progress of the organizing of the Commonwealth Games and meet with members of the Organizing Committee. If the Organizing Committee is not in place before his visit, India will cut a very sorry figure and a negative report by him to the Executive Board and General Assembly Meetings of the Commonwealth Games Federation, which will be held in Melbourne in the first week of April, 2005, may result in India losing the Games.

I shall be very grateful if you could kindly instruct the Sports Ministry to send the names of their nominees as soon as possible and to co-ordinate with the Indian Olympic Association to make the Commonwealth Games a great success.

With Kind Regards

Yours sincerely,

Randhir Singh

(RANDHIR SINGH)

Dr. Manmohan Singh
Hon'ble Prime Minister of India
7, Race Course Road
New Delhi

C.C. to: *Shri Pulok Chatterjee, Jt. Secretary, PM Office, South Block, New Dehi*

Gate No. 25, Jawaharlal Nehru Stadium, New Delhi - 110 003 Tel : 91-11-4366950, 4366951, 4366952
Fax : 91-11-4365953, E-mail: ioa@nde.vsnl.net.in

COMMONWEALTH GAMES FEDERATION
CGF

2nd FLOOR
138 PICCADILLY
LONDON, W1J 7NR
UNITED KINGDOM
T: +44 (0)20-7491 8801
F: +44 (0)20-7409 7803
E: office@thecgf.com
www.thecgf.com

31 July 2009

Dr. Manmohan Singh
Hon. Prime Minister
Government of India
7 Race Course Road
New Delhi 110001
INDIA

Dear Prime Minister

CHOGM Sports Breakfast – TRINIDAD & TOBAGO, 28 NOVEMBER 2009

During the forthcoming Commonwealth Head's of Government meetings the Commonwealth Games Federation along with the Hon. Patrick Manning, the Prime Minister of Trinidad & Tobago will be hosting a Sports Breakfast at the CHOGM retreat venue for Heads of Government, from 8.00am to 9.30am on November 28th.

These "Sports Breakfast's" have, with the support of the Commonwealth Secretariat and its Secretary General, become a regular feature at CHOGM's since Coolum in 2001. The last such occasion was in Kampala, Uganda where during the breakfast President Yoweri Museveni hosted and spoke as did the British Prime Minister Gordon Brown..

With India hosting the 2010 Commonwealth Games in Delhi we believe this represents an excellent opportunity to once again profile not only the Games themselves but also to highlight India's commitment to the Games movement directly to the Heads of Government and in this regard we would very much appreciate your agreeing to make a brief presentation during the function on the forthcoming Games with a particular focus on legacy benefits and the rapid growth of the city as a consequence.

I look forward to receiving your advice on this matter.

Yours sincerely

Michael Fennell
President

CC: Suresh Kalmadi M.P., Chairman, Organising Committee Commonwealth Games Delhi 2010

सत्यमेव जयते

प्रधान मंत्री
Prime Minister

New Delhi
August 9, 2006

Dear Prof. Malhotra,

I have received your letter of August 5, 2006 regarding the preparations for the Commonwealth Games 2010.

With regards,

Yours sincerely,

(Manmohan Singh)

Prof. Vijay Kumar Malhotra, MP
6, Dr. Bishamber Dass Marg
New Delhi – 110 001

विजय कुमार मलहोत्रा
संसद सदस्य
VIJAY KUMAR MALHOTRA
M.P.
Dy. Leader & Spokesman
B.J.P. Parliamentary Party (Lok Sabha)
Chairman
Public Accounts Committee (Lok Sabha)

सत्यमेव जयते

6, डॉ. बिशम्बर दास मार्ग,
नई दिल्ली - 110001
6, Dr. Bishamber Dass Marg
New Delhi-110 001 (India)
Tel. : 23715051, 23715070
Fax : 91-11-23715045

August 5, 2006

Dear Dr. Manmohan Singh Ji,

Kindly refer to my earlier letter dated June 10, 2006 drawing your attention towards the host of Committees being constituted in the name of Commonwealth Games 2010. I once again give below the list of Committees constituted by various bodies.:

1. Commonwealth Games Organizing Committee and Executive Board of Commonwealth Games headed by Shri Suresh Kalmadi, President, Indian Olympic Association.
2. Group of Ministers Co-ordinating Committee for Commonwealth Games under the Chairmanship of Union Minister for Human Resource Development, Shri Arjun Singh.
3. Co-ordinating Committee under the Chairmanship of Lt. Governor of Delhi.
4. A Co-ordinating Committee under the Chairmanship of Chief Minister of Delhi
5. A High-powered Apex Committee under the Chairmanship of Union Minister of Youth Affairs & Sports.
6. Various other Committee of Finance Ministry, HRD Ministry, Sports Ministry, DDA, NDMC, MCD and other local bodies.

To add more confusion to the already chaotic situation, one more Department of International Sports Co-ordination is being created under the Ministry of Youth Affairs & Sports only to accommodate a few more Officers, apparently to co-ordinate with all the participating Countries in the Commonwealth Games 2010. Organizing Committee and its Executive Board is constituted with the sole responsibility of hosting the Games. Constitution of several Committees with over-lapping powers would be counter-productive.

As mentioned in my earlier letter, the whole attention of the Central Govt and the Govt of NCT of Delhi is towards creation of more and more infrastructure. It is amazing to know that the Govt. of NCT has planned to spend Rs,26,808 Crores for preparation of Delhi City for hosting the Commonwealth Games 2010 for which Rs.770 Crores will be given as Central Assistance. Similarly, Delhi Development Authority is planning to spend Rs.1082 crores for its various Projects at Akashardham for which DDA will get Rs.446 crores as Central Assistance. Over-emphasis on infra-structure development has side-lined the much needed attention on preparation of Indian Teams for such mega Sports Events

2

विजय कुमार मलहोत्रा
संसद सदस्य
VIJAY KUMAR MALHOTRA
M.P.
Dy. Leader & Spokesman
B.J.P. Parliamentary Party (Lok Sabha)
Chairman
Public Accounts Committee (Lok Sabha)

सत्यमेव जयते

6, डॉ. बिशम्बर दास मार्ग,
नई दिल्ली - 110001
6, Dr. Bishamber Dass Marg
New Delhi-110 001 (India)
Tel. : 23715051, 23715070
Fax : 91-11- 23715045

-: 2 :-

I am surprised to note that there is no provision in the Central Budget for MYAS to nurture the sport talent and prepare Indian Teams as a part of preparation for the Commonwealth Games. It is needless to mention that India being the Host Country, it is important to improve its medal tally in the Commonwealth Games 2010. However, I regret to mention that instead of improving its medal tally, India is sliding down in the overall ranking. This is happening due to lack of any long term programme to identify the talent, nurture them and prepare them for international competitions.

While development of infrastructure is desirable as well as essential for the Capital, however, the infrastructure alone will not fetch medals for the Country. If not 10%, at least 5% of the entire infrastructure budget for the Commonwealth Games 2010 should be spent for development of sports training facilities and nurturing of the talent towards winning record number of medals in the Commonwealth Games 2010. The irony of the fact is that while we spent hundreds of crores of rupees on a single fly-over or tunnel, however, when it comes to sports promotion, we become extremely frugal and provide shoe-string budget for the same and expect India to win International Medals!

You are, therefore, requested to kindly intervene so that huge amount being spent on host of Committees could be diverted to nurture and prepare the Indian talent for the Commonwealth Games. It is requested that the allocation under Sports in the Annual Budget for MYAS may be enhanced to Rs.1000.00 crores per annum with modification in the Guidelines to increase the number of days for National Camps, increase in the number of International exposures, provision to send talented Seniors and Juniors abroad for training-cum-competition stint, improvement in the training facilities, import of modern equipment, etc.

I once again request you to kindly look into the matter and ensure that the preparation work for hosting the Commonwealth Games 2010 is taken up in the right earnest by giving emphasis on preparation of the Indian Teams instead of constituting several Committees with over-lapping powers.

With kind regards,

Yours sincerely,

(VIJAY KUMAR MALHOTRA)

Dr. Manmohan Singh,
Prime Minister,
Govt. of India,
New Delhi.

सत्यमेव जयते

प्रधान मंत्री

Prime Minister

New Delhi
June 14, 2006

Dear Shri Malhotra,

I have received your letter of June 10, 2006 regarding the preparations for the Commonwealth Games 2010.

With regards,

Yours sincerely,

(Manmohan Singh)

Shri Vijay Kumar Malhotra, MP
6, Dr. Bishamber Dass Marg
New Delhi-110001

विजय कुमार मलहोत्रा
संसद सदस्य
VIJAY KUMAR MALHOTRA
M.P.
Dy. Leader & Spokesman
B.J.P. Parliamentary Party (Lok Sabha)
Chairman
Public Accounts Committee (Lok Sabha)

6, डॉ. बिशम्बर दास मार्ग,
नई दिल्ली - 110001
6, Dr. Bishamber Dass Marg
New Delhi-110 001 (India)
Tel. : 23715051, 23715070
Fax : 91-11- 23715045

June 10, 2006

Dear Dr. Manmohan Singh Ji,

I would like to draw your attention towards the series of Committees being formed in the name of Commonwealth Games 2010. Recently, one more Apex Committee has been added vide Gazette Notification No:70-312-SP-II dated 23rd May 2006 under the Chairmanship of Union Minister for Youth Affairs & Sports with members from various walks of life. As you are aware, many Committees have already been constituted such as:

1. Commonwealth Games Organizing Committee and Executive Board of Commonwealth Games headed by Shri Suresh Kalmadi, President, Indian Olympic Association.

2. Group of Ministers Co-ordinating Committee for Commonwealth Games under the Chairmanship of Union Minister for Human Resource Development, Shri Arjun Singh.

3. Co-ordinating Committee under the Chairmanship of Lt. Governor of Delhi.

4. A Co-ordinating Committee under the Chairmanship of Chief Minister of Delhi

5. A High-powered Committee under the Chairmanship of Union Minister of Youth Affairs & Sports.

6. Various other Committee of Finance Ministry, HRD Ministry, Sports Ministry, DDA, NDMC, MCD and other local bodies.

Since the Commonwealth Games are allotted to the National Olympic Committee of the host Country and it is the collective responsibility of the National Olympic Committee and the Govt. of the host Country to supervise and host the Games in the most befitting manner so as to uphold the prestige of the host Country. Hence, it is the prerogative of the National Olympic Committee to form the Organizing Committee for which consultation with the Central Govt. State Govt. and other bodies is obvious.

विजय कुमार मलहोत्रा
संसद सदस्य
VIJAY KUMAR MALHOTRA
M.P.
Dy. Leader & Spokesman
B.J.P. Parliamentary Party (Lok Sabha)
Chairman
Public Accounts Committee (Lok Sabha)

सत्यमेव जयते

6, डॉ. बिशम्बर दास मार्ग,
नई दिल्ली - 110001
6, Dr. Bishamber Dass Marg
New Delhi-110 001 (India)
Tel. : 23715051, 23715070
Fax : 91-11-23715045

-2-

Thus, Organizing Committee and its Executive Board is constituted with the sole responsibility of hosting the Games. Constitution of several Committees with over-lapping powers would be counter-productive.

I may further add that I am the Senior Vice President of Indian Olympic Association and Vice Chairman of the Organizing Committee, Commonwealth Games 2010 constituted by IOA. I get the information of most of the decisions taken by the various authorities through the Press and media only. Commonwealth Games should be a National endeavour and not a Party affair.

I am sure that you will look into the matter and ensure that the preparation work for hosting the Commonwealth Games 2010 is taken up in the right earnest instead of constituting several Committees with over-lapping powers.

With kind regards,

Yours sincerely,

(VIJAY KUMAR MALHOTRA)

Dr. Manmohan Singh,
Prime Minister,
Govt. of India,
New Delhi.

सत्यमेव जयते

प्रधान मंत्री

Prime Minister

New Delhi
31 October, 2007

Dear Dr. Karan Singh ji,

I have received your letter of 24 October, 2007 regarding objections raised by the environmentalists in respect of siting of the Games Village for the forthcoming Commonwealth Games 2010.

With regards,

Yours sincerely,

(Manmohan Singh)

Dr. Karan Singh, MP
3, Nyaya Marg, Chanakyapuri
New Delhi-110021

Dr. Karan Singh
MEMBER OF PARLIAMENT
(RAJYA SABHA)

3, NYAYA MARG
CHANAKYAPURI
NEW DELHI - 110 021

24 October 2007

My dear Prime Minister,

Some environmentalists met me recently and raised certain serious objections with regard to the siting of the Games Village for the forthcoming Commonwealth Games 2010. They strongly suggest that the present site on the riverbed of Yamuna will have extremely negative environmental implications, and that the colony could easily be located at Dwarka. In the worst case scenario they suggest that only temporary structures could be made which can then be dismantled after the games are over.

Quite clearly they have raised certain significant points which deserve your urgent consideration. I am enclosing the papers given by them with this letter.

I leave late tonight to accompany Shrimati Sonia Gandhi on a 5-day visit to China.

With warm regards,

Yours sincerely,

Karan Singh

Dr Manmohan Singh
Prime Minister
South Block
New Delhi

Encl: as above

Tel. : 2611-1744, 2611-5291 Fax : 2687-3171
E-mail : karansingh@karansingh.com

Yamuna Abhiyaan

18 October 2007
YJA/CORRES/10/07

To,

Dr. Karan Singh, MP
'Mansarover' 3, Nyay Marg
Chanakyapuri
New Delhi

Respected Sir,

Greetings

This is to thank you for sparing your valuable time at a short notice and giving us a patient hearing in the matter of ill advised and wrong siting of the Games Village in the river bed of river Yamuna by the state for the forthcoming Commonwealth Games 2010.

As advised, please find enclosed a brief note on why the said step of the government is wrong.

We hope that your good self would be able to convince the powers that since there is still time to the Games in October 2010, the site may be changed. In the worst case if there is indeed a compelling reason and the state is not in a position to change the site then only temporary 'dismantable' structures as was advised by the Ministry of Environment and Forests, MOEF itself be adopted.

With warm regards,

Manoj Misra
Convenor

Encl: As above

Advisors Samar Singh H S Panwar Sureshwar D Sinha
Members CMS Environment / LIFE / Matu People's Organisation / Pani Morcha / PEACE Institute / Ridge Bachao Andolan / Toxics Link

Secretariat 178-F, Pocket - 4, Mayur Vihar - I, Delhi - 110 091 Telefax 91-11-22719005
e-mail : yamunajiye@gmail.com
www.peaceinst.org / www.toxicslink.org

Say NO to 'constructions' in the river bed

a) RIVER YAMUNA – CITY'S LIFE LINE

The Yamuna river bed along with Ridge is an irreplaceable and most 'valuable' natural resource in the city

- Yamuna bed and flood plain (remaining) between the two embankments in east and west cover 9700 ha area (Zone O in the MPD 2021) in two separate parts with little sub-surface inter connectivity
- More than 50% of the water needs of the city is met (and this will only increase) from underground sources
- Ground water is already over extracted compared to its annual recharge
- Flood plains need to be secured zealously (**not concretized in any manner**) to enable flood waters to spread and percolate down on an annual basis during monsoons
- According to an estimate by Prof. Vikram Soni of NPL, Yamuna flood plains and the Ridge together are worth Rs. 21,000 crore annually just on the basis of their ground water recharge potential.

The Yamuna river bed is an insurance against devastation wrought by menacing flood waters (remember 1978, 1988, 1995, Mithi river in Mumbai in 2005, and river Thames in London in 2007)

Any construction (Multi stories buildings, Malls, Elevated Metro etc) on river bed and flood plain is a sitting duck in the event of even a medium sized earthquake (remember Mexico in 1985 and Kobe in 1995)

Let us not forget that what we do to the river Yamuna in Delhi impacts both upstream and down stream of its passage in Delhi. So we in Delhi have to act responsibly.

b) BUT DOES THE STATE NOT HAVE ALL THE APPROVALS FOR ONGOING AND PLANNED CONSTRUCTIONS IN THE RIVER BED?

No, the state neither has nor can have permissions and approvals as per law and rules and regulations in vogue.

Any such construction would also need the following approvals

1) Yamuna Standing Committee (MOWR) from flood impact angle - NO
2) Central Ground Water Authority (MOWR and MOEF) for permission to extract ground water for various uses - NO
3) Delhi High Court appointed committee to over see removal of encroachments from the river bed - NO
4) Environment Impact Assessment (MOEF) – YES ? (*RTI response from Ministry of Environment and Forests (MOEF) shows that the so called clearance was not based on merit but extraneous considerations like lack of time and national prestige*)

ANY CONSTRUCTION IN THE RIVER BED NEEDS TO TAKE INTO ACCOUNT THE RESULTS OF AN EXTENSIVE STUDY OF THE RIVER CONDUCTED BY NATIONAL ENGINEERING RESEARCH INSTITUTE (NEERI) IN 2005 **(COMMISSIONED BY THE DDA)** WHICH CLEARLY STATED:

""No permanent structures of residential or industrial nature should be raised in the river bed"

Against the above what is under construction / planned are the following:

a) DMRC Yamuna Depot, polluting coach cleaning facility, elevated line (52 ha)
b) TRANSCO building, Power plants, Solid waste dumps, highways,
c) High rise (8,7,6 and 4 stories flats for 8500 athletes and officials) multi storied flats, Malls, and other residential infrastructure for the Commonwealth Games Village (47 ha)
d) Pawan Hans Heliport over 40 acres

Above is just the beginning.

Most unfortunately the example of Akshardham which itself was the last government's worst folly is being cited by the present government of Delhi to build the Games Village in the river bed.

c) BUT DO WE NOT NEED COMMONWEALTH GAMES AND THE LIKE?

Yes, certainly we do.

But most certainly NOT at the cost of our life - line (river) or the security of our life and property !

a) Importantly when safe '**alternatives**' exist in the city for the Games Village.

b) Above all certainly not based on '**lies**'. We had promised to the world at Jamaica in November 2003 (when the CG 2010 was voted for Delhi) that the Games Village would be build at safe and pleasant site **(The site is risky, disturbed, dangerous and in the river bed)**; would be proximate to the Airport **(Airport is nowhere proximate to the river bed)**; would become University accommodation **(Post Games the Village is planned to be sold out and converted into private residential colony)** and the buildings would be low cost, low rise and low end **(The planned buildings are high rise and high end)**.

Clearly none of what was promised by the Indian Olympic Association (IOA) in Jamaica at the time of voting for selecting a host city for Commonwealth Games 2010 is proving to be true at the current site in the river bed.

D) BUT IS THE COMMONWEALTH GAMES FEDERATION (CGF) NOT SUBSIDISING INDIA FOR THE GAMES PREPARATIONS INCLUDING INFRASTRUCTURAL DEVELOPMENT IN DELHI?

NO. This is a POPULAR myth !

There is not a paisa coming to the Indian Olympic Association (IOA) who is the games host or the city of Delhi or the Government of India.

On the contrary the **tax payer in India is paying for the following** (promised by the IOA to voting members at Jamaica under whose authority?):

a) Payment of USD 100,000 (approx. Rs 4 crore) to each of the 72 members of Commonwealth Games Federation (CGF) which includes rich countries like UK, Canada and Australia. (Kind of a soft bribe?)
b) Costs of free travel (to and fro) and stay in Delhi for almost 25 days to all the 8500 plus athletes and officials who are expected to come for participation at the Games from all over.

Let us also not forget that like the Cricket World Cup (organised by BCCI), Commonwealth Games 2010 or any such sporting event (10- 15 day event) is basically a private affair (IOA's baby). The government of India and in turn the **tax payer is heavily subsidizing** (approx to the tune of 23,000 crores plus), the IOA for the same.

E) BUT WILL THE GAMES NOT PAY FOR THEMSELVES?

NO.

Statistics reveal that none of these sporting events (including the Olympics) with the sole exception of Los Angeles Olympics in 1984 has ever been a profit making venture.

It is estimated that for the CG 2010 against an approx. expenditure of Rs 23,000 crores the best case scenario for revenue (from tourism and advertisements) in Delhi is a mere Rs 4550 crore.

F) DO WE HAVE TIME TO SHIFT THE GAMES VILLAGE AWAY FROM THE RIVER BED

YES.

There are still 3 years to go for the Games in the October 2010.

Even otherwise, why cannot the state abide by the advice of the Expert Appraisal Committee (EAC) of the Ministry of Environment and Forests, MOEF for

..... adopt 'dismantable' temporary structures for the 10 day sporting event so that the river bed could be restored to the river.....

सत्यमेव जयते

प्रधान मंत्री

Prime Minister

New Delhi
15 May, 2008

Dear Ambika ji,

I have received your letter of 12 May, 2008 regarding a new road alignment for the Commonwealth Games 2010.

With warm regards,

Yours sincerely,

(Manmohan Singh)

Smt. Ambika Soni
Minister of Tourism & Culture
New Delhi

पर्यटन एवं संस्कृति मंत्री
भारत सरकार
नई दिल्ली-110 115
MINISTER OF TOURISM & CULTURE
GOVERNMENT OF INDIA
NEW DELHI-110 115

अम्बिका सोनी
Ambika Soni

No. F-24/24/2006 - 07
May 12, 2008

Respected Prime Minister,

I enclose for your kind information a letter written by me on 11th April 2008 to Shri Arjun Singh, Minister of Human Resource Development and Chairman, Group of Ministers for Commonwealth Games 2010. This was in the context of a new road alignment in preparation for the 2010 Commonwealth Games which is expected to pass over or close to certain protected monuments. Since I was unable to attend, Archaeological Survey of India (ASI) was represented and this point of view was put across.

Since then we have received a formal proposal from the Delhi Administration and the process of considering the proposal is on in the ASI, even though, I understand, there are differing views on this proposal.

This is for your kind information.

With regards,

Yours sincerely,

(Ambika Soni)

Dr. Manmohan Singh,
Hon'ble Prime Minister,
Government of India,
South Block,
New Delhi.

F. No. 24/24/...

पर्यटन एवं संस्कृति मंत्री
भारत सरकार
नई दिल्ली-110 115

MINISTER OF TOURISM & CULTURE
GOVERNMENT OF INDIA
NEW DELHI-110 115

सत्यमेव जयते

अम्बिका सोनी
Ambika Soni

April 11, 2008

Dear Shri Arjun Singh ji,

I enclose a note with reference to the GOM meeting held on 9.4.08, under your Chairmanship where certain decisions were taken with regard to a new road alignment, in preparation for the 2010 Commonwealth Games, which is expected to pass over or close to certain protected monuments under the ASI.

I had barely just returned to Delhi from an official visit abroad and was unable to attend the meeting. Therefore, I would like to make a few observations for your consideration.

We would be happy to provide all assistance in ensuring the success of these games. However, certain statutory obligations need to be kept in view with regard to the archaeological monuments which are in the vicinity of the proposed elevated road. The processes that have to be followed by the ASI, even to modify the existing policy in this regard, can be initiated only if Government direct the ASI to do so.

With best wishes,

Yours sincerely,

(Ambika Soni)

Shri Arjun Singh,
Hon'ble Minister for Human Resource Development and
Chairman, Group of Ministers for Commonwealth Games 2010,
Shastri Bhavan,
New Delhi.

Ministry of Culture
Shastri Bhavan
***

This is with reference to the discussions held in the meeting of the Core Group of Ministers (GOM) constituted for carrying out the work relating to organization of Commonwealth Games 2010, held under the Chairmanship of Hon'ble Minister for HRD on 9 April 2008. In the meeting, the GOM granted its approval to the proposal made by Govt. of NCT of Delhi (GNCTD) to construct an elevated corridor over Barapula Nala to ensure connectivity between the Games Village and the Jawaharlal Nehru Stadium. It was also decided that a necessary modification to the existing notifications under the Ancient Monuments and Archaeological Sites and Remains Act, 1958 may be carried out, or a new notification issued, to ensure that the permission granted for construction of this new corridor remains within the legal parameters. In connection with the above, the following aspects of the matter are brought to notice for consideration.

The GNCTD has not submitted any formal proposal relating to the proposed project for consideration of Archaeological Survey of India (ASI). The presentation made by GNCTD was based on discussions held with the representatives of ASI in a meeting called by Delhi Urban Arts Commission. It may be seen from the Minutes of 1191st meeting of DUAC (copy enclosed for ready reference) that the representative of PWD of GNCTD accepted the views of ASI and DUAC and the Engineer-in-Chief PWD agreed to review the proposal on these lines. GNCTD, however, has taken up the matter to GOM without first consulting ASI.

A scrutiny of the project details to ensure its compliance with law is not only a statutory requirement under the Ancient Monuments and Archaeological Sites and Remains Act, 1958 and rules framed there under and the notifications issued, but also essential for imposing necessary conditions and safeguards to be followed by GNCTD while implementing the project in this archaeologically rich area. A copy of the relevant extract of the Act, Rules and the 1992 Notification are enclosed for ready

2

reference. Without getting the full project details, ASI is neither in a position to identify all the monuments whose prohibited/regulated areas the road alignment might pass through nor able to appreciate the possible impact on these monuments. A preliminary assessment indicates that the number of such monuments may be larger than the two monuments mentioned in the presentation.

For the above reasons it is necessary that GNCTD submits a formal proposal to ASI under the relevant provisions of law.

As regards the issue relating to amendment of the notification, it may be stated that such a modification of notification, whether involving a change in the protected status of a monument or involving a change in the prohibited/regulated area around it, even if to accommodate the needs of a development project, would be an unprecedented move. The two monuments in question were notified as protected monuments in 1915 and 1916 respectively. Both are of great archaeological importance and are architecturally unique. However, if the Government were to decide on this course of action taking into account a larger public interest, appropriate instructions may kindly be communicated to this Ministry.

अगाथा संगमा
AGATHA SANGMA

ग्रामीण विकास
राज्य मंत्री
भारत सरकार
नई दिल्ली - 110 001
MINISTER OF STATE FOR
RURAL DEVELOPMENT
GOVERNMENT OF INDIA
KRISHI BHAWAN, NEW DELHI-110 001

24 June 2009

Respected Prime Minister,

We are indeed grateful to your goodself that every effort is being made by the Government of India, under your stewardship, to make the Commonwealth Games 2010 a grand success.

I understand the grandeur will include several cultural programmes representing different cultures of our country. I am of the opinion that it would be in the fitness of things if the traditional Garo Dance "WANGALA", a speciality from the North Eastern region in general and Meghalaya in particular is included in the cultural events, so that it can be displayed before the international audience and receive their acclamation.

I am sure, you will appreciate the aspirations of the youth of the North East to showcase their cultural finesse and the proposal receives your blessings.

With best regards,

Yours sincerely,

Agatha Sangma
(Agatha Sangma)

Dr. Manmohan Singh,
Hon'ble Prime Minister of India,
7, Race Course Road,
New Delhi.

02 Aug 2010 17:39 HP LASERJET FAX p.1

सत्यमेव जयते

SANJAY RAUT
MEMBER OF PARLIAMENT Rajya Sabha
EXECUTIVE EDITOR Saamana

Member :
Standing Commitee : Ministry of Home Affairs
Consultative Commitee : Ministry of Civil Aviation
11, Ferozshah Road, New Delhi - 110001.
Tel.: Res. 011-23382999 Fax : 011-23382000

2nd August, 2010

Dear Prime Minister Ji,

As you are aware about the CVC Report on rampant corruption in Commonwealth Games, which is appeared in various national newspapers / media. I need not to elaborate all the discrepancies in awarding of the works at higher rates and grant of works to ineligible agencies involving huge expenditure.

In view of the issue of public importance, I had an oppourtunity to raise the issue in Rajya Sabha during Zero Hour and demanded action against the culprit (s) through investigation by a C. B. I. Enquiry. Commonwealth Games is one of the prestigious and important games in international arena. Such allegation of corruption for the preparation of CWG , especially from CVC is very depressing. Seeing the seriousness of the concerns of the CVC in the issue as also public demand, It will be in the fitness of the things , if you could kindly agree to refer the matter for the consideration and through investigation by a Joint Parliamentary Committee (JPC).

With warmest regards,

Yours sincerely,

(Sanjay Raut)

Dr. Manmohan Singh,
Hon. Prime Minister,
P.M.O., South Block,
New Delhi.

सामना
Resi.: "Maitree" Bunglow, Friends Colony, Bhandup (East), Mumbai - 400 042. Tel.: 022-2593 3636, Fax 022-2592 3636
Off.: Sadguru Darshan, Nagu Sayaji Wadi, Dainik Saamana Marg, Prabhadevi, Mumbai - 400 025.
Tel.: 022-2437 0591, Fax 022-2436 5308*, E-mail : s.raut@sansad.nic.in

प्रधान मंत्री

Prime Minister

New Delhi
30 September, 2010

Dear Shri Thomas,

I have received your letter of 25 September, 2010 regarding the Commonwealth Games.

With regards,

Yours sincerely,

(Manmohan Singh)

Shri P.T. Thomas, MP
Puthiyaparambil
P.O. Thodupuzha
Distt. Idukki
Kerala – 685584

P.T. THOMAS
member of Parliament
(Lok Sabha)
Idukki (Kerala)

34, South Avenue,
New Delhi-110011
Phone: 011-23010594
Mobile: 9013180092

PT/PM/662/2010 25th September, 2010

To

Dr.Manmohan Singh,
Hon'ble Prime Minister of India
South Block, New Delhi

Respected Prime Minister,

I am to draw your kind attention to the following grave issue of utmost importance.

A high level trans- national conspiracy had evidently been taken place in order to malign the image of India by manipulating the Commonwealth Games news by an unscrupulous minority among the media. The manipulation of Commonwealth Games news has striking similarity with an incident happened in Hyderabad in which a man was set on fire by himself. In the above said incident, the poor man was encouraged to torch himself by two T.V journalists after having given him false assurance of dousing the fire for the sake of 'a live news item'. Similarly, some pictures of filthy toilets 'said to have taken this week' from the Common wealth games Village were leaked to BBC and other channels. Adhering to the journalistic ethics, BBC and other channels are bound to reveal the name of the person who has taken the pictures, the exact time and date of capturing of the pictures.

The other defamatory news pertaining to the Commonwealth games was of dogs soiling the beds of the athletes. It could also be a well fabricated one. Just as the man has been encouraged to torch himself for the sake of 'news', the dogs, in all possibility, were enticed to enter the room after having put eatables on the bed. However, with the aid of unauthenticated photos, they could start a malicious attack on an emerging Asian country which in true spirit of hospitality spent heavy amount for hosting the Commonwealth games.

As far the Commonwealth Games are concerned, I am not denying awesome shortcomings caused by the Committee concerned which is about to be investigated /enquired into. My request is that along with that investigation/enquiry, the international conspiracy perpetrated possibly by heavily financed transnational business companies to defame India and Indian Business companies doing business in other countries must also be enquired into.

Puthiyaparambil, Thodupuzha P.O., Idukki (Dt.), Kerala-685584
Tel. No. 04862-229595, Mob.: 9447029595

P.T. THOMAS
Member of Parliament
(Lok Sabha)
Idukki (Kerala)

34, South Avenue,
New Delhi-110011
Phone: 011-23010594
Mobile: 9013180092

Some international companies clandestinely encouraging racism for the sake of advancement of their business seem to have played a joint role in spearheading anti-India campaign in the wake of Commonwealth Games.

It is a fact that stray incidents occur everywhere despite our strenuous efforts. Previous Commonwealth Games and Asian Games were not exception in terms of infrastructure and the better facilities offered to athletes. But stray incidents should not be at the heart of a general conclusion. Had not a man on the street mysteriously entered the private room of Queen Elizabeth some years back? Does it mean that Buckingham Palace is without security? Few months back, an uninvited couple crossed all security barriers of white house and participated in the party hosted by Barrack Obama. Does it mean that White House is devoid of security?

By citing stray incidents of dogs soiling the beds (which was manipulated) and the pictures of filthy toilets (which was also manipulated), the trans-national forces target India's prestige and ridicule crores of Indians here and millions of Indians who do business and live in every nook and corner of the world. I humbly request you to give immediate attention to the issue raised here. A speedy enquiry should also be conducted to check the veracity of photos - when the photo was taken and by whom - and to bring to light the tacit understanding between a section of trans-national media and International Business Companies involved in anti-India campaign particularly in the specific context of Common wealth Games.

Thanking you,

Yours sincerely,

(P.T.THOMAS)

Puthiyaparambil, Thodupuzha P.O., Idukki (Dt.), Kerala-685584
Tel. No. 04862-229595, Mob.: 9447029595 E-mail: ptthomasidk@gmail.com

Office of MOS (Planning & Parliamentary Affairs)

Subject: Review of Prasar Bharati's preparedness for hosting the Commonwealth Games

Today, i.e., on 10.09.2010, I had reviewed the Prasar Bharati's preparedness for Commonwealth Games telecast. Doordarshan as the broadcaster for the Games is responsible for production and coverage of the Games from 16 games venues and two road events in High Definition.

2. Prasar Bharti has informed that the customization of broadcast compounds at all the venues has been done and broadcasting equipments have been shifted to seven venues as on date. The production and coverage of the events has been contracted to SIS Live and they have moved their equipments at 10 venues and would be completing shifting to five more venues by the end of today, i.e., 10.9.2010. Doordarshan has drawn monitoring chart venue wise and is being reviewed on a daily basis. The status as on 08.09.2010 is enclosed.

3. The CEO, Prasar Bharati has indicated that due to delays in making the venues available to the Prasar Bharati as per agreed timelines, there has been a considerable delay in establishing their facilities. However, CEO has assured that they are working round-the-clock to make up for the lost time and has assured that by 15th September, 2010 all works would be completed by them. He, however, highlighted the following issues which need to be addressed and resolved immediately by the Organizing Committee:

(i) Lack of availability of synchronized power supply with DG sets at all the venues (as on date synchronized power with DG set in place is available at 2 venues only).

(ii) Water logging in the trenches at venues is causing problems for cable connection as water needs to be pumped out from the trenches.

(iii) Water logging is also creating health hazards due to mosquito breeding, which is discouraging the foreign experts from visiting the venues for their work.

(iv) Facilitation for issuance of visas to SIS Professionals.

3. I am taking up the above issues with Shri Suresh Kalmadi, Chairman, Organizing Committee of Commonwealth Games, 2010.

4. The International Broadcasting Center is ready. I propose to visit the International Broadcasting Center as well as couple of games venues on 15th September, 2010 to assess the situation on the ground.

5. Submitted for kind information of Hon'ble Prime Minister.

(V. Narayanasamy)
Minister of State
(Planning & Parliamentary Affairs)
10.9.2010

Hon'ble Prime Minister

सत्यमेव जयते

प्रधान मंत्री

Prime Minister

New Delhi
26 November, 2010

Dear Dr. Gupta,

I have received your letter of 20 November, 2010 regarding Shri V.K. Verma, Director General, Commonwealth Games Organising Committee Office.

With regards,

Yours sincerely,

(Manmohan Singh)

Dr. Akhilesh Das Gupta, MP
11, Lodhi Estate
New Delhi – 110 001

Dr. Akhilesh Das Gupta
M.B.A, LL.B, Ph. D.
(Ex-Minister, Govt. of India & Ex-Mayor Lucknow)

सत्यमेव जयते

EX-CHAIRMAN
Parliamentary Standing Committee or
INDUSTRY

सत्यमेव जयते
Member of Parliament
(Rajya Sabha)

CONFIDENTIAL

November 20, 2010

Respected Pradhan Mantri ji

Reg: Missing of Tenders related files at Commonwealth Games Organizing Committee (CGOC) Office

1) The leading newspapers have reported that the tenders related files and important documents are not available in the office of Commonwealth Games Organizing Committee. This news is very shocking and gives wrong signals and sets bad precedent.

2) As per the Constitution of CGOC, few officials are appointed on Honorary basis, whereas the Director General, CGOC, MR. V.K. VERMA is the senior most PAID OFFICIAL ON HEAVY MONTHLY SALARY BASIS. As DG, he is the actual custodian of all the files and documents and it is his duty to ensure safe custody of the same and make it available to the investigating agencies for fair inquiry.

3) If the files and documents are missing from the CGOC office, it could only be possible under the guidance and connivance of Mr. V.K. Verma only. Obviously, he could do it to stall the inquiry process against him.

4) I would request you to kindly issue necessary instructions to deal this matter in a very strict manner because missing of files and documents itself is a big SCAM.

Kind Regards

(Dr. Akhilesh Das Gupta)

Dr. Manmohan Singh,
Hon'ble Prime Minister,
Govt. of India, South Block,
New Delhi

120, Parliament House Annexe, New Delhi 110 001 (India) Tel.: 23034120 Tele fax: 23017779
Res.: 11, Lodhi Estate, New Delhi (India) 110 003 Tel.: 24645049, 24641809, Fax: 24698432
55, Babu Banarasi Das Nagar (Purana Kila), Lucknow 226 001 (U.P.). Tel.: (0522)

दिलीप गांधी
DILIP GANDHI
संसद सदस्य
MEMBER OF PARLIAMENT

MEMBER :
- **Committee on Petroleum and Natural Gas**
- **Consultative Committee on Civil Aviation**

सत्यमेव जयते

चेयरमैन : नगर अर्बन को-ऑप. बैंक लि.
(शेडयुल्ड बैंक), अहमदनगर, महाराष्ट्र
CHAIRMAN
NAGAR URBAN CO-OP. BANK LTD.
(SCHEDULED BANK), AHMEDNAGAR

पूर्व केन्द्रीय पोत परिवहन राज्य मंत्री
भारत सरकार
EX-MINISTER OF STATE FOR SHIPPING
GOVERNMENT OF INDIA
Director : National Oilseeds and
Vegetable Oils Development Board

Sh. T.K.A. Nair,
Principal Secretary
Prime Minister of India,
South Block, New Delhi

Sub: Apathetic attitude of various agencies involved in Common Wealth Games – pertaining to the residents of Vasant Kunj, New Delhi

Dear Shri Nair,

In view of prevailing conditions of un-preparedness of the various agencies for completion of various infrastructure projects for the coming Common Wealth Games, it is heartening to note that the Prime Minister of India had to undertake a visit to various common wealth games sites in order to assess the preparedness of the various agencies involved for completion of the various projects. The performance of the various agencies is a glaring example of negligence and un-responsible approach towards such a mega event which is highlighted day-in-day-out by the various media agencies.

2. I am construined to bring to your notice and for further directions to the agencies concerned for doing the needful to solve the serious issues which have been highlighted by me through my various letters mentioning the apathetic approach towards the day-to-day problems being faced by the residents of the Vasant Kunj, New Delhi. I am listing below the problems as well as the agencies concerned supposed to take the action in the matter and inspite of my various letters to these agencies they have not acted to mitigate the sufferings of the residents.

(i) As everybody knows that the DDA is constructing big housing project at Vasant Kunj in order to accommodate the *participants of the Common Wealth Games* and the Nelson Mandela Marg is the main arterial road connecting Ring Road (R.K. Puram) to Vasant Kunj. It will not be out of place to mention that this main Nelson Mandela Road which is approximately 4 kms long and starts from Vasant Kunj Flyover and connects Munirka (outer ring road) is in a very bad shape and there is lot of garbage / mulba scattered at various locations on both sides of the road, the footpath in front of the C-3 Block Vasant Kunj starting from Police Station upto the flyover is broken at many places, curb stones are missing, the side drains inlet are chocked and filled with mulba left over by the contractor, thorny bushes are protruding on the inner roads parallel to the Nelson Mandela Marg, there is a garbage dump and rubbish lying just at the junction of the Nelson Mandela Marg and the Flyover which is very near to the Common Wealth Games Flats under construction. The Nelson Mandela Marg is considered the Mall Road of Vasant Kunj and the pathetic conditions of this 4 kms stretch is unimaginable by any standards when such an important event is going to take place. The road development is looked after by PWD, Delhi sanitation by MCD, Delhi, the DDA looks after the development of the interior roads and DDA Market opposite Police Station, Vasant Kunj.

(ii) Inspite of having a written a number of letters to Vice-Chairman, DDA, Commissioner, MCD and Commissioner, Delhi Police, the DDA market near Apollo Clinic opposite Police Station, Vasant Kunj is a host to unauthorized open air restaurant serving non-vegitarian delicacies in the evenings giving rise to unsanitary conditions turning the place to look like a Paharganj or old Delhi with mosquitoes and flies around covering the floor like a carpet due to the left over non-veg food, dogs and cats relishing the bones and meat pieces. The DDA market is in a very bad shape and the floor tiles are broken and flooring has sunk at many places there is a stagnant water giving rise to breeding of mosquitoes due to chocked manholes and sewerlines. It is quite questionable as to how the Police Station, Vasant Kunj is turning a blind eye by allowing unauthorized activities on govt. land in connivance with the MCD and DDA Officials. The residents of the Vasant Kunj are facing problems due to the smoke and bad smell which generates while cooking or frying non-veg. food and the smell is unbearable which can be felt upto a distance of 200 meters. There is also a van serving non-veg. food near Apollo Clinic permanently parked opposite Police Station, Vasant Kunj. *This market is on the main Nelson Mandela Road, the approach to the venue of Common Wealth Games Village and all these activities are going on under the protection of the Police Station, Vasant Kunj.*

6, डा॰ राजेन्द्र प्रसाद रोड, नई दिल्ली - 110 001
'देवेन्द्र' बंगला, आनंदऋषिजी मार्ग, अहमदनगर, महाराष्ट्र
दूरभाष : ऑ. (0241) 2451444/2451595/2452231 मोबाईल : ......

दिलीप गांधी
DILIP GANDHI
संसद सदस्य
MEMBER OF PARLIAMENT
MEMBER:
- Standing Committee on Petroleum and Natural Gas
- Consultative Committee on Civil Aviation
- National Oilseeds and Vegetable Oils Development Board
- Hindi Salahakar Samiti, Ministry of Shipping

सत्यमेव जयते

पूर्व चेयरमैन : नगर अर्बन को-ऑप. बैंक लि.
(शेड्युल्ड बैंक), अहमदनगर, महाराष्ट्र
EX-CHAIRMAN
NAGAR URBAN CO-OP. BANK LTD.
(SCHEDULED BANK), AHMEDNAGAR

पूर्व केन्द्रीय पोत परिवहन राज्य मंत्री
भारत सरकार
EX-MINISTER OF STATE FOR SHIPPING
GOVERNMENT OF INDIA

(iii) There is a beautiful park opposite DPS, Vasant Kunj called Vasant Vatika opposite C-1,C-2 block Vasant Kunj, which is maintained by DDA and the road parallel to the park is maintained by MCD. Hundreds of the residents of the vasant kunj visits the park in the morning and evening and the road is in a very bad shape with lot of mulba and garbage strewen all over and the roads have been dug up there. There is a huge pit in the Vasant Vatika Park which has turn into lake due to the sewage being discharged into that pit and it has became a place for breeding of dengue mosquitoes. It has became an drainage pond and it is so deep that anybody can be drowned. MCD is least bothered to prevent the breeding of mosquitoes in this pond inside the park.

(iv) The footpath in front of Police Station, Vasant Kunj has become a junkyard as the Police Station has dumped accidented vehicles which are rusting for the last many years and it is on the main Nelson Mandela Marg giving a look of Kabadi Bazar. It is surprising that the senior officers of Delhi Police who visit police Station, Vasant Kunj do not visualize this pathetic conditions in front of the police station.

(v) The foot path and the road leading to DPS, Vasant Kunj is also in a very bad shape and the side drains are chocked and have become a breeding place for mosquitoes, bushes and wild grass is mushrooming all around, filth is strewen is all over. A large of residents of C-1,C-2 & C-3 blocks of Vasant Kunj have become victims of Dengue Fever due to the breeding of mosquitoes in the stagnant water.

(vi) The residents of C-1 block Vasant Kunj opposite the flyover are facing a very peculiar problem of cow dung getting collected outside their houses (as there is a masood pur dairy nearby) upto the level of 3 feet during the rainy season as the sewerage system and manholes start over flowing. MCD / DDA have failed to take any action in the matter despite many representations by the RWA.

I earnestly request that a serious view may be taken on the issues highlighted above as my numerous correspondences with the various agencies mentioned above have brought no change in the situation. I may kindly be communicated about the action taken in the matter as it is not only the residents of the Vasant Kunj who are suffering but also involves the prestige connected with the Common Wealth Games as deligates and the atheletes will be staying in the flats under construction in the Vasant Kunj.

With regards,

Yours sincerely,

(Dilip Gandhi)
6, Dr. Rajender Prasad Road,
Opposite Shashtri Bhawan,
New Delhi-110001

Distribution:-

1. Ms. Sheila Dixit,
Chief Minister of Delhi,
Chief Minister Office,
Level-3, A-Wing, Delhi Secretariat,
I.P. Estate, New Delhi
2. Sh. Tejender Khanna,
Lieutenant Governor Delhi,
Rajnivas Marg, Court Lane,
Delhi-110054

Date:- 06.09.2010

6, डा. राजेन्द्र प्रसाद रोड, नई दिल्ली-110001
दूरभाष : 011-23357732, 23354246
'देवेन्द्र' बंगला, आनंदऋषिजी मार्ग, अहमदनगर, महाराष्ट्र
दूरभाष : ऑ. (0241) 2451444, 2451515, 2452231 मोबाईल : 09422226070, 09013180296

सत्यमेव जयते

प्रधान मंत्री

Prime Minister

New Delhi
31 August, 2010

Dear Dr. Gupta,

I have received your letter of 29 August, 2010 regarding Shri V.K. Verma, Director General, Commonwealth Games.

With regards,

Yours sincerely,

(Manmohan Singh)

Dr. Akhilesh Das Gupta, MP
Chairman
Committee on Industry
120, Parliament House Annexe
New Delhi – 110001

Dr Akhilesh Das Gupta
M.B.A, LL.B, Ph. D.
(Ex-Minister, Govt. of India & Ex-Mayor Lucknow)

CHAIRMAN
Parliamentary Standing Committee on
INDUSTRY

Member of Parliament
(Rajya Sabha)

29 August 2010

Hon'ble Sir,

Sub:- **Financial irregularities in hiring London based AM Films Ltd.- by Mr. VK Verma, DG, CWG.**

This is in continuation of my earlier letter of 31st July'10.

From very reliable sources and on the basis of documentary evidence, it has been confirmed that certain officials of the Organizing Committee, CWG, in order to divert the attention from their corrupt activities involving contracts worth thousands of crores, highlighted certain allegation through the media regarding a contract worth around 2 crores only. In this regard, the role of Mr. V.K. Verma, Director General, OC; Mr. M. Jeychandran, Jt. DG (Finance & Accounts) and Mr. R.K. Sacheti, Jt. DG, is instrumental. I would like to highlight the following facts for your kind attention and consideration:-

i) Mr. V.K. Verma, DG, had constituted an Empowered Committee headed by Mr. M. Jeychandran, Jt. DG(F&A) with DDGs Mr. Sanjai Mahendru and Mr. Sudhir Verma as Members. It was the decision of this empowered committee under the guidance of DG, Mr. VK Verma which led to the hiring of the services of M/s AM Films (copy of the minutes indicating the decision and subsequently release of advance/ payment is enclosed).

ii) Mr. Darbari's role was only restricted to ceremonial, protocol and coordination with the government agencies WITHOUT any financial transaction, tender process etc.

iii) It is most unfortunate that the empowered committee of three members was constituted by Mr. V.K. Verma, DG, who are involved

120, Parliament House Annexe, New Delhi 110 001 (India) Tel.: 23034120 Tele fax: 23017779
Res.: 11, Lodhi Estate, New Delhi (India) 110 003 Tel.: 24645049, 24641809, Fax: 24698432
5, Babu Banarasi Das Nagar (Purana Kila), Lucknow 226 001 (U.P.), Tel.: (0522) 2613917, 2274020 Fax: 2628030
E-mail: bbdnd08@gmail.com, bbdnd@hotmail.com

Dr. Akhilesh Das Gupta
M.B.A, LL.B, Ph. D.
(Ex-Minister, Govt. of India & Ex-Mayor Lucknow)

CHAIRMAN
Parliamentary Standing Committee on
INDUSTRY

Member of Parliament
(Rajya Sabha)

- 2 -

in corruption but none of these officers have been suspended nor terminated (only one member Mr. Sanjay Mahendroo resigned himself earlier). But, instead, another officer Mr. T.S. Darbari, who was not even member of this committee and had no access to the finances, has been made a scapegoat. While the fact is that he was neither responsible for hiring AM Films nor was he involved in any price negotiation or disbursement of advances/ payment etc.

iv) Whereas, the fact is that Mr. V.K. Verma, though sitting in Delhi, was directly monitoring all the committee members, in touch with each other, through email, SMS, telephones, blackberry, internet phones and other means of communication. Hence, it is quite evident that the real offenders and scamists are Mr. VK Verma, DG, Mr. M. Jeychandran, Chairman of Empowered Committee and the Members Mr. Sudhir Verma & Mr. Sanjay Mahendroo

We all have extreme faith in your integrity and leadership. I would strongly urge that the above guilty officials, involved in decision making, should be terminated immediately before they could destroy the evidences by diverting the attention on an innocent and unconnected official like Mr. T.S. Darbari who had no role in the episode whatsoever.

Regards

(Dr. Akhilesh Das Gupta)

Dr. Manmohan Singh,
Hon'ble Prime Minister,
Government of India,
New Delhi

120, Parliament House Annexe, New Delhi 110 001 (India) Tel.: 23034120 Tele fax: 23017779
Res.: 11, Lodhi Estate, New Delhi (India) 110 003 Tel.: 24645049, 24641809, Fax: 24698432
Babu Banarasi Das Nagar (Purana Kila), Lucknow 226 001 (U.P.), Tel.: (0522) 2613917, 2274020 Fax: 2628030
E-mail: bbdnd08@gmail.com, bbdnd@hotmail.com

Role and involvement of Mr. M. Jeychandren, OSD (F & A) in the contracts relating to M/s AM Cars/ M/s AM Films during QBR London launch, October, 2009 and also in SMAM Contract.

1. M/s AM Van and Car Hire and M/s AM Films were given business worth GBP 2,38,093.56 and GBP 146868.80 **by the empowered committee under the chairmanship of the then Jt. DG (F & A), Mr. M. Jeychandren.** This empowered committee was duly constituted by the competent authority i.e. **Mr. V.K. Verma, DG OC who had instructed "an empowered committee headed by the Jt. DG (F& A), Shri Jeychandren who will be in London during the QBR negotiates with the suppliers of branded buses and taxis and any other head where due to paucity of time tender procedures could not be followed".** Thus, in both the above contracts it is the responsibility of the committee headed by Mr. Jeychndren to conduct proper procedures, opening of the bids, preparation of the minutes and the recommendations thereof, finalization of the suppliers, price negotiations with the supplier, disbursement of advance etc., and to put up the recommendations to the competent authority i.e. DG, who had constituted this committee.This was the duty of Mr. Jeychandren as the Chairman of the Empowered Committee, deciding on the above contracts.

2. The other role of Mr. Jeychandren was, in capacity as Jt. DG (Finance & Accounts) and Head of the Finance & Accounts Department, where he is personally responsible to ensure proper procedures followed by the Committee and presence of all essential documents on file, before releasing the payments and advances.

3. The third role of Mr. Jeychandren was in his capacity as Member-Secretary of the OC Finance Committee, which approved of the enhanced Budget for the QBR London launch, on confirmation/certification that the President of India shall be participating in this function. This OC Finance Committee approved the enhanced budget for the event at its 7th meeting held in September, 2009. This OC Finance Committee was headed by Mr. V.K. Verma DG OC who is also the Chairman of the OC Finance Committee.

4. The QBR London launch function in October 29, 2009 involved two functional areas – i.e. the QBR Budget and the Ceremonies Department for conducting the cultural element of the function. Both these functional areas dealt with this; on files, and therefore the M/s Jack Morton Worldwide (JMW) contract was dealt with these two departments and the files are maintained with them. The Chairman Secretariat was NOT the concerned functional area, as Mr. Jeychandren normally claims to deflect his responsibilities.

5. As regards his role in the SMAM contract, though the contract was initially signed on 25th July, 2007 by Mr. Lalit Bhanot, Secretary General and Mr. R.K. Sacheti, Jt. DG, the revised contract was formulated, negotiated and dealt with by Mr. Jeychandren Currently he is in charge of all matters relating to SMAM.

प्रधान मंत्री

Prime Minister

New Delhi
31 October, 2010

Dear Shri Javadekar,

I have received your letter of 22 October, 2010 regarding servicing of the Shunglu Committee by the Cabinet Secretariat.

With regards,

Yours sincerely,

(Manmohan Singh)

Shri Prakash Javadekar, MP
24, Mahadeo Road
New Delhi – 110001

Prakash Javadekar
- Member of Parliament
- Spokesperson, BJP

सत्यमेव जयते

Date: 22.10.10

To
Dr. Manmohan Singh ji,
Prime Minister,
New Delhi.

Respected Sir,

Sub: Servicing of Shunglu Committee by Cabinet Secretariat.

Sir, you have appointed a committee to go into the irregularities in the CWG under the chairmanship of Ex-CAG Mr. Shunglu. You have given it a time frame of 3 months to complete the investigation.

Normally, this committee will be serviced by the Ministry of Sports. I request you to ponder over following facts;

I. Sports Secretary, Mrs. Khullar was on the executive board of OC of CWG. Thus, she is partied to all the decisions taken by the OC.

II. Joint Secretary, Mr. Rahul Bhatnagar of ISD in the Sports ministry was member of the finance committee of the OC. This committee decided about all the tenders.

You will appreciate that in such a situation the sports ministry should not be servicing the Shunglu Committee as actions of these officers and others will be under scanner of the committee.

I demand therefore that Shunglu committee should be serviced by the cabinet secretariat for the purpose of transparent and impartial enquiry.

Thanking you,

Yours truly,

(Prakash Javadekar)

Res.: 24, Mahadeo Road, New Delhi-110001, Phone : 011-23352124 Fax : 011-23765111
e-mail:pjavadekar@gmail.com

सत्यमेव जयते

प्रधान मंत्री

Prime Minister

New Delhi
6 August, 2010

Dear Dr. Gupta,

I have received your letter of 31 July, 2010 alleging irregularities by the Director General, Commonwealth Games.

With regards,

Yours sincerely,

(Manmohan Singh)

Dr. Akhilesh Das Gupta, MP
Chairman
Parliamentary Standing Committee on Industry
120, Parliament House Annexe
New Delhi – 110001

Dr. Akhilesh Das Gupta
M.B.A, LL.B, Ph. D.
(Ex-Minister, Govt. of India & Ex-Mayor Lucknow)

CHAIRMAN
Parliamentary Standing Committee on
INDUSTRY

Member of Parliament
(Rajya Sabha)

PERSONAL/ CONFIDENTIAL

July 31, 2010

Hon'ble Sir,

Sub: Illegal cash payment to London based AM Films UK Limited by Director General Commonwealth Games, Mr. V.K. Verma.

In the above context I wish to draw your kind attention to the following:

1. I have gone through today's the Hindustan Times and other newspapers wherein a detailed report about illegal cash payments by Commonwealth Games Organsising Committee have been published. Copies of some such reports are attached herewith for your ready reference.

   It has been brought to my notice that the real perpetrator of this offence is Director General Commonwealth Games, Mr. V.K. Verma.

3. For this very purpose, the Director General had personally visited UK and is believed to have settled with the officials of AM Films, UK Ltd, flouting all norms of Money Laundering Act, 2002.

4. Prior to his present posting Mr. V.K. Verma was Director (Commercial), Air India. At that time also a CBI inquiry had been constituted against him, which is

120, Parliament House Annexe, New Delhi 110 001 (India) Tel.: 23034120 Tele fax: 23017779
Res.: 11, Lodhi Estate, New Delhi (India) 110 003 Tel.: 24645049, 24641809, Fax: 24698432
bu Banarasi Das Nagar (Purana Kila), Lucknow 226 001 (U.P.), Tel.: (0522) 2613917, 2274020 Fax: 2628030
E-mail: bbdnd08@gmail.com, bbdnd@hotmail.com

Dr. Akhilesh Das Gupta
M.B.A, LL.B, Ph. D.
Ex-Minister, Govt. of India & Ex-Mayor Lucknow)

सत्यमेव जयते

CHAIRMAN
Parliamentary Standing Committee on
INDUSTRY

Member of Parliament
(Rajya Sabha)

still pending. This goes to show that Mr. V.K. Verma is a habitual offender.

5. In the capacity of Director General Commonwealth Games, Mr. V.K. Verma is also handling many more tasks. He is also believed to have done grave financial irregularities in those transactions.

6. Sir, you would agree that this incident of siphoning off the money has brought immense shame to the country.

In view of the seriousness of the offence committed by the Director General Commonwealth Games, I would request you to kindly immediately advise the concerned authorities to take appropriate action against the Director General. Any delay in taking action will give him sufficient time to destroy the evidences. I am sure that a thorough investigation of the Director General will give details of many more illegal activities.

Regards

(Dr. Akhilesh Das Gupta)

Dr. Manmohan Singh
Hon'ble Prime Minister
Govt. of India
New Delhi

120, Parliament House Annexe, New Delhi 110 001 (India) Tel.: 23034120 Tele fax: 23017779
Res.: 11, Lodhi Estate, New Delhi (India) 110 003 Tel.: 24645049, 24641809, Fax: 24698432
bu Banarasi Das Nagar (Purana Kila), Lucknow 226 001 (U.P.), Tel.: (0522) 2613917, 2274020 Fax: 2628030
E-mail: bbdnd08@gmail.com, bbdnd@hotmail.com

List of Officials of Commonwealth Games 2010

(a) S.No. 1 to 5 are permanent employees of CWG-OC on monthly salary + perks basis.

(b) S.No. 6 to 23 are designated as Technical Officials for CWG and their duties are till 15th October'10. They all are getting To & Fro Air Tickets, Free Accommodation + Food + Rs.1500 per day and a Kit costing Rs.25000/- per head.

S.No	Name	State	Designation
1	Shri V.K. Verma	New Delhi	President, BAI & DG-OC, CWG,
2	Shri S. Muralidharan	Kerala	Vice President, BAI
3	Shri K.Ch.Punnaiah Choudary	Andhra Pradesh	Jt. Secretary, BAI
4	Shri T.P.S. Puri	Chandigarh	Vice President, BAI
5	Shri S.P. Singh	New Delhi	Jt. Secretary, BAI
6	Shri S.A. Rawal	Gujarat	Vice President, BAI
7	Shri Sanjay Mishra	Chattisgarh	EC Member, BAI
8	Shri S.T. Desai	Gujarat	EC Member, BAI
9	Dr. O.D. Sharma	J & K	Vice President, BAI
10	Shri K. Prabhakar Rao	Jharkhand	Jt. Secretary, BAI
11	Shri Anil K. Choughule	Madhya Pradesh	EC Member, BAI
12	Shri Malsawmika	Mizoram	Council Member, BAI
13	Shri K.K. Sharma	Rajasthan	Jt. Secretary, BAI
14	Shri B.S. Mankoti	Uttarakhand	Council Member, BAI
15	Shri Dilip Pinge	Maharashtra	EC Member, BAI
16	Dr. Manjit Singh	Haryana	EC Member, BAI
17	Shri Krishnand Jaiswal	Bihar	EC Member, BAI
18	Shri K. Liam Hming Thanga	Mizoram	Council Member, BAI
19	Shri S.A. Shetty	Maharashtra	EC Member, BAI
20	Shri Rajesh Kamal Rajput	Meghalaya	EC Member, BAI
21	Shri Syed Iqubal Raheman	Orissa	EC Member, BAI
22	Shri Anand Khare	Air India	Council Member, BAI
23	Shri Chunni Lal	Himachal Pradesh	EC Member, BAI

The above Members & Office Bearers of BAI will attend the Extraordinary General Meeting of BAI on 12th Oct. 2010.

Mohammed Azharuddin
Member of Parliament
(Lok Sabha)
MURADABAD CONSTITUENCY
MEMBER :
• Standing Committee on Energy
• Consultative Committee on Youth Affairs & Sports

सत्यमेव जयते

C-322, Defence Colony,
New Delhi - 110 024
Cell : 09013180193
09935523456

October 03, 2010

Hon'ble Sir,

Subject:- Mr. V.K. Verma, Director General, Commonwealth Games NOW TRYING TO SABOTAGE THE GAMES

With reference to the above subject, I am with a heavy heart giving you the following information:-

1) Because of the incompetence and corrupt functioning of some of the main officials of Commonwealth Games Organizing Committee (CGOC), your goodself has rightly entrusted the entire responsibility of conducting the ensuing Commonwealth Games to a **"high power committee"** consisting of two senior Union Cabinet Ministers, Cabinet Secretary and other very senior officials in order to salvage the prestige of the country.

2) The CGOC with Mr. Suresh Kalmadi and his associates, specially the Director General Mr. VK Verma, are obviously unhappy with the new arrangement of the Government and, hence, a series of mismanagement and disruption by the coterie of few people in the CGOC is being planned to sabotage the games for ensuring that the blame goes to the said **high power committee** constituted by your goodself.

3) **Here is the latest example of sabotage plan of Mr. VK Verma**

a) While the Commonwealth Games will be on its peak specially on 12th, 13th and 14th October 2010, Mr. VK Verma, who is also the President of Badminton Association of India (BAI) has called up

Mohammed Azharuddin
Member of Parliament
(Lok Sabha)
M..ADABAD CONSTITUENCY
MEMBER :
• Standing Committee on Energy
• Consultative Committee on Youth Affairs & Sports

सत्यमेव जयते

C-322, Defence Colony,
New Delhi - 110 024
Cell : 09013180193
09935523456

-2-

an Extraordinary General Meeting of BAI on 12th October 2010 and that too in the Conference Hall of the HQ of Commonwealth Games at Jai Singh Road, New Delhi. (A copy of the notice dated 11th Sept. 2010 for holding this meeting is enclosed). Here the question is that when BAI has an independent office in New Delhi, then why the EGM of BAI is proposed to be held at a very sensitive place - the Headquarters of Commonwealth Games?

b) The most alarming and interesting part of this meeting is that the 23 members of the General Council of BAI are either permanent or temporary officials on the pay roll of CGOC till 15th October 2010 atleast. (A copy of the list of these 23 members is enclosed for your kind perusal).

c) Holding Extraordinary General Meeting of BAI on a day when the interest in Commonwealth Games will be at peak, is a clear-cut case of sabotage of Commonwealth Games. This must be examined in the perspective that how the said 23 technical officials, who are getting handsome payments and perks from the CGOC, instead of giving priority to their respective duties in successfully organizing the Commonwealth Games till 15th October 2010, have been asked to leave their duties on 12th October 2010 and go to attend the Extraordinary General Meeting of the Badminton Association of India? Clearly, to help the agenda and intention of Mr. VK Verma. Isn't it the specific

Mohammed Azharuddin
Member of Parliament
(Lok Sabha)
MURADABAD CONSTITUENCY
MEMBER :
• Standing Committee on Energy
• Consultative Committee on Youth Affairs & Sports

आत्मदेव जयते

C-322, Defence Colony,
New Delhi - 110 024
Cell : 09013180193
09935523456

-3-

case of sabotage, high-handedness, mismanagement and serving own vested interests of the DG, OC, Mr. Verma & Company?

d) It is also apprehended that in the proposed meeting of BAI, there can be stiff opposition of Mr. VK Verma which may cause exchange of blows between two groups and even violence can take place. But, Mr. VK Verma has nothing to loose in it and he seems to be not bothered even if the games are sabotaged. This shows his irresponsible and indifferent attitude towards his duties.

4) I, therefore, suggest that, in view of his overall performance and attitude, Mr. V.K. Verma may be relieved of all his authorities so that he may not cause any further embarrassment and sabotage the Commonwealth Games.

With regards,

Yours sincerely,

(MOHAMMED AZHARUDDIN)
Member of Parliament (Lok Sabha)

Dr. Manmohan Singh,
Hon'ble Prime Minister
Govt. of India, South Block,
New Delhi-1

MOHAMMED AZHARUDDIN
Member of Parliament
(Lok Sabha)
MORADABAD CONSTITUENCY

MEMBER :
- Standing Committee on Energy
- Consultative Committee on Youth Affairs & Sports

C-134, Defence Colony,
New Delhi - 110 024
Cell : 09013180193
09935523456

सत्यमेव जयते

November 15, 2010

Mr. T.K.A. Nair,
Principal Secreatary
Prime Minister's Office
Govt. of India, South Block,
New Delhi-1

Dear Sir,

Subject:- **Gross Financial/ Tender Irregularities and criminal conspiracy done by Mr. V.K. Verma, D.G. and Mr. R.K. Sacheti, Jt. DG, Organizing Committee Commonwealth Games Delhi 2010 – Siphoning of Funds and Money Laundering in Foreign Currency to the tune of more than Rs.200 Crores.**

With reference to the above subject, I am writing in continuation of my earlier complaints against Mr. V.K. Verma. The details of corruption committed by him are as under:-

1) Mr. V.K. Verma, who is a habitual offender under FEMA, is known for hiring middlemen in Switzerland, USA and UK for his corrupt activities, causing crores of rupees of financial loss to the Government exchequer, both during his stint in Air India and now in the Organizing Committee of Commonwealth Games where he is in charge of important tenders worth crores of rupees and operates in connivance with Mr. R.K. Sacheti, Jt. DG.

2) **Timing, Scoring and Result System (This is Rs.112 Cores of Payout and Money Transfer in Swiss Francs)**

RFP for this was issued as a global tender with stipulation that the bidder must have games time experience (Olympics, Commonwealth Games etc.). Only two bids were received from (i) M/s Swiss Timing and (ii) M/s MSL. The committee evaluating the RFP had differences of opinion among the members. However, in the final analysis, the bid of M/S MSL was rejected saying that they did not meet the evaluation criteria.

Contd.....2

MOHAMMED AZHARUDDIN
Member of Parliament
(Lok Sabha)
MORADABAD CONSTITUENCY

MEMBER :
• Standing Committee on Energy
• Consultative Committee on Youth Affairs & Sports

सत्यमेव जयते

C-134, Defence Colony,
New Delhi - 110 024
Cell : 09013180193
09935523456

-2-

The contract was later awarded to M/s Swiss Timing at a cost of Rs.112 crores. It was always talked about that, since it was practically a single bid, the price quoted was so high. **Had it been a competitive bidding, the price would have been in the range of Rs.25-30 Crores.** Here, it is important to note that world-wide the prices of technological equipments are coming down because of advance technology. But, the above TSR contract has been awarded 5 times more than the prices of same work in Melbourne Commonwealth Games 4 year back.

The funds available were only 102 Crores. The DGOC Mr. VK Verma added Rs. 7.7 Crores given by the Ministry of Sports for purchase of Legacy Equipment for Athletics, Swimming and Cycling for SAI stadia, even though this purchase was not a part of this proposal and asked the vendor to offer 1 Million Swiss Franc discount.

The Ministry kept suspecting that DGOC had misrepresented the figures but could never nail him down. Two crimes committed by the above officials:

a) The technical specifications were so drawn that for all practical purposes it was a single bid and obviously at four times the present cost and five times the amount paid at Melbourne for the similar work, while the worldwide cost of technical equipments are coming down due to technology advancement.

b) Funds were not available but the figures were misrepresented to the finance sub-committee for approval.

The above has resulted in wrongful financial gain to Mr. Verma and Sacheti in Swiss Francs. It would be interesting to investigate the role of middlemen like (i) Hiren (Henry) Seth of Mumbai, a close associate of Mr. Verma and (ii) Mr. Neil Kothari of Chicago, USA, and their dealings with Swiss Banking Corporation at its main branch in Zurich, Switzerland – the persons and channels who find a mention in the CBI's FIR filed in Mumbai in 1998 in the Pennsylvania Woven Carpet Mills' case where Mr. Verma was responsible for causing a loss of Rs.250 Lacs on a purchase order of carpets for AI aircrafts in gross violation of Stores and Purchase procedures as investigated by CBI.

3) Similarly, the other contract relating to the **Games Management System** was awarded at **three times the market price.**

MOHAMMED AZHARUDDIN
Member of Parliament
(Lok Sabha)
MORADABAD CONSTITUENCY

MEMBER :
• Standing Committee on Energy
• Consultative Committee on Youth Affairs & Sports

C-134, Defence Colony,
New Delhi - 110024
Cell : 09013180193
09935523456

- 3 -

4) **Ticketing Contract worth Rs.15 Crores**: Mr. VK Verma manipulated the committee for finalization of this tender to award the contract to the L2 party despite it being at least 50% more than the L1 bidder. Further, he forced the committee to take all the 4 bidders to the commercial stage despite the fact that only 2 parties were capable of delivering the exact requirements. Under the garb of public sector, he has taken undue benefits in excess of Rs.5 Crores from M/s Broadband and M/s Ticket Pro (both foreign companies) and consortium partners of M/s IRTC. Incidentally, these companies were positioned by Verma to work with IRTC.

5) **Verma & Sacheti's role in accreditation card deals worth crores**:

Each of the ID card/ Accreditation card has a Lanyard (ribbon) so that it could be hung around the neck. To limit the competition and increase the cost of this item, the specifications were so prepared that only those supplier, whose Lanyard (ribbon) can withstand 80 degree centigrade, could compete. It may be noted that the plastic lamination and the paper would get burnt at about 70-80 degree centigrade and the person wearing the lanyard would also get burnt, but this lanyard (ribbon) would survive. It priced about Rs.70/- each and around 1.5 Lac accreditation cards were printed and each having a Rs.70 ribbon.

6) **Purchase of Hova Courts for Badminton Stadium**:

a) Mr. VK Verma managed to purchase 26 synthetic hova courts from Yonex for the game of badminton.

b) There was no need to purchase such a big quantity. Instead only 10 hova courts were sufficient, out of which 6 hova courts are still lying idle in Mr. Verma's custody.

c) Moreover, six hova courts were already purchased few months back by the Badminton Association of India (BAI) and the entire funds for the same were given as subsidy by Govt. of India. In fact, there was no need of synthetic hova courts.

d) These hova courts though technically purchased by DDA but so called "technical advice" was managed by Mr. Verma who is also the President of BAI.

MOHAMMED AZHARUDDIN
Member of Parliament
(Lok Sabha)
MORADABAD CONSTITUENCY

MEMBER :
• Standing Committee on Energy
• Consultative Committee on Youth Affairs & Sports

सत्यमेव जयते

C-134, Defence Colony,
New Delhi - 110 024
Cell : 09013180193
09935523456

-4-

e) He fraudulently managed & manipulated to make DDA understand that no tendering was required because the Badminton World Federation (BWF) had authorized only Yonex by saying on record that Yonex is the only approved supplier of hova courts and no other hova courts are allowed internationally. Whereas on the website of WBF, there is a list of 18 potential suppliers from whom such courts could be purchased.

f) Further, the Commonwealth Games does not come under BWF games charter. Even if somebody says it is allowed to purchase from Yonex, even then it is wrong statement because Yonex was not allowed to write its name on the hova courts as there was written only "Commonwealth Games 2010 .

g) Even in ensuing Asian Games in China, hova courts are not being used. It is well known in the badminton world that VK Verma took bribe of more than Rs.60 Lacs which has been paid to him partly in Kualalumpur (Malaysia) and partly in London and America, where his wife is having bank accounts and his 3 children are studying there. The said bribe has been transferred in their accounts. In this deal alone, a loss of more than Rs.1.25 Crore was done to the public exchequer.

7) **<u>Project of Cleaning and Waste Management</u>:**

For this work, more than Rs.60 Crores have been spent, whereas this could entirely be done within Rs.15-20 Crores, and Mr. Verma was head & in charge of this project. It is well known to everyone that cleaning & waste management work in the entire games village and other places was very poor and Verma took heavy commissions in this account also.

8) **<u>Networking, IT and Computerization Contract during Games</u>:**

On the face of it, this contract was given to MTNL for more than Rs.650 Crores. But before giving contract on nomination basis, VK Verma managed and made it confirmed that sub-contract on back to back basis was given to private operators like HCL and CISCO. A Rs.150 Crores contract for supply of hardwares was given to Telecom Consultants India Ltd. (TCIL) which was finalized by Mr. VK Verma. This hardware contract was also given back to

MOHAMMED AZHARUDDIN
Member of Parliament
(Lok Sabha)
MORADABAD CONSTITUENCY

MEMBER :
- Standing Committee on Energy
- Consultative Committee on Youth Affairs & Sports

C-134, Defence Colony,
New Delhi - 110 024
Cell : 09013180193
09935523456

- 5 -

back to a private party engaged by Mr. Verma. Before giving the above contract to MTNL, Mr. Verma in connivance and in hand-in-gloves with MTNL officials managed back to back arrangement for Rs.650 crores software contract to HCL and CISCO. In this deal alone, more than Rs.150 Crores have been taken as commission by VK Verma alongwith the officials of MTNL and some other officials of CWGOC. It has been reported that this amount has been received by them through the route of Mauritius, Switzerland, USA and someother countries which are enjoying tax exemption.

9) **Contract of International TV Broadcasting Rights**:

Though the local contract within India for broadcasting the games was given to Prasar Bharati, the international TV broadcasting rights were given by CGOC and the contract was finalized by VK Verma. This contract was for around Rs.300 Crores. Here also malpractice revealed and heavy commission has been taken in this particular deal.

10) **Queen's Baton Relay**:

This controversial matter is now much publicized and both in & outside India, this arrangement was finalized by VK Verma. He himself was going to join the baton relay function in London but, at the last moment, he did not attend. Instead, he formed a three-member committee who was reporting to him on each & every step through backberry chating, SMS etc. while Mr. Verma, sitting in Delhi, was directly monitoring the function in London and giving direction to the said committee members who were in touch with each other and every on the spot decision was taken directly with the approval of VK Verma. It is infact the show managed by VK Verma only and he is the real scamist in this matter. Few months after the above event, he personally went to London in May-June 2010 to "settle" the account.

11) **Printing of publicity material for Commonwealth Games 2010**:

The entire general printing jobs of all kinds, other than ticketing, like bill boards, Shera boards, pamphlets etc. were sanctioned by VK Verma on much higher prices than the market rates and he received huge bribe in this work.

12) **Sponsorship of Premier Brand**: This is also an area where VK Verma has managed sponsorship of his choice in which he has taken huge commission.

MOHAMMED AZHARUDDIN
Member of Parliament
(Lok Sabha)
MORADABAD CONSTITUENCY

MEMBER :
• Standing Committee on Energy
• Consultative Committee on Youth Affairs & Sports

सत्यमेव जयते

C-134, Defence Colony,
New Delhi - 110 024
Cell : 09013180193
09935523456

- 6 -

13) **Favouritism and Corruption in the Appointments of Staff, technical officials etc.**: Mr. VK Verma was keyman in the recruitment process of staff, full time/ part time, and technical officials at different level who were appointed on very high salaries and perks. It has been reported that all kinds of corruption, favouritism, turpitude have been done in engaging the technical staff and work force, in far more than the required numbers, at the time of conducting the games for which very high amounts were paid. Each & every officer/ technical official from outside Delhi was paid air fare, boarding, lodging, free kits plus Rs.1500 per day. It has been reported the only 30% of the employed force was genuine and the rest 70%, including some technical officials, was excessive & unfair which was just to favour relatives/ friends and to extort money at different levels.

14) **Purchase of Souvenir, Gifts, Shera and Kits**:

It has been reported that around fifty thousand numbers of these items were got prepared/ purchased for volunteers, technical officials, players etc. and VK Verma was the key man in all these purchases, reportedly in large than the required quantity and at much higher prices, obviously to get heavy kickbacks.

15) **Investment in Properties by Mr. VK Verma**: He has made huge insvestments in properties worth crores, of rupees in his name, benami and several properties & cash balances in the name of his two sons & one daughter studying abroad. He has also purchased a big penthouse on a plot of 800 Sq.Yds. in the posh colony of Maharanibagh in Delhi at a cost of more than Rs.20 crores. This purchase was done by him just after his retirement from Air India. After becoming Director General, Commonwealth Games Organizing Committee, he has recently got well-furnished his house with very costly interiors etc. of more than Rs.5 crores. Further, he has also purchased a big farm house at a cost of Rs.40 crores, for the time being in the name of one of his close friends in Pushpanjali scheme of Ansals in Delhi. He has also bought some commercial properties in Delhi, Saharanpur and in Kualalumpur (Malaysia). He has also purchased residential property for his son in Washington and a 3-bedroom flat for himself in London.

16) Mr. VK Verma, DG, CWG, used to claim openly that he knew the entire tendering and purchasing systems of government because he had been in different public sector undertakings like Air India (where he faced CBI's charge sheet for his corrupt practices) and how to manage the tender for his personal

MOHAMMED AZHARUDDIN
Member of Parliament
(Lok Sabha)
MORADABAD CONSTITUENCY

MEMBER :
• Standing Committee on Energy
• Consultative Committee on Youth Affairs & Sports

सत्यमेव जयते

C-134, Defence Colony,
New Delhi - 110 024
Cell : 09013180193
09935523456

- 7 -

gains. He also claimed that he would design such kind of system in which CBI and other investigating agencies would not be able to find any malpractice. He also used to say that he already had faced inquiry agencies like CBI and there is nothing new which might bother him.

17) A note containing serious charges of corruption with documentary evidence relating to VK Verma's crimes committed in Air India, causing crores of rupees financial loss to the government and public exchequer, with details of his receiving commissions in foreign banks, is enclosed for a thorough probe by CBI, DRI and ED.

There is a huge list of corruption done by Mr. VK Verma, besides above. I would earnestly request you to order for a free & fair inquiry immediately to be conducted by CBI, ED, Income Tax and Customs Dept. and/or other concerned investigating agencies in the interest of justice and of government as well.

Thanking you,

Yours sincerely.

(MOHAMMED AZHARUDDIN)

Encl: as above

Corrupt & Dubious Background of Mr. V.K. Verma
Director General, Commonwealth Games 2010

1. **His initial appointment in Air India was illegal:** Although no post of Sports Executive existed in the Standard Force of Air India, in 1992, Mr. V.K. Verma, in gross violation of laid down procedures, was interviewed for the post of Deputy Controller of Sports, that too without advertising the post either in national news papers or in any internal notification. More surprising is the fact that although Mr. V.K. Verma was interviewed for the post of Deputy Controller of Sports, he was appointed -Controller of Sports. This issue was raised in Lok Sabha in 1992, but the Ministry did not give suitable reply.

2. **He caused loss to Air India of more than Rs. 225 lacs in the purchase of carpets:** During 1993-95, Mr. V.K. Verma was Dy. Director (Stores & Purchase). In gross violation of stores & purchase procedures, he placed an order for carpets for Air India aircrafts with a U.S. based company namely Pennislvenia Woven Carpet Mill's (PWCM).

   This corruption was investigated both by Air India's Vigilance Department and the CBI. CBI even filed an FIR against Mr. V.K. Verma in Mumbai in 1998. However, under pressure of Air India's the then Director Vigilence Mr. SPS Yadav, IPS and others, the investigations were blocked. The enquiries have revlealed that in violation of PSU regulations on purchase procedures, two middlemen were roped in to finalise the deal. CBI, during investigations had unearthed this fact. Please see para 1 to 9 of the attachement 1.

   CBI's investigation of the above case revealed that one of the middlemen was one Mr. Hiren (Henry) Seth, a resident of Mumbai and a close aquitance of Mr. VK Verma. The U.S. company in the case in the New York Court of Law had admitted that they were instructed by Mr. Seth to transfer USD 116,232 to the Swiss Banking Corporation at its main branch in Zurich, Switzerland.

- 2 -

Other middleman was an NRI, namely, Mr. Neil Kothari, a resident of Chicago, USA. Involvement of both middlemen was recorded in the CBI's FIR filed in Mumbai in 1998. Please see paras 6 to 12 of attachment 1. Please also see news clipping on "the carpet that AI never rolled out" which appeared in the Indian Express, Mumbai on 11th July 2002 (attachment 2).

Consequently, Mr. SPS Yadav was prematurely repatriated to his home state – Maharashtra, although he had completed only 18 months of his 3 years posting with Air India. Please see the attahched cuttings published in various newspapers in Mumbai.

It is relevant to note that even though Mr. SPS Yadav challenged his premature transfer and secured CAT and a High Court order for his reinstatement in Air India, these orders have not been implemented.

3. **Submitting false medical certificates to cover an alleged illness during the period October 2000 – May 2001**: Under instructions of the Ministry of Civil Aviation, Mr. VK Verma was transferred from the post of Director (Planning) to Director (Corporate Affairs). Thereafter, Mr. Verma reported sick for a period of six months between October 23, 2000 and May 21, 2001. In support of his faked illness he submitted some medical certificates allegedly signed by Doctors in All India Institute of Medical Sciences, New Delhi.

On investigation by Director (Vigilence), Mr. SPS Yadav, IPS, these certificates were found to be false. Therefore, action was initiated against Mr. Verma. However, no action has actually materialised against Mr. Verma.

4. **Sale of Bilateral Traffic Rights:** As Commercial Director of Air India in the 7 years period, March 2000 to Dec.2007, Mr. VK Verma was responsible for granting traffic rights and clearly for financial considerations to foreign airlines based on recommendations made to

- 3 -

the Ministry of Civil Aviation from time to time. These recommendations were made with the active support of the Air India's the then Director (Planning) Mrs. Shireen Lalwani and assistance from a Delhi based middlemen Mr. Deepak Talwar, owner of Deepal Talwar and associates, located at 4 D, White House, 10-Bhagwan Das Road, New Delhi.

Please see Table-1 which clearly illustrates the reckless manner in which the bilateral traffic rights were sold. An exmination of the table will reveal that the almost 300% increase over 4 years translates to an average annual rate of increase of 32% per annum, year on year. Please also see Table-2 and 3 which show further increases.

5. **Accumulation of disproportionate assets by Mr. VK Verma**: As mentioned above, Mr. VK Verma was appointed in Air India in 1992 in questionable manner. As Controller of Sports in Air India, he requested the then Director (HR) to allot a car. He was advised to purchase a car or a second-hand vehicle. He responded that he did not have the finances to buy the vehicle. This statement should be viewed in the context of the fact that during the course of his 18 odd years with Air India, he has amassed vast financial assests such as :-

a) Maruti Bolero which has now been upgraded to the latest model of Honda.
b) Many plots in his home town Saharanpur in the name of his parents and 2nd wife Mrs. Renu Arora whom he married in 1983.
c) Educating his daughter Radhika Verma in London. He spent atleast UK Pounds 30,000 on her 2 years education.
d) Educating his son Vikram Arora Verma in USA for 4 years and spent atleast USD 80,000.

Despite various requests by the Vigilance Dept. of Air India to inquire into his disproportionate assets, no steps have been taken due to his political clout.

सत्यमेव जयते

प्रधान मंत्री

Prime Minister

New Delhi
24 November, 2010

Dear Shri Azharuddin,

I have received your letter of 15 November, 2010 regarding Shri V.K. Verma, Director General and Shri R.K. Sacheti, Joint Director General, Organizing Committee, Commonwealth Games 2010.

With regards,

Yours sincerely,

(Manmohan Singh)

Shri Mohammed Azharuddin, MP
C-14, Lodhi Estate
New Delhi

D.O.No.293...Min,(PR,YA&S) / 06

मणि शंकर अय्यर
MANI SHANKAR AIYAR

मंत्री
पंचायती राज और युवा कार्यक्रम एवं खेल
भारत सरकार
नई दिल्ली-110 001
Minister
Panchayati Raj and Youth Affairs & Sports
Government of India
New Delhi-110 001

9 March 2006

Subject : Expenditure projections for Commonwealth Games-2010

I write to seek a meeting with you to discuss the gargantuan gap between the expenditure projections given in the 2003 Note for Cabinet on the basis of which approval was accorded for us to bid for the Commonwealth Games-2010 and the present projected figures of expenditure. The gap is not only gargantuan, it also seems to be growing. As against the figure of Rs.150 crore for physical infrastructure projected in 2003, current estimates have been ramped up to over Rs.5000 crore. On the organization of the games, the 2003 expenditure projection of Rs.250 crore has already been ramped up to nearly Rs.900 crore.

After the formation of our Government, Cabinet sanction has also been accorded for us to bid for the Asian Games 2014 on the basis of the relatively modest expenditure projection which was given in the Note for Cabinet. However, going by the experience of the Commonwealth Games, and previous such mega sports events, I apprehend that we will once again witness a gargantuan gap between projected and actual expenditure. Indeed, the prospective bid for the Asian Games is being used to justify the vast gap between earlier and present projections for the Commonwealth Games. There seems to be a desire also to build up a campaign for the Olympic Games, even perhaps as early as 2016. All these ambitions are feeding on each other to justify an expenditure of tens of thousands of crores of rupees.

I would like to discuss with you the ethics of embarking on such a course.

Perhaps large-scale expenditure on Delhi-centric sports events which have an essentially middle class appeal could rest easier on our conscience if there were a corresponding scheme to meet the crying need

401-सी, शास्त्री भवन, नई दिल्ली–110 001 दूरभाष : 011-23386520, 23384183, फैक्स : 011-2338[illegible]
401-C, Shastri Bhawan, New Delhi-110 001 Tele. : 011-23386520, 23384183, Fax : 011-2338-[illegible]

for sports facilities in the rural areas which I have personally experienced both as a constituency MP and as Minister of Panchayati Raj. I would, therefore, also wish to discuss with you, in the context of expenditure on the Commonwealth Games, a proposal I am formulating for a Panchayat Khel-Khud Abhiyan.

I should be grateful if you would kindly find a few minutes in your extremely busy schedule for me to secure your personal guidance on these matters.

With respectful regds.

Yours sincerely,

Dr.Manmohan Singh
Hon'ble Prime Minister
South Block
New Delhi.

D.O.No. 725 Min, (YA&S) 06

मणि शंकर अय्यर
MANI SHANKAR AIYAR

मंत्री
पंचायती राज और युवा कार्यक्रम एवं खेल
भारत सरकार
नई दिल्ली-110 001
Minister
Panchayati Raj and Youth Affairs & Sports
Government of India
New Delhi-110 001

3 July 2006

Respected Prime Minister, Sir,

Chairman, Organizing Committee, has sent me a copy of his letter to you dated 9 June requesting representation for OC in the Committee of Secretaries appointed for the Commonwealth Games. May I take the liberty of saying I do not think the suggestion merits acceptance.

Yours sincerely,

Dr. Manmohan Singh
Hon'ble Prime Minister
South Block
New Delhi

401-सी, शास्त्री भवन, नई दिल्ली–110 001 दूरभाष : 011-23386520, 23384183, फैक्स : 011-23381898
Shastri Bhawan, New Delhi-110 001 Tele. : 011-23386520, 23384183, Fax : 011-23381898

D.O.No. 820 Min, (YA&S)/06

मणि शंकर अय्यर
MANI SHANKAR AIYAR

मंत्री
पंचायती राज और युवा कार्यक्रम एवं खेल
भारत सरकार
नई दिल्ली-110 001
Minister
Panchayati Raj and Youth Affairs & Sports
Government of India
New Delhi-110 001

11 July 2006

Respected Prime Minister, Sir,

Subject : Visit to the United Kingdom – 4-9 July 2006

I visited the United Kingdom for nearly a week from 4-9 July and returned yesterday. As my visit covered all three of my Ministerial responsibilities, I am summarising below the outcome with respect to each of these portfolios.

Sports

During the course of my visit, I met Mike Fennell and Mike Hooper, Chairman and CEO respectively of the Commonwealth Games Federation. I also met with Tessa Jowell, Secretary of State for a variety of subjects, including the London Olympics 2012, and her Minister of State for Sports, Richard Caborn. Both were prepared to consider exchange of expertise and information on the Commonwealth Games/Olympics under the Trade Agreement signed between our Minister of Commerce and their Secretary of State for Trade and Industry in November last year. The details are to be worked out by the Indian High Commission in London but we have the go-ahead for continuing the joint work now initiated. Together, the British Ministers and I attended the anniversary celebrations at Trafalgar Square of London being selected as the venue for the Olympic Games 2012. Prime Minister Tony Blair was present on the occasion and kindly took care to make a special mention of my presence in his speech. In addition, I visited Manchester, venue of the Commonwealth Games 2002 and held detailed discussions with all concerned, collected a vast amount of documentation and saw for myself the various venues for those Games and the use being made of them now as the Commonwealth Games legacy. Back in London, I met with officials concerned with the London Olympics, including the Chairman of the Organising Committee, Lord Sebastian Coe.

The following important conclusions arise with respect to Delhi hosting the Commonwealth Games 2010 :

(i) Analogous to the manner in which the UK government has designated the Secretary of State herself as the Cabinet Minister in charge of the London Olympics, we need to immediately set up a

401-सी, शास्त्री भवन, नई दिल्ली-110 001 दूरभाष : 011-23386520, 23384183, फैक्स : 011-2338...
401-C, Shastri Bhawan, New Delhi-110 001 Tele. : 011-23386520, 23384183, Fax : 011-23381...

Department of Commonwealth Games in the Ministry of Youth Affairs and Sports to exclusively concentrate on coordinating and overseeing all the different authorities involved with the Games. GoM have already approved the establishment of a new post of Joint Secretary, International Sports. But after having been in charge of this Ministry for the better part of half a year, and comparing our organisational arrangements for CWG 2010 with those in the UK, I am persuaded that the current Secretary, Youth Affairs and Sports has far too full an agenda to be able to devote the time and attention required for pulling together the various different strands of our organisational arrangements for the Commonwealth Games 2010. Accordingly, I will be moving a Note for Cabinet for the creation of a Department of Commonwealth Games that, in due course, might be converted, if required, into a Department of International Sporting Events.

(ii) The concept of a Games "legacy" has a completely different meaning, connotation and significance in the UK to the manner in which we are conceiving "legacy" in India. There, the aim of the Games in Manchester was to transform the most derelict part of the city, East Manchester, in the interests of the most disadvantaged section of society – laid off workers from the declining textiles and heavy engineering industries, many of whom had been unemployed for two generations or more – to be resettled in a renewed way of life with much better housing, superior community facilities and remunerative employment in light industries in the same place where their families had lived for years. The transformation is spectacular, in both human and environmental terms. The same legacy objective is aimed at for the Lea Valley on the outskirts of London where six of the worst-affected boroughs of London City are set to be transformed into a garden suburb thanks to the London Olympics. The equivalent would be a complete makeover of the trans-Yamuna East Delhi slums into a garden suburbia, not for the benefit of the upper middle class but for the lakhs of rural immigrants now living there in sub-human conditions. By coincidence, while I was in London *The Times* carried a front- page story on the escalation in costs of the Olympic Games but it turned out on a close reading that the additional investment was essentially aimed at rehabilitation on a spectacular scale for the seriously disadvantaged people now living there.

(iii) As regards the sports legacy, such as the stadia and other venues, in Manchester detailed planning had been done in advance, and conscientious implementation has followed, to involve the local community as fully as possible in the community use of this legacy. In sharp contrast to the limited public use to which we have put our National Stadium or the Jawaharlal Nehru Stadium or the Indira Gandhi Stadium, the stadia and venues at Manchester are so thoroughly used for community purposes, including the most disadvantaged and excluded, that, for example, to ensure access for Muslim women to the swimming pool, special hours are reserved for their exclusive use with women staff, women coaches and women life-guards in attendance. Similar forethought for giving disadvantaged sections of our community, especially poor children and student and non-student youth, access to these facilities after the Games are over is, in my view, essential.

(iv) Massive private sector investment, through donations, direct investments, investments in partnership with public authorities, sponsorship/advertising/merchandising characterised the financing of the Commonwealth Games at Manchester. A similar effort has been mounted for the London Olympics. In consequence, while expenditure on Government account is held down, public expenditure is more than balanced by private investment and private sector involvement. In association with the Organising Committee of our own Games, we need to do something similar in India.

(v) With respect to both the Manchester Games and the forthcoming London Olympics, there is a determined endeavour to make people all over the United Kingdom have a sense of involvement in the mega event so as to transform what is essentially a city event into a national event. In the context of our Commonwealth Games, I believe the launch of the Panchayat Yuva Khel Abhiyan in the context of the Commonwealth Games will make this mega sports event in our capital city meaningful and relevant to the nation as a whole, especially to the many millions who live in rural areas and urban slums and have thus far being given little or no access to organised sports and games. Later this week, I will be circulating a Concept Note on the proposed Abhiyan and subsequently a Note for Cabinet.

(vi) Four years of detailed preparation and persuasion with all the authorities concerned went into putting forward Manchester's candidacy for the Commonwealth Games, 2002. It was only after a minute examination of a detailed feasibility report, prepared by consultants of international repute, that the go-ahead was given for holding the Commonwealth Games in a provincial city and promoting it as an all-UK event that would restore Manchester's 19th century reputation as a leading 21st century business hub. Similar due diligence is, I believe, the need of the hour before we take decisions on our final bid for the Asian Games 2014 or the Olympics 2016.

Youth Affairs

I had a substantial meeting with David McKinnon, Secretary General of the Commonwealth, on the follow-up to the Nassau Youth Ministers meeting in respect of which I had had a prior discussion when the Secretary General visited New Delhi in February, a few months before the Nassau meeting. The discussion with McKinnon complemented the meeting I had had earlier with Tessa Jowell.

Based on the Nassau communique, the Secretary General has nominated Andrew Simmons as the pointsman in his personal office to liase with us through the Indian High Commission on Commonwealth assistance to, and involvement with, the leveraging of the Commonwealth Youth Programme - Asia Centre, Chandigarh, as the platform for interaction among elected youth members of Panchayati Raj Institutions in different States of North India and the Rajiv Gandhi National Institute of Youth Development, Sriperumbudur for States in South India. Progressively this could be expanded to inter-country exchanges within the Asian Commonwealth and, possibly, beyond.

Secretary of State Tessa Jowell and the Department of Environment, Food and Rural Affairs (DEFRA) were also supportive of the role which the Commonwealth could play in youth development generally and youth in local governance, in particular. This preliminary sounding might prove useful when the Nassau communiqué comes up for Heads of Government approval at the CHOGM Summit in Uganda next year.

Panchayati Raj

I attended a Round Table on "Local Governance, Democracy and Sustainable Development" specially convened for me by DEFRA to provide a platform for interaction with Department officials, local government enthusiasts and activists, academic experts, and local government authorities, including the Deputy Mayor of London. The suggestions emanating from the Round Table, including the establishment of an Indo-UK Local Government Forum, particularly with the participation of British local government representatives of South Asian origin, came up for detailed discussion. Based on these suggestions, DEFRA is considering appropriate steps to operationalise these proposals under the general aegis of the agreement reached with our Minister of Environment and Forests during Premier Tony Blair's visit last year. Our High Commissioner in London felt this would be in order but I am writing separately to our Minister of Environment and Forests and MEA for their concurrence before moving further in the matter.

I also participated in the Wilton Park Conference of the UK's partner countries in their Dialogues on Sustainable Development (Brazil, China, India, Mexico and South Africa). My particular theme was on the role of the States and local government, Panchayats in particular, in ensuring sustainable development. I dwelt in particular on Panchayati Raj in Fifth Schedule Areas as the issue had been raised by previous speakers. I think I was able to dispel some of the misinformation being spread by a particularly offensive don, Prof. R. Grove. It was also useful to exchange views with the Brazilian participants as Brazil seems to have considerable experience in dealing with local communities residing in forests. They will be sending me documentation which might be of use in our consideration of PESA-related issues and the pending Bills on Forest Rights and Resettlement.

With respectful regards,

Yours sincerely,

Dr.Manmohan Singh
Hon'ble Prime Minister
South Block
New Delhi.

D.O.No. 2666 ...Min. (YA&S) 06

मणि शंकर अय्यर
MANI SHANKAR AIYAR

मंत्री
पंचायती राज और युवा कार्यक्रम एवं खेल
भारत सरकार
नई दिल्ली-110 001
Minister
Panchayati Raj and Youth Affairs & Sports
Government of India
New Delhi-110 001

8 March 2007

Respected Prime Minister,

Shri Suresh Kalmadi, Chairman, Organizing Committee, Commonwealth Games 2010 called on me yesterday to ask whether we could furnish him with an additional sum of Rs.5 crores to enable him to pursue New Delhi's bid for the Asian Games 2014.

He was initially sanctioned the Rs.2 crore which he had asked for. He has already supplemented this with a further sum of Rs.3 crore from CM, NCT Delhi. He is now seeking a further sum of Rs. 3 crore from the Government of NCT Delhi. He wants us to top it up with another Rs.2 crore from the Government of India, making a total of Rs.10 crore. Thus, against his initial projection of a requirement of Rs. 2 crore on pre-bid expenditure, he has upped the ante to Five times the initial figure. This is of a pattern with everything else connected with his involvement in mega sports events.

On being asked the rationale for this request, he indicated that the Republic of Korea is relentlessly pursuing its bid for Incheon and has been making promises to various countries, particularly the poorer countries of South East Asia such as Cambodia and Laos. In contrast to the optimism he earlier exuded, it now appears that our bid is far from tied up as earlier indicated. He was unable to give me any details of how he has spent, or proposes to spend the additional Rs.8 crore he has sought or is seeking to push our bid through. I told him that in all my four decades of experience as a diplomat, I could not recall such large sums of money being spent on pre-bid exercises. He will be furnishing his requirements in writing.

I also found that as against SAI's estimate that about Rs.300 crore would be required for the special training of talented athletes to increase our medal tally at the Commonwealth Games 2010, Kalmadi's projection has now been raised from Rs.1,000 crore to Rs.1,500 crore! Once again, there is no detailed justification.

Finally, I must mention the apprehension informally conveyed to me by the Commonwealth Games Federation that if India were to succeed in getting the Asian Games 2014, Kalmadi's Organizing Committee might be too distracted to give the concentration required to the Commonwealth Games.

1

401-सी, शास्त्री भवन, नई दिल्ली–110 001 दूरभाष : 011-23386520, 23384183, फैक्स : 011-23381898
Shastri Bhawan, New Delhi-110 001 Tele.: 011-23386520, 23384183, Fax : 011-23381898

4361/AS(P)/S/07 651/JS(M)/07 2081/DS(US) VIP

All these developments reinforce my conviction that we should gracefully withdraw from the race for the Asian Games 2014.

Yours sincerely,

Dr. Manmohan Singh
Hon'ble Prime Minister
South Block
New Delhi

D.O 4661/MYAS/07
14/c

मणि शंकर अय्यर
MANI SHANKAR AIYAR

मंत्री
पंचायती राज, युवा कार्यक्रम एवं खेल और
उत्तर-पूर्वी क्षेत्र विकास
भारत सरकार
नई दिल्ली-110001
Minister
Panchayati Raj, Youth Affairs & Sports and
Development of the North Eastern Region
Government of India
New Delhi-110 001

Secret

23 October 2007

Dear Pulok,

At 5.00 pm day-after-tomorrow, Thursday, 25 October, the Prime Minister has convened a meeting to review the arrangements for the Commonwealth Games. This is the first review at his level after a lapse of over a year.

2. My officers have done all they can to alert Government, specifically the Cabinet Secretariat and PMO, to a number of our extremely serious concerns which have only been mounting over the past year. I fear that if these concerns are not met in the meeting day- after-tomorrow, we may find ourselves irretrievable damaged.

3. My primary concern is that, in sharp distinction to the structure of the Special Organising Committee for the Asian Games, 1982, which was chaired by the Minister of State for Sports, Sardar Buta Singh, and packed with Government Ministers, MPs and Government officials, the Executive Committee for the Commonwealth Games 2010, chaired by Suresh Kalmadi, has no Government Ministers, just one back-bench MP and only two Government Secretaries, and they too lack veto powers; almost all decisions are taken in the committees of the Executive Board that do not include these Government officials; and the Executive Board does not report the decisions of these committees to the Ministry of Youths Affairs and Sports. In consequence, money is being squandered, such as appointing Mike Hooper of the Commonwealth Games Federation as an international consultant with *monthly* first-class air passages for him, and sometimes his wife, between London and Delhi and a farm house in Delhi to live in with scores of air-conditioners, at a total estimated cost of some Rs. 2 crore! Other international consultants have been appointed at a cost of up to $ 5,000 *per day*.

4. Also, unlike the Special Organising Committee of the Asian Games, 1982 which had a large number of distinguished and powerful public-minded representatives, including Shri Rajiv Gandhi, then a back-bench MP, to guide the Executive Board, the present Organising Committee is packed with yes-men (and a few yes-women) and has no one with any influence on the Executive Board or its Committees to press an alternative opinion, leaving the Chairman with virtually dictatorial powers. Without a drastic overhaul of both the Executive Board and Organising Committee for the Commonwealth Games, I fear it will prove to be practically impossible for the Government to significantly address the excesses of Chairman Suresh Kalmadi and his cohorts.

401-सी, शास्त्री भवन, नई दिल्ली-110001 दूरभाष : 011-23386520, 23384183 फैक्स: 011-23381898
401-C, Shastri Bhawan, New Delhi-110001 Tele :011-2338 6520, 2338.4183, Fax : 2338 1898

:2:

5. Moreover, the direct and indirect costs of CWG have already soared to over Rs. 20,000 crore! The total expenditure on the Asian Games 1982 was of the order of Rs. 55 crore. *O tempora! O mores!*

6. My Ministry has suggested three alternatives of dealing with the situation, any one of which could retrieve the situation even at this juncture:

(a) Since Chairman Kalmadi insistently maintains that Commonwealth Games revenues will substantially exceed expenditures by the Organising Committee, he may be invited to take his 'bankable' propositions to financial institutions or commercial banks and raise the required finances from the market, thus releasing the Government of any expenditure on the Organising Committee and any responsibility to Parliament for the antics of its Executive Board.

Or :

(b) A Minister of State for International Sporting Events may be appointed Chairman of the Organising Committee with an adequate number of Government nominees on the Executive Board, including influential sports-minded back-bench MPs, with the power of veto over inappropriate decisions taken by the Board or any of its committees. And:

(c) Recasting the Organising Committee and the Executive Board for the Commonwealth Games to conform to the pattern that was so successfully evolved for the Asian Games 1982.

6. If at all possible, I would appreciate an opportunity to meet Madam on Thursday, 25 October in the forenoon to discuss with her the line I should be taking in the Prime Minister's meeting in the afternoon of the same day.

With all good wishes,

Yours sincerely,

Shri Pulok Chatterji
Additional Secretary
Prime Minister's Office
South Block
New Delhi

मणि शंकर अय्यर
MANI SHANKAR AIYAR

मंत्री
पंचायती राज, युवा कार्यक्रम एवं खेल और
उत्तर-पूर्वी क्षेत्र विकास
भारत सरकार
नई दिल्ली-110001
Minister
Panchayati Raj, Youth Affairs & Sports and
Development of the North Eastern Region
Government of India
New Delhi-110 001

D.O. No. 4672 min, (YA&S)/07

Secret

25 October 2007

Respected Prime Minister, Sir,

Sub: Commonwealth Games, 2010

I grow increasingly alarmed at the profligacy of the Chairman of the Organising Committee of the Commonwealth Games 2010, especially after learning from General Susheel Gupta, Deputy Chief of Army Staff, that the total expenditure on the Military Games recently held in Hyderabad, with nearly three quarters the number of athletes and officials expected for CWG, came to *under* Rs.200 crore. Present projections of expenditure on the Commonwealth Games and CWG-related expenditure have topped Rs.20,000 crore!

2. A recent example of this profligacy is the contract signed with Mike Hooper, a serving official of the Commonwealth Games Federation, to appoint him as an international consultant at a cost of Rs.1.5-2 crore! Unsurprisingly, Hooper has been converted, overnight as it were, from a trenchant critic of our arrangements to an avid enthusiast!

3. While I am glad to report that arrangements for the physical infrastructure are well underway and we can confidently expect all the infrastructure to be completed well in time for the Games in October 2010, my Ministry has failed to establish a genuinely cooperative working relationship with the Organising Committee. This has happened despite my personal decision to not operationalise the Apex Committee authorised by GoM after Kalmadi's vociferous opposition to the Apex Committee at the meeting in August 2006 convened at your level. I thought if I kept out of the picture and left it entirely to my officials to handle matters in the Cabinet Secretary's Committee and the Executive Board of the Organising Committee, personality clashes could be avoided. But abuse and scorn continue to be heaped at the Ministry in public statements made by the Chairman who stoops so low as to describe us as "cartoons sitting in one room in Shastri Bhavan".

401-सी, शास्त्री भवन, नई दिल्ली-110 001 दूरभाष : 011-23386520, 23384183, फैक्स : 011-23381898
Shastri Bhawan, New Delhi-110 001 Tele.: 011-23386520, 23384183, Fax: 011-23381898

4. Such offensive language would not have mattered if at least there were some understanding of General Financial Rules and Government of India procedures in asking for ever-escalating sums of money, usually with no detailed explanation and, when such explanations are insisted on, supplied with much resentment and after long delays. Finding that even the presence of a mere two Secretaries to the Government of India in the Executive Board is an impediment to the virtually dictatorial functioning of the Chairman, he is increasingly resorting to establishing sub-committees of the Executive Board which exclude the Government nominees, take decisions endorsed by the Chairman alone and without referring even the minutes to the Ministry. If I may mix my metaphors, the Chairman sees the Ministry as a milch cow to extract as much money as he can and a rubber-stamp to endorse every spending decision he takes, however outrageous. GoM meetings are hardly constructive because of the stand-off between the OC Chairman and the Ministry which has unfortunately become a standard feature of the often acrimonious proceedings.

5. My Secretary has, therefore, suggested that since the Chairman of the Organising Committee believes his proposals to be 'bankable', it might be best for him to raise the required finances in the open market rather than have Government fund his demands and then be held responsible before Parliament. Although this suggestion has been formally put to the Cabinet Secretariat and PMO, we are yet to receive a response.

6. In my humble view, and on the basis of nearly two years of closely monitoring developments, I am persuaded that whereas, thanks to the agencies concerned, the physical infrastructure will go up as scheduled and will substantially meet exacting international quality requirements, the organisation of the Games in an economic, efficient and tasteful manner cannot be assured with the present organisational structure.

7. I have, therefore, consulted the record and spoken to Sardar Buta Singh, who, as you might remember, was Minister of State for Sports during the run-up to the Asian Games 1982. Raja Bhalinder Singh was then the President of the Indian Olympic Association.

8. During Raja Bhalinder's Presidentship, there were three successive Chairpersons of the Special Organising Committee (SOC) for the Asian Games: S/Shri Vijay Malhotra, VC Shukla and, finally, Sardar Buta Singh. Under all three, the IOA President served on the Organising Committee as a special invitee and did not himself head the Committee. Moreover, the SOC, headed by the Minister in charge, was given a great deal of financial and organisational autonomy. The supervisory role for CWG 2010 given to GoM, which meets but sporadically, is a departure from the more successful model adopted for the Asian Games 1982.

2

Moreover, the SOC for the Asian Games contained a large number of prominent and influential public personalities, including Shri Rajiv Gandhi, then a back-bench MP, and other prominent personalities such as S/Shri Arun Nehru and Arun Singh, and was packed with senior civil servants capable of taking decisions within the Rules and implementing them expeditiously. The Asian Games 1982, universally applauded as an outstanding success, cost the exchequer under Rs.55 crore.

9. I urge the imperative need of recasting the Organising Committee for CWG 2010 and its Executive Board. I know that this has to be done keeping in view the provisions of the Olympic Charter. But as no one suggested that the organisational structure for the Asian Games 1982 was in transgression of the Olympic Charter, perhaps that is the precedent for us to bear in mind.

10. I am far too occupied with my multifarious Ministerial responsibilities to offer myself as Chairman of the Organising Committee for CWG 2010. But I would suggest that a Minister of State for International Sporting Events be appointed from amongst our younger MPs to take over as Chairman of a revamped Executive Board of a rejigged Organising Committee and thus ensure that the organisation of the Games is delivered economically, efficiently and with good taste. I think the Minister for Youth Affairs and Sports should keep himself distanced from the day-to-day work of the Games and confine himself to major decisions of a policy or operational kind.

11. I should be grateful to be afforded an opportunity to discuss these suggestions with the Prime Minister at his earliest convenience.

With respectful regards,

Yours sincerely,

Dr Manmohan Singh
Prime Minister
Prime Minister's office
South Block
New Delhi-110 011

3

D.O. No.....5153.....min, (YA&S) 0'

मणि शंकर अय्यर
MANI SHANKAR AIYAR

सत्यमेव जयते

मंत्री
पंचायती राज, युवा कार्यक्रम एवं खेल और
उत्तर-पूर्वी क्षेत्र विकास
भारत सरकार
नई दिल्ली-110001
Minister
Panchayati Raj, Youth Affairs & Sports and
Development of the North Eastern Region
Government of India
New Delhi-110 001

8 January 2008

Respected Mr. Chairman,

I am constrained to bring to your attention with the deepest regret the continuing non-cooperation of the Chairman of the Organising Committee with the Ministry of Youth Affairs & Sports, the latest instance of which is Organising Committee's failure to invite Secretary, Youth Affairs & Sports, who is a Member of the Executive Board, to a meeting of the Executive Board that was held today. I enclose a copy of a communication I have sent in this regard to Shri Suresh Kalmadi.

With respectful regards,

Yours sincerely,

Shri Arjun Singh
Minister of Human Resource Development
Shastri Bhavan
New Delhi

401-सी, शास्त्री भवन, नई दिल्ली-110001 दूरभाष : 011-23386520, 23384183 फैक्स: 011-23381898
401-C, Shastri Bhawan, New Delhi-110001 Tele : 011-2338 6520, 2338 4183, Fax : 2338 1898

D.O. No. 5531 PS to Min, (YA&S)OE

मणि शंकर अय्यर
MANI SHANKAR AIYAR

सत्यमेव जयते

D.O.No.70-15/2008 CWG

मंत्री
पंचायती राज, युवा कार्यक्रम और खेल
उत्तर-पूर्वी क्षेत्र विकास
भारत सरकार
नई दिल्ली-110 001
Minister
Panchayati Raj, Youth Affairs & Sports and
Development of the North Eastern Region
Government of India
New Delhi-110 001

19 March 2008

Respected Prime Minister, Sir,

I am bringing to your kind notice an important matter related to the Organizing Committee (OC), Commonwealth Games, 2010.

2. An application seeking details under RTI Act was received by the MoYAS during April 07 and as the subject matter concerned OC, we had requested them to furnish the required details immediately. However, OC refused to provide the required details on the ground that OC was not a "Public Authority" under the Act. The advice of the Ministry of Law & Justice, Department of Legal Affairs was obtained in this matter and they were also of the opinion that OC falls within the purview of the definition of Public Authority under the RTI Act. Accordingly, we declared the OC as a Public Authority on 1.11.2007 and requested OC to appoint a Central Public Information Office and an Appellate Authority and comply with other obligations of the RTI Act while providing the required details to the Applicant without any further delay.

3. Instead of complying with this advice, the OC has filed a petition before the Hong'ble High Court of Delhi against the decision of MoYAS for declaring OC as a Public Authority. We now have no alternative but to strongly defend our case before the Hon'ble High Court.

Yours sincerely,

Dr. Manmohan Singh
Hon'ble Prime Minister
South Block
New Delhi

401-सी, शास्त्री भवन, नई दिल्ली-110001 दूरभाष : 011-23386520, 23384183 फैक्स: 011-23381898
401-C, Shastri Bhawan, New Delhi-110001 Tele :011-2338 6520, 2338 4183, Fax : 2338 1898

D.O. No. ...

डॉ० एम० एस० गिल
D M. S. GILL

युवा कार्यक्रम एवं खेल
राज्य मंत्री (स्वतंत्र प्रभार)
भारत सरकार,
शास्त्री भवन, नई दिल्ली-110 115
MINISTER OF STATE (INDEPENDENT CHARGE)
YOUTH AFFAIRS & SPORTS
GOVERNMENT OF INDIA
SHASTRI BHAWAN, NEW DELHI-110 115

18th October 2008

Dear Prime Minister,

I enclose a note of things done, in the months since I have been in this job, to improve the situation for sports, and sportspersons.

Yours sincerely,

(M S Gill)

Dr Manmohan Singh
Prime Minister of India
South Block
New Delhi

Office : 401-C, Shastri Bhawan, New Delhi-110 115. Tele. : 011-2338 6520, 2338 4183, Fax : 011-2338 1898

HIGHLIGHTS OF THE STEPS TAKEN BY DR M S GILL, MINISTER OF STATE (I/C), FOR YOUTH AFFAIRS & SPORTS

Commonwealth Games, 2010

1 Road linkage between Games Village and Jawaharlal Nehru Stadium

The contentious issue of road link between Games Village, and Stadium was not getting resolved, for a long time, causing critical delay in construction of games venues. Within three days, of the assumption of the Charge as Minister, the Group of Ministers (GOM) was scheduled to take a decision, in the matter. In order to, resolve the issue amicably, I conducted, a meeting, with Delhi Government officials, before the GOM, and settled, most of the contentious issues, at the official level first. Following that, in the GOM meeting held on 9th of April 2008, we could get a unanimous decision from GOM, for construction of elevated road over *Barapulla Nullah*. In the meeting, other issues such as, pending litigation in the Delhi High Court, relating to the Games Village, were also discussed. As there is no stay, by the Delhi High Court, clear directions, were given for taking up, construction activities, in the Games Village.

2 Starting of Monthly Meeting with Chief Minister, Delhi, and Chairman, Organising Committee, Commonwealth Games

There was clear lack of coordination between Sports Ministry, Delhi Government and Organising Committee. So, I started a new initiative of monthly meeting with CM, Delhi, and Chairman, Organising Committee, to discuss all issues relating to CWG. The Secretary (Culture), Secretary (Urban Development), Secretary (Tourism) and Joint Secretary (Cab Secretariat) and other senior officials of GOI, also attend the meetings, and have started lending their support for smooth implementation of Commonwealth Games related infrastructures. In these meetings, harmonious, and unanimous decisions are taken, which are also monitored regularly.

3 Field inspection of Commonwealth Games Venues

Construction works, in different stadiums were stalled due to differences, over designs & specifications between National Sports Federations (NSFs), Organising Committee (OC), and Sports Authority of India (SAI), over designs & specifications. On 13th June 2008, I visited, and inspected the construction work at

Jawaharlal Nehru Stadium and National Stadium, along with engineers and consultants. Following, the visit, and after discussing the engineers, I have set, a dead line, of November 2009 for handing over, the venues, for trial runs, before the games.

I have followed this with a visit to Dr Karni Singh Shooting Ranges on 17th June 2008, where work was yet to start, again due to non finalization of design. After detailed discussion with National Rifle Association of India, Indian Olympic Association, Engineers and SAI officials, the layout of the shooting range was finalized, and CPWD was given 'go-ahead' to start the work immediately.

Similarly, the issue of cycle velodrome was discussed with all stakeholders and the designs for Velodrome, was also finalized to the satisfaction of Commonwealth Games Federation, and CPWD was directed to start the work, immediately.

I have followed this with regular visits to the other sites, i.e. Dr Shyama Prasad Mookherjee (Talkatora) Swimming Pool, and Rugby Stadium, at Delhi University ground, and sorted out the problems, relating to flow of funds etc for smooth completion of works.

4 Visit to Commonwealth Youth Games, 2008, Pune

The Commonwealth Youth Games, Pune scheduled from 12-18 October 2008, was in jeopardy, as not a rupee was released for the same even till July 2008. On 30th July 2008, I visited Pune, for on the spot, review of the progress, for preparation of Commonwealth Games at Pune. I reviewed, and ordered for immediate release of funds for the Youth Games, which were held up till then. I also agreed for review of the budget, after a realistic assessment of their demands. On 3rd October 2008, I have been able to get Cabinet Approval for the enhancement of budget, from Rs 66.5 crores to Rs 110 Crores. Because of these proactive steps, the games could be held on schedule. I also attended the Opening Ceremony of the Games, at Pune, which was inaugurated by the President of India.

5 New Scheme for preparation of Teams, for Commonwealth Games

After, a lot of discussion with National Sports Federations, I have been able to get the approval of the Cabinet, amounting to Rs 678 crores, for a new scheme, for preparation of Teams for Commonwealth Games 2010.

After the Cabinet Approval, the selection process, for various teams, has started. We are identifying about 1300 elite players, in 17 disciplines, 250 coaches (*both Indian & Foreign*), and about 80 supporting personnel (Physiotherapists, Psychologist, Masseurs etc). The first round of selection process of elite players, in disciplines such as Archery, Badminton, Boxing, Hockey, Shooting, Squash, Table Tennis, Tennis, Weightlifting, and Wrestling is over. These elite players will be fully funded by the Government, for intensive training of 305 days, in a year, both within, and outside the country. They will also be provided state of art, equipments, & training venues and take part in international tournaments. The players will be assessed at regular intervals, through pre-decided monitor-able parameters, till their final selection for Commonwealth Games, in 2010.

<u>Sports</u>

6 Pension to Medal Winners, doubled

There have been much criticism of government apathy towards our past sports achievers, such as P T Usha, and others, as they were getting a meager amount of Rs 4,000/- p.m. as pension to meritorious sportspersons. The rates of pension for medalists, have been increased by two folds, w.e.f. 1.7.2008.

S No.	Category of Meritorious Sportspersons	Existing rates of pension (Rs /pm	Enhanced rates of pension (Rs/pm)
1	Medalists at the Olympic Games	5000	10000
2	Gold Medalists at the World cup/World Championships in Olympic and Asian Games disciplines	4000	8000
3	Silver and Bronze medalists at the World Cup/World Championships in Olympic and Asian Games disciplines	3500	7000
4	Gold medalists of the Asian/Commonwealth Games	3500	7000
5	Silver and Bronze medalists of the Asian/Commonwealth Games	3000	6000
6	Gold medalists of Para Olympic Games	2500	5000
7	Silver medalists of Para Olympic Games	2000	4000
8	Bronze medalists of Para Olympic Games	1500	3000

Following the enhancement, the ministry is continuously receiving large number of thanks/congratulatory letters, from common people, and sportspersons, alike to this act of government.

7 Award money increased for olympic medal winners

After the best ever performance, of India at the Beijing Olympics, the ministry organized special reception, of the olympic medal winners, and arranged their visits, to high dignitaries in Delhi. After discussion, with the Prime Minister, the award money for olympic medal winners, were increased as follows.

S no.	Category	Award money Earlier	Award money increased
1	Gold Medalist in Olympics	Rs 30 lakhs	Rs 50 lakhs
2	Silver Medalist in Olympics	Rs 18 lakhs	Rs 30 lakhs
3	Bronze Medalist in Olympics	Rs 12 lakhs	Rs 20 lakhs

Shri Abhinav Bindra, Shri Vijender Singh, and Shri Sushil Kumar have been handed over the cheques, by me in a special ceremony, held in the Ministry.

8 Promotion of Games, in schools and colleges

The Inter-University Games were stopped, few year back, due to various administrative reasons. I have ordered for special recognition to 'Association of Indian Universities' (AIU), as National Sports Promotional Organisation (NSPO), which will make them eligible, to receive funds, from the Ministry and organize the prestigious Inter-Universities Sports, and Games, in the country both at Zonal and at National level. Similarly, there were disputes in the School Games Federation, between two factions, as a result, the school games were not taking place. The issue has been resolved and the recognition of School Games Federation of India, has now been restored. This has made them eligible to receive grants, for conducting sports & games at the school level, throughout the country.

9 Enhancement of MAKA Trophy award money

Until now, the best sports university in the country, were awarded the Maulana Abul Kalam Azad Trophy (MAKA) Trophy, with a financial assistance of Rs 2 lakhs, Rs 1 lakh, and Rs 50,000/- as I, II & III Prizes, respectively. This award money, was considered meager in view of the huge amount of effort to be taken up

4

by Universities. I have increased the MAKA trophy prize money to Rs 10 lakhs, Rs 5 lakhs, and Rs 3 lakhs, w.e.f. current financial year, so that this works, as an incentive for promotion of sports infrastructure/events in Universities.

10 Issue of pending sports infrastructure in the States, settled

The erstwhile Sports Infrastructure Schemes that were transferred to the State Sector w.e.f. 1.4.2005. As a result, a huge number of sports infrastructures, such as Stadia, Swimming pools, multipurpose halls etc, were abandoned, in a half constructed stage. Almost, all State Governments have been approaching the Central Government, for meeting the committed liabilities of Govt of India, to these incomplete sports infrastructures, in the States. I have pursued this matter with Deputy Chairman, Planning Commission, & Finance Ministry. They have now agreed on my request, to fund the past committed liabilities of Govt of India, through Additional Central Assistance (ACA)/State Plan Assistance (SPA).

11 Two to Four times, increase in the financial assistance to sports persons, for medical treatment etc.

The Ministry has a scheme, under which financial assistance is provided to meritorious sports persons/coaches, who get injured/incapacitated, for their medical treatment. The amount of assistance were not revised, for a number of years. I held wide ragingly discussions with all concerned, and the following decisions have been taken.

- Eligibility ceiling for sportspersons in indigent circumstances revised from Rs 36,000 per annum to Rs 2 lakh per annum.
- Definition of 'Outstanding sportsperson' simplified and liberalized.
- Assistance for fatal injury to sportspersons raised from Rs 1 lakh to Rs 5 lakh.
- Assistance for sustaining injury other than a fatal injury enhanced from Rs 40,000 to Rs 2 lakh
- Pension for permanent incapacitated sports person increased from Rs 2,500 per month to Rs 10,000 per month.
- Pension in other cases enhanced from Rs 2000 per month to Rs 8000 per month
- Assistance to families of indigent sportspersons increased from Rs 40,000 to Rs 2 lakh
- Assistance for medical treatment increased from Rs 40,000 to Rs 2 lakh

5

- Assistance to eminent coaches, referees, and umpires enhanced from Rs 20,000 to Rs 50,000

12 Sports Promotion in Ladakh

Recently, I spent six days in Ladakh, interacting with youths, sports persons, mountaineers, in that region. As a follow up, I had taken the following decisions, for promotion of sports, in Ladakh.

- Grant of Rs 2.5 lakhs sanctioned for the Ladakh Polo Tournament, which is unique in the country. This will be an annual grant, on regular basis.
- Supply of equipments, for Archery, Fencing, Ice Hockey & Figure Skating to sports club in Ladakh.
- Provisions made for grant for Ice Hockey Tournament at Leh, the only of its kind in the country. For this year Rs 2.00 lakhs, has been sanctioned for conducting tournaments. It will also be an annual grant on regular basis.
- Setting up of SAI Training Centre/Day Boarding Centre at Leh.
- Promotion of Adventure (*high altitude mountaineering)*, in Leh
- Organisation, of two National Integration Camps, in Leh & Nubra valley, and Sending more number of youth from Ladakh region to different parts of the country
- Rs 25,000/- has been sanctioned to Ms Padma Chorol, a girl of 12 years, in the Moravian School, who is an outstanding figure skater, with potential, under National Sports Development Fund, of the Ministry.
- An amount of Rs one lakh, is being sanctioned to Tsering Ladol, a student of class XII, in Govt Girls Senior Secondary School, Leh, who climbed Mt. Everest, as a member of NCC expedition team. Ms Ladol has been sent by my ministry, to Korea, as a member of Indian Youth delegation from 16th October to 25th October 2008.

13 Anti Doping Measures

In a significant achievements for the entire South Asia region, the National Anti Doping Agency (NADA), of India has got accreditation, from World Body i.e. World Anti Doping Agency (WADA). I have pursued this prestigious matter in sports, on the sidelines of the Beijing Olympics. That was followed up, with very pro active steps, by the ministry, such as setting up of Laboratory, nominating the best medical professionals, in the country to be incharge of NADA.

As a result, we have been able to get the accreditation of the WADA on 20th September 2008. I have directed that we must use NDTL, for entire dope testing protocols, during the Commonwealth Youth Games, Pune, being held from 12th to 18th October 2008. A full team of NDTL is now camping at Pune, and taking hundreds of samples everyday, and reports are given within 24 hours. This has been highly appreciated by the members of Commonwealth Games Federation.

The National Anti Doping Agency (NADA) has been reconstituted, by inducting eminent medical experts, and sports persons, in the country. Dr P Rama Rao, Director NIPER, Dr Manmohan Singh, Chairman, Medical Commission of IOA, Dr H S Phoolka, Advocate, eminent Jurist, from Delhi High Court, and Director General, Health Services, have been made new members of NADA, Governing Body.

Similarly, the National Dope Testing Laboratory (NDTL) has been made to be the best in the world by providing them, the state of art, equipments, and medical professionals. Four doctors, i.e, Dr Prof S D Seth from ICMR, Dr Y K Gupta from AIIMS, Prof N K Ganguly, former DG, ICMR, and Dr Manmohan Singh, Chairman, Medical Commission of IOA, have been taken as new members of NDTL.

14 Doping issue of Monika Devi

The Monika Devi's doping case had agitated the entire Manipur State, and had created law & order problem similar to Amarnath Shrine Board, in J&K. On my return from Beijing Olympics, the same day I talked to Chief Minister, Manipur, and also, gave personal hearing to Monika Devi, to hear her grievances. I also requested Shri T S Krishnamurthy, Former Chief Election Commissioner of India to inquire into all aspects of the issue and submit his report within a month. This has contained the situation, which might otherwise, have been difficult to handle. Shri Krishnamurthy took up the case immediately, and after hearing all concerned, submitted a report within 20 days, and the following actions have been taken promptly by the Ministry:

- Specific protocols prescribed, for treatment, testing, and hearing of elite players, in international events. Specific mention has been made in the protocol, to treat elite players, with due respect.
- Doping procedure made transparent, accountable, and time bound. It has now been made sure, that the player is kept informed at every stage of the dope testing, and reporting.

7

- As recommended by Shri Krishnamurthy, the 'B' sample, of Ms Monika Devi is being sent to Tokyo for testing. Ms Monika Devi has also been allowed to be present during the Testing, at Tokyo, or send her representative, if she feels so.

15 Panchayat Yuva Krida aur Khel Abhiyan

In order to provide universal access to sports and games, especially in rural areas, the Government has come out with a scheme, titled Panchayat Yuva Krida aur Khel Abhiyan (PYKKA), in an effort to broad base sports, through grassroot sports activity throughout India. Involving an outlay of Rs 1500 crores for the XI Plan Period, it provides basic sports infrastructure and equipment at panchayat level, and conducts annual competitions, at block and district levels, leading broadbasing of talent. This will lead to better performance of our sports persons, in national and international events. I believe that the London Olympic medals will come from village India.

I organized, the State Sports Ministers' Conference, after a gap of nearly six years, for grounding of this flagship sports scheme of UPA government, on 9th July 2008. All the States, have promised to give full support for the implementation, of the new scheme of the Government of India, for development of rural sports, in the country. So far, approximately Rs 70.00 crores has been sanctioned to 06 states i.e. Andhra Pradesh, Bihar, Orissa, Punjab, Haryana and Mizoram. Six more states i.e. Maharashtra, J&K, Gujarat, Rajasthan, Nagaland and West Bengal, are under examination. Those who have not submitted, their Plans, are pursued, for the same

16 Other sports activities

- Hockey, Football, Swimming, Basketball, Cycling, Volleyball, School/University Games, which were in 'Others' category have been promoted to priority category. This will provide them much higher funding, international exposure and visits.

- I have requested the Railway Minister, for doubling the railway concessions, given to Arjuna Awardees, Rajiv Gandhi Khel Ratna Awardees, Dronacharya Awardees, and Tenzing Norgay National Adventure Awardees.

Sports Authority of India (SAI)

8

17 Laying of astroturf, by SAI

In order to strengthen the training, and playing facilities for hockey, I have reviewed the issue of laying of astroturf by SAI. So far, SAI has been focusing on laying only full length astroturf, which are not only expensive, but also requires huge amount of money for its up keep, and maintenance. As a result, only few astroturf could be laid with the limited funds available. I set up an Expert Committee, of Former Hockey Captains, and after detailed deliberation by them, as well as with Technical Officers, it has now been decided to provide smaller turf', for training centers, while full length turf could be provided for Centre of Excellences, and match/tournaments venues. As a result, with the same amount of finance, SAI will be able to lay smaller turfs', called six-a-size astroturf, four times more in number, for training purposes, as against the earlier. Along with this policy decision, it has also been decided that initially SAI will lay 20 astroturf, on priority basis that will provide training grounds, for the hockey players, in Tier II cities, and SAI training centres.

18 Promotion of Coaches

Coaches are the backbone of Sports Authority of India, who provide training, and grooming of sports talent, so as to enable them to reach, their highest potential. However, for more than ten years, there has been no promotion, among coaches. As a result, the entire cadre was de-motivated, and stagnated. I have directed SAI, to immediately take up their pending issues of promotions, and after clearance by the Departmental Promotion Committee, 205 coaches have been empanelled for promotion, out of which 118 Grade-I coaches, have been promoted to the Selection Cadre, in the first phase. Consequently, vacancies of Grade-I coaches, will be filled up by promotion from the Feeder Cadre. This will give the much needed boost, to the morale of the coaches, whose services will be very much required, for preparation of teams, for Commonwealth Games, as well as implementation of PYKKA, in the states.

19 Recruitment of Coaches

The Sports Authority of India has a cadre strength of 1953 coaches, in 19 disciplines. However, due to ban, in the recruitment, and other various reasons, there are only 1336 coaches in position, which severely limits the functioning ability of the SAI. The Ministry has recently approved the proposal for filling up the vacancy of about 256 coaches. The proposal to this effect is being taken up with Finance Ministry for their approval.

9

Nehru Yuva Kendra Sangathan (NYKS)

20 Re-organisation of NYKS

In a major restructuring of the Nehru Yuva Kendra Sangathan (NYKS), it has now been decided that instead of 18 Zonal Offices, all the 28 States, will have the State level offices, to be headed by Zonal Director. This will provide the much needed coordination with the State Governments, for strengthening youth works, by NYKS. Further the Ministry has approved the setting up of 123 new Nehru Yuva Kendras, in the uncovered districts. The proposal to this effect, has been sent to the Finance Ministry, for approval.

21 Promotion of Sports Clubs in Rural Area

From this year onwards, the NYKS, will provide financial assistance to 100 sports clubs, in each district for purchase of sports material, and conducting village games. These Sports Clubs will work as a nursery, for sporting talents, under National Rural Sports Programme, which is otherwise called PYKKA.

22 J & K Youth Exchange Programme

The NYKS is taking Kashmiri Youth to various parts of the country, under JK Youth Cultural Exchange Programme, funded by Home Ministry. I have requested the Home Ministry, to double the number of youth so that more number of Kashmiri youths, can visit the other parts, of the country. I have also asked NYKS, to organize 'Kashmir Dastkar Mela' in New Delhi in November, 2008, specifically for the youth of J&K.

23 Special Programme for girls, in border districts

NYKS has been running, a short term Vocational Training Programme, for rural youth. In the context of Eleventh Fice Year Plan, these programmes have been closed. Since these programmes were highly beneficial, for rural youth, specially girls, I have re-introduced few of the vocational training programmes specifically earmarked, for girls, such as sewing, knitting, tailoring, embroidery etc, in a pilot scale, from out of NYKS's own programme fund. These programmes will be implemented in only 100 districts, selected from border areas, tribal & hilly districts, in the country, on part funding by NYKS & part payment basis, by the girl trainees.

__Youth__

24 Introduction of National Programme for Youth & Adolescent Development

The ministry has been implementing four, 100% Centre Schemes, for promotion of national integration, adventure, vocational training, and Development of Adolescents. In order to reduce the multiplicity of schemes, with similar objectives and in the context of Eleventh Fice Year Plan, a composite scheme has been introduced, by the ministry for 'National Programme for Youth & Adolescents Development', with effect from 2008-09. I have held detailed discussions, on this scheme, with the State Youth Ministers. Following my meeting with the States, the ministry has now started the proposals, and funds are being released to the Project Implementing Agencies, in the states.

25 Youth exchange programme with China

As a part of Agreement, between the Prime Minister of India, and the President of China, 100 member youth delegation, visited China, from 29th June to 8th July 2008. The youth delegation was very carefully selected, to cover all States/UTs, and with 50:50 boys & girls. This has a very good positive effect, towards the improvement of youth to youth relations, between India & China. The Ministry is expecting, a return visit of 100 Chinese Youth, to India from 11th to 20th November 2008. The delegation will be visiting New Delhi, Mumbai, Pune, and Jaipur. All arrangements are being made by the Ministry, for making it a successful visit.

26 Increase in honorarium, for National Service Volunteers

The ministry, through NYKS and NSS engages, about 7000 National Service Volunteers (NSV), each year, who are graduates, annd interested in social/youth works in Block/Village level. The objective is to engage willing young people in nation building activities for a period of one year, extendable upto 2 years in deserving cases. These NSVs were paid an paltry honorarium of Rs 1,000/, so far to meet their travel & pocket expenses. As the amount was too less, I have now doubled, their honorarium to Rs 2,000/- and also provided the additional Rs 500/- per month to meet their travel expense, within their work area. This will motivate a lot of rural youth, to work as NSV, who are our social engineers, in rural areas,

National Service Scheme (NSS)

27 Enhancement of cost norms, for NSS activities.

The National Service Scheme (NSS) provide a platform for students to do, community service, while under-going their higher education, in colleges/universities. This is perhaps, the oldest scheme, in the Ministry, operating successfully since 1969. However, due to very meager financial norms, most colleges/universities have not been able to conduct quality programmes, in the field. Taking this into account, the ministry has doubled, the cost norms for most of their regular activities, and special camping programme. It has, however, been made clear that the contribution of Govt of India, will remain same but the colleges/universities, having NSS, are allowed to mobilize additional resources so that they can meet the additional requirement, and organize meaningful, and qualitative programmes.

We have also introduced the concept of self finance units, of NSS, so that the private & other cash rich institutions can take benefit of this, unique student volunteer-ship programme, in the country.

Rajiv Gandhi National Institute of Youth Development (RGNIYD)

28 Deemed University Status to RGNIYD

The Rajiv Gandhi National Institute of Youth Development, Sriperumbudur, Tamilnadu, is an autonomous organization of the Ministry, working as a think-tank for the Ministry. We have taken all necessary steps, for up-gradation of this institute, to a Deemed University status, and making it an International Centre of Excellence, on youth development. The notification by Ministry of Human Resource Development is expected shortly.

****

D/L

No. NYAS/10/C.O./09

डॉ० एम०एस० गिल
Dr. M.S. GILL

युवा कार्यक्रम एवं खेल मंत्री
भारत सरकार
नई दिल्ली-110 115
MINISTER FOR YOUTH AFFAIRS & SPORTS
GOVERNMENT OF INDIA
NEW DELHI-110 115

CONFIDENTIAL

26th September 2009

Subject : Commonwealth Games – October 2010, and Fennell letter.

Dear Prime Minister,

You are aware of the controversies and concerns, that have come up on the Fennell letter, which points to serious doubts, about the capacity of the 500 member Organising Committee, under Shri Suresh Kalmadi, to deliver the conduct of the Games, from the 3rd of October 2010 to the 16th, when they all finally depart.

The 1982 Asian Games in Delhi, held 28 years ago, on a much smaller scale, than any current games, were a great success. The main reason was that, as in all Games anywhere, then and now, the preparation and conduct was entirely in government's hands. Shri Rajiv Gandhi was a unique point of authority, able to break any inter-ministerial or other road blocks. The actual work was given to the then Home Minister Shri Buta Singh, and a selected group of twenty odd officials. The Games were a great success, and are admired. Today the Asian Games, after such a long interval, are very much bigger, and more complex. The Commonwealth Games of course, are in the big league.

The then Government of India and the Government of Delhi, alongwith the IOA, signed the agreement, taking the Games, in 2003 The original signed document had a government Chairman, but later somehow that was changed. The basic design of these games, requires that nine major stadiums, are funded and built by the Government through the Central PWD. Some lesser stadiums are being built by the DDA, and other Delhi Government authorities, through the State PWD. The Athletes village, unfortunately, across the river, is being built by a Dubai Company under the DDA. The Delhi Government and Chief Minister, are undertaking a major infrastructure improvement effort, for the city of Delhi. All the work of Delhi authorities, is funded through, and linked to the Urban Development Ministry. The security is the responsibility of the Home Ministry and the Lt Governor, Delhi. The Nine Government Stadiums, are being built with all the energy, at our command. Though I have to point out that work was slow, till I took over on 6th April 2008.

The Shooting, Cycling and Swimming Stadiums had not even been started, due to internal arguments. Nor had the bridge, to bring the athletes across the river from the village, to the Stadium. These were immediately got started, and under constant supervision, will be got ready, in time. The time lost in the past cannot be recovered. The Delhi Chief Minister is also pushing all the infrastructure in every possible way. We would like to see you, to discuss all this, and at that time, will make a presentation on this work, if permitted.

Contd on page 2

Continuation Sheet

-2-

But the most vital part, that of the conduct of the Games, from 3rd to 16th October 2010, is the sole responsibility of the Organising Committee of 500, and such staff as they appoint – currently about 400, and said to come up to even 1200. The Ministry of Sports, ensures that the funds as necessary, are promptly provided. At the time of the Agreement, they were to be about 200 crores, are now something less than 800 crores, and we are coming to Cabinet soon, for something above 1600 crores.

The Organising Committee has an Executive Committee of 15 Members, with three from the Commonwealth Games Federation, include one Mr Hooper, looked after by the Organising Committee, and based in Delhi, since long; the Chairman Shri Kalmadi with four other colleagues from the IOA and five Government Officers, namely Secretary (Sports), Secretary (Urban Development), Chief Secretary (Delhi), Principal Secretary to CM, Delhi, and Additional Secretary (Finance) Govt of India. In the past, the Committee rarely met and generally endorsed post-facto decisions, taken in a highly centralised system. When I came in on 6th April 2008, I pushed with my Secretary, to get some order, insisting on regular meetings, with minutes, advanced agenda etc. Finance Committees too, were set up for greater financial control, and concurrent audit was brought in. Some order has been restored.

But the question raised by Fennell is, about the ability and the capability of the Organising Committee and its higher staff, to deliver the Games, to the quality expected. They are expected to lookafter 17000 sports persons and officials, from the time, they leave they countries, their travel cost, unfortunately being our burden, to the 16th of October, when they depart. Every aspect of their living in Delhi, and their competitions are to be organized with clock work precision. The OC have 23 Sub Committees, which have rarely met, or performed in the situation described above. Yesterday 25th September 2009, the Chairmen of all these Committees were called by the OC Chairman, I suppose in view of the current controversy, and given an exhortation, in the hope that they will buckle down to the job. The competence of the Committees, and the decentralization, necessary for them, to function effectively, is yet to be seen.

In this background, I have had intensive meetings with Shri Kalmadi and Shri Randhir Singh the Secretary General, and with the Delhi Chief Minister, the Cabinet Secretary, and Shri T K Nair. We have devised a line of action, to strengthen the management, inside the Organising Committee, immediately. The structure cannot be changed, but this is the essential minimum now, with no time to lose. [The Cabinet Secretary has identified individuals, and I agree with him.] This first step needs to be taken without delay, and then we will go on, from there. I may also mention that I had asked for a detailed written report from Shri Kalmadi, on the Fennell letter, and he has now put in a formal request to my

Contd on page 3

Continuation Sheet

-3-

Secretary, asking for senior staff injection, into the OC. It will be necessary that the persons asked to undertake this fire fighting job, are fully backed by the Minister of Sports, and Yourself, in order to be effective and do the job to the country's satisfaction.

I would request an early meeting, alongwith the Delhi Chief Minister, with the Cabinet Secretary and Shri Nair, being present. We will also make a presentation on the progress of the construction, if allowed.

With regards

Yours sincerely,

(M S Gill)

Dr Manmohan Singh
Hon'ble Prime Minister of India
7, Race Course Road
New Delhi

SPORTS-GILL-SJFI

SJFI poll agrees with Sports Minister Gill

Panaji, May 7 (UNI) Union Sports Minister M S Gill today received a huge boost with the leading sports journalists of the country strongly supporting his efforts to put reigns over the IOA and the various National Sports Federations.

The sports journalists from all over the country who are here in connection with the 34th National convention of the Sports Journalists' Federation of India (SJFI) have virtually given their thumps up to Gill and his efforts to fix age limit and tenure limit over the office bearers of office bearers of the various sports federations.

Asked to comment on a simple one-liner, 'do you agree with Sports Minister, Gill's move to limit tenures of National federation heads', over 99 per cent of the 70-odd journalists from 16 States attending the convention felt that what the Sports Minister was doing was right. Only less than one per cent said they did not agree with the move.

The opinion poll was the second to be done at the convention in as many days. On the opening day when asked, 'will the Indian Premier League continue to flourish even in the absence of the now suspended Lalit Modi', 94 per cent of the participants picked up 'yes' as their response while the rest said 'no'.

UNI XC HSB CS HS15 19

CONFIDENTIAL

D.O. No.35(co) Min.(YA&S)

डॉ॰ एम॰एस॰ गिल
Dr. M.S. GILL

युवा कार्यक्रम एवं खेल मंत्री
भारत सरकार
नई दिल्ली-110 115
MINISTER OF YOUTH AFFAIRS & SPORTS
GOVERNMENT OF INDIA
NEW DELHI-110 115

सत्यमेव जयते

18th February 2010

Subject : Serving of Beef in the Commonwealth Games

Dear Prime Minister,

A question has recently been raised, asking the Organisers, not to serve beef, during the Commonwealth Games. It seems the matter was also raised, in the Delhi Corporation, and Congress Members, perhaps had to support the point. This was informally discussed, in the Group of Ministers' Meeting, which includes Shri Kalmadi, the Chairman of the Organising Committee. For the moment, it was simply deferred. It appears to me, that it is going to be difficult to answer. The Opposition will press their points, and the Organising Committee will have difficulty, with the Commonwealth Games Federation. whose agreement, with the OC, includes necessary provisions for suitable foods, as needed and asked for. The issue is going to require, a wider consultation, and some decision in the near future.

Representations have also been received, against the presence of Shri Sajjan Kumar and Shri Jagdish Tytler, in the Games Committees. Shri Sajjan Kumar was in the Organising Committee, and I am told that he has been removed, since he is not an MP. I am confirming this. Shri Tytler as President of the Judo Federation, is the Chairman of the Committee, training the 35,000 young volunteers. He too, is of course, not an MP. This issue continues to figure on Punjab TV, and in the press with statements, from various people. It may come up in the coming Budget Session, in questions or in debate.

I am writing this to keep you informed. We will bat, as best we can.

With respect

Yours sincerely,

(M S Gill)

Dr Manmohan Singh
Hon'ble Prime Minister of India
7, Race Course Road
New Delhi

D.O. No.109.(Co)...Min.(YA&S)10

डॉ० एम०एस० गिल
Dr. M.S. GILL

युवा कार्यक्रम एवं खेल मंत्री
भारत सरकार
नई दिल्ली-110 115
MINISTER OF YOUTH AFFAIRS & SPORTS
GOVERNMENT OF INDIA
NEW DELHI-110 115

CONFIDENTIAL

6th September 2010

Subject : Commonwealth Games

Dear Prime Minister,

We are 27 days away, from the Commonwealth Games. Today, I decided to go to the Cabinet Secretary's office, and hold a meeting, with the 13-14 officers, appointed by him, each incharge of one venue, to supervise intensive work. We spent almost three hours, going over in great detail, all the problems, and the work being done, whether at the Games Village, various stadiums, and the current laying out of the cables, fitting and equipment, for the international broad cast, by the Prasar Bharti, and relevant corporations. There have been delays particularly, in the broad casting aspect, due to some internal problems, and external coordination. We have pushed all these items, as hard as, we can. I am heartened, that the injection of these officers, by the Cabinet Secretary, has had a very positive effect. Each is hands on, and pushing hard, for the completion of every little job.

At 4 pm, we had a three hour meeting of the Group of Ministers, where we spent most of the time, going over the Opening and Closing ceremonies, the music, dance and other aspects of the programme, and the current schedule. We took note of the weather problems, with many rainy days, still to come, and assessed as to how, we would modify the schedule, and even the basics of the opening ceremony, if needed. The Aerostat Balloon has been spread out in the Nehru Stadium, and next steps are being taken to fill and float it. We are keeping a close watch over everyday's weather and work, and will react to the situation, as it emerges.

I also have the impression now, that at this stage, the Organising Committee and its staff, is working in coordination with the Government Officers, that have been injected, into the situation. This was not quite so, when Jarnail Singh, and the other three officers were sent, but now resistance has greatly reduced, and work is going forward. The Cabinet Secretary's Officers have also been told to assert themselves, and push action without delay, as there is no time. Over all, I am hopeful, and wait for a turn in the weather.

With regards

Yours sincerely,

(M S Gill)

Dr Manmohan Singh
Hon'ble Prime Minister of India
7, Race Course Road
New Delhi

21/c

O/o MOS (I/C) for Youth Affairs &Sports
Shastri Bhawan, New Delhi
**

As Hon'ble Prime Minister is kindly aware, Shri Suresh Kalmadi has been removed from the posts of Chairman of the Organizing Committee, CWG, Delhi 2010 and from the position of Chairman, Executive Board of the Organizing Committee, CWG, 2010. Shri Lalit Bhanot has, similarly, been removed from the posts of Secretary General of the Organizing Committee, CWG, 2010 and from the position of Secretary General, Executive Board of the Organizing Committee, CWG, Delhi, 2010 on 24.1.2011.

2. In this connection, I would like to apprise Hon'ble Prime Minister that pursuant to a request from Director, CBI to the Cabinet Secretary on 8.12.2010 requesting for removal of Shri Kalmadi and Shri Bhanot in order to ensure a free and impartial investigation, the sequence of steps taken by this Ministry in consultation with the Ministry of Law and Ld. Attorney General till 24.1.2011 is detailed out in the enclosed statement for your kind perusal.

Ajay Maken

(Ajay Maken)
Minister of State (I/c)
25.1.2011

Hon'ble Prime Minister

SEQUENCE OF EVENTS

DATE	EVENT
8.12.2010	Director, CBI writes to the Cabinet Secretary requesting for removal of Shri Kalmadi and Shri Bhanot to ensure a free and impartial investigation
10.12.2010	The request was forwarded by the Cabinet Secretary to Secretary (Sports)
16.12.2010	A meeting was held by Secretary, Sports with the Registrar of Societies on 16.12.2010 seeking advice on the status of Organizing Committee as a registered society.
16.12.2010	Secretary (Sports) wrote to Cabinet Secretary indicating that Ministry of Law would be consulted on further course of action.
23.12.2010	The file was sent to Law Ministry for their advice by the Secretary (Sports).
31.12.2010	the file was sent by the Law Minister to Ld. Attorney General
10.1.2011	The Ld. Attorney General sent the file to Secretary (Sports) alongwith his advice
14.1.2011	The file was submitted to the then Minister of Youth Affairs & Sports(Shri M.S.Gill).
21.1.2011	The file was resubmitted to me on assumption of charge as MoS(I/c) YAS for further directions
22.1.2011	A meeting was held by the Cabinet Secretary in which Ld. Attorney General, Law Secretary and Secretary (Sports) were present. The file was referred back to the Law Secretary for further advice in the matter.
23.1.2011	Ld. Attorney General gave his further advice.
24.1.2011	Orders issued to remove Shri Suresh Kalmadi and Shri Lalit Bhanot from their respective posts

24/c

O/o MOS (I/C) for Youth Affairs &Sports
Shastri Bhawan, New Delhi
**

As Hon'ble Prime Minister would be aware, the issue of outstanding payments to various firms including Australian firms for works/services contracted to them by the Olympic Committee (OC), CWG was raised by the Australian authorities with Hon'ble External Affairs Minister, Shri S.M.Krishna on the day that I took charge of this Ministry i.e. 20.1.2011.

2. I had immediately issued directions on the same day that all pending **legitimate dues** should be settled after **thorough verification** within a period of ten days.

3. I also reviewed the position of outstanding payments on 24.1.2011 with the OC officials in which Secretary (Sports) was also present. In the meeting, the OC officials informed that they had an elaborate internal system in place to ensure thorough verification of all claims.

4. Hon'ble Prime Minister would be happy to know that OC, CWG has now informed that they have made payments to 36 out of 45 foreign vendors by 31.1.2011 (including 8 vendors to whom payments have been made between 24.1.2011 and 31.1.2011). The total amount paid till date to all foreign vendors is Rs. 305.95 crores and only a balance of Rs.17.80 crores has been withheld to 9 foreign vendors on account of non-performance of contracts.

YOUTH AFFAIRS & SPORTS MINISTER OF STATE (I/C) ★ Dy. No. 44 Date 01|2|11

5. A Press Communique today has been issued by the OC in this regard, a copy of which is enclosed for kind perusal of Hon'ble Prime Minister.

-sd-
(Ajay Maken)
Minister of State (I/c)
1.2.2011

Hon'ble Prime Minister

Copy to: External Affairs Minister (Sh. S.M.Krishna)

Ajay Maken

PRESS COMMUNIQUE

The Organising Committee, Commonwealth Games 2010 Delhi contracted 45 Foreign Vendors for the conduct of the Commonwealth Games. Out of these 45 Foreign Vendors, payments equal to Rs.114.84 crore have been made to 36 Foreign Vendors by 31st January, 2011 (This includes eight Vendors to whom payments have been made between 24th January to 31st January, 2011).

The part payments to the following nine Foreign Vendors have been withheld because of non-performance of the contracts. These nine Vendors have been already paid Rs.191.11crore and balance Rs.17.80 crore has been withheld.

1. Swiss Timing
2. Infostrade Sports
3. K Events SRL
4. Mark Fisher
5. Great Big Event
6. Spectek Production
7. Production Resource Group
8. EKS Workforce
9. E&Y Workforce (Consortium with EKS)

In addition, there are 71 Commonwealth Games Associations (CGAs) to whom a total travel grant equivalent to Rs.16.74 crore were payable. Out of these 71 CGAs, 64 CGAs have been fully paid amounting to Rs.14.95 crore, and the balance payment to 7 CGAs amounting to Rs.1.79 crore will be released by 7th February, 2011.

Note for Press Communique

There were 45 foreign vendors who were contracted for Commonwealth Games Delhi 2010. Out of these 45 foreign vendors, payments have been made as under:

1. Payments made till 24-1-2011 ________ 28
2. Payment processed and made Between 24-1-2011 and 31-1-2011 ________ 08
3. Payments withheld because of disputes due to non-performance of contracts ________ 9
4. In addition to above, there are 71 Commonwealth Games Associations (CGAs) to whom travel grants amounting to Rs. 16.74 Cr. were payable. Out of these 71 CGAs, 64 CGAs have been fully paid amounting to Rs. 14.95 Cr. and Rs. 1.79 Cr. due to balance 7 CGAs will be released before 7-2-2011.

(Jarnail Singh)
CEO &Chairman
OC, CWG D2010

Secretary (Sports)

Travel Grant Due to CGAs		
Country	Amount Due In 30% payout after deducting the adjustments (USD)	Amount Due In INR
Canada	231948.89	10574550
New Zealand	120425.07	5490179
St. Helena	1276.50	58196
Guernsey	12465.00	568279
Isle Of Man	10120.00	461371
Jersey	6016.00	274269
Northern Ireland	10062.00	458727
Total	392,313.46	17,885,570

Statement for Payments

Department of Sports (Government of India) had a meeting on 24th January, 2011 with the Organizing Committee to expedite legitimate dues of tr foreign vendors. Against a list of 45 foreign vendors, actual payments have been completed in respect of 35 vendors. The payments of th remaining 9 vendors, as per details given below, are withheld on account of disputes relating to contractual obligation/under performance: -

Sr. No.	Name of the Vendor	Total Contract Value	Amount Paid till date	Amount Paid in INR	Balance to be paid	Prevailing rate (INR)	Balance due in INR
1	Swiss Timing	CHF 2,49,90,000	CHF 23740500	103.15 Cr	CHF 1249500	47.52	59,376,240
2	Infostrada Sports	USD 20,60,000	USD 1442000	6.72 Cr	USD 618000	45.59	28,174,620
3	K Events SRL	EURO 58,72,265	EURO 5578652	33.60Cr	EURO 293613	61.98	18,198,134
4	Mark Fisher	USD 199500	USD 149625	0.69 Cr	USD 49875	45.59	2,273,801
5	Great Big Event	USD 850000	USD 765000	3.48 Cr	USD 85000	45.59	3,875,150
6	Spectek Production	USD 2295000	USD 1969875	8.98 Cr	USD 325125	45.59	14,822,449
7	Production Resource Group	USD 3500000	USD 3150000	14.36 Cr	USD 350000	45.59	15,956,500
8	EKS Workforce	USD 2592959	USD 2074367	9.45 Cr	USD 518592	45.59	23,642,609
9	E&Y Workforce	Rs. 118540306	Rs. 106774175	10.68 Cr	Rs. 11766131		11,766,131
	Grand Total			**191.11 Cr**			**178,085,634**

(Jarnail Si
CEO & Chair
Organising Committee Commonwealth Games, 20

Sr. No.	Name of the Vendor	Total Contract Value	Amount Paid	Amount Paid in INR	Balance to be paid
1	Samantha Cotterell	US $ 30,000 per month Net of Taxes, later reducd to USD 22500/- Pm.	USD 465000	21390000	No balance due
2	David Payne	US $ 2,96,600.00	USD 295700	13602200	No balance due
3	Patrick & Pauline Furlong	US $ 10,000 Net of Taxes for min. 5 days from 01.06.2007, and US $24000 Net of Taxes for min. 12 days from 01.05.2009 to 31.10.2010 -	USD 662000	30452000	No balance due
4	Greg Bowman	USD 17200PM	USD 163123	7503658	CONTRACT TERMINATED no balance due
5	Bruce Wilkie	USD 214400.00	USD 185300	8523800	CONTRACT TERMINATED no balance due
6	John Lade	Consultancy fee is AUD 1600 p.d & Per Diem is USD 50 p.d, upto 22nd Oct. 2010	AUD 208143.63	9366463.35	No balance due
7	Brain Nourse	AU $ 3,82,560.00	AUD 241507	11109322	CONTRACT TERMINATED no balance due
8	Clint Flood	CAN $ 185775.00	CAD 185775	8545650	No balance due
9	Vasileios P Kalaitzis	USD 8000/- pm plus taxes	USD 144000	6480000	No balance due
10	John Pauline	USD 98500 plus taxes	USD 98500	4432500	No balance due
11	Yiannis Roussakis	USD 7500/- p.m. plus taxes	USD 26250	1181250	No balance due

Statement of Payments made to Foreign Vendors/Consultants

Sr. No.	Name of the Vendor	Total Contract Value	Amount Paid	Amount Paid in INR	Balance to be paid
12	Dennis Meredith	USD 26250 plus taxes	USD 26250	1181250	No balance due
13	Matthew Jankowski	USD 38000 plus taxes	USD 38000	1710000	No balance due
14	Alexandros Louris (Foreign Consultant)	USD 5000 pm plus taxes	USD 12250	551250	No balance due
15	Scott Willsallen	USD 73500.00	USD 73500	3307500	No balance due
16	PKL	GBP 1270377.00	GBP 1270377	92737521	No balance due
17	EKS (PPM)	USD 5007656.00	USD 5007656	225344520	No balance due
18	EnY (PPM)	Rs. 95441110.00	Rs. 95441110.00	Rs. 95441110.00	No balance due
19	Maxxam Intt.	USD 20,00,000.00	USD 2000000	90000000	No balance due
20	Stage One	GBP225963.61	GBP 225963.61	16495343.53	No balance due
21	Howard & Sons	USD 750000.00	USD 750000	33750000	No balance due
22	Piears Sheppard	USD 160475.00	USD 160475	7221375	No balance due
23	Richard Hartman	USD 120750.00	USD 120750	5433750	No balance due.

Statement of Payments made to Foreign Vendors/Consultants

Sr. No.	Name of the Vendor	Total Contract Value	Amount Paid	Amount Paid in INR	Balance to be paid
24	Andrew Garrod	USD 109200.00	USD 109200	4914000	No balance dua
25	Lawrence Estrin	USD 175957.5	USD 175957.5	7918087.5	No balance due
26	Ian Baldwin	USD 104400.0	USD 104400	4698000	No balance due
27	Aaron Felkar	USD 96500.00	USD 20500	943000	CONTRACT TERMINATED no balance due
28	Durham Marenghi	USD 350740.00	USD 156026	7177196	CONTRACT TERMINATED no balance due
29	Tarm Show	EURO 267890.00	EURO 241101	14948262	CONTRACT TERMINATED no balance due
30	GEO Fabrics	USD 387694.68	USD 387694.68	17446260.6	No balance due
31	Delaware North	AUD 1790000.00	AUD 1790000	80550000	No balance due
32	Great Big Event (A)	USD 502000.00	USD 313800	14434800	CONTRACT TERMINATED no balance due
33	EKS part A	USD 1157100.00	USD 1157100	52069500	No balance due
34	EKS part C	USD 2910000.00	USD 2910000	130950000	No balance due
35	Sarah Grubb	USD 40000	USD 40000	1800000	No balance due

Statement of Payments made to Foreign Vendors/Consultants

Sr. No.	Name of the Vendor	Total Contract Value	Amount Paid	Amount Paid in INR	Balance to be paid
36	Gold Medal System	USD 46,72,669	USD 4672669	210270105	No balance due
	Grand Total			1148438564	Nil

प्रधान मंत्री
Prime Minister

New Delhi
12 November, 2008

Dear Dr. Gill,

Please refer to the news item on Commonwealth Games published in the Hindustan Times of today. The report says that the Chairman of the Commonwealth Games Federation's Coordination Committee has expressed concern about the preparations for the 2010 Commonwealth Games scheduled to be held in Delhi. The report also states that the Commonwealth Games Village site is the subject matter of a judicial proceeding and this could complicate matters in so far as the completion of the Games Village is concerned.

You would agree that it is of utmost importance that all preparations for the 2010 Commonwealth Games are completed on time. I shall be grateful if you could look into the matter and also give a detailed status report on the preparations for the Games.

With regards,

Yours sincerely,

(Manmohan Singh)

Dr. M. S. Gill
Minister of State for Youth Affairs
and Sports (Independent Charge)
New Delhi

अजय माकन
AJAY M AKEN

सत्यमेव जयते

D.O. No. 1010 MOS(IC)/YA&S/20...
युवा कार्यक्रम एवं खेल
राज्य मंत्री (स्वतंत्र प्रभार)
भारत सरकार
नई दिल्ली–110 115
MINISTER OF STATE (INDEPENDENT CHARGE)
FOR YOUTH AFFAIRS & SPORTS
GOVERNMENT OF INDIA
NEW DELHI-110 115

Respected Prime Minister,

0 8 जुलाई JUL 2011

You are aware of the issues regarding the Common Wealth Games, CWG 2010, emanating out of letters written by Shri Mani Shankar Aiyer and the position/ role of Shri Suresh Kalmadi in the conduct of the Games.

With reference to the same and in repose to the largely media issues related to Shri Aiyer's letters, I am attaching a detailed note containing my summarized observations under broad content specific categories of; 1. Administrative Structure, 2. Ideological issues and opposition to bidding for Asian Games 2014 and the Olympics, and 3. Financial Management.

It is prefaced that, Shri Kalmadi's appointment and continuation as the Chairman of the Organizing Committee (OC) of the CWG 2010 was obligated by the contracts and agreements entered into by the previous BJP regime in September 2003.

Similarly, Shri Aiyer, as Minister in-charge for about two years ironically played an irreparable obstructionist role that led to inordinate delays resulting in huge cost and time over runs. This, even as he kept writing to the Prime Minister, saying that the infrastructure works were satisfactorily under progress.

With kind regards

Yours Sincerely,

Ajay Maken
(AJAY MAKEN)

Dr. Manmohan Singh
Hon'ble Prime Minister

Report on CWG related issues

Prime Minister is aware that almost all the controversies surrounding the Common Wealth Games pertain to Corruption charges (emanating essentially out of the inordinate delays in the execution of various infrastructure projects), and the high handedness and unaccountable behavior of Shri Suresh Kalmadi. The delays were caused much because of Shri Mani Shankar Aiyer's obstructionist ways, even as he kept presenting a rosy picture about preparedness of infrastructure, as detailed in his letter to PM Dt. 25.10.2007. (at Annexure-I)

Similarly, the facts behind the appointment and continuation of Shri Suresh Kalmadi as the Chairman of the Organizing Committee (OC) of the Common Wealth Games 2010 (CWG 2010) clearly state that he owed his position in the OC singularly to a favorable clique of the Sports Minister and Sports Secretary during 2003 i.e. during the BJP led regime of that time.

In continuation of the same and with reference to the media issue arising out of the letters written by the then Minister of Youth Affairs & Sports, Shri M S Aiyer to you, it is stated that the issues being raised by him- so prominently being aired in the Media are non issues which have no basis or substance.

Even as I attach a copy of all his letters with their attachments along with the observation of the Ministry on them, for the purpose of general clarity I am detailing my summarized comments, premising them under the broad content specific categories of; 1. Administrative Structure, 2. Ideology and opposition to bidding for Asian Games 2014 and Olympics, and 3. Financial Management.

1. **Administrative Structure**
   a. It is reiterated that the appointment and continuation of Shri Kalmadi as the Chairman of OC was necessitated, as indeed obligated by the "Host City Contract"(HCC) signed by the previous NDA Government and approved by its Cabinet on **11th September, 2003** as an obligatory international instrument. The HCC stipulated that the head of the National Common Wealth Association- in our case, the Indian Olympic Association (IOA)- should be the head of the OC of the CWG, and Shri Kalmadi, who was the elected President of IOA was accordingly nominated so.

   b. The Host City Contract, which is the legal document governing the Commonwealth Games, and, to which Government of India is also a signatory, states:

"The Federation shall entrust the Commonwealth Games Association (CGA)[1] of the Host country with the organization of the Games. The CGA shall establish an OC, which shall have legal status and shall delegate the organization of the Games to the OC, which shall work in conjunction with its CGA, and shall be jointly and severally responsible with the CGA for all commitments including financial commitments in regard to the organization and staging of the games" (Protocol 2, Para 1.1)

c. According to the Host City Contract the Organising Committee was to be constituted within six months of signing of the Contract, which was subsequently extended by the Common Wealth Games Federation (CGF) until December, 2004. The obligations under the Host City Contract- which was approved by the Cabinet- categorically required that the Organising Committee can be formed by the Indian Olympic Association (IOA) to be approved by its General Assembly. The CGF had confirmed at that time that the responsibility for establishing the final structure of the Organising Committee rests with the IOA.

d. The intriguing nature of the signatory of the HCC is also pointed out at this stage. While in the case of Olympics 2012 at London, the signatory on behalf of the host city is the Greater London Development Authority and the British Olympic Association, in case of CWG 2010, the signatory was Shri Rajiv Srivastava, the Secretary, Sports, GoI in 2003 along with the then Delhi Lt. Governor, Shri Vijay Kapur and the IOA, President Shri Suresh Kalmadi. Shri Srivastava was later in 2004, inducted into the OC by Shri Kalmadi in a classic case of Quid-pro-Quo, you scratch my back, I will scratch your's. He continued with him till 2010.

e. In this regard, the observations of the Shunglu HLC on the role of Secretary (Sports) and the Sports Ministry are worth noting; the same is attached at Annexures. "The Secretary, signing on behalf of the government of India, committed the Government to;

   i. Responsibility for all commitments including without limitation financial commitments relating to the organization and staging of the Games,
   ii. Support, facilitate and finance the organization of the games,
   iii. Ensure free access to the host country, minimize the imposition of taxes and
   iv. Ensure appropriate and necessary security".

[1] **CGA**: For India is the Indian Olympic Association.

f. Moreover, the very provisions of the Host City Contract, that ensured Shri Kalmadi's appointment as well as survival, strangely do not find comparable equivalent in the Contract signed for the London Olympics between the hosts and the International Olympic Committee (IOC). The contract document for London says, '**The OCOG-Organizing Committee Olympic Games shall include, among the members of its board of directors and executive committee, the IOC member or members in the host country, the President and Secretary General of the NOC, an athlete having competed in the previous edition of the Olympic Winter Games or the Games of the Olympiad and at least one member representing, and designated by the City,**" Clearly, it did not stipulate the President of the NOC as the Chairman of the Organizing Committee. (The London host City Contract document is attached at Annexure-II)

g. While this on one hand squarely debunks the theory that his appointment was as per provisions of the Olympic Charter, on the other hand it clearly establishes complicity between the then Government, its Ministers, the Secretary (Sports) and Shri Suresh Kalmadi.

h. The Shunglu HLC in the Second Chapter of its Sixth Report has at length outlined the role of Shri Kalmadi right from the outset when the bids for CWG were being pitched by him in collaboration with the then BJP led Government of India.

The High Level Committee, it its Sixth and Main Report has pointedly observed about the conundrum that the Government found it self viz-a-viz Shri Kalmadi :

Chapter 7.18 "The remaining option was to appoint Shri Kalmadi or some other person. There does not seem to have been any other candidate besides Shri Kalmadi. He also 'claimed' to possess impeccable credentials, Member of Parliament, as President of Indian Olympic Association he had succeeded in winning CWG – 2010 for India and had been Minister of State for Railways. It is still possible to criticize this selection; but with the benefit of hindsight. What is in question are not his credentials but his conduct of the Games."

i. As Prime Minister is aware, subsequently in January 2011, Shri Suresh Kalmadi was removed from the position of Chairman, Organizing Committee. Prior to taking the decision, my **Ministry had consulted the Attorney General. (AGs opinion is annexed at Annexure-III) He had advised that the Chairman [OC] and the Secretary General [OC] could and should be**

removed from the Organizing Committee by the Government. In his view, "in any case, the Games are now over and the Host City Contract Clause would be applicable only till such time as the Games were to be organized and conducted." It had not been found feasible to replace Shri Kalmadi between 2005 and 2010, because doing so would have placed the Games in severe jeopardy, besides being legally untenable in light of the fact that the binding obligations of the Host City Contract was in effect till the games were over.

j. I am also attaching my earlier note in this regard for details about inevitable circumstances created by the previous NDA Government led by BJP for appointment of Shri Kalmadi and his colleagues as Chairman and office bearers of the OC of CWG 2010.

2. Ideology

a. As the Minister in-charge of Sports, Shri Aiyer was at the helm implementing our National Sports Policy that entails Excellence in Sports- an integral component of which is hosting of International Sporting Events. The hosting of CWG 2010 were pretty much an exercise in this professed policy direction and any opposition to this was nothing but pure rhetoric. Moreover, it may be recalled that our Government had hosted the Asiad in 1951 and in 1982, even after the previous Janata Party Government had opposed the latter- these were events hosted at a time when our economic prosperity was far below today's levels.

b. Even as the issue of hosting the CWG 2010 was counter argued by Shri Aiyer by the need for utilizing funds for broad basing of Sports in India, it may be seen that this counter argument was fully acknowledged and substantially disposed by the means of the Panchayat Yuva Khel Krida Abhiyan (PYKKA). The PYKKA, credit for which is taken so ardently by Shri Aiyer was approved by the Cabinet, headed by the PM in March 2007 and entails development and promotion of sporting infrastructure and sports at the Panchayat, Block and District levels in rural areas at a cost of Rs. 5000 Cr. It is only ironical that a complaining Shri Aiyer never deemed it proper to thank the PM or Hon'ble Congress President for PYKKA, which was declared a flagship program of the UPA Government.

c. Similarly, with regards to the bidding for the Asian Games 2014, the Cabinet had taken a decision to do so in 2005 and reiterated it with all of Shri Aiyer's concerns incorporated in 2007. Even as he wrote rhetorical and whimsical letters against the decision, he was an integral part and partial of the same Cabinet that had approved the bidding decisions in the first place. It may be noted here that his dissent, if any, in the Cabinet were never aired by him in the media. I deem it proper to mention here that Shri Aiyer's letters were widely quoted and used to scuttle our bid for Asian Games 2014- a situation that should have arisen only if Shri Aiyer, in all his professed righteousness had first resigned from the Cabinet.

3. Financial Management

a. Shri Aiyer has maliciously opined in the Media that he forewarned about escalation of budgetary sanctions of the OC- an issue that not only does not stand subject to factual verification, but also appears frivolous. Even as he wrote about increased financial sanctions to the OC, Shri Aiyer as Minister in-charge approved, duly the Cabinet note giving Rs. 767 Cr to the OC.

b. It is common knowledge that supposed irregularities, as pointed out by the Shunglu HLC are much more quantified in the domain of "Infrastructure" related to the Games. However, Shri Aiyer did an extremely dichotomous, contradictory and self indicting job of dealing with them. While undue cost escalation for various infrastructure projects have been attributed to inordinate delays in their execution, he wrote to the PM on October 25, 2007 detailing that he was **"glad to report that arrangements for physical infrastructure are well underway and we can confidently expect all infrastructure to be completed well in time for the Games in October 2010". In the same letter, he further writes , " In my humble view, and on the basis of nearly two years of closely monitoring developments, I am persuaded that whereas, thanks to the agencies concerned, the physical infrastructure will go up as scheduled and will substantially meet exacting international quality requirements, the organization of the Games in an economic, efficient and taste ful manner cannot be assured with the present organizational structure".** I underline that while the Games did happen, they certainly did not have the advantage of successful preceding infrastructural time lines irrespective of his assurances to the PM on the contrary.

c. Even as Shri Aiyer kept presenting a rosy picture to the PM about the progress in infrastructure preparedness, he actually did everything to hinder and obstruct work which eventually led to delays and huge cost escalations.

d. As far as Shri Aiyer's concerns regarding restructuring of the organizational set up is concerned, the PM, even bound by the sweeping limitations of the afore mentioned HCC took detrimental measures that ensured significant slashing of approved as well as sanctioned budgets of the Organizing Committee (OC). While Jarnail Singh was appointed CEO of the OC with full executive powers, S. Ramachandran, Secy. UD was appointed head of the steering committee on Finance. The Addl. Secy. (Finance) was made member of the Executive Board and request of Shri Kalmadi for including a member of the OC on the Committee of Secretaries (CoS) was not acceded to by the PM. A representative of the OC could only make issue related presentations in meetings of the CoS.

e. It is also beyond comprehension as to by Shri Aiyer chose not to operationalize the "Apex Committee" that was supposed to lord over the OC, even after holding three of its meetings, decisions taken by which were duly adhered to.

f. May I also point out that in expressing his inability to head that the OC through a communication to you, Shri Aiyer displayed gross irresponsibility of a shirker rather than a leader who could take charge and deliver.

Yours Sincerely,

(AJAY MAKEN)

0707.2011

Shri Manmohan Singh
Hon'ble Prime Minister

13

Government of India
Ministry of Youth Affairs & Sports
International Sports Division

On this file, Ministry had sought the advice of the Ministry of Law on the following two points:

(i) Given the structure, legal status, composition of the existing OC and the decision with regard to appointment of Chairman, etc., under what process would it be possible to remove the Chairman and Secretary General from their posts held in the OC and replace them with some other persons within the existing framework of the OC.

(ii) The legal possibility/tenability of superseding the OC, CWG 2010 and replacing it with another legal personality which would continue further to discharge the liabilities and complete the winding up process of the existing OC.

2. This had been done in the context of the letter of Director, CBI addressed to Cabinet Secretary which had been received in the Ministry from the Cabinet Secretariat in which he had stated that Shri Suresh Kalmadi, Chairman OC and Shri Lalit Bhanot, Secretary General, OC were reportedly intimidating officers and witnesses and preventing production of relevant documents which were critical to the investigation. Director, CBI had requested that Shri Suresh Kalmadi, Chairman and Shri Lalit Bhanot, Secretary General, OC may be relieved of their posts in the OC to ensure a free and impartial investigation.

3. The advice from the Law Ministry has been received which may kindly be perused on pre pages. The Learned Attorney General has advised in respect of the above points as under:

(i) **"Yes, The Chairman and the Secretary General can and should be remoeved by the Government. The Government has appointed them at the first instance and has the power to remove them and the apprehension of the CBI must be immediately addressed.**

(ii) **Does not really arise. However, it is the obligation of the Organizing Committee as a society registered under the Societies Registration Act to do all things as are necessary in order to wind up their affairs since the Commonwealth Games have been concluded."**

4. In respect of the advice given by Learned Attorney General of India, it is stated that the decision to appoint Shri Suresh Kalmadi, Chairman OC and Shri Lalit Bhanot, Secretary General, OC, was taken by the Group of Ministers.

14

5. The sequence of events that led up to the decision of the Group of Ministers is as below:

(i) On 3rd September, 2004, Cabinet Secretariat issued orders for constitution of a Core Group of Ministers (GOM) for coordinating the work relating to the organization of the Commonwealth Games 2010 with the approval of the Hon'ble Prime Minister.

(ii) First Meeting of the GOM was held on 25.10.2004 under the chairmanship of the Hon'ble Prime Minister.

(iii) Agenda for the aforesaid Meeting of the GOM was prepared by the Ministry of Youth Affairs & Sports in the form of a Note For The Group of Ministers on Preparations for Commonwealth Games 2010 at New Delhi. Vide Para 16.1 of the said Agenda Note, approval/decision of the GOM was solicited, inter alia, on:

a) Constitution of an Organizing Committee in the form of a Registered Society with Minister, Youth Affairs & Sports as Chairperson; and

b) Constitution of an Executive Board with Minister Youth Affairs & Sports as Chairperson.

(iv) Minutes of the aforesaid 1st Meeting of the GOM, as approved by the Hon'ble Prime Minister, were received from the Cabinet Secretariat through their OM dated 9.11.2004 for further necessary action and circulation to all concerned. In the Minutes sent by the Cabinet Secretariat to this Ministry, there was no decision on the above mentioned two Agenda Items.

(v) The aforesaid Minutes of the GOM held on 25.10.2004 were not issued as the then Minister, YAS, Shri Sunil Dutt had taken up the matter with the Prime Minister and Minister for HRD (Chairman, GOM). Letters dated 11.11.2004 and 14.11.2004 written by the then Minister, YAS to the HRD Minister (Chairman, GOM) and the Hon'ble Prime Minister in this regard refer.. The then Secretary, Sports, had also minuted that the Minutes of GOM dated 25.10.2004 were not issued as Minister (YAS) had written to PM on the subject and mentioned that Minutes are not being issued.

(vi) Thereafter, an ID Note dated 6.12.2004 from PMO addressed to Cabinet Secretary with copy to PS to HRD Minister was received in this Ministry from OSD to HRD Minister with directions that the same is to be considered as an agenda item for the GOM Meeting. The aforesaid PMO ID Note laid down institutional arrangements evolved for the conduct of the

-21-

OFFICE OF SHRI G E VAHANVATI
ATTORNEY GENERAL FOR INDIA
SUPREME COURT, NEW DELHI 110 001
[AG Dy. No. 21/R dt. 22.1.11]
(FTS No. LS Dy No. 216/11 dt. 22.1.11 - Min./Y.A. & Sports)

1. I have seen the further reference dated 22nd January, 2011 which deals with issues which arose after the meeting held with the Cabinet Secretary yesterday. I have also gone through the Host City Contract. I have gone through the Common Wealth Games Federation Constitution, Games Management Protocols, Regulations and the Code of Conduct dated July 2002.

2. Section B contains Games Management Protocols. Para 1.1 of Protocol 2, which deals with duties of the Commonwealth Games Association of the Host Country and of the Organizing Committee reads as under:

> "1.1 The Federation shall entrust the CGA of the host country with the organisation of the Games. The CGA shall establish an OC, which shall have legal status and shall delegate the organization of the Games to the OC, which shall work in conjunction with its CGA, and shall be jointly and severally responsible with the CGA for all commitments including financial commitments in regard to the organisation and staging of the games."

3. As mentioned in my opinion dated 10th January, 2011, the recognition of the Organizing Committee by the GOM in its decision dated 29th January, 2005 was even before the Organizing Committee was registered as a Society on 10th February, 2005. The decision does not require constitution of a Registered Society but obviously, this was practically the way to go forward. The recognition of the Organizing Committee by the Government is not based on the above clause 1.1 of the Protocol. In any case, the games are now over and clause 1.1 would be applicable only till such time as the games were to be organized and conducted. It, therefore, cannot come in the way of the exercise of powers by Government today.

4. Turning now to the resolution of the IOA at its AGM held on 1st November, 2004, it is obvious, in the facts and circumstances of the case that in the event what transpired prior to 29th January, 2005 is not conclusive. The appointment by the IOA of Shri Suresh Kalmadi as the Chairman of the Executive Board of the Organizing Committee was not considered as being a fait accompli or binding on the Government. The Government took an independent decision to appoint him as Chairman of the OC after the meeting of the GOM held on 29th January, 2005, *de hors* the resolution passed on 1st November, 2004. This, therefore, also cannot come in the way of exercise of powers for removal of Shri Kalmadi as the Chairman of the Organizing Committee.

5. As far as the MOA/Rules and Regulations of the Organizing Committee as a Registered Society are concerned, I have already dealt with the same in my earlier opinion dated 10th January, 2011.

6. Considering the aforesaid, the advice that I have given in my earlier note dated 10th January, 2011 remains unaltered.

(Goolam E. Vahanvati)
Attorney General for India
23.1.2011

JS&LA (Shri M.K. Sharma)

JS May kindly see.

24-1-11

AS (L&RLK)

24/1

M/o Youth Affairs + Sports (Sh. Rahul Bhatnagar) JS

8/c

SECRET

अजय माकन
AJAY MAKEN

युवा कार्यक्रम एवं खेल
राज्य मंत्री (स्वतंत्र प्रभार)
भारत सरकार
नई दिल्ली-110 115
MINISTER OF STATE (INDEPENDENT CHARGE)
FOR YOUTH AFFAIRS & SPORTS
GOVERNMENT OF INDIA
NEW DELHI-110 115

D.O.No. 70-97/2011-CWG (Pt) /118

Dated the 22nd July, 2011

Respected Prime Minister,

The Fourth Report of the High Level Committee under the chairmanship of Shri V.K.Shunglu, former Comptroller and Auditor General to look into issues relating to the organizing and conduct of Commonwealth Games - Delhi 2010 relating to 'Games Venues' has been examined in detail. The views of Venue Owners and Executive Agencies and Officials were sought and their comments have been taken into account. I enclose a Brief which clearly indicates that the executive agencies have not agreed with the findings of the HLC in its Fourth Report on Games Venues.

With kind regards,

Yours sincerely,

Ajay Maken

(AJAY MAKEN)

Dr. Manmohan Singh,
Hon'ble Prime Minister,
South Block, New Delhi

5/7

Government of India
Ministry of Youth Affairs and Sports
(International Sports Division)

BRIEF ON OBSERVATIONS OF HIGH LEVEL COMMITTEE (HLC) IN 4th Report (SPORTS VENUES) AND COMMENTS OF VENUE OWNERS/EXECUTING AGENCIES.

Chapter No/Agency	Para Numbers with Category of Comments received from Venue owners/Agency	Brief of disagreement by Venue Owners/ Agency
Executive Summary	Summary of the main observations in respect of all the Chapters.	Comments and disagreement of various agencies involved i.e. venue owners, construction agencies etc have been given in the respective Chapters.
1 **Introduction**	Paragraphs 1.1 to 1.17 deals with general description of the Venue Owners, Role of Venue Owners, Scope of Report Methodology.	These paragraphs are of introductory nature and are factual and these are no comments or remarks to offer.
2 **Venue Briefs**	Main Observation of HLC is that i) the process of preparation and finalization of Venue Briefs for various Games Venues was inordinately delayed; ii. More time and effort was spent in favouring EKS than completion of Venue Briefs in time; iii. Venue Owners unjustifiably protracted the process; iv. This resulted in bunching, resort to 'emergency' procedures in contracting, inflated tender prices and enabled agencies to take full advantage of the situation to the detriment of Government.	Necessary comments in respect of observations have been given by the Venue Agencies and Venue construction agencies and are incorporated against the respective Chapters.

CPWD		
3 JLN Sports Complex	**Part 3.1 - Construction of New Fixed Tensile Membrane Roofing over the seating area in JNS** **Agree with the findings of HLC** NIL **Under investigation –** NIL **Factual** Paras 3.1.1, 3.1.4 relate to general scope of work and tendering process and award of contract. Paras 3.1.5 to 3.1.7 are regarding the pre qualification process. **Disagree** 3.1.2, 3.1.3,3.1.8 to 3.1.32 **Part 3.2 – Laying of IAAF** **Agree with the findings of HLC** Paras 3.2.2, 3.2.5, 3.2.9, 3.2.10 relates to general steps taken for preparation for tendering. **Under investigation** NIL **Factual** Paras 3.2.1, 3.2.4, 3.2.11, 3.2.12, 3.2.13 to 3.2.15 **Disagree** 3.2.3, 3.2.6 to 3.2.8, 3.2.16 to 3.2.36 **Part 3.3 Providing and laying Flat Lawn greens over compatible sub – base in stadia for Lawn Bowls**	Part 3.1, 3.4, 3.5 &3.6 have brought ou irregularities in the contract for th construction of New Fixed Tensile Membrane Roofing over seating area in JNS Weightlifting Auditorium, DG Sets for SA Stadia and Purchase of Un-interrupted Power Systems (UPS) for CWG Venues respectively. C.P.W.D. in their detailed replies have not accepted these irregularities. The issues raised are extremely technical and legal in nature covering interpretation of CPWD Manual, the actual contract, reimbursement of Service Tax, points of negotiation with the successful bidder, cost derived from Import Bills etc. Part 3.2 and 3.3 Irregularities pointed out in the contract for laying of IAAF approved synthetic athletic track at JN Stadium have not been accepted by CPWD. The issues raised are technical and legal in nature covering interpretation of CPWD Manual, cost derived from Import Bills etc. **These issues may be specifically looked by a Technical Committee which could examine the responses of the CPWD vis-a-vis the findings of the HLC for fixing responsibility if any.**

	Agree with the findings of HLC NIL **Under investigation** NIL **Factual** 3.3.10 to 3.3.24 Para 3.3.16 to 3.3.24 Relates to creation of facilities in excess of requirement resulting in extra expenditure in the development of extra greens and location of two bowling pitches HLC has not raised question on any policy decision taken by MoYAS and hence the views of CPWD cannot be agreed to. **Disagree** 3.3.1 to 3.3.9, 3.3.25 to 3.3.38 **Part 3.4 Weight Lifting Auditorium** **Agree with the findings of HLC** Paras 3.4.6, 3.4.8 relate to nonproduction of certain contract files and delay in completion. **Under investigation** NIL **Factual** 3.4.1, 3.4.2, 3.4.5, 3.4.7 **Disagree** 3.4.3, 3.4.4, 3.4.9 to 3.4.22 **Part 3.5 – DG Sets for SAI Stadia** **Agree with the findings of HLC** NIL **Under investigation** NIL **Factual** 3.5.1 to 3.5.4 **Disagree** 3.5.5 to 3.5.23	

- 2 -

Ajay Maken

	Part 3.6 Purchase of UPS for CWG Venues **.Agree with the findings of HLC** NIL **Under investigation** NIL **Factual** **Disagree** 3.6.1 to 3.6.17	
4 **Major Dhyan Chand National Stadium**	**Agree with the findings of HLC** Paras 4.13, 4.14, 4.25, 4.33 Relates to acceptance of lowest negociated amount, re-negociation with L1, justification on the high cost and award of contract and returning of venue brief of CPWD. **Under investigation** The files relating to the contract for construction of this Stadium had earlier been seized by the CBI (para 4.3) **Factual** 4.1 to 4.4, 4.11, 4.12, 4.20, 4.24, 4.27 **Disagree** 4.5 to 4.10, 4.15 to 4.19, 4.21 to 4.23, 4.26, 4.28 to 4.32, 4.34 to 4.36	Irregularities regarding short listing/finalising/ of brands of turf, rates accepted, negotiation of the rates, award of contract, bungling in estimation of rates, etc., pointed by HLC have not been accepted by CPWD and hence **these issues may be specifically looked afresh by a Technical Committee which could examine both, the findings of High Level Committee and the replies of CPWD.**
5 **Dr.SPM Swimming**	**Agree with the findings of HLC** NIL **Under investigation** NIL **Factual** 5.2, 5.4, 5.5 to 5.9, 5.11, 5.14, 5.16, 5.24, 5.29, 5.30 **Disagree**	Irregularities pointed out by HLC regarding extensive renovation of the stadium, return venue brief, preparation of cost justification, comparison of rates of other contracts for similar items, undue benefit extended to the contractor by way of escalation payment/ additional questionable payments made to the contractor etc have not been accepted by CPWD and hence **these issues may be specifically looked at by the Technical**

-4-

(c) Ajay Maken

	5.1, 5.3, 5.10, 5.12, 5.13 5.15, 5.17 to 5.23, 5.25 to 5.28, 5.31 to 5.44	**Committee which could examine both, the High Level Committee findings and the replies of CPWD.**
6 **Dr. Karni Singh Shooting Range**	**Agree with the findings of HLC** Paragraphs 6.4 to 6.6, 6.8, 6.12, 6.16, 6.18, 6.19 deals with venue briefs, provision of separate shooting ranges, survey by consultants, preparation of lay out plan by CPWD, change in scope of work resulting in revised technical sanction, tendering and award of contract., **Under investigation** NIL **Factual** 6.2, 6.3, 6.7, 6.10, 6.11, 6.14 **Disagree** 6.1, 6.9, 6.13, 6.15, 6.17 , 6.22, 6.23, 6.24 , 6.25, 6.26, 6.27	Irregularities have been pointed in the works carried out at Dr. Karni Singh Shooting Ranges which included Construction of Ranges of 10 M, 25M, 50M, Trap, Skeet, Final Range and Armoury Building including Development of Complex (Civil and Electrical) relating to adding on unwarranted elements of cost causing wasteful expenditure by awarding the contract at higher cost . CPWD in their detailed replies have not accepted these irregularities **As stated above the issues may be specifically looked at by a Technical Committee which could examine both, the High Level Committee findings and the replies of CPWD.** Comments of MoYAS (6.17) CPWD in response to para 6.17 of the Report of HLC has stated that this para is to be addressed by MYAS. HLC in their findings has observed that JS(ISD), MYAS informed the Government that the requirement of the Federation and the Commonwealth Games Federations necessitated major changes in design and construction of shooting ranges. The position of the case is that JS(ISD) informed in the meeting of EFC held on 20/25th February, 2009 that large scale variations in two venues mainly K.S. Shooting Range and Cycling Velodrome which involve major changes in design and scope. However many changes and approval of specification came about in the course of detailed meetings with the OC and were not necessarily processed for approval on file. In view of this the observations of HLC viz that variations noticed in the venue briefs cannot be considered as objectionable.

-5-

Ajay Maken

7 Cycling Velodrome	**Agree with the findings of HLC** Paragraphs 7.12, 7.13, 7.17 relate to short listing of experts for design and construction, tendering and award of contract and negotiation with L 1. **Under investigation** NIL **Factual** 7.2 to 7.8, 7.10 to 7.11, 7.14, 7.18, 7.26, 7.27, 7.30, 7.34 **Disagree** 7.1, 7.9, 7.16, 7.19, 7.20 to 7.29, 7.31 to 7.7.33, 7.35 to 7.39	Irregularities have been pointed out in the works carried out at Indira Gandhi Sports Complex – Cycling Velodrome which included the contract relating to design, fabrication, supply and construction of permanent timber track including supporting structure of the indoor Cycling Velodrome. This according to HLC resulted in the contractor favoured with **'undue gains'** of over Rs. **13 crore** and this has become possible due to complicity of senior CPWD officers. CPWD in their detailed replies have not accepted these irregularities **As stated above the issues may be specifically looked afresh by a Technical Committee which could examine both, the High Level Committee findings and the replies of CPWD.** Comments of MoYAS (7.19) CPWD in response to para 7.19 of the Report of HLC has stated that this para is to be addressed by MYAS. HLC in their findings has observed that JS(ISD), MYAS informed the Government that the requirement of the Federation and the Commonwealth Games Federations necessitated major changes in design and construction of shooting ranges. The position of the case is that JS(ISD) informed in the meetings of EFC held on 20/25th February, 2009 that large scale variations in two venues mainly K.S. Shooting Range and Cycling Velodrome which involve major changes in design and scope. However many changes and approval of specification came about in the course of detailed meetings with the OC and were not necessarily processed for approval on file. In view of this the observations of HLC viz. that variations noticed in the venue briefs cannot be considered as objectionable.

GNCTD		
Thyagaraj Sports Complex (A)		(B) The Government of National Capital Territor of Delhi has denied the irregularities whic have been pointed out by the High Leve Committee in respect of the Thyagraj Sport Complex. According to GNCTD, the HLC is not correct in suggesting that conceiving the whole project in two packages (basic structure and civil and electrical work) and awarding the work at different points of time was bad planning. They have stated that in fact, it is a sound principle of construction management and planning that a project is divided into convenient activities according to sequence of occurrence and taken up one by one instead of working on all activities simultaneously. HLC has given no explanation for its conclusion that Package II was 13 percent higher in cost than Package I. **Package I and Package II have entirely difference items. Therefore, comparison of rates of items of Package I and Package II is just not possible.** One week for Package-I was good enough as this package contained items like excavation, plain cement concrete, reinforced cement concrete, steel reinforcement, structural steel work and roofing only with which all the construction agencies are familiar. In response to the HLC's observation that the contract for Dual Fuel turbine was awarded to the single bidder the GNCTD has replied that wide publicity was given in leading news papers as well as on website. Seven tenderers (comprising of almost all the major International Agencies dealing in such kind of work) purchased the bid document and five agencies attended the pre-bit meeting where issues raised by them were addressed to their satisfaction. **Laid down process and approval of single tender under the Works Manual was duly followed. Due care was**

-7-

		taken to ensure that the tender wa awarded at reasonable rates. Regarding HLC;s observation abou retractable seating the GNCTD has stated tha the retractability and movability of the seats ensures that the field of play can be used fo various sporting and non-sporting events which make the stadium a truly multi-purpose stadium in legacy use. Due to the retractability of the seats, the indoor field of play can be converted into a large hall of 100mX40m size by moving the dividing central array of seating to the wall without sacrificing the seating capacity. In response to the observations of the HLC regarding award of contract for IMW Solar Power there was a representation from L2 bidder which was not disposed of in a satisfactory manner, it has been stated that as per the standard practice of the department comparative statement was prepared considering all the items contained in the bill of quantity and the lowest bidder was also decided considering all the items. It would have been incorrect and objectionable, if the comparative statement was prepared and lowest bidder decided by ignoring a particular item of bill of quantity. As such, the representation of L2, that for deciding the L1, item No. 11 of bill of quantity should not be considered, was unreasonable, unacceptable and beyond the standard practice prescribed by the CPWD Manual. Accordingly the representation of L2 was not accepted. The supplier of the maple wood was pre qualified by the OC. PWD did not have the option to open all the tenders. Regarding late start of the project it is stated that the Final Venue Brief was received from OC as late as December 2006. Thereafter the

		concept plans were immediately submitted to OC in December 2006 itself, which were approved only on May 9, 2007 by them. **GNCTD have stated that they are totally at a loss to appreciate the thinking behind the observations of HLC in so far as they relate to Thyagraj Sports Complex. The only venue assigned to the Delhi government emerged as a prime instance of excellence in conception and timely execution.** **In view of the non acceptance of the findings of the HLC and also the matter is technical it is desirable to get this investigated by a Technical Committee.**
NDMC		
9. **Shivaji Stadium**	**Agree with the findings of HLC** Paras 9.12, 9.38, 9.67, 9.68 relate to revision of estimates, procurement of material on behalf of Foreign firm by the Indian contractor, irregular payments and recovery thereof. **Under Investigation** Disciplinary proceedings had been initiated against officials of NDMC who have been alleged to be involved in the omissions and commissions in execution of the construction works and under investigation by CBI/CTE. CBI has registered three FIRS on 9.3.2011. **Factual** 9.1 to 9.11, 9.14 to 9.15,	Reasons given in respect of the paragraphs of **chapter 9 and 10** mainly consist of points justifying the action taken by NDMC regarding the necessity for improvement/upgradation of Shivaji Stadium though it was not ready for CWG 2010. Justification detailing that there was no instances of collusion between officials of the NDMC and other parties such as consultant and contractor, which have been stated to have resulted in appointment of an ineligible consultant as well as contractor, as also unwarranted expenditure on this project, and Disputing the other anomalies such as omission of the escalation clause for steel reinforcement bars and cement (10CA) from contract, and tampering with justified rates in order to fit the bid within 10% above the justified rates. **Since the matter is stated to be under investigation of CBI, the outcome of the investigation may have to be awaited.**

	9.21, 9.22, 9.24, 9.25, 9.27 to 9.29, 9.31, 9.32, 9.34, 9.35, 9.40, 9.42 to 9.44, 9.49, 9.57, 9.58, 9.60, 9.66, 9.72 and 9.75 **Disagree** 9.13, 9.16 to 9.20, 9.23, 9.26, 9.30, 9.33, 9.36, 9.37, 9.39, 9.41, 9.45 to 9.48 9.50to 9.56, 9.59, 9.61 ti 9.65, 9.69 to 9.71, 9.73, 9.74, 9.76 to 9.80	
10 **Talkatora Indoor Stadium**	**Agree with the findings of HLC** Paras 10.64 to 10.66, 10.71 Relates to poor workmanship, delays in completion and rectification of electrical works. **Under Investigation** 10.63 CTE has objected to lower quality of material of material and hence part payment only has been released. **Factual** 10.2 to 10.9, 10.11 to 10.18, 10.35 to 10.38,10.43, 10.46 to 10.47, 10.51, 10.63, 10.67, 10.70, 10.75 to 10.81 **Disagree** 10.1, 10.10,10.19 to 10.29, 10.34, 10.39 to 10.42, 10.44 to 1045, 10.48 to 10.50, 10.52, 10.54 to 10.62, 10.68 to 10.69, 10.72 to 10.74, 10.82	
DDA		
11 **Siri Fort**	**Agree with the findings of**	Reasons given in respect of Paragraphs of

-10-

Ajay Maken

Sports Complex	**HLC** Para 11.65 to 11.68 relate to quality issues during the construction of the competition venue. **Under Investigation** 11.33 and 11.34 The matter regarding unlawful financial advantage by the DDA officials is under Departmental investigation. **Factual** 11.1 to 11.11, 11.13 to 11.18, 11.20 to 11.21, 11.26, 11.36 to 11.38, 11.43, 11.48, 11.49, 11.57 to 11.61 and 11.69 **Disagree** 11.12, 11.19, 11.22 to 11.25, 11 27 to 11.32, 11.35, 11.39 to 11.42, 11.44 to 11.47, 11.52 to 11.56, 11.62 to 11.64, 11.70 to 11.75	chapter 11 and 12 mainly consist of points relating to methodology followed in preparation of RFP for invitation of bids for the works ,evaluation of bids and weightage given for the two bid system, rates determination for preparation of tender documents by market rates instead of rates of schedule of rates of CPWD, and wasteful expenditure on account of variations in the execution and change of specification during execution of the work **It is desirable to get the points of views of HLC and DDA examined by a technical committee to arrive at the final conclusion to fix responsibility for omissions and commissions of the executives if any,**
12 **Yamuna Sports Complex**	**Agree with the findings of HLC** Paras 12.11 to 12.13, 12.21, 12.29, 12.34, 12.46 sub contract for DG Sets, running of the DG Sets, Illumination of external parking facility, acceptance of tender under emergency, Time over-runs in tendering for DG sets, and change in design of flooring. **Under Investigation** Nil **Factual** 12.2 to 12.6, 12.8, 12.15 to 12.16, 12.26, 12.28, 12.33, 12.38, 12.41 to 12.45, 12.49 to 12.50, 12.54 to 12.55, 12.57, 12.60 to 12.61, 12.63	Same as the contents against Chapter 11

	to 12.64 **Disagree** 12.1, 12.7, 12.9,12.10, 12.14, 12.17 to 12.20,12.22 to 12.25, 12.27, 12.30 to 12.32, 12.35 to 12.37, 12.39 to 12.40, 12.46 to 12.48, 12.51 to 12.53, 12.56, 12.58 to 12.59, 12.62, 12.65 to 12.70	
AITA		
13 **R.K Khanna Tennis Stadium**	**Agree with the findings of HLC** Paras 13.42 to 13.51 relates to procurement of tennis surfaces. **Under investigation** Nil **Factual** 13.1 to 13.16, 13.18, 13.21, 13.24, 13 36 to 13.40 **Disagree** 13.17, 13.19, 13.20, 13.22, 13.23, 13.25, 13.26 to 13.31-13.33, 13.34 to 13.35 and 13.41	The irregularities pointed out by the HLC relating to revenue generation out of scrap,, accounting , utilisation certificate, avoidable visit of officials abroad, staff salary accounting, award of work have been denied by AITA.
Delhi University		
14 **Competition & Training Venues**	**Agree with the findings of HLC** NIL **Under Investigation** NIL **Disagree** 14.1 to 14.84	General Comments: The report of the HLC is one sided and no opportunity was given to the University to respond and clarify the points raised which would have sorted out many of the observations. Appointment of EIL has been done in accordance with GFR 2005.(14.18) MOUs have been signed for three venues under the direct control of DU. Legacy use also has begun. The colleges have been asked to sign the MOU.(14.11, 14.12 Maple wood flooring was done as per requirement of OC.) General Comments of EIL:

		After going through the observations of HLC, it is observed that most of the issues have been interpreted on presumptions which are contrary to the facts. 1. All the details /documents desired by the HLC team during the audit were provided so **it is not fair to mention at many locations that 'the details were not made available to the committee'.** 2. The estimates have been prepared on standard concept and are put in place before opening of price bids after approval of competent authority. No justification has been made thereafter so **it is not fair to say that the estimates have been inflated.** 3. The expenditure done for the project is within the approved sanctioned budget by EFC. The venues have been developed as per the requirement of OC, security, trtaffic, health etc. To conduct successful games & to have better legacy use for student community of Delhi University. **It is unfair to term the part of expenditure as wasteful.** 4. Though a detailed discussion was held to clarify all the points related to tendering wherein the HLC team acknowledged the clarifications, **so it is surprising that many such issues have again been pointed out in the report.** 5. Appointment of consultat has been done on a standard methodology of deposit concept and on fair basis. 6. All jobs have been awarded through fair competitive bidding after getting approvals of

Ajay Makan

		competent authority.
Jamia Milia Islamia		
15 **Training Venue for Rugby**	**Agree with the findings of HLC** Paras 15.2, 15.3, 15.4 relate to role in relation to CWG. **Under investigation** Nil **Factual/No comments** 15.1, 15.6, 15.7 **Disagree** 15.5, 15.8 to 15.16	The estimation and execution of work was based on the directions of the Venue Briefs and Return Venue Briefs supplied by the OC. Some of the bills in respect of ECIL, RITES and other parties are under preparations. Once the final bills are settled the unutilized amount will be returned to the MoYAS. As the HLC has not asked for the photographs the same were not made available to them. The draft MOU was sent to JMI on 8.4.2010 and the same was signed on 8.7.2010. The work has now been handed over to JMI by RITES completely. The old seating facility in the JMI required to be replaced. The provision of DG sets was necessary because of the frequency of power breakdown.
Delhi Public School R.K Puram		
Training Venue for Lawn Bowls Synthetic Surfaces		The sports surfaces have been used by the Indian Lawn Ball teams and trainees of India and various countries before and during the CWG 2010. The venue is being used by the School children and will be made available as and when required by MYAS and SAI or Organisations authorised by the MYAS.
Kadarpur Shooting Range		
The Big Bore Shooting Range at CRPF		The Range is being maintained by CRPF as per MOU signed with MYAS and is used for National/International competitions. The All India Police Shooting Competition and

-14-

Kadarpur		National Big Bore Shooting Championship have been recently held at this facility,(Chapter 17- Par 17.1 to 17.10
Chapter 16 Main findings		SAI/CWPD have informed that the estimates prepared by SAI/CPWD which were appraised by the EFC in September, 2006 were tentative estimates, since at that time the venue briefs from OC and their consultants were not available to them. Detailed/accurate estimates could only be prepared much later when detailed venue briefs and drawings had been made available. There was an urgency to get the work commenced for which the demolition of the existing structures had to be done first and foremost which was also a time consuming process and simultaneously the process for statutory/regulatory clearances had to be commenced and that would not have been possible unless approval of the competent authority in this case the Cabinet, had been obtained for this work. Regarding HLC;s observation of rewarding contract at high rates CPWD have informed that all the codal formalities were followed unscrupulously, so it is not correct to say that the emergency procedures were adopted in contracting and hence no compromise was done from the established procedure. Regarding HLC;s observation on security expenditure it is stated that the cameras and other security gadgets were installed as per the directions of the Security Agencies. It is beyond the jurisdiction of HLC assess 'Threat' perception and such decision are best taken by agencies who have been entrusted with this responsibility. As regards the HLC's observations regarding 'No dearth of money syndrome' it is stated that a realistic and firm estimate was prepared based on the requirements projected by OC/SAI The cost estimation required techno-commercial study of the items such as

		providing Membrane roofing in JLN. These were approved by EFC and then approved by the Competent Authority **In regard to HLC's findings of irregularities of an amount of Rs.113 crores in a contract of Rs.350 crores, CPWD has stated that this is not a fixed cost contract and there is a provision in contract for payment of escalation and hence the payment of Rs. 29.70 crores can not be termed as irregular. Further regarding fully locked cable HLC Report has not taken into account import of 335.116 MT of cable(value Rs. 16.35 crores). Further the HLC findings have not considered cost of membrane (Rs. 16.49 crores), crane hire charges (Rs. 20 Crores), labour transportation (Rs. 4.41 crores) etc. And hence HLC had overlooked a number of vital facts and figures.** CPWD have stated in their response that most CWG projects executed by CPWD involved components (being special type of structures and also specific games related provisions) requiring specialized skill and it is not proper to terms these as normal Civil constructions. The estimates were not prepared in perfunctory manner and these were prepared as per the CPWD procedure. The actual expenditure can never be expected to be exactly the same as the estimated cost. It is likely to be either more than or less than the sanctioned estimated cost. The HLC;s observations regarding undue benefits given to the contractor is not correct and is based on wrong presumption overlooking the number of vital facts and figures. Only bonafide payment as admissible under the contract has been released to him. The CPWD have further stated that the basement parking (below Weight lifting Venue) has been constructed as per Layout Plan approved by MCD/DUAC. Hence it was not a wasteful expenditure. The basement parking at MDC National Stadium is near India Gate, and the costliest land in area.

Ajay Malik

		Basement provided are very useful for parkin during any event in stadium and at the time (trade fair at ITPO. The tendering proce: followed by CPWD is as per the procedure lai down for the purpose and it is not correct t say that undue benefits have been given to . particular contractor. No Bid documents were tweaked to provid for escalation as alleged in the HLC report and the CTE and CAG has also examined and nowhere ever the issue of escalation clause was raised, as it had the approval of the tender acceptance authority –Central Works Board. The CPWD has further stated that the H.L.C. has made some observations related to award of contract for Timber cycling track at I.G. Stadium Complex and drawn conclusion in their main findings para 16.42 that there is an undue benefit of Rs. 3 crores passed on to the contractor by accepting a higher bidder. The observations of the HLC are denied in view of the detailed clarifications given below. The timber track contract was decided after following a very transparent and competitive bidding process in spite of a strong recommendation from the OC and the International Cycling Union to nominate M/s Schuermann only. The Most transparent and competitive bidding process was followed. Regarding bidding process for the up gradation of the Dr. Karni Singh Shooting Range **C.P.W.D.** has stated that the most transparent and competitive bidding process was followed. Regarding the report of HLC on DG sets it is stated by the **CPWD** that comparison of rates have not been properly done as HLC has not considered duties, taxes, cost of essential components etc for operationalization of DG Set. Similarly in the case of UPS also HLC has failed to make proper comparison as tender specification are much higher than the

-17-

specification considered by HLC fi comparison of rates. Hence no loss is cause to Government on this part of work and also n procedural lapses on part of any official ar sustained. Hence the report of HLC on DG se and UPS is an exercise in futility.

Regarding renovation/construction of **Shivaj Stadium and Talkatora Stadium (NDMC)**i is stated that the matter is under investigation by CBI/CTE.

Regarding Siri Fort Complex which has been constructed/renovated by **DDA** the matter is under investigation.

The irregularities pointed out by the HLC in case of Yamuna Sports Complex have been denied by the **DDA** and stated that the proper procedure was followed and the work has been carried as per the requirement.

The report of HLC is one sided as per the Statement of **Delhi University** and they have not given any opportunity to respond and clarify the points raised by them. The EIL has stated that all the work was done through fair competitive bidding after getting the approval of the competent authority.

Regarding **Jamia Milia Islamia** stated that the work was done in the University as per the Venue Brief and Return Venue Brief supplied by the OC.

(C) **Since the irregularities pointed out by the High Level Committee have not been agreed to by the executive agencies (CPWD, DDA, NDMC, RITES, EIL etc), these issues may be specifically looked afresh by a Technical Committee which could examine both the High Level Committee Report and replies of the executing Agencies.**

-18-

Organising Committee
Commonwealth Games 2010 Delhi

Suresh Kalmadi *M.P.*
Chairman, Organising Committee
Commonwealth Games 2010 Delhi
&
President, Indian Olympic Association

January 18, 2005

Reg: Commonwealth Games 2010

Dear Shri Vikram Doraiswamy

It is unfortunate that the Indian Olympic Association, which has been awarded the Commonwealth Games, has not been invited for both the GoM Meetings and we have not been given an opportunity to give our point of view.

1. It is a matter of regret and concern that the directions of the Prime Minister's Office finalized after a series of meetings by the GoM, Cabinet Secretary, Sports Ministry, Indian Olympic Association and other departments, have not been implemented and are constantly being stalled by the Ministry of Sports for one or the other reason. The directions of the PMO are in keeping with the autonomy of the Indian Olympic Association and the resolutions passed at its General Assembly Meeting of the Indian Olympic Association held on Nov. 1, 2004 regarding the Chairmanship of the Organising Committee are acceptable to us. <u>Any other format will be unacceptable to the Indian Olympic Association.</u>

2. We have lost lot of time in our preparation for the Commonwealth Games due to delaying tactics of the Ministry of Sports. The Commonwealth Games Federation is constantly reminding the Indian Olympic Association to meet our obligations and deadlines, and we are far behind schedule. <u>The President of the Commonwealth Games Federation, Mr. Mike Fennel is due to arrive at Delhi on February 2, 2005</u> and the country would face lot of international disrepute and loss of face if the issues were not settled by that date. <u>We would face the risk of the Commonwealth Games being shifted to some other country.</u>

Gate No. 25, Jawaharlal Nehru Stadium, Lodhi Road, New Delhi-110003. India.
Tel.: +91-11-24366950, 51, 52. Fax : +91-11-24365395
e-mail : ioa@nde.vsnl.net.in website : www.cwgdelhi2010.com

2010 COMMONWEALTH GAMES DELHI

Organising Committee
Commonwealth Games 2010 Delhi

Suresh Kalmadi *M.P.*
Chairman, Organising Committee
Commonwealth Games 2010 Delhi
&
President, Indian Olympic Association

: 2 :

3. I understand that Mr Sunil Dutt, Minister for Sports has raised certain issues relating to the Commonwealth Games 2010 during the meeting of the GoM held on January 14, 2005. Whereas the enclosed note gives our views, I would however like to emphasize the following: -

(a) The Indian Olympic Association is an autonomous body governed by the Olympic Charter and our autonomy is important for the Olympic movement and there can be no compromise on this.

(b) The games have been allotted to the Indian Olympic Association and the Organizing Committee formation rests with the Indian Olympic Association and not with the Ministry of Sports.

(c) I was unanimously elected as Chairman of the Organizing Committee and the Executive Board of the Commonwealth Games 2010 at the General Assembly Meeting of the Indian Olympic Association held on Nov. 1, 2004 and authorised to finalise the Organizing Committee, its Executive Board and other Committees in consultation with other Members of the Indian Olympic Association. I was further authorized to deal with the Government of India and the Government of NCT, Delhi regarding the Commonwealth Games (copy of the Resolution enclosed).

(d) In case of 1982 Asian Games, Mr Buta Singh was elected as the Chairman of the Organizing Committee in his capacity as President of the Amateur Athletic Federation of India, and not as a Minister, by the General Assembly of the Indian Olympic Association.

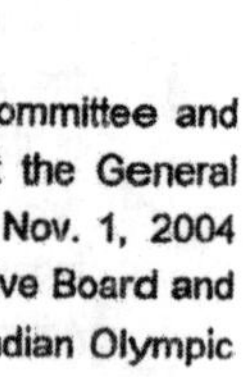

Gate No. 25, Jawaharlal Nehru Stadium, Lodhi Road, New Delhi-110003. India.
Tel.: +91-11-24366950, 51, 52. Fax : +91-11-24365395
e-mail : ioa@nde.vsnl.net.in website : www.cwgdelhi2010.com

Organising Committee
Commonwealth Games 2010 Delhi

Suresh Kalmadi *M.P.*
Chairman, Organising Committee
Commonwealth Games 2010 Delhi
&
President, Indian Olympic Association

: 3 :

(e) Any contractual obligation derives only from the Host City contract, which has been duly signed by the then Secretary, Sports, the Lt. Governor of Delhi and the Indian Olympic Association. There has been no changes in this document, which clearly states that the games belong to the Indian Olympic Association.

(f) The Bid Document kept getting changed from time to time till the Commonwealth Games Federation was satisfied on all counts. The Initial bid documents, the bid updates 1 and 2, and the consolidated updated bid document were prepared and presented by the Indian Olympic Association to the Commonwealth Games Federation at various times. The bid documents were discussed and finalized between the Indian Olympic Association and Commonwealth Games Federation. The Ministry of Sports, Government of Delhi and DDA were consulted from time to time as per requirement and at no stage they have differed from the views of the Indian Olympic Association.

(g) The issue of the Chairmanship of the Organizing Committee in the Initial Bid Document came up during the visit of the Commonwealth Games Federation Evaluation Commission and suggestions of some of the friendly Member countries who were Voters at Montego Bay General Assembly to drop the "Government Nominee" suffix as it would enhance our bid prospects and would be in keeping with the principles of autonomy was accepted. This change was part of the final presentation at Montego Bay General Assembly held on 13th November 2003 by me as Chairman, Bid Committee was duly acknowledge and is now part of the final Bid Document. The then Secretary

Gate No. 25, Jawaharlal Nehru Stadium, Lodhi Road, New Delhi-110003. India.
Tel.: +91-11-24366950, 51, 52. Fax : +91-11-24365395
e-mail : ioa@nde.vsnl.net.in website : www.cwgdelhi2010.com

Organising Committee
Commonwealth Games 2010 Delhi

Suresh Kalmadi *M.P.*
Chairman, Organising Committee
Commonwealth Games 2010 Delhi
&
President, Indian Olympic Association

:4:

(Sports), Mr Rajiv Srivastava who is a signatory to the Host City contract and who represented the Sports Ministry in all discussions, is aware of this position. The Sports Ministry Officials were also present at the Commonwealth Games General Assembly Meeting at Athens on 17th August 2004 where the final Bid Document was presented and accepted by the House. At no stage the Government objected, we are surprised that this matter has been brought up now at this stage at the GoM. Mr Mike Fennell, President, Commonwealth Games Federation has already sent congratulatory messages to me for being elected Chairman of the Organising Committee.

I seek your intervention in the matter so that the Commonwealth Games are not jeopardized and Prime Minister's order is implemented.

Regards

Yours sincerely,

(SURESH KALMADI), M.P.
Chairman, Organizing Committee,
Commonwealth Games 2010
President, Indian Olympic Association.

Shri Vikram Doraiswamy
Private Secretary to the Prime Minister
7, Race Course Road
New Delhi

This is same note I have sent to Mr Arjun Singh who is heading the GoM for your understanding

Gate No. 25, Jawaharlal Nehru Stadium, Lodhi Road, New Delhi-110003, India.
Tel.: +91-11-24366950, 51, 52. Fax : +91-11-24365395
e-mail : ioa@nde.vsnl.net.in website : www.cwgdelhi2010.com

COMMONWEALTH GAMES FEDERATION
CGF

26 UPPER BROOK STREET
LONDON, W1K 7QE
UNITED KINGDOM
T: +44 (0)20-7491 8801
F: +44 (0)20-7409 7803
E: office@thecgf.com
www.thecgf.com

2 September 2004

Suresh Kalmadi
President
Indian Olympic Association
Gate No.25 Jawaharlal Nehru Stadium
Lodhi Road
New Delhi - 110 003
India

Dear Suresh

Organising Committee - Delhi 2010 Commonwealth Games

Further to our recent discussions in Athens and in particular those related to the formation of the Organising Committee we appreciate very much the presentation given by you and your colleagues to the CGF Executive Board which included your confirmation that the Organising Committee will be formed no later than 31 December 2004.

As advised in Athens and indeed in our earlier discussions leading up to the award of the Games last year in Jamaica responsibility for establishing the final structure of the Organising Committee rests with the Indian Olympic Association and we look forward to receiving your formal advice having regard to the liability issues raised by our President and Honorary Legal Adviser.

Insofar as the Executive Board of the Organising Committee is concerned, consistent with the bid, in our letter of June 14th we confirmed our representatives i.e. our President Michael Fennell, Vice President HRH Tunku Imran and myself, the remaining members are of course a matter for the IOA to determine with its partners.

We look forward to receiving your advice on this matter at your earliest convenience.

Kind regards

Michael Hooper
Chief Executive Officer

APPENDIX 5

F.70-10/2004-SP.II
Government of India
Ministry of Youth Affairs and Sports

Dated: 8th September, 2004

To

The Secretary General,
Indian Olympic Association,
Jawaharlal Nehru Stadium,
Lodhi Road, New Delhi

Subject: Updated Bid Document for Commonwealth Games, 2010

Sir,

I am directed to refer to Director (Coordination)'s letter No. Nil dated 6th September, 2004 wherein an "Updated Bid Document" was enclosed. In the letter a brief summary of the salient changes incorporated in the Bid Documents has been given.

2. It has been observed from the above letter that some items may have additional financial implications and no approval of the Government was obtained.

3. The Government had approved the budget estimates submitted by IOA vide its letter dated 27th August, 2004. The budget estimates were of the order of Rs 399.05 crores against expected revenue generation of US $ 100 million by the Organising Committee Projected expenditure, inter-alia, included an amount of Rs.48 crores towards travel grant.. The details for this grant were not spelt out at that point of time. You may please clarify whether the details spelt out now in your letter under the head of Travel Grant would have additional financial implications. Similarly, clarification may please be given as to whether the details given under the head of Accommodation would have additional financial implications.

4. Under para 8 of the letter mentioned above, a mention has been made on a new training site for the sport.' This is rather vague. The proposal may please be amplified with a clarification as to whether this also involves financial implications.

5. You will kindly appreciate that it would not be possible for the Government to approve of any expenditure on items which were not indicated at the time of submission of budget estimates and, therefore, not approved. An early response in this regard will be highly appreciated.

Yours faithfully

(R.K. Mishra)
Joint Secretary to the Govt. of India

Organising Committee
Commonwealth Games 2010 Delhi

Suresh Kalmadi *M.P.*
Chairman, Organising Committee
Commonwealth Games 2010 Delhi
&
President, Indian Olympic Association

January 18, 2005.

Dr. Manmohan Singh Ji,
Hon'ble Prime Minister of India,
7-Race Course Road,
New Delhi.

Urgent

Dear Dr Manmohan Singh ji

Reg: Commonwealth Games 2010.

A delegation of the Indian Olympic Association would like to meet you regarding Commonwealth Games 2010 Delhi. The order regarding the institutional arrangements for the Commonwealth Games 2010 dated 6th December 2004 issued by the Prime Minister's office has not been implemented as yet. The President of the Commonwealth Games Federation, Mr. Mike Fennel is due to arrive at Delhi on February 2, 2005 and the country would face lot of international disrepute and loss of face if the issues were not settled by that date. We would face the risk of the Commonwealth Games being shifted to some other country.

I request you to kindly give some time at the earliest.

Regards and Best wishes

Yours sincerely,

(SURESH KALMADI), M.P.
Chairman, Organizing Committee,
Commonwealth Games 2010
President, IOA

Gate No. 25, Jawaharlal Nehru Stadium, Lodhi Road, New Delhi-110003. India.
Tel.: +91-11-24366950, 51, 52. Fax : +91-11-24365395
e-mail : ioa@nde.vsnl.net.in website : www.cwgdelhi2010.com

2010 COMMONWEALTH GAMES DELHI

Organising Committee
Commonwealth Games 2010 Delhi

Suresh Kalmadi *M.P.*
Chairman, Organising Committee
Commonwealth Games 2010 Delhi
&
President, Indian Olympic Association

January 31, 2005

Dr Manmohan Singh
Hon'ble Prime Minister of India
7, Race Course Road
New Delhi

Dear Dr Manmohan Singhji,

Mr Michael Fennell, President Commonwealth Games Federation is visiting Delhi in the first week of February 2005.

Mr Michael Fennell would like to call on you along with myself and Mr Randhir Singh Secretary General IOA on any day and time convenient to you from 6th to 8th February 2005.

I request you to give time at the earliest. This courtesy call will go a long way in further strengthening India's bonds with the Commonwealth Games Federation.

Regards

Yours sincerely,

Suresh Kalmadi

(SURESH KALMADI), M.P.
Chairman, Organising Committee
Commonwealth Games 2010 Delhi

c.c. to

Shri Vikram Doraiswamy
Private Secretary to the Prime Minister
7, Race Course Road, New Delhi

Gate No. 25, Jawaharlal Nehru Stadium, Lodhi Road, New Delhi-110003. India.
Tel.: +91-11-24366950, 51, 52. Fax : +91-11-24365395
e-mail : ioa@nde.vsnl.net.in website : www.cwgdelhi2010.com

भारतीय ओलम्पिक संघ
Indian Olympic Association

March 23, 2005

Dr Manmohan Singh
Hon'ble Prime Minister of India,
New Delhi.

Dear Dr Manmohan Singhji,

Thank you very much for the interest taken by you for the Commonwealth Games 2010. We have to utilize the Commonwealth Games 2010 to build up Olympic Sports in the country. Some of the very important steps which needs to be taken care of urgently are as follows:

1. **Sports Budget**

   The Sports Budget for the year 2005-06 is Rs. 312.79 Crores (which includes Rs 45.5 Crore for Commonwealth Games) against the Budget for the year 2004-05 of Rs 269.48 Crores. If we take out the Commonwealth Games Budget, the Sports Budget has gone down.

   - **Budget for the National Sports Federations**

     Budget for the National Sports Federations have been reduced from Rs. 50.31 Crore to Rs. 48.00 Crore.

   - **Budget for the Commonwealth Games**

     The Planning Commission had agreed to earmark Rs 115 Crore for the Commonwealth Games 2010 but in the final budget Rs 45.5 Crore has been allocated.

2. **Rs 200 Crore per year to get medals at the Commonwealth Games 2010**

   The expenditure for the Commonwealth Games 2010 need not only be on the infrastructure alone but we have to see India is on top of the medals tally. We have requested Rs 200 Crore per year to be allocated up to year 2010 for training of Athletes, Coaches, foreign exposure etc.

Cont.......P/2

JAWAHARLAL NEHRU STADIUM, NEW DELHI-110 003 (INDIA)
Tel. : (91-11) 4366950, 4366951, 4366952 Grams : INDOLYMPIC Fax : (91-11) 4365953
E-mail : ioa@nde.vsnl.net.in

भारतीय ओलम्पिक संघ
Indian Olympic Association

:2:

3. **Incentive for Industry**

Industry should also come forward to promote sports in the country. It is proposed that 200% tax exemption may be given up to the Commonwealth Games 2010. to all companies investing in olympic sports upto a maximum of 10% of their profits

4. **Cabinet Approval for Asian Games 2014 and in Principle Approval for 2016 Olympic Games**

Sports Ministry has forwarded a Cabinet Note for approval of bidding for Asian Games 2014. The approval is needed urgently as last date for submission is 31 March, 2005.

Indian Olympic Association has also sent a proposal to the Sports Ministry for the bidding for 2016 Olympic Games. **The President of India has also mentioned in his address to the joint session of Parliament that India will stake its claim to host the 2016 Olympic Games.**

We request that **in principle approval** may be given for 2016 Olympic Games Bid so that no other country of Asia, Africa and Commonwealth Countries may not their claims.

5. **Sports in Concurrent List- Opposed by States & IOA**

The Ministry of Sports had called for a meeting of all the States Sports Ministers to get the support for bringing the sports in the Concurrent List of the Constitution. The move was apposed by most of the State Sports Ministers, which was violative of the spirirt of the constitution and was also vitiative to our Federal Structure. It is also against the spirit of the Olympic Charter so the Indian Olympic Association can not support such a move.

Thanking you.

With best wishes

Yours sincerely,

Prof. V K Malhotra
Sr. Vice President, IOA

(Suresh Kalmadi), M.P.
President, Indian Olympic Association

JAWAHARLAL NEHRU STADIUM, NEW DELHI-110 003 (INDIA)
Tel. : (91-11) 4366950, 4366951, 4366952 Grams : INDOLYMPIC Fax : (91-11) 4365953
E-mail : ioa@nde.vsnl.net.in

Organising Committee
Commonwealth Games 2010 Delhi

CWG / 2010 / Infra/ November 07, 2005

Dear Shri Nair,

As you are aware that Delhi would be hosting the Commonwealth Games in 2010. For providing the world class infrastructure we held series of discussions with DDA, NCT of Delhi, Sports Authority of India, Indian Olympic Association and the National Federations concerned. The Organising Committee engaged the Event Knowledge Services (EKS) to guide us on selecting the best venues for holding Commonwealth Games.

Based on the views of the organizations mentioned above I have prepared a **DRAFT REPORT** on Sport Venues a copy of the same is sent herewith for your comments.

The Organising Committee solicits your valuable suggestions on sports venues by ***17th November, 2005*** .

Regards

Yours sincerely,

SURESH KALMADI, M.P.
CHAIRMAN
ORGANISING COMMITTEE
COMMONWEALTH GAMES 2010 DELHI

Shri T.K.A.Nair,
Principal Secretary to the Prime Minister,
Prime Minister's Office,
South Block,
New Delhi

Gate No. 25, Jawaharlal Nehru Stadium, Lodhi Road, New Delhi-110003. India.
Tel.: +91-11-24366950, 51, 52. Fax : +91-11-24365395
e-mail : ioa@nde.vsnl.net.in website : www.cwgdelhi2010.com

2010 COMMONWEALTH GAMES DELHI

Organising Committee
Commonwealth Games 2010 Delhi

Suresh Kalmadi *M.P.*
Chairman, Organising Committee
Commonwealth Games 2010 Delhi
&
President, Indian Olympic Association

25th August,2005

CWG/2010/PM/National Teams

Dear Dr Manmohan Singhji,

I am happy to appraise you of the progress on the preparations for 2010 Commonwealth Games. We had recently held the meetings of the Executive Board and Organizing Committee of the Commonwealth Games. Games Secretariat started functioning in J.N. stadium. Discussions are being held with DDA, NCT of Delhi and Sports Authority of India (SAI) to finalise the infrastructure requirements for the Games.

On 15th & 16th Sept. 2005 the Executive Board of Commonwealth Games Federation will be meeting in Delhi which would be attend by the President of the Commonwealth Games Federation. Baton carrying the message of the Queen Elizabeth II to the athletes of all the 71 Commonwealth countries will be arriving into Delhi on 13th September, 2005.

The Organizing Committee of the 2010 Commonwealth Games in its meeting held on 11th August, 2005 resolved the following to showcase Delhi and India and requested me to bring to the notice of the Hon'ble Prime Minister for kind patronage.

1. To provide the State of Art Sports infrastructure for holding the **competitions** and **training** of participating teams prior to and during the Games.

2. To give top priority for training of our National teams for 2010 Commonwealth Games as well as Asian Games which are held with in a span of 45 days.

3. To engage best Indian coaches to train our National teams.

4. To engage foreign coaches as at **annexure-I** for various disciplines of the Commonwealth Games and Asian Games from the countries leading in respective sports disciplines to train our National teams along with the Indian coaches.

5. To engage Sports Scientists (Indian & Foreign) as indicated in **annexure-II** to provide Scientific support to the National teams.

Cont....P/2

Gate No. 25, Jawaharlal Nehru Stadium, Lodhi Road, New Delhi-110003. India.
Tel.: +91-11-24366950, 51, 52. Fax : +91-11-24365395
e-mail : ioa@nde.vsnl.net.in website : www.cwgdelhi2010.com

Organising Committee
Commonwealth Games 2010 Delhi

:2:

6. **To treat all disciplines of the Commonwealth Games and Asian Games as priority disciplines and extend full financial support for their training and competitions in India and abroad, holding of more domestic competitions and International competitions with in the country.**

7. To provide the best quality sports equipment to our sports persons for their training and competitions.

8. To strengthen the Sports Sciences centers of SAI and set up new centers in Pune, Hyderabad and Chennai where the National teams could be trained.

9. Develop the existing High altitude center at Shilaroo (HP) by providing synthetic Athletic track and set up a new center in Uthagamandalam (TN). At Uthagamandalam the high altitude training could be held round the year since it is free from snow.

10. Each of the 36 discipline of Commonwealth Games and Asian Games may be sanctioned on an average of Rs. Five (5) crores per annum for holding the domestic competitions and International competitions in India for strengthening the performance of our teams and to upgrade the knowledge of Indian Technical Officials.

11. The budget requirements worked out in consultation with the concerned National Federations to prepare the National teams (Senior & Junior) and for conducting competitions amounting to Rs. 1227.76 crores for 5 years from 2006-07 to 2010-11 financial years is at **Annexure-III & IV** for making provision in the annual budget of each year.

12. **Govt. staff for Games Secretariat:** As done for 1982 Delhi Asian Games the services of the staff required from various Ministries/Departments for specific works may be spared to the Organizing Committee of 2010 Commonwealth Games meeting their salaries by the respective Ministries/Departments.

As the Chairman of the 2010 Commonwealth Games Organizing Committee and the President of the Indian Olympic Association, I would solicit the Hon'ble Prime Minister kindly to approve the requirements projected and to advise the Ministry of Youth affairs and Sports to take action immediately on each issue.

Regards

Yours sincerely,

Suresh Kalmadi

(Suresh Kalmadi), M.P.

Dr. Manmohan Singh,
Hon'ble Prime Minister of India,
South Block,
New Delhi.

Gate No. 25, Jawaharlal Nehru Stadium, Lodhi Road, New Delhi-110003. India.
Tel.: +91-11-24366950, 51, 52. Fax : +91-11-24365395
e-mail : ioa@nde.vsnl.net.in website : www.cwgdelhi2010.com

APPENDIX – 5

F.70-10/2004-SP.II
Government of India
Ministry of Youth Affairs and Sports

Dated: 8th September, 2004

To

The Secretary General,
Indian Olympic Association,
Jawaharlal Nehru Stadium,
Lodhi Road, New Delhi

Subject: Updated Bid Document for Commonwealth Games, 2010

Sir,

I am directed to refer to Director (Coordination)'s letter No. Nil dated 6th September, 2004 wherein an "Updated Bid Document" was enclosed. In the letter a brief summary of the salient changes incorporated in the Bid Documents has been given.

2. It has been observed from the above letter that some items may have additional financial implications and no approval of the Government was obtained.

3. The Government had approved the budget estimates submitted by IOA vide its letter dated 27th August, 2004. The budget estimates were of the order of Rs 399.05 crores against expected revenue generation of US $ 100 million by the Organising Committee. Projected expenditure, inter-alia, included an amount of Rs.48 crores towards travel grant., The details for this grant were not spelt out at that point of time. You may please clarify whether the details spelt out now in your letter under the head of Travel Grant would have additional financial implications. Similarly, clarification may please be given as to whether the details given under the head of Accommodation would have additional financial implications.

4. Under para 8 of the letter mentioned above, a mention has been made on a new training site for the sport.' This is rather vague. The proposal may please be amplified with a clarification as to whether this also involves financial implications.

5. You will kindly appreciate that it would not be possible for the Government to approve of any expenditure on items which were not indicated at the time of submission of budget estimates and, therefore, not approved. An early response in this regard will be highly appreciated.

Yours faithfully,

(R.K. Mishra)
Joint Secretary to the Govt. of India

APPENDIX – 6

No.F.70-19/2002-SP-II
Government of India
Ministry of Youth Affairs and Sports

Dated : 24th May, 2003

To,

The Secretary General,
Indian Olympic Association,
J.N. Stadium,
New Delhi.

Sub: **Bid for hosting Commonwealth Games, 2010**

Sir,

I am directed to refer to this Ministry's letter of even number dated 9th May, 2003 regarding proposed holding of XIX Commonwealth Games at New Delhi in the year 2010.

2. The Government has approved the proposal of the IOA for holding the Commonwealth Games, 2010. A letter from Union Minister for Youth Affairs and Sports addressed to Chairman, Commonwealth Games Federation indicating the Government support for bid of the City of Delhi to host the Games, guarantee for free entry to India of all accredited athletes and delegation of the participating countries and further guarantee to the effect that the Games will be organized in accordance with the constitution, protocols and regulations of the Commonwealth Games Federation is enclosed.

3. As regards financial assistance to IOA towards bidding of Commonwealth Games, the matter is under consideration of the Government. The decision regarding financial assistance for bidding for the Commonwealth Games will be taken by the Ministry in consultation with Ministry of Finance. As soon as a decision in this regard is taken, IOA will be intimated accordingly.

Yours faithfully,

(B.K. Das)
Joint Secretary (Sports)

Organising Committee
Commonwealth Games 2010 Delhi

Suresh Kalmadi *M.P.*
Chairman, Organising Committee
Commonwealth Games 2010 Delhi
&
President, Indian Olympic Association

Urgent

January 18, 2005

Reg: Commonwealth Games 2010

Dear Mr Pulok Chatterjee

It is unfortunate that the Indian Olympic Association, which has been awarded the Commonwealth Games, has not been invited for both the GoM Meetings and we have not been given an opportunity to give our point of view.

1. It is a matter of regret and concern that the directions of the Prime Minister's Office finalized after a series of meetings by the GoM, Cabinet Secretary, Sports Ministry, Indian Olympic Association and other departments, have not been implemented and are constantly being stalled by the Ministry of Sports for one or the other reason. The directions of the PMO are in keeping with the autonomy of the Indian Olympic Association and the resolutions passed at its General Assembly Meeting of the Indian Olympic Association held on Nov. 1, 2004 regarding the Chairmanship of the Organising Committee are acceptable to us. Any other format will be unacceptable to the Indian Olympic Association.

2. We have lost lot of time in our preparation for the Commonwealth Games due to delaying tactics of the Ministry of Sports. The Commonwealth Games Federation is constantly reminding the Indian Olympic Association to meet our obligations and deadlines, and we are far behind schedule. The President of the Commonwealth Games Federation, Mr. Mike Fennel is due to arrive at Delhi on February 2, 2005 and the country would face lot of international disrepute and loss of face if the issues were not settled by that date. We would face the risk of the Commonwealth Games being shifted to some other country.

Gate No. 25, Jawaharlal Nehru Stadium, Lodhi Road, New Delhi-110003. India.
Tel.: +91-11-24366950, 51, 52. Fax : +91-11-24365395
e-mail : ioa@nde.vsnl.net.in website : www.cwgdelhi2010.com

Organising Committee
Commonwealth Games 2010 Delhi

Suresh Kalmadi *M.P.*
Chairman, Organising Committee
Commonwealth Games 2010 Delhi
&
President, Indian Olympic Association

: 2 :

3. I understand that Mr Sunil Dutt, Minister for Sports has raised certain issues relating to the Commonwealth Games 2010 during the meeting of the GoM held on January 14, 2005. Whereas the enclosed note gives our views, I would however like to emphasize the following: -

(a) The Indian Olympic Association is an autonomous body governed by the Olympic Charter and our autonomy is important for the Olympic movement and there can be no compromise on this.

(b) The games have been allotted to the Indian Olympic Association and the Organizing Committee formation rests with the Indian Olympic Association and not with the Ministry of Sports.

(c) I was unanimously elected as Chairman of the Organizing Committee and the Executive Board of the Commonwealth Games 2010 at the General Assembly Meeting of the Indian Olympic Association held on Nov. 1, 2004 and authorised to finalise the Organizing Committee, its Executive Board and other Committees in consultation with other Members of the Indian Olympic Association. I was further authorized to deal with the Government of India and the Government of NCT, Delhi regarding the Commonwealth Games (copy of the Resolution enclosed).

(d) In case of 1982 Asian Games, Mr Buta Singh was elected as the Chairman of the Organizing Committee in his capacity as President of the Amateur Athletic Federation of India, and not as a Minister, by the General Assembly of the Indian Olympic Association.

Gate No. 25, Jawaharlal Nehru Stadium, Lodhi Road, New Delhi-110003. India.
Tel.: +91-11-24366950, 51, 52. Fax : +91-11-24365395
e-mail : ioa@nde.vsnl.net.in website : www.cwgdelhi2010.com

2010 COMMONWEALTH GAMES DELHI

Organising Committee
Commonwealth Games 2010 Delhi

Suresh Kalmadi *M.P.*
Chairman, Organising Committee
Commonwealth Games 2010 Delhi
&
President, Indian Olympic Association

: 3 :

(e) Any contractual obligation derives only from the Host City contract, which has been duly signed by the then Secretary, Sports, the Lt. Governor of Delhi and the Indian Olympic Association. There has been no changes in this document, which clearly states that the games belong to the Indian Olympic Association.

(f) The Bid Document kept getting changed from time to time till the Commonwealth Games Federation was satisfied on all counts. The Initial bid documents, the bid updates 1 and 2, and the consolidated updated bid document were prepared and presented by the Indian Olympic Association to the Commonwealth Games Federation at various times. The bid documents were discussed and finalized between the Indian Olympic Association and Commonwealth Games Federation. The Ministry of Sports, Government of Delhi and DDA were consulted from time to time as per requirement and at no stage they have differed from the views of the Indian Olympic Association.

(g) The issue of the Chairmanship of the Organizing Committee in the Initial Bid Document came up during the visit of the Commonwealth Games Federation Evaluation Commission and suggestions of some of the friendly Member countries who were Voters at Montego Bay General Assembly to drop the "Government Nominee" suffix as it would enhance our bid prospects and would be in keeping with the principles of autonomy was accepted. This change was part of the final presentation at Montego Bay General Assembly held on 13th November 2003 by me as Chairman, Bid Committee was duly acknowledge and is now part of the final Bid Document. The then Secretary

Gate No. 25, Jawaharlal Nehru Stadium, Lodhi Road, New Delhi-110003. India.
Tel.: +91-11-24366950, 51, 52. Fax : +91-11-24365395
e-mail : ioa@nde.vsnl.net.in website : www.cwgdelhi2010.com

Organising Committee
Commonwealth Games 2010 Delhi

Suresh Kalmadi *M.P.*
Chairman, Organising Committee
Commonwealth Games 2010 Delhi
&
President, Indian Olympic Association

: 4 :

(Sports), Mr Rajiv Srivastava who is a signatory to the Host City contract and who represented the Sports Ministry in all discussions, is aware of this position. The Sports Ministry Officials were also present at the Commonwealth Games General Assembly Meeting at Athens on 17th August 2004 where the final Bid Document was presented and accepted by the House. At no stage the Government objected, we are surprised that this matter has been brought up now at this stage at the GoM. Mr Mike Fennell, President, Commonwealth Games Federation has already sent congratulatory messages to me for being elected Chairman of the Organising Committee.

I seek your intervention in the matter so that the Commonwealth Games are not jeopardized and Prime Minister's order is implemented.

for your kind intervention otherwise the Commonwealth Games would be shifted to Canada

Regard

Yours sincerely,

(SURESH KALMADI), M.P.
Chairman, Organizing Committee,
Commonwealth Games 2010
President, Indian Olympic Association.

Shri Pulok Chatterjee
Joint Secretary
Prime Minister's Office,
South Block,
New Delhi.

Gate No. 25, Jawaharlal Nehru Stadium, Lodhi Road, New Delhi-110003. India.
Tel.: +91-11-24366950, 51, 52. Fax : +91-11-24365395
e-mail : ioa@nde.vsnl.net.in website : www.cwgdelhi2010.com

2010 COMMONWEALTH GAMES DELHI

Organising Committee
Commonwealth Games 2010 Delhi

Suresh Kalmadi *M.P.*
Chairman, Organising Committee
Commonwealth Games 2010 Delhi
&
President, Indian Olympic Association

August 8, 2006

Dr. Manmohan Singh Ji,
Hon'ble Prime Minister of India
South Block
New Delhi- 110011

Dear Dr Manmohan Singh ji

I hope this letter finds you in the best of health.

I thank you once again for your initiative to call a review meeting of the Commonwealth Games.

We are committed internationally to give the best Commonwealth Games ever, but the experience over the last one year has seen multiplicity of agencies resulting in slow pace on the infrastructure front.

There is a need to allocate specific responsibilities to the concerned agencies. In this connection, I would like to suggest the following:

1. The Group of Ministers for the Commonwealth Games be empowered with the powers of the Cabinet and a separate secretariat attached to it. The Committee of Secretaries to implement the decisions of the Group of Ministers.
2. Restore and Implement the Institutional arrangements suggested by the

PMO in December 2004 after taking into account the views expressed by the Group of Ministers, Minister for YA & Sports and Indian Olympic Association (copy of note of Dec 6, 2004 enclosed). Under these suggestions which are clear, precise and workable, the work relating to the construction of the stadias and any other infrastructure facilities required for the games was allotted to the Minister of YA & Sports and the Organising of the Games to the Chairman of the Organising Committee. Somehow this direction was modified by the Group of Minister which led to the multiplicity of the agencies (GoM Minutes of January 29, 2005 enclosed)

Organising Committee
Commonwealth Games 2010 Delhi

Suresh Kalmadi *M.P.*
Chairman, Organising Committee
Commonwealth Games 2010 Delhi
&
President, Indian Olympic Association

: 2 :

3. Recently Union Cabinet has cleared Sports Ministry's proposal for creation of a International division headed by a Joint Secretary with staff strength of 13 members. The Minister for Sports now feels that since the work load of Secretary Sports has increased, a separate department headed by a Secretary Govt. of India may be created for the Commonwealth Games. Instead of over loading the present Sports Ministry, we would suggest that a separate Ministry for the Commonwealth Games be created as was the case with the Commonwealth Games 2006 at Melbourne. Creation of a Ministry for the Commonwealth Games will also send a message across the World of Sports that India is taking Sports seriously and means business. This would also enhance our chances to host 2014 Asian Games and 2016 Olympics. Creation of such a Ministry would in no way effect the role of the Ministry of YA & Sports as they would continue to handle Youth Services, Nehru Yuva Kendra Sangathana, Sports Authority of India, National Anti Doping Agency, Sports Science Centres, Panchayati Raj Khel Khud Abhiyan and assist in training of athletes. coaching facilities etc.

These measures which are workable, will give specific responsibility to all concerned.

For your kind and early consideration.

Regards

Yours sincerely,

Suresh Kalmadi

(SURESH KALMADI), M.P.
Chairman, Organising Committee,
Commonwealth Games 2010 Delhi

2010 COMMONWEALTH GAMES DELHI

Organising Committee
Commonwealth Games Delhi 2010

Suresh Kalmadi M.P.
Chairman, Organising Committee
Commonwealth Games Delhi 2010
&
President, Indian Olympic Association

December 7, 2006

Shri T.K.A. Nair
Principal Secretary to
the Prime Minister of India
South Block
New Delhi

Sub: **Commonwealth Games 2010 Delhi**
Hotels in Luytyen's Building Zone

Dear Mr TKA Nair,

As you are aware Commonwealth Games are scheduled to be held in 2010 in New Delhi. This is an event of national importance and prestige. Successful hosting of these games may lead to a successful bid for India to host the Asian Games 2014 and World Olympics 2016.

India's growing stature in the international sporting arena will be greatly enhanced if we win in our attempt to hold the games in India. As you know China has already been selected for World Olympics 2008.

The pride of Delhi is the Lutyen's Building Zone in which there are a few hotels which are in need of modernization and enhancement of room capacity. During the Asian Games in 1982 many relaxations were given to enable the existing hotels like Hotel Taj Mahal and Hotel Le-Meridien to add to their room capacity. It is therefore requested that existing hotels in LBZ like Hotel Imperial and Hotel Janpath may be granted a relaxation in their FAR to international level i.e. 4 times the plot area.

Contd...P/2

Organising Committee
Commonwealth Games 2010 Delhi

:P/2:

Needless to add that the Government can ensure that the new hotels coming into this zone will adhere to the Lutyen's architectural theme and space planning so as to enhance the character of the LBZ and create outstanding properties for our important visitors to go back with happy and memorable experience after visiting New Delhi the capital city of India.

We hope this decision can be taken urgently since time at our disposal is very limited if the deadline for 2010 is to be met.

Regards

Yours sincerely,

(SURESH KALMADI), M.P.
Chairman, Organising Committee
Commonwealth Games 2010 Delhi

भारतीय ओलम्पिक संघ
Indian Olympic Association

Suresh Kalmadi,
Member Of Parliament
President

May 6, 2010

Dear Dr Manmohan Singhji

I am happy to inform you that the Coordination Commission (CoCOM) of the Commonwealth Games Federation (CGF) was here in Delhi for five days and at the end of their visit, they have given us a thumping report. Based on our presentations and meetings, the CoCOM have publically announced that they are satisfied with the performance of the Organising Committee for the successful conduct of the Games and they will not be visiting Delhi anymore, prior to the Games.

This has reference to our meeting on 5th of May 2010. I reiterate that all efforts are being made to make the Commonwealth Games 2010 Delhi a roaring success. We have the highest commitment to our nation's prestige and to your goodself and, on behalf of all National Sports Federations(NSFs) and the Organising Committee, I assure you that Delhi will stage the best ever Commonwealth Games.

Sir, you were kind enough yesterday to give us a hearing when I and a few senior representatives of national Sports Federations brought to your notice the avoidable tension created by the unwarranted and untimely guidelines issued by the Ministry of Sports. These guidelines even violate the statutes of International Federations which govern the working of our National Sports Federations and any violation can lead to losing recognition from international bodies under IOC Charter.

Sir, let me bring to your notice that all National Sports Federation have voluntarily accepted the RTI Act and have been having their accounts audited by the CAG. Selection of all national teams is done by ex-international sports persons and audited by the Govt observer.

The Sports Ministry has announced that they are sending officials to the International Olympic Committee to ascertain if the issuance of these guidelines is legitimate. Under the circumstances, we request you to advise the Sports Ministry that

(i) They file the affidavit which will reflect the decisions of the Government after they ascertain the position from International Olympic Committee, and

(ii) Defer the effective date of these guidelines until the Commonwealth Games, by which time the consultations with the IOC, the International Federations and national Sports Federations can be held for creating a harmonious environment.

Olympic Bhavan , B-29, Qutub Institutional Area, New Delhi 110 016 (INDIA)
Tel : (91 11) 2685 2480-84 Fax : (91 11) 2685 2386
E-mail : ioa@nde.vsnl.net.in Website : www.olympic.ind.in

भारतीय ओलम्पिक संघ
Indian Olympic Association

Suresh Kalmadi,
Member Of Parliament
President

Sir, there is no doubt that utmost transparency and efficiency has to be maintained by all stake-holders and that sports can flourish in India only when there is positive and healthy communication, a conducive administrative environment and respect for statutes of national and international bodies.

India, with the issuance of these guidelines, is seriously threatened of sanctions and ban on participation of its sportspersons/teams given the statutes of International Olympic Committee and that of by most International Federations.

We earnestly request you to advice the Sports Ministry on the above lines.

With respects

Suresh Kalmadi
SURESH KALMADI, M.P.

Dr.Manmohan Singh
Hon'ble Prime Minister of India
New Delhi

'Olympic Bhavan', B-29, Qutub Institutional Area, New Delhi 110 016 (INDIA)
Tel : (91 11) 2685 2480-84 Fax : (91 11) 2685 2386
E-mail : ioa@nde.vsnl.net.in Website : www.olympic.ind.in

भारतीय ओलम्पिक संघ
Indian Olympic Association

Suresh Kalmadi,
Member Of Parliament
President

22nd May 2010

Dear Mr Nair,

I am enclosing herewith a copy of the latest reply received from International Olympic Committee, with regard to the letter sent by the Ministry of Sports to the "International Olympic Committee" regarding autonomy. The matter is being taken up in the 'International Olympic Committee Executive Board Meeting' in June 2010.

I am extremely worried about the situation and this needs to be defused immediately, otherwise it will have the direct impact on the successful delivery of the "Commonwealth Games Delhi 2010".

I request this may be intervened at the highest level.

Regards

Suresh Kalmadi, M.P.

Shri T. K. A. Nair
Principal Secretary, to Prime Minister
South Block.
New Delhi

'Olympic Bhavan', B-29, Qutub Institutional Area, New Delhi 110 016 (INDIA)
Tel : (91 11) 2685 2480-84 Fax : (91 11) 2685 2386
E-mail : ioa@nde.vsnl.net.in Website : www.olympic.ind.in

INTERNATIONAL
OLYMPIC
COMMITTEE

Dr Manohar Singh Gill
Minister of Youth Affairs & Sports
Government of India

Mr Suresh Kalmadi, MP
President
Indian Olympic Association

NOC Relations Department
Ref. No. 2010/PMS/jpy

Lausanne, 21 May 2010

Dear Sirs,

This is in reference to the letter dated 12 May which we received from Mr Injeti Srinivas, Joint Secretary of the Ministry of Youth Affairs & Sports in India.

As you are well aware, the IOC / OCA joint position in this matter has been already clearly expressed in previous letters (attached hereto for reference purposes). This stance is based on the Olympic Charter which all national sports organisations which choose and decide freely to belong to the Olympic Movement must respect, and be in a position to respect.

In addition, we have taken note of the unanimous position taken recently by the Indian Olympic Association and the National Sports Federations in India against the directives issued by the Ministry of Youth Affairs and Sports on 1st may 2010.

In view of this, we would like to remind you, once more, that in the event where the directives issued by the Ministry of Youth Affairs and Sports would be imposed on the Olympic Movement in India (even for future elections), we would be forced to report this case to the next IOC Executive Board meeting (in June) according to the rules of the Olympic Charter, in particular Rule 28.9 which states:
"Apart from the measures and sanctions provided in the case of infringement of the Olympic Charter, the IOC Executive Board may take any appropriate decisions for the protection of the Olympic Movement in the country of an NOC, including suspension of or withdrawal of recognition from such NOC if the constitution, law or other regulations in force in the country concerned, or any act by any governmental or other body causes the activity of the NOC or the making or expression of its will to be hampered. [...]".

We count on your understanding and cooperation in order to resolve this issue amicably and to ensure that the autonomy of the Olympic Movement in India is fully respected in accordance with the Olympic Charter.
We thank you for your kind attention to this matter and for taking all appropriate steps.

Yours sincerely,

Pere MIRÓ
NOC Relations Director
International Olympic Committee (IOC)

Husain Al-MUSALLAM
Director General & Technical Director
Olympic Council of Asia (OCA)

Cc:
- Jacques ROGGE, IOC President
- Sheikh Ahmad Al-Fahad AL-SABAH, OCA President
- Raja Randhir SINGH, IOC Member
- Association of Summer Olympic International Federations (ASOIF)
- Commonwealth Games Federation

DELHI 2010

Organising Committee
Commonwealth Games Delhi 2010

Suresh Kalmadi M.P.
Chairman, Organising Committee
President, Indian Olympic Association

28th March 2008

Dear Dr Manmohan Singhji,

I wish to draw your attention to the issue related to coverage of Indian Olympic Association (IOA) under R.T.I. act 2005 wherein an impression has been created that we have initiated a legal battle with Government of India on this matter.

In this regard, I must clarify first that IOA/OC has no intention to get into any legal battle with Government of India. In fact, we are aware that on the basis of nature of relation with IOA, Ministry of Youth Affairs and Sports had opined that IOA did not fulfill the criterion of "Public Authority" as defined in R.T.I. Act 2005. However, Central Information Commission decided to treat us as "Public Authority". As you are also aware that financial support by Government of India to O.C. is not a grant but a Loan with interest and therefore, O.C. cannot be treated as "Public Authority" (Note enclosed). It was on this context that, we had to seek judicial interpretation on the matter.

In the light of above, I once again would like to clarify that it is never our intention to go to Court against Government of India. I hope this clarifies our position.

Regards

Suresh Kalmadi

SURESH KALMADI, M.P.

Dr. Manmohan Singh
Hon'ble Prime Minister of India
New Delhi

Gate No. 28A, Jawaharlal Nehru Stadium, Lodhi Road, New Delhi-110003, India.
Tel.: +91-11-24307000, 24367928 / 29/30, Fax: +91-11-24307040
e-mail: suresh.kalmadi@cwgdelhi2010.org

IOA, being an 'Apex Umbrella Body' does not receive any funds from the Government of India to conduct its own operations. Whatever funds are placed at its disposal are in the form of reimbursement of travel costs (directly paid to the designated travel agency by the Ministry), kits for the athletes and daily allowance to the athletes participating in international sporting events.

Since no running / operational cost of IOA is met by the Government, IOA cannot be termed as "PUBLIC AUTHORITY" under Section 2 (h) of RTI Act 2005. It is only on this basic premise that the Hon'ble High Court of Delhi has given stay to the erroneous decision of the Ministry in declaring IOA as a "PUBLIC AUTHORITY".

DECLARATION OF ORGANISING COMMITTEE COMMONWEALTH GAMES DELHI 2010 (OC CWG DELHI 2010) AS PUBLIC AUTHORITY UNDER RTI ACT 2005 BY MINISTRY OF YOUTH AFFAIRS AND SPORTS

BASIC FACTS

1. OC is a Society established by the Indian Olympic Association (IOA) in accordance with the Article 27 (C) of the Constitution of Commonwealth Games Federation (CGF) to conduct Commonwealth Games in Delhi.

2. CGF, IOA, OC, Government of India and Government of National Capital Territory of Delhi are five independent legal entities who have bound themselves in a contractual agreement through Host City Contract with respect to discharge of their roles and responsibilities related to the organization of the Commonwealth Games.

3. The decisions pertaining to appointment of Chairman / composition of OC emanates from Memorandum of Association and Rules & Regulations of the OC, registered as Society under the Societies Registration Act 1860.

4. The funding of GOI is not by way of a grant to the OC, but a loan to be repaid with interest.

DECISION OF MINISTRY OF YOUTH AFFAIRS & SPORTS

The suo moto decision taken by the Ministry of Youth Affairs & Sports, without being even considerate enough to hear OC's view point on the matter, in declaring the OC as "PUBLIC AUTHORITY" under section 2(h) of the RTI Act 2005 is based on completely misplaced reasons both on the issue of law as well as issue of facts. A cursory perusal of OC's letter dated 20th June, 2007 (Annex-I) in response to Ministry's letter dated 29th May, 2007 (Annex-II) establishes the above contention. Rather than examining the contention of OC rationally Ministry not only decided to approach Ministry of Law and Justice for confirming its decision, but refused to entertain the request of the OC to share the documents related to its brief before the Ministry of Law & Justice, and the consequent advice received by it.

ACTION TAKEN BY OC

Frustrated with the obstinate stand taken by the Ministry, OC was constrained to seek judicial remedy on the matter.

The Executive Board of the OC is represented by the representatives of CGF and also people of eminence like Prof. V.K. Malhotra MP and Mr. Digvijay Singh MP, and its decisions are guided by collective views of these dignitaries.

REMARKS

While the OC is committed to maintain its credibility through adoption of good governance ethics and practices and dissemination of maximum possible information to generate interest in the Games world wide as well as amongst potential sponsors, it cannot afford to accept such erroneous and misplaced decisions. It also needs to be borne in mind that OC is a short lived, event specific organization and many of its decisions, specially, the revenue generating agreement with competing sponsors, are and will be guided by Non-Disclosure Agreements.

SURESH KALMADI
Member of Parliament, India
Chairman, Organising Committee
Commonwealth Games 2010 Delhi

DELHI 2010
XIX COMMONWEALTH GAMES

August 8, 2010

Dear Dr Manmohan Singhji

There are 39 days left for the Games Village to be opened on September 16, 2010 when 8000 athletes and officials from 71 Commonwealth nations and territories start arriving to participate in the XIX Commonwealth Games 2010 Delhi.

The Organising Committee Commonwealth Games 2010 Delhi with a workforce of more than 2000 is working day and night to ensure the successful delivery of the Games. We are focussed on the task of conducting the Games well and making India proud.

Suddenly, last week, attempts were made to defame the Commonwealth Games 2010 Delhi and the Chairman of the Organising Committee Commonwealth Games 2010 Delhi.

We shall place some important facts for your perusal before we address the attempt to defame.

GAMES STRUCTURE

The original signatories to the Host City Contract were Government of India, Government of NCT of Delhi, Commonwealth Games Federation and Indian Olympic Association. The contract was signed in November 2003.

Organising Committee Commonwealth Games 2010 Delhi was registered as a society on February 10, 2005 and thereafter became a signatory to the Host City Contract.

In the overall scheme of preparation for the Commonwealth Games 2010 Delhi, the Government laid down the following institutional arrangement:

- Sports Infrastructure is to be developed by Government agencies and funded directly by Government.
- The responsibility for the Conduct and delivery of the Games is of the Organising Committee Commonwealth Games 2010 Delhi. The Organising Committee is funded upfront by the Government as a loan to be recouped on the basis of revenue neutrality.
- The development, upgradation and improvement of the city infrastructure are to be done by the Government of Delhi with the support of the Government of India.

City Centre-II, (NDCC Towers), Opp. Jantar Mantar, Jai Singh Road, New Delhi - 110001, India
Tel.: +91 11 23438000 Fax : +91 11 23438004 Email: secy.chairman@cwgdelhi2010.org Website : www.cwgdelhi2010.org

DELEGATION OF FINANCIAL POWERS

The Organising Committee Commonwealth Games 2010 Delhi has checks and balances built into the accounting processes.

- In keeping with the Government of India's direction in letters dated July 18, 2005 and February 7, 2006, the Financial and Administrative Guidelines are a practical and prudent mix of Government's financial rules and the rules of the Commonwealth Games Federation, within the overall parameters of generally accepted accounting and auditing standards.

- **The Chairman of the Organising Committee Commonwealth Games 2010 Delhi has no financial powers**

- The following table shows the Competent Financial Authority

No.	Approving Authority	Monetary Limit Upto 31 March 2010	Monetary Limit From 1 April 2010
1.	Chief Executive Officer		Upto 25 lakh
2.	Expenditure Approval Committee comprising of Secretary-General, Treasurer, CEO and Director General	Up to to Rs 50 lakh	Upto Rs 50 lakh
3.	Executive Management Committee comprising of Chairman, Vice-Chairman, Secretary General and Treasurer, CEO and Special Director General (Finance & Accounts)	Upto Rs 3 crore	Upto Rs. 6 crore
4.	Executive Board of 15 members (including representatives of the Commonwealth Games Federation, office-bearers of the Organising Committee, two representatives of the Government of India, two representatives of the Government of NCT of Delhi and representatives of the National Sports Federations and CEO.	Above Rs 3 crore	Above Rs 6 crore

GAMES BUDGET

The budget provided for by Government of India for the Commonwealth Games 2010 is Rs 11,494 crore. This includes the budget of a number of Ministries, departments and institutions. **Of this, the budget of the Organising Committee Commonwealth Games 2010 Delhi is Rs 1620 crore. This has been given as a loan to the Organising Committee Commonwealth Games 2010 Delhi.** In addition, Overlays has been sanctioned a budget of Rs 687 crore. **Usually, Overlays are provided by venue owners.**

Of the Rs 1620 crore, Organising Committee Commonwealth Games 2010 Delhi has received Rs 900 crore from the Government of India so far. It has also raised the following revenues of Rs 700 crore as follows:

- **Sponsorship commitments** — **Rs 450 crore**
- **Sale of Broadcasting rights** — **Rs 250 crore**

As of now, we are also expecting the following additional revenues from:

- **Ticketing** — **Rs 100 crore**
- **Merchandise** — **Rs 50 crore**

The Comptroller and Auditor General of India (CAG) has conducted three audits of the Organising Committee Commonwealth Games 2010 Delhi and has not come out with any major objection on its functioning.

There have been some media reports alleging irregularities on three major issues:

1. Launch of Queen's Baton Relay 2010 Delhi in London in October 29, 2010.
2. Overlays contracts
3. M/s Sports Marketing and Management (SMAM) being paid commission for securing sponsorship from Public Sector Undertakings.

1. OVERLAYS:

The media has also highlighted that the Overlays contracts have been highly inflated and have quoted some items with their prices. **The fact is the media has been quoting figures from an offer document rather than the actual contract.**

Overlays means whatever is not permanently provided in the Stadia and secured on rent by the Organising Committee Commonwealth Games 2010 Delhi for the successful delivery of the Games. It consists of around 1000 different items to be placed over 60 venues, 4000 rooms and in external places to be used by security personnel, athletes, volunteers, Games Family, VIPs, workforce etc

The process for hiring of Overlays started in 2009 when an Express of Interest was issued. DMRC (Delhi Metro Rail Corporation) was consulted during the formulation of RFP. **The bids were invited cluster wise (each cluster consists of a few venues).** It is on turnkey basis for all items in a cluster.

3

Accordingly, rounds of negotiations were held with the lowest bidder for each cluster and the proposals were considered and approved by

i. OC Finance Committee with two representatives of Government.
ii. Finance Sub-Committee formed by the Cabinet. It includes three Government of India Secretary level officers and the CEO of the Organising Committee.
iii. Executive Board of OC CWG 2010 Delhi.

The contracts were allotted on the competitive bidding basis. The lowest bidder for each cluster on the basis of all items was further negotiated. The location and site conditions and quantity patterns at different venues are also factors responsible for different prices for different clusters.

The following is what the media has said about some of the items:

No.	Allegation	Fact
1.	Toilet Rolls being got for Rs 3751 each!	The Rs 3751 is for cartons of 100 rolls each. The price works out to Rs 37.51 per roll.
2.	Umbrellas	The patio umbrellas are required to provide shades in open areas. They are large in size (2.4m diameter), 100 per cent water-proof, fire-retardant and come with counter weight to withstand high wind velocity.
3.	Treadmills costing Rs 1 lakh in the market being rented for Rs 9 lakh	The treadmill spoken of is a high-end anti-gravity treadmill and was used in Beijing Athletic. The purchase price is Rs 29 lakh (approx). The rental was to be Rs 9 lakh. **In the final Bill of Quantity sent to the vendors, we have not ordered this treadmill at all.**
4.	Air-Conditioners costing Rs. 50,000 in the market being taken on rent for exorbitant amounts	The orders were for 11-ton air-conditioners to be put in large tents. The rentals include cost of mounting arrangement in tents, air ducts, cabling and captive power supply with Generator back-up, operation and maintenance on turnkey basis.

To augment world class stadia and to deliver a world class games, we needed to contract vendors who have provided such Overlay services at the Commonwealth, Asian or Olympic Games. We **want to ensure that the effort gone into building world class stadia is not compromised with inferior Overlay work that does not meet international standards.**

The overall cost of overlays includes transportation from the city of origin to Delhi and back, the cost of technical personnel for installation, maintenance, dismantling etc.

2. Queen's Baton Relay launch in London:

The launch was held successfully at the Buckingham Palace in London on October 29, 2009, with Queen Elizabeth II handing over the baton to Hon'ble President Smt. Pratibha Devisingh Patil. The event was attended by a number of dignitaries from India, Britain and the Commonwealth Games Federation.

Last week, some media reports alleged about Money Trails from the Organising Committee Commonwealth Games 2010 Delhi to M/s. AM Cars and Vans Hire Ltd as well as AM Films UK Ltd. Two concerned officers of the Organising Committee Commonwealth Games 2010 Delhi produced copies of e-mails that were purportedly written by a staffer of the High Commission of India in London recommending AM Cars and Vans as an approved supplier.

In order to find out the truth, the Organising Committee Commonwealth Games 2010 Delhi instituted an inquiry. CEO Mr. Jarnail Singh, IAS (retd) headed the panel that included Special Director General (Finance and Accounts), Mr. GC Chaturvedi, IAS, and Chief Vigilance Officer Ms, Gurjyot Kaur, IDAS. **Based on the interim report, the Executive Board of the Organising Committee Commonwealth Games 2010 Delhi decided to suspend two officers (a third officer had resigned from his position three months ago).** The guilty will not be spared.

3. SMAM Contract

At the outset, we would like to clarify that Organising Committee Commonwealth Games 2010 Delhi has not paid any commission to SMAM for Delhi 2010.

Sports Marketing and Management (SMAM), a reputed company, was engaged by the Organising Committee as consultants to help secure sponsorships. The company's track record in Commonwealth Games at Manchester and Melbourne was impressive.

The Contract with SMAM had been entered into after a global tender. The offers were evaluated by duly-nominated committees and the Executive Board of the Organising Committee, in which there are five Government officers as members, has been apprised of at every stage of the process.

The allegation is that SMAM was being paid commission up to 23 per cent even on the sponsorships obtained from the PSUs and Railways. **We would like to clarify that as per the contract with SMAM, there was no commission payable on the following:**

5

"Grant, funding, donation or contribution received by the Organising committee by the federal or the State Government or their respective department or local statutory bodies being of a non commercial nature".

There was no commission payable for sponsorship by Railways.

The management fee covered strategic planning, inter-departmental co-ordination, delivery of rights and benefits, sponsorship services, documentation and post-event reporting.
As per the revised contract, for all the sponsorship revenues and Value in Kind (VIK) generated from PSUs, SMAM was entitled to a management fee, which is 7.5% upto $ 50 million sponsorship value, 10% for amounts between $ 50 and 100 million sponsorship value and 11.25% for amounts more than $ 100 million sponsorship value.

Organising Committee Commonwealth Games 2010 Delhi contemplated terminating the agreement even earlier. But if such termination had been done before August 1, 2010, it would have involved long notice to be given to SMAM and referral to Commonwealth Games Federation President and even Arbitration.

Organising Committee Commonwealth Games 21010 Delhi obtained legal advice on how to terminate the contract because of non-performance. We were advised that the period of rectification needed to be given was only three days if the contract was terminated after August 1, 2010 **Accordingly, the Executive Board of the Organising Committee Commonwealth Games 2010 Delhi decided on August 5, 2010 to terminate the contract with SMAM on account of non-performance.**

SMAM was served a termination notice on August 6, 2010.

Even in the latest CVC report, the Organising Committee Commonwealth Games 2010 Delhi has not been mentioned.

We hope that the above facts clarify the misgivings raised in the media and elsewhere. These are totally baseless and unfounded.

Organising Committee Commonwealth Games 2010 Delhi has already stated that we are ready for any enquiry – CAG or Judicial.

I seek your co-operation and best wishes in making the Games a success.

Regards

SURESH KALMADI, MP

Dr. Manmohan Singh
Hon'ble Prime Minister of India
7, Race course Road,
New Delhi

SURESH KALMADI
Member of Parliament, India
Chairman, Organising Committee
Commonwealth Games 2010 Delhi

DELHI 2010

Personal & Confidential

October 17, 2010

Dear Dr Manmohan Singhji

The Commonwealth Games have been successfully conducted dispite all the challenges, delays, aspersions and a campaign of vilification, serious doubts were created whether India had the ability to host the games and ensure safety of the participants. The people of India the sports persons workforce of the OC and thousands of volunteers have done us proud. The credit belongs to the country. I have been deeply anguished for months by wild allegations and judgmental observations as I was challenged in my capacity as Chairman, Organising Committee that the games are held successfully, my priority was to ensure the same, I kept quiet not giving any controversies to snowball. It is sad that it was mistaken as an admission of any wrong doing on my part, irrespective of the fact that I was President of the Indian Olympic Association who successfully brought the Games to the country. I have been humiliated after the conclusion of the Games. The action of Dr. M.S. Gill in trying to bask in the glory and insult the Indian Olympic Association by not taking us with the athletes to the Hon'ble Prime Minister has appauled all the sports Association in the world. Such treatment has never been given to the Olympic Association in any country, which has hosted a multi sport games. The Prime Ministers enquiry is on and I welcome it and I insist that every aspect of the Games should be looked into. The Organising Committee has the responsibility for the conduct of the Games which includes the Opening & Closing ceremony. These have been seen and applauded around the world. I am as proud an Indian as any other citizen. I must mention that for one who has seen action in two wars to defend the country in 1965, 1971 as a pilot in the Indian Air Force the honour of my country is supreme. The Chief Minister of Delhi by her statement seems to take the entire credit and then prejudicing the enquiry by making irresponsible observation has done a great damage to the country, Government Image and the image of my Congress Party. I was constrained to issue a statement which I enclose for your attention.

Regards and Best wishes

Kalmadi

(SURESH KALMADI), MP

Dr. Manmohan Singh
Hon'ble Prime Minister of India
7, Race course Road,
New Delhi

City Centre-II, (NDCC Towers), Opp. Jantar Mantar, Jai Singh Road, New Delhi - 110001, India
Tel.: +91 11 23438000 Fax: +91 11 23438004 Email: secy.chairman@cwgdelhi2010.org Website: www.cwgdelhi2010.org

Organsing Committee
Commonwealth Games 2010 Delhi

NDCC II, Jai Singh Road, New Delhi 110 001

MEDIA RELEASE

Delhi Chief Minister Mrs. Shiela Dikshit's aspersions on corruption in the Organising Committee Commonwealth Games 2010 Delhi are most disappointing and uncalled for. It is not right to deflect and point fingers at others when she must indulge in self-reflection on corruption in her own departments. She has said that the ways of the Organising Committee are mysterious whereas the Commonwealth Games chief Mr. Michael Fennell declared the conduct of the Games as exceptional and successful.

We have already welcomed the Prime Minister's decision to set up a probe panel and have said that we will support it. We are sure that the Terms of Reference of the Shunglu Committee will include not just the scope of work undertaken by the Organising Committee at a budget of Rs 1620 crore but also the Rs 16,000 crore spent by Delhi Government.

Despite a series of attacks in the run up to the Games, I was quiet as I wanted the Games to succeed. Keeping quiet should not be interpreted as a sign of weakness. Nor should patience be seen as a sign of guilt. It was more important to focus on the task of conducting the Games well.

National pride was at stake and I didn't want that to be affected. Our challenge was to keep the morale of our workforce of over 4000 high. We succeeded in doing that and ensuring the smooth delivery of the largest ever Commonwealth Games. But, on Dasara day, I owe to the Organising Committee that we speak out. We don't want to be the scapegoats anymore.

In 2005, in the overall scheme of preparation for the Games, Government laid down the following institutional arrangement:

- Sports Infrastructure is to be developed by Government agencies and funded directly by Government.
- The development, upgradation and improvement of the city infrastructure are to be done by the Government of Delhi with the support of the Government of India.
- The responsibility for the Conduct and delivery of the Games is of the Organising Committee Commonwealth Games 2010 Delhi.

I am proud that the world has declared that conduct of the Games was faultless, with all competitions being held as per schedule. A massive amount of work was done in planning and preparing for the Games by innumerable people under the guidance of the Indian Olympic Association and National Sports Federations. The execution of these plans was impeccable. It led Organising Committee to deliver spectacular Opening and Closing Ceremonies that were overseen by the Group of Ministers.

The Games have succeeded because of the efforts of Team India, including a large number of people and agencies and not any individual. Mrs. Dikshit's attempt to take credit for getting the Games Village ready in time does not fit with the team concept. The Lieutenant Governor of Delhi and the Organising Committee, who were preparing the Village for over two years, co-ordinated the work of a number of agencies to ensure that it was entirely ready to welcome the athletes.

The Organising Committee was constantly being criticised for delays and shoddy work when we were not at all involved in any construction activity. Unmindful, we kept defending the venues and infrastructure and reassured the Games Family that everything would be ready in time for the Games.

When the foot overbridge near the Jawaharlal Nehru Stadium collapsed, it led to doubts about the safety of the people. Reports of delays in getting the city ready also caused many teams to believe that Games could not be held. We had to do a lot of hand-holding and cajoling to ensure that the full complement of 71 nations and territories took part in the Games.

We would like to point out that all decisions in the Organising Committee are made by the Executive Board, which includes two representatives each of the Central and Delhi Governments. And the Prime Minister's Office deputed a number of Government officers, including the CEO Mr, Jarnail Singh, to work with the Organising Committee.

Transparency and accountability remain the watch words in the Organising Committee. We are confident that the guilty will not be spared irrespective of which agency they belong to.

Suresh Kalmadi, MP
Chairman
Organising Committee
Commonwealth Games 2010 Delhi

October 17, 2010
New Delhi

SURESH KALMADI
Member of Parliament, India
Chairman, Organising Committee
Commonwealth Games 2010 Delhi

DELHI 2010
XIX COMMONWEALTH GAMES

07 April 2010

Dear Mr. S M Krishna,

Sub: Prime Minister receiving the Queen's Baton at Wagah Border

As you are aware, Commonwealth Games Delhi 2010 is the most prestigious sporting event being held in the history of India, after the conduct of 1982 Asian Games.

The Queen's Baton Relay, an integral part of the Commonwealth Games, symbolizes the coming together of all the Commonwealth nations for a festival of sport, showcasing the rich diversity of the Commonwealth to the host nation and around the world.

The Baton Relay which was launched by Her Majesty, Queen of England and Hon'ble President of India from Buckingham Palace on 29th October 2009 with a message from Her Majesty, the Queen, after travelling a distance of 170000 kilometers across 70 countries over 240 days, would be arriving in India through Wagah Border on 25th June 2010. The historic occasion also coincides with "100 days to for the Games". This is an important milestone that calls for an appropriate celebration. It is proposed to receive the Baton at Wagah border ceremonially and organise a function from 0930 hrs to 1030 hrs on 25th June 2010.

Since the Commonwealth Games 2010 Delhi are also an occasion to promote friendship through sports, it is appropriate that the Hon'ble Prime Minister receives the baton from the Prime Minister of Pakistan. This will give a boost to the Queen's Baton Relay in building up the hype and tempo for the Games and also send a message to the whole world regarding India's intention of improving relations with its neighbors through sports and diplomacy.

In a meeting with Dr. Manmohan Singh, the Hon'ble Prime Minister on 2nd April 2010, I had broached the subject of receiving the baton by the Hon'ble Prime Minister of India from the Prime Minister of Pakistan at Wagah border, and, he has advised me to take the subject forward with the External Affairs Ministry.

I shall be grateful if you could kindly take the above proposal forward and indicate the date and time convenient to you to discuss the modalities.

Regards,

Suresh Kalmadi, MP

Shri S M Krishna
Hon'ble Minister for External Affairs
South Block, New Delhi

Copy to: Shri. TKA Nair, Principal Secretary to Prime Minister.

New Delhi City Centre - Tower II, Opposite Jantar Mantar, Jai Singh Road, New Delhi 110001, INDIA
91 11 23482000, 23482008 F: +91 11 23438004 E: secy.chairman@cwgdelhi2010.org W: www.cwgdelhi2010.org

Organising Committee Commonwealth Games 2010 Delhi

DELHI 2010

17 April 2010

Dear Smt Nirupama Raoji

I am writing this with reference to our discussions yesterday regarding invitation to Heads of States of select Commonwealth Nations for the Commonwealth Games 2010.

Enclosed herewith is a list of 25 Commonwealth countries whose Heads could be considered for the invitation. These are the countries wherefrom we are expecting participation on a big scale as well as the business delegations are also visiting during the Games time.

The Commonwealth Games Delhi 2010 is the most prestigious sporting event being held in the history of India. In addition to promoting sports and camaraderie amongst the Commonwealth countries, the Games also provide a great opportunity to showcase Indian heritage and culture. The Games will also be a platform to demonstrate India's progress as nation specially in the field of ICT based technologies.

The event, most importantly, also offers excellent opportunities for India to improve and deepen bilateral relations with a host of countries in the backdrop of this sporting and cultural extravaganza.

In addition, Brazil's Head of State should also be invited it being the host country for the 2016 Olympic Games. Also, Heads of States from the other BRIC countries, viz. Russia and China may also be invited. Besides, as reported in the Newspapers, the PM has said that the President of the United States may visit India during that time and he may also, therefore, be invited to attend the Opening Ceremony of the Games as a 'goodwill gesture'.

Regards

SURESH KALMADI, MP
CHAIRMAN

Smt. Nirupama Rao, IFS
Foreign Secretary,
Ministry of External Affairs,
South Block, New Delhi.

Copy to: Shri T.K.A. Nair, Principal Secretary to PM, Prime Minister's Office, South Block, New Delhi.

New Delhi City Centre - Tower II, Opposite Jantar Mantar, Jai Singh Road, New Delhi 110001, INDIA
T: +91 11 24500400 F: +91 11 24500451 E: info@cwgdelhi2010.org W: www.cwgdelhi2010.org

Most Immediate

PRIME MINISTER'S OFFICE

South Block
New Delhi - 110 101

Please find enclosed herewith a copy of the Record of Discussions of the meeting chaired by the Principal Secretary to PM on 16.10.2009 to discuss overseas promotional and publicity activities for the Commonwealth Games, 2010.

(Sanjay Mitra)
Joint Secretary
☎: 23018876

Shri Suresh Kalmadi, Chairman, Organising Committee, Commonwealth Games, 2010
Secretary, Department of Sports, New Delhi
Secretary, Ministry of Tourism
Shri B.N. Puri, Sr. Consultant, Planning Commission

PMO ID No.570/31/C/26/2009-ES.2 Dated: October 19, 2009

Encl: As above.

Record of Discussions of the meeting chaired by Principal Secretary to PM on 16.10.2009 at 11.30 am at PMO to discuss promotional and publicity activities for Commonwealth Games, 2010 in overseas markets.

A meeting to discuss promotional and publicity activities for Commonwealth Games, 2010 in overseas markets was convened under the chairmanship of Principal Secretary to PM on 16.10.2009 at 11.30 am at PMO. The list of participants is annexed.

2. After going through the letter addressed by the Minister of Tourism to the Prime Minister in this regard, it was noted that the Group of Ministers constituted for the Commonwealth Games, 2010 had decided that the Ministry of Tourism would be responsible for overseas publicity in coordination with Organising Committee (OC), and Planning Commission would allocate additional funds to the Ministry of Tourism for the purpose. However, as the Department of Expenditure was of the view that additional funds cannot be provided, Planning Commission indicated that promotional and publicity activities for the CWG, 2010 be undertaken by the OC from funds already provided to it.

3. Secretary, Ministry of Tourism submitted that the Ministry's budgetary allocation has remained unchanged as compared to last year and that it has sought of additional funds to the tune of Rs. 60 crores for the activities in connection with the Commonwealth Games. The Ministry was willing to undertake overseas promotional and publicity activities provided funds are made available either by the Planning Commission or the OC.

4. Secretary, D/o Sports submitted that the revised budget for the OC to the tune of Rs. 1620 crores has been cleared by the EFC and would be coming up for Cabinet's consideration during the next week. However, the revised budget does not have a provision for the purpose under discussion. She also stated that funds being provided to the OC were in the nature of a loan and it would be difficult for the OC to accommodate the additional cost.

5. Keeping in view the paucity of time and urgency of the matter and after speaking to the Secretary, Finance, it was decided that the Ministry of Tourism will undertake overseas promotional and publicity activities for CWG, 2010 to the tune of Rs. 50 crores, from its existing outlay which would be adjusted subsequently at the R.E stage. Modalities and details will be settled between the Department of Sports and the Ministry of Tourism

(Action: Ministry of Tourism, Department of Expenditure, Department of Sports)

DELHI 2010

COME OUT AND PLAY

Organising Committee
Commonwealth Games Delhi 2010

Suresh Kalmadi, M.P.
Chairman, Organising Committee
President, Indian Olympic Association

URGENT
for Cabinet Tomorrow

April 2, 2008

Dear Shri B.V.R. Subrahmanyam ji

I take this opportunity to draw your kind attention on the Cabinet note proposed by Ministry of Youth Affairs and Sports with regard to a "Draft Comprehensive National Sports Policy 2008".

At the outset, the IOA and all NSFs reiterate their considered view that with just 200 days to go for Commonwealth Youth Games 2008 and 900 odd days to go for Commonwealth Games 2010, it is more critical to put in place a comprehensive, integrated action plan focused on enhancing India's Medal tally rather than diverting the attention and resources in proposing a new National Sports Policy. I would like to highlight here that despite the decision in the Committee of Secretaries meeting to seek the Cabinet approval, by 1st week of March 2008, for the proposed special scheme of preparation of Indian Teams for 2010, the scheme is yet to see the light of the day. Further, with just four months left for Beijing Olympics 2008 there is gross uncertainty regarding the provision of equipment / ammunition support to our shooting team which is India's best bet for Medals in the coming Olympics. As a result, the National Federation has announced to withdraw the Shooting Team from coming Olympics. It is needless to emphasis that the Ministry of Youth Affairs and Sports needs to priorities its obligations.

In order to deliberate and suggest the draft Sports Policy a joint working group comprising the representatives of various stakeholders including IOA and NSFs was constituted. Incidentally, the first meeting of joint working group was scheduled to be held on 29th February 2008 which happen to the Budget Presentation Day. As a result, neither me nor Shri Vijay Kumar Malhotra M.P., Mr. Digvijay Singh M.P. could attend the meeting. In addition, the Ministry could not circulate any discussion paper for the meeting therefore, the first meeting could not take place. No communication has been received from the Ministry for the next meeting. However, we understand that Ministry is contemplating to do away with the joint working group and proceed further without completing the consultation process. In this regard, I would also like to bring to your kind notice that the International Sports bodies have serious apprehension about the autonomy of the National Olympic Committees. The letters received from International Sports Bodies are enclosed for your kind perusal.

1052622 ES2/VIP/3945/08

DELHI 2010

Organising Committee Commonwealth Games Delhi 2010

Suresh Kalmadi M.P.
Chairman, Organising Committee
President, Indian Olympic Association

In the light of our serious concern, at this juncture, about the performance of India in the coming Olympics in August 2008, Commonwealth Youth Games 2008 and Commonwealth Games 2010 and the fact that the consultation process through joint working group has not taken place at all, I request you to direct the Ministry to first finalise and launch the proposed scheme of preparation of Indian Teams without loosing any more time; to address the issues related to supply of necessary items including ammunition to the Indian Team for Olympics; and, thereafter, complete the consultative process through the joint working group constituted for finalisation of proposed Sports Policy, before cabinet takes up the matter. The previous Sports Policy of 2001 is good that should be reviewed. A new Sports Policy is not required.

Regard

SURESH KALMADI, M.P.

Shri B.V.R. Subrahmanyam
Private Secretary to PM
7, Race Course Road,
New Delhi.

Gate No. 28A, Jawaharlal Nehru Stadium, Lodhi Road, New Delhi-110003, India.
Tel.: +91-11-24307000, 24367928 / 29/30, Fax: +91-11-24307040
e-mail: suresh.kalmadi@cwgdelhi2010.org

DELHI 2010

Organising Committee
Commonwealth Games Delhi 2010

Suresh Kalmadi M.P.
Chairman, Organising Committee
President, Indian Olympic Association

28th March 2008

Dear Mr T K A Nair ji

I take this opportunity to draw your kind attention to the exercise being undertaken by Ministry of Youth Affairs and Sports with regard to proposing a new Sports Policy.

At the outset, the IOA and all NSFs reiterate their considered view that with just 200 days to go for Commonwealth Youth Games 2008 and 900 odd days to go for Commonwealth Games 2010, it is more critical to put in place a comprehensive, integrated action plan focused on enhancing India's Medal tally rather than diverting the attention and resources in proposing a new National Sports Policy. I would like to highlight here that despite the decision in the Committee of Secretaries meeting to seek the Cabinet approval, by 1st week of March 2008, for the proposed special scheme of preparation of Indian Teams for 2010, the scheme is yet to see the light of the day. Further, with just four months left for Beijing Olympics 2008 there is gross uncertainty regarding the provision of equipment / ammunition support to our shooting team which is India's best bet for Medals in the coming Olympics. As a result, the National Federation has announced to withdraw the Shooting Team from coming Olympics. It is needless to emphasis that the Ministry of Youth Affairs and Sports needs to priorities its obligations.

In order to deliberate and suggest the draft Sports Policy a joint working group comprising the representatives of various stakeholders including IOA and NSFs was constituted. Incidentally, the first meeting of joint working group was scheduled to be held on 29th February 2008 which happen to the Budget Presentation Day. As a result, neither me nor Shri Vijay Kumar Malhotra M.P., Mr. Digvijay Singh M.P. could attend the meeting. In addition, the Ministry could not circulate any discussion paper for the meeting therefore, the first meeting could not take place. No communication has been received from the Ministry for the next meeting. However, we understand that Ministry is contemplating to do away with the joint working group and proceed further without completing the consultation process. In this regard, I would also like to bring to your kind notice that the International Sports bodies have serious apprehension about the autonomy of the National Olympic Committees. The letters received from International Sports Bodies are enclosed for your kind perusal.

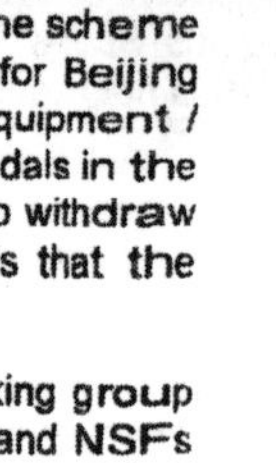

Gate No. 28A, Jawaharlal Nehru Stadium, Lodhi Road, New Delhi-110003, India.
Tel.: +91-11-24307000, 24367928 / 29/30, Fax : +91-11-24307040
e-mail: suresh.kalmadi@cwgdelhi2010.org

Organising Committee
Commonwealth Games Delhi 2010

Suresh Kalmadi M.P.
Chairman, Organising Committee
President, Indian Olympic Association

In the light of our serious concern, at this juncture, about the performance of India in the coming Olympics in August 2008, Commonwealth Youth Games 2008 and Commonwealth Games 2010 and the fact that the consultation process through joint working group has not taken place at all, I request you to direct the Ministry to first finalise and launch the proposed scheme of preparation of Indian Teams without loosing any more time; to address the issues related to supply of necessary items including ammunition to the Indian Team for Olympics; and, thereafter, complete the consultative process through the joint working group constituted for finalisation of proposed Sports Policy.

Regards

SURESH KALMADI, M.P.

Shri T. K. A. NAIR
Principal Secretary to the Prime Minister of India
New Delhi

Gate No. 28A, Jawaharlal Nehru Stadium, Lodhi Road, New Delhi-110003, India.
Tel.: +91-11-24307000, 24367928 / 29/30, Fax : +91-11-24307040
e-mail: sureshkalmadi@cwgdelhi2010.org

The Olympic Council of Asia

Founded 1982

Aomori Resolution
20th OCA General Assembly
16th May, 2002, Aomori.

It has come to the notice of the Olympic Council of Asia (OCA) that of late aggressive interference is being made in the autonomy of many Member NOCs by the Governmental bodies of their countries.

The General Assembly of OCA therefore, reaffirms that in keeping with the spirit of the Olympic Charter all the NOCs must preserve their autonomy as envisaged in Rules 31.5 of the said Charter. Any violation of the rules of the Olympic Charter shall result in withdrawal of recognition by OCA.

It is therefore resolved that this decision of the General Assembly be brought to the notice of all the Member NOCs of OCA.

Sheikh Ahmad Al-Fahad Al-Sabah
President. OCA.

16th May 2002.

P.O. Box: 6706 Hawalli – 32042, Kuwait
Telex: 30401 OCA KT.

Tel.: (965) 5717196 – 5726600 – 5734972
Fax: (965) 5726622 – 5734973
Email: info@ocasia.org

Olympic Council of Asia

OCA/20
August 24, 2007

Mr. Suresh Kalmadi
President
Indian Olympic Association

Re: Autonomy of the Indian Olympic Association

Dear Mr. Kalmadi

I present to you my best greetings and would like to refer to different reports coming out in media with regard to a move by the Government of India to interfere in the autonomy and the functioning of the Indian Olympic Association and the National Sports Federations of India.

I would like to reiterate the Aomori declaration (copy enclosed) as well as the Olympic Charter and the OCA Constitution Article 13 Bye-law (2) which clearly state that:

> "All Member NOCs must preserve their autonomy as envisaged in the OCA Constitution & Rules and in the Olympic Charter. There should be no interference from the Government and its agencies in the functioning of the NOC. However strong and cordial relationship should be maintained with the Government and its agencies. Any violation of the rules of the OCA Constitution/Olympic Charter shall result in suspension/withdrawal of recognition by OCA."

I would appreciate if you would take appropriate measures to maintain the autonomy of the Indian Olympic Association.

With kind regards
Yours sincerely,

Sheikh Ahmad Al-Fahad Al-Sabah
President OCA
C.C: Raja Randhir Singh – IOC Member & Secretary General OCA.

P.O.Box: 6706 Hawalli – Zip Code 32042, Kuwait – Tel.: +965 5734972 – Fax: +965 5734973
E-mail: info@ocasia.org – Website: www.ocasia.org

Suresh Kalmadi
Member of Parliament
INDIA

Note on "F-1"

I would like to state that Indian Olympic Association had only received a 'Way Forward' letter and not a contract from the FOA. The "Way Forward" letter dated 1st June 2007 clearly states "This letter does not constitute an offer capable of acceptance, nor is it intended to create legally binding relations." and was *subject to contract*. This understanding was a time bound understanding with clear deliverables to be met before 30th Sept 2007 dead line. A copy of this letter was distributed in the press in 2007. IOA was in touch with various state governments/private developers in efforts to procure huge capital investment and land as well as providing a standby letter of credit to FOA of US $35 million. However IOA could not deliver within the time frame because of the nature of huge capital investment. Also IOA was unable to acquire land from the government for purpose of the track. The IOA has not spent any money on this project. After expiry of the offer to IOA, the FOA was free to deal with anybody in India. Thereafter the role of IOA in bringing Formula 1 to India came to an end.

During early 2007 several private sector corporate were speaking to FOA to tie up with them. Subsequent to the lapsing of the offer to the IOA on 30th September 2007, M/s Jaiprakash Group approached Mr. Bernie Ecclestone along with Mr Sundar Mulchandani. Mr Mulchandani is well known to the FOA and had been trying to get Formula one to India for a long time including at Hyderabad. FOA awarded the Formula One Circuit Rights to M/s Jaiprakash Associates ltd. through their subsidiary, M/s JPSK Sports Private Limited, a company registered under the Company's Act, after JPSK fulfilled all the conditions, including financial terms, of the FOA agreement and entered into contract with them. The subscribers/ initial shareholders of M/S JPSK Sports Private Limited were Mr. Jaiprakash Gaur (JP), Mr. Suresh Kumar (SK) Mr. Sameer Gaur, Mr. Sunder Mulchandani and Mr. Harish Vaid. Mr. Sameer Gaur and Mr. Sunder Mulchandani signed the contract on behalf of M/S JPSK Sports Private Limited with Formula One administration (FOA) for Formula One Circuit rights for India.

Subsequently on their return to India Mr. Sunder Mulchandani approached my family, who have been involved in the Automobile business for over a decade to invest in this company and share the risk and involvement in the project. The expensive motor track infrastructure requires automotive manufacturer contacts for using the track for the rest of the 360 days for automotive testing, trials, auto expositions, go karting 2 wheeler racing etc as well as event management expertise for conducting large scale events. The Shareholders agreement was signed with a condition that if the Company (JPSK) was not able to get the Land transferred by 30th September 2008, this agreement would 'automatically stand terminated forthwith without any action being necessary on the part of parties hereto'. Since the Land could not be transferred to the Company by 30th September 2008, the shareholders agreement stands terminated. It is quite apparent that if my family were in dictating terms of this arrangement we would never have accepted a termination clause. There have been no monies earned whatsoever by my family, individually or through M/s Sulba Realty Pvt. Ltd. towards this agreement. Subsequent to the above deadline not being met, the rights of the family in the shareholders agreement stand terminated.

Information regarding Directors and shareholders in Sulba Realty is publicly available information. M/S JPSK Sports Private Ltd is a 100% subsidiary of M/s Jaiprakash Associates Ltd., in which the Jaypee group has absolute control, Mr. Sameer Gaur is the Managing Director of the Company and Mr Manoj Gaur is the chairman of the company.

भारतीय ओलम्पिक संघ
Indian Olympic Association

Statement on F1 Event:

22nd August 2009

Taking note of the news item in Indian Express on 22nd August, 2009 wherein IOA is dragged into unnecessary controversy at a time when India is organising Commonwealth Games Delhi 2010.

The clarification of IOA on the factual position is as follows: -

1. IOA received a letter from Mr. Bernie Ecclestone, Head of FOA on 1st June, 2007 indicating the "Way Forward" for a possible F1 event to India subject to following stringent conditions -

   (a) IOA will get the support of Government of India/State Government to get a circuit constructed at a site acceptable to FOA;

   (b) IOA will take the responsibility to raise necessary financing including a Letter of Credit for an amount of USD 35 Million as first year's license fee to be furnished by 30th September, 2007 along with an Agreement confirming all the commitments.

2. While IOA took various parallel steps to process the letter of FOA, due to following constraints, IOA failed to comply with the deadline of 30th September,2007 set by FOA to meet the conditions -

   (a) Despite pursuing the matter with various Governments, IOA was unable to get the necessary support in this regard within the timeframe.

   (b) There was no way IOA could have either taken the responsibility of highly capital intensive premise of acquisition of land, construction of circuit and raising millions of dollars every year to conduct the race;

3. **Thus, the facilitating role of IOA in bringing this prestigious event to India came to an end at a premature stage itself resulting in automatic termination of further communication on this issue with FOA by IOA in September, 2007. And, thereafter, IOA has had no further involvement in the matter.**

Tarlochan Singh	A.K. Mattoo	Dr. Lalit K. Bhanot	Harish Sharma
Vice-President	Treasurer	Jt. Secretary	Jt. Secretary

22/8/09

'Olympic Bhavan', B-29, Qutub Institutional Area, New Delhi 110 016 (INDIA)
Tel : (91 11) 2685 2480-84 Fax : (91 11) 2685 2386
E-mail : ioa@nde.vsnl.net.in Website : www.olympic.ind.in

Suresh Kalmadi

Member of Parliament (LS)

April 8, 2011

Dear Shri T. K. A Nairji

My attention has been drawn to media reports on the High Level Committee's report on the conduct of the Commonwealth Games 2010 Delhi.

I met Mr V K Shunglu and Mr Shantanu Counsul in their office at Vigyan Bhavan on March 18, 2011 and requested them to give me an opportunity to answer any queries they may have for me. It appears as if the High Level Committee has submitted its reports to the PMO without giving me a chance to explain my role in the Organising Committee Commonwealth Games 2010 Delhi.

I request you to give me a copy of the HLC reports and the annexures so that I can submit a response to you, especially on issues that concern me as an individual, as President of the Indian Olympic Association and as Chairman of the Organising Committee Commonwealth Games 2010 Delhi for six years.

From the media reports, it appears as if the basis for the HLC reports is a forensic report submitted by KPMG. Since HLC has relied on documents and reports and data collected by KPMG, it will be only fair that I should be provided with a copy of all documents and annexures and the report prepared by KMPG for HLC.

Regards

Yours sincerely,

(SURESH KALMADI), M.P.

Shri T K A Nair
Principal Secretary
Prime Minister's Office
South Block, **New Delhi**

Delhi : 2, K. Kamraj Lane, New Delhi-110011 Phone. 011-23792539, 23793699 Fax : 011-23793709 E-mail: skalmadi@sansad.nic.in
Pune : Kalmadi House, 42/8, Dr. Ketkar Road Erandvane, Pune-4 Phone. 020-25431161, 25433033, Fax : 020-25433072

भारतीय ओलम्पिक संघ
Indian Olympic Association

IOA/RTI/159/2011/ 430 October 21, 2011

To

Shri Vivek Garg
18/1, Ground Floor
Shakti Nagar
Delhi 110007

Sir,

Reference your RTI application dated 06/08/2011 forwarded by the Ministry of Youth Affairs & Sports vide letter no. 70-94/2011-CWG-I dated 12th September, 2011. Available information as per record is furnished below.

With regard to your above application, statement of expenditure for the Commonwealth Games 2010 Bid with relevant details (six pages) are enclosed herewith.

First Appellate Authority of Indian Olympic Association

Mr. Rakesh Gupta
Appellate Authority (RTI Cell)
Indian Olympic Association
B-29, Qutub Institutional Area
New Delhi 110 016

Yours faithfully,

George Mathew

(George Mathew)
CPIO

Encl: as above

'Olympic Bhavan', B-29, Qutub Institutional Area, New Delhi 110 016 (INDIA)
Tel : (91 11) 2685 2480-84 Fax : (91 11) 2685 2386
E-mail : ioa@nde.vsnl.net.in Website : www.olympic.ind.in

Statement of Expenditure for the Commonwealth Games 2010 Bid

Income			Expenditure		
SR. NO.	PARTICULARS	AMOUNT	SR. NO.	PARTICULARS	AMOUNT
1	FUNDS SANCTIONED FOR CWG 2010 BIS - AS PER SANCTION LETTER NO. F.70-19/2002 SP -II (VOL II) DATED 08.09.2003 OUT OF THE SANCTIONED AMOUNT RS.1,34,69,301 HAS ALREADY BEEN RELEASED	16,000,000.00	1	BID DOCUMENTS, PUBLICITY EXPENSES FOR LONDON COURIER CHARGES FOR BID DOCUMENTS & EXPENSES ON LONDON VISIT FOR BID SUBMISSION, EXPENSES ON EVALUATION COMMITTEE VISIT, SHOW BY MINISTRY OF SPORTS AT HOTEL ASHOKA	9,000,771.00
2	Delhi Government's Share	2,000,000.00	2	ADVANCE VISIT TO JAMAICA (PARA-2 / ANNEXURE-1)	188,617.00
			3	UPDATE OF BID BROCHURES (PARA-3 / ANNEXURE-1)	521,950.00
			4	COURIER CHAREGS- BID UPDATE (PARA-3b/ ANNEXURE-1)	1,45,008.00
3	Deficit	16,199,502.00	5	CGA MEMBERS VISIT TO DELHI (PARA -4 /ANNEXURE -1)	2,611,133.00
			6	PRESENTAION AT MONTEGO BAY (PARA 5/ANNEXURE 1)	21,732,023.00
		34,199,502.00			34,199,502.00

TREASURER - IOA SECRETARY GENERAL -IOA PRESIDENT -IOA

AUDITORS CERTIFICATE

We have examined the above Income & Expenditure statement of Indian Olympic Association pertaining to Commonwealth Games 2010 Bid and found the same correct in accordance with the documents / papers/ vouchers presented before us for verification and also in terms of letter no.F-70-19/2002-SP-II VOL.II DATED 08/11/2003 of Ministry of Youth Affairs and Sports stating that out of the sanctioned amount of Rs.2 crores. 80% of it will be borne by Ministry of Youth Affairs and Sports and the balance amount will be borne equally by Delhi Government and IOA.

Dinesh Mehta & Co.
Chartered Accountants

Dinesh Mehta
Partner 9.1.2004

Dinesh Mehta & Co. Darya Ganj New Delhi Chartered Accountants

Date : 9.1.2004
Place :

INDIAN OLYMPIC ASSOCIATION

S No	Accounts Heads	Expenditure
1	Expenditure incurred up to Evaluation visit audited accounts submitted	8,900,771
1a	Presentation at Hotel Ashoka by MoYAS	100,000
2	Advance visit to Jamaica visit to Jamaica (Air fare + Misc. + Pocket All.)	188,617
3	Update of Brochures	521,950
3b	Courier Charges(bid update to all CGA Members)	145,008
4	CGA Members visit to Delhi Hotel Meridian Air Fare reimburesment to delegates Transport Agra Visit Delegates Kit Media Kit & other expenses Publicity Misc. Expenses	2,611,133
5	Presentation at Montego Bay	
	Air Fare	4,186,802
	Boarding & Lodging	2,330,555
	Cultural Programme /Decor of Hospitality Area	3,198,556
	India Night and Joint Lunch & Dinner	4,049,487
	Publicity Material, Brochures, CDs Films, Exhibition Hall, Material, Photographs cutouts, etc.	2,362,446
	Mementos / Uniforms/ Media Kit Gifts - Elephant Balzer and Trousers Kurata Pajama Media Folders T. Shirts Caps / Leather Folders	913,661
	Transport	229,797
	Exhibition Hall/ Hospitality Area villa 60 Exp.	854,434
	Consultancy Charges TSE Consulting	2,186,647
	Rent of Electronic AV Equipment (Beta Film)	99,739
	Loss due to Foreign Exchange Rate	34,261
	Cargo charges & excess baggage charges	1,183,945
	Mobile Charges	101,693
		34,199,502

Dinesh Mehta & Co.
Chartered Accountants

INDIAN OLYMPIC ASSOCIATION

Statement of Expenditure for the Commonwealth Games 2010 Bid till visit of Evaluation Committee

Income			Expenditure		
SR. NO.	PARTICULARS	AMOUNT	SR. NO.	PARTICULARS	AMOUNT
1	FUNDS TO BE RECEIVED AS PER SANCTION FOR LONDON VISIT FROM MINISTRY OF YOUTH AFFAIRS AND SPORTS VIDE SANCTION LETTER NO. F-70-19/2000-SP-II DATED 13/9/2003	4,370,000.00	1	BID DOCUMENTS, PUBLICITY EXPENSES FOR LONDON, COURIER CHAGRES FOR BID DOCUMENT AND EXPNESES ON LONDON VISIT FOR BID SUBMISSION (Annexure - A, B, C & D)	5,633,441.00
2	FUNDS TO BE RECEIVED AS PER SANCTION FOR EVALUATION COMMISSION VISIT FROM MINISTRY OF YOUTH AFFAIRS AND SPORTS VIDE SANCTION LETTER NO. F-70-19/2000-SP-II DATED 13/9/2003	3,200,000.00	2	EXPENSES ON EVALUATION COMMITTEE VISIT (Annexure - E)	3,267,330.00
	Deficit	**1,330,771.00**			
		8,900,771.00			8,900,771.00

TREASURER - IOA

SECRETARY GENERAL IOA

AUDITORS CERTIFICATE

We have examined the above Income & Expenditure statement of Indian Olympic Association pertaining to Commomwealth Games 2010 Bid and found the same correct in accordance with the documents / papers/ vouchers presented before us for verification and as well letter of Ministry of Youth Affairs and Sports sanctioning the amount incurred and to be incurred vide their letter no. F-70-19/2000-SP-II DATED 13/9/2003

Dinesh Mehta
Partner
Dinesh Mehta & Co.

Date 4.10.03
Place Delhi.

Dinesh Mehta & Co. Darya Ganj New Delhi Chartered Accountants

EXPENDITURE STATEMENT FOR BID 2010 COMMONWEALTH GAME

ANNEXURE -A

SR. NO	PARTICULARS		AMOUNT INCURRED & PAID 1	PAYMENT TO BE MADE 2	TOTAL AMOUNT (1+2)
1	AIR FARE & VISA FEE Delhi London Delhi		839,629	-	839,629.00
2	HOTEL ACCOMMODATION IN LONDON GBP 9780/-		752,571	-	752,571.00
3	POCKET ALLOWANCE		377,425	-	377,425.00
4	CULTURAL PROGRAMME AT MARLBOROUH, DINNER & Cultural Programme at hotel Hilton		1,502,488	-	1,502,488.00
5	MISC EXPENSES AT LONDON				
	Transportation-	GBP 935.70	77,773.00	-	77,773.00
	Typing & Photocopy-	GBP 97.16	7,476.00	-	7,476.00
	Mobile- (Three Phone)		15,449.00	-	15,449.00
8	UNIFORMS TO DELEGATES		94,553.00		94,553.00
9	METROLOGICAL DEPARTMENT		1,835.00	-	1,835.00
10	PRESENT FOR DELEGATES		20,893.00	-	20,893.00
			3,690,092.00	-	3,690,092.00

NOTE :

1) GBP stands for Great Britain Pound

2) The above formate has been adopted for the presentation of statement of actual expenses incurred (paid & due, based on the budget estimate presentaed by IOA to the Ministry of Youth Affairs & Sports.

ANNEXURE B

SR.	PARTICULARS	Actual Incurred	Payment to be made	TOTAL AMOUNT
	BID DOCUMENTS cost of Bid document, cost of 250 CDs 250 Media Kit (Leather Folders, Pad & Pen) Two type of Posters, logo & Mascot)	1,269,773	—	1,269,773.00

For INDIAN OLYMPIC ASSOCIATION

Treasurer Secretary General President

Dinesh Mehta & Co. Chartered Accountants New Delhi

ANNEXURE C

SR.	PARTICULARS	Actual Incurred	Payment to be made	TOTAL AMOUNT
	PUBLICITY MATERIAL			
	FILM (BETA FORMATE AND VHS AND 200 COPIES IN CDS)	200,000.00	–	200,000.00
	BROCHURES (16 PAGES)	107,600.00	–	107,600.00
	DIGITAL BANNER etc.	73,602.00	–	73,602.00
		381,202.00	-	381,202.00

ANNEXURE D

SR.	PARTICULARS	Actual Incurred	Payment to be made	TOTAL AMOUNT
	COURIER CHARGES FOR SENDING BID DOCUMENTS TO 71 CGA COUNTIRES		292,374	292,374.00
		-	* 292,374	292,374

NOTE: * SINCE PAID BY IOA

ANNEXURE -E

SR.	PARTICULARS	Actual Incurred	Payment to be made	TOTAL AMOUNT
1	Airfare Delegates	1,018,846	0	1,018,846
2	Publicity Expenses	1,373,149	297396	1,670,545
3	Accommodation	476,400	0	476,400
4	Transportation	23,729	0	23,729
5	Photographs	11,670	0	11,670
6	Gift to Delegates	50,000	0	50,000
7	TA/DA to members for visit to Delhi for presentation	16,140	0	16,140
		2,969,934	297,396	3,267,330

ANNEXURE B

SR.	PARTICULARS	Actual Incurred	Payment to be made	TOTAL AMOUNT
	BID DOCUMENTS cost of Bid document, cost of 250 CDs 250 Media Kit (Leather Folders, Pad & Pen) Two type of Posters, logo & Mascot)	1,209,773	–	1,289,773.00

For INDIAN OLYMPIC ASSOCIATION

Treasurer Secretary General President

Dinesh Mehta & Co. Darya Ganj New Delhi Chartered Accountants

No.F.70-19/2002-SP-II (Vol.II)
Government of India
Ministry of Youth Affairs & Sports

New Delhi : 8th November, 2003

To

The Pay & Accounts Officer,
Pay & Accounts Office (Sports)
Shastri Bhavan,
New Delhi.

Sub: Indian Olympic Associaion – Grant-in-aid towards the expenditure incurred on Commonwealth Games, 2010 Bid.

Sir,

I am directed to say that Government of India has approved a total budget of Rs.2,00,00,000/- (Rupees two crores only) and out of this Government of India's has agreed to bear an expenditure of Rs.1,60,00,000/- (Rupees one crores & sixty lakhs only)) as its share. The release of Rs.1,60,00,000/- (Rupees one crores & sixty lakhs only)) will be as under:-

Total Government of India's share	:	Rs.1,60,00,000/-
Already released vide Sanction No.F.70-19/2002-SP-II Vol.II 24.10.2002 (on the basis of audited accounts for London visit and visit of evaluation team)	:	Rs. 58,77,202/-
Balance to be released:	:	Rs.1,01,22,798/-
75% to be released as first installment	:	Rs.75,92,099/-

2. Accordingly, I am directed to convey the sanction of the President to the payment Rs.75,92,099/- (Rupees seventy five lakhs ninety two thousand and ninety nine only) to Secretary General, Indian Olympic Association, J.N. Stadium, New Delhi for the purpose of Commonwealth Games Bid, 2010. This is a non-recurring grant.

F. No. 7/79/2011-NS.II
Ministry of Finance
Department of Economic Affairs
(Budget Division)

North Block, New Delhi,
Dated the 9th January, 2012

To
Shri Vivek Garg
18/1, GF, Shakti Nagar
Delhi-110007

Subject: Information under RTI Act, 2005.

Sir,

With reference to your RTI application No. RTI/M/oFin-Delhi/2011/702 dated 16-12-2011, received on 16-12-2011 in this Department, so far as NS-I and NS-II Section, Budget Division, Department of Economic Affairs is concerned, a copy of D.O. letter No. 167/PRNCM/10 dated 21-4-2010 from Chief Minister of Delhi to Union Finance Minister and a D.O. letter dated 8-7-2010 from Finance Minister to Chief Minister of Delhi, are enclosed herewith.

2. Appeal, if any, can be preferred under section 19 A of the RTI Act within 30 days from receipt of this letter to: Shri Ritvik Pandey [Deputy Secretary & Appellate Authority], Department of Economic Affairs, Ministry of Finance, R. No. 168-A, North-Block, New Delhi, Tele: 23093810 [ritvik@nic.in].

Yours faithfully,

(M.A. Khan)
Under Secretary & CPIO (NS)
Tele: 23093035

Copy to: Ms. Sadhna Sharma, S.O. (RTI Cell), D.E.A.,M/o Finance, North Block, New Delhi [w.r.t. I.D. No. 2/196491/RTI/11 dated 19-12-2011] for information.

GOVT. OF NATIONAL CAPITAL TERRITORY OF DELHI
DELHI SECRETARIAT, I.P. ESTATE, NEW DELHI-110113
PHONE : 23392020, 23392030 FAX : 23392111
D.O.NO.: 167|PRNCM|10
Dated : 19-03-2010

SHEILA DIKSHIT
CHIEF MINISTER

सत्यमेव जयते

Dear respected Pranabda,

DY. No. 764424 FMN/F/2010
21 APR 2010

I am indeed grateful to you for accepting my request for re-appropriation of Additional Central Assistance provision of Rs. 1,000 crores from JNNURM to Additional Central Assistance for Commonwealth Games to Delhi Government under R.E. 2009-10 as requested vide my letter dated 19th October, 2009. This enhanced allocation for Commonwealth Games has enabled us to provide the necessary funds for completion of all the Commonwealth Games related projects which have to be completed by July/August, 2010. However, the Budget 2010-11 indicates that there is a provision of only Rs. 50 crores as Additional Central Assistance for Commonwealth Games for the year 2010-11.

The Commonwealth Games projects are in advanced state of completion and I am personally monitoring each of these projects. Delhi Government's mandate is to improve the city infrastructure to support the Games activities at the Games venues and this includes inter-alia provision of adequate water, power, transport facilities, streetscaping, street furniture, preparing the training venues and two Games venues, taking care of volunteer programme as partners with Organizing Committee and Government of India's Department of Sports, as well as cultural programmes. The expenditure on the Commonwealth Games projects which are now under implementation and which have to be completed under any circumstances by July - August, 2010, is Rs. 1,800 crores for the year 2010-2011. While the Government of India allocated Rs. 350 cores during 2007-08, Rs. 400 crores during 2008-09 and Rs. 2000 crores during 2009-10, the allocation of only Rs. 50 crores against the minimum requirement of Rs. 1045 crores for completing the on going works (after taking into account allocation under JNNURM for 2010-11) is grossly insufficient.

In addition to the committed expenditure indicated above, we are sacrificing our revenue by way of grant of luxury tax exemption to all the players, sports organizations etc. during the games period, making provision for free buses for the various test events as well as the games. To reduce congestion on city roads we are providing free use of public transport to ticket holders during the Games. This is being done as per international practice for hosting such events.

-:2:-

We have provided in the normal budget, provisions for qualitative improvement in areas of education and health which are priority areas for the national government. We have also launched a number of programmes to improve the efficiency of integrated delivery of welfare services to the economically weaker sections and vulnerable sections of our society as a part of our policy to have sustainable growth through the Mission Convergence programme which was inaugurated by the Hon'ble President of India on 14th August, 2009. The health sector requires major investments to improve access to health care to millions of people in Delhi. All these would require our entire resources to meet the socio-economic objective of providing a caring and efficient governance for the national capital.

In this scenario, a sudden reduction in the Central assistance for the Commonwealth Games to Rs. 50 crores would be a major setback in honouring our commitments to complete all the preparations for the Games. You will appreciate that in organizing such an international event, there are unforeseen demands which are being made on us like exemption for VAT, exemption for Entertainment Tax, unforeseen expenditure on organizing for volunteer programme, civic awareness campaign, implementing an efficient transport plan to ensure smooth and efficient movement of sports personnel and also upgrading the health facilities for sports injuries infrastructure. All these are our international commitments. I would, therefore, sincerely request you to kindly review the provision of Rs. 50 crores and enhance the Additional Central Assistance for Commonwealth Games to Government of Delhi in 2010-11 to Rs. 1,000 crores so that we are in a position to complete all the projects in the next six months.

With regards,

Yours sincerely,

Sheila Dikshit

(SHEILA DIKSHIT)

Shri Pranab Mukherjee,
Hon'ble Union Finance Minister,
North Block,
New Delhi – 110 001.

प्रणब मुखर्जी
PRANAB MUKHERJEE

सत्यमेव जयते

वित्त मंत्री, भारत
FINANCE MINISTER
INDIA

8 JUL 2010

Dear Sheila ji

Please refer to your D.O. letter No.167/PRNCM/10 dt.19.3.2010 requesting for enhancement of the Additional Central Assistance for Commonwealth Games to Government of NCT of Delhi in 2010-11 to Rs.1000 crore.

Ministry of Home Affairs is the administrative Ministry in respect of Demand No.55- Transfers to UT Governments under which the Additional Central Assistance for Commonwealth Games to NCT of Delhi are made. Any proposal for enhancement under a Plan scheme/project should be routed through MHA, in consultation with Planning Commission. Hence, the comments of MHA were obtained in the matter. MHA has indicated that since that Ministry does not have the details of the ongoing works and no information is available on the project-wise breakup and the physical progress on the amounts released from 2007 till date, they are unable to support the proposal for additional allocation of central funds over and above Rs.50 crore already provided in the budget.

In view of the above, I would request you to take up the matter with Ministry of Home Affairs with the requisite details.

With regards,

Yours sincerely,

(Pranab Mukherjee)

ISSUED

Smt. Sheila Dikshit,
Chief Minister,
Delhi Secretariat, I.P. Estate,
New Delhi

Office : Room No. 134, North Block, New Delhi-110001 Ph. : 23092810, 23092510 Fax : 23093289
Residence : 13. Talkatora Road, New Delhi-110001 Tel. : 23737623, 23323042, 23737658

D.O.No.2(39)-B(CDN)/2006

वित्त मंत्री
भारत
नई दिल्ली - 110001
FINANCE MINISTER
INDIA
NEW DELHI-110001

August 21, 2008

Dear [illegible]

Please refer to your letter dated 30th July, 2008 seeking 'in principle' approval of the Ministry of Finance, for providing accumulated unspent balances of Rs.4051.38 crore from CRF in RE 2008-09 for disbursement to States/UTs for State Road projects.

2. As you may be aware, allocations from the Central Roads Fund (CRF) are governed by the Central Road Funds (CRF) Act 2000 and the CRF State Roads Rules, 2007. The Rules also prescribe the process for release of funds to the States. In accordance with the Act and the Rules, Rs.1781.56 crore has been provided as grants to States for "State Road Works" in 2008-09.

3. In so far as disbursement of unspent balances of previous years is concerned, it would be necessary to first have an account – State-wise and year-wise – of the funds allocated/released to the various States/UTs in previous years, in order to determine the entitlement of each State/UT for further release of funds from the unspent balances in accordance with the Rules. I would, therefore, request that the Department of Road Transport and Highways prepare a statement of account as indicated above to enable this Ministry to take a view on the quantum of additional funds to be released from the CRF during the current financial year.

4. I may add that any release from unspent balances would also require appropriation through Parliament. This can be done, at the earliest only when presenting the Supplementary Demands for Grants during the next session of Parliament.

With regards,

Yours sincerely,

(P. Chidambaram)

Thiru T.R. Baalu,
Minister of Shipping, Road Transport & Highways,
Transport Bhawan,
New Delhi.

D.O.No.2(39)-B(CDN)/2006

वित्त मंत्री
भारत
नई दिल्ली - 110001
FINANCE MINISTER
INDIA
NEW DELHI-110001

August 21, 2008

Dear Shri Dev,

Please refer to your letter No.846/M(HI&PE)/VIP/0/2008 dated July 31, 2008 drawing attention to the grant of funds for road projects in Silchar in the State of Assam.

2. As you may be aware, allocations from the Central Roads Fund (CRF) are governed by the Central Road Funds (CRF) Act 2000 and the CRF State Roads Rules, 2007. The Rules also prescribe the process for release of funds to the States. In accordance with the Act and the Rules, Rs.1781.56 crore has been provided as grants to States for "State Road Works" in 2008-09.

3. Your letter refers to the "unspent balances" of previous years. Allocation in previous years would have been done under the CRF Act and the funds would have been released according to the Rules for specific road projects. If some of the funds allocated/released have not been spent, I assume there will be an account for such funds in respect of each of the previous years. Before Ministry of Finance responds to your request, we would like to have an account – State- wise and year-wise - of the funds allocated/released to the various States. Once we have such a statement of account, it would be possible to determine the entitlement of each State for further funds from the unspent balances in accordance with the Rules.

4. I may add that any release from unspent balances would also require appropriation through Parliament. This can be done, at the earliest, only when presenting the Supplementary Demands for Grants during the next session of Parliament.

5. Meanwhile, I have requested that the Department of Road Transport and Highways, Ministry of Surface Transport to prepare a statement of account as indicated in paragraph 3 above. Once the statement of account is received, we shall advise you on the course of action to be adopted.

With regards,

Yours sincerely,

(P. Chidambaram)

Shri Sontosh Mohan Dev,
Minister of Heavy Industries & Public Enterprises,
Udyog Bhawan,
New Delhi.

SE

D.O. No.2(39)-B(CDN)/2006

August , 2008

Dear

Please refer to your letter No.RW/G-20016/5/2006-W&A dated 18th July 2008 regarding additional requirement of Rs.2326.52 crore from the unspent balances of Central Road Fund (CRF) in Public Account Major Head 8224 for disbursement to States/UTs during the current financial year.

2. As you are aware, allocations from the Central Road Fund (CRF) are governed by Section 10 (sub Section VII) of the CRF Act 2000. Section 11 read with Section 6 & 9 of the CRF (State Roads Rule) 2007 defines the process of release of funds to States. In FY 2008-2009, an amount of Rs.1781.56 crores has been provided as grant to States for State road works.

3. It would therefore, be advisable for the Department of Road Transport and Highways to first undertake an assessment - State wise and year wise - of the actual trend of expenditure against the funds allocated released to various States to determine the entitlement of each State for further release of funds from the unspent balances within the provisions of the relevant CRF Act Rules. Thereafter, the Department of Road Transport and Highway may bring up the proposals for the drawal of unspent balances to augment the existing budgetary provisions for State Road Projects which would require Parliament approval through Supplementary Demand for Grants.

With regards,

Yours sincerely,

SE

Shri Brahm Dutt,
Secretary,
Ministry of Shipping & Road Transport & Highways,
Transport Bhawan,
New Delhi

Annexure-2
3

GOVT. OF NATIONAL CAPITAL TERRITORY OF DELHI
DELHI SECRETARIAT, I.P. ESTATE, NEW DELHI-110002

SHEILA DIKSHIT
CHIEF MINISTER

D.O.NO.: 231/PRNCM/08
Dated: 17-03-2008

H. R. M. OFFICE
RECEIVED
18 MAR 2008
NEW DELHI

Dear respected Arjun Singhji,

I am writing to you in connection with the urgent need to ensure a very good connectivity between the Games Village with the Jawahar Lal Nehru Stadium for the Commonwealth Games, which are to be held in October 2010. Various alternatives for providing the connectivity have been considered over the past one year but two alternatives are considered to be the most feasible. One is the Tunnel Road alignment from Nizammudin Bridge to Jawahar Lal Nehru Stadium, which has legacy value. The other is the alignment of a road on the Barapulla Nalla from Ring Road to Jawahar Lal Nehru Stadium, which does not have much legacy value.

I am enclosing a note, which outlines the entire issue. Since this requires immediate resolution, I urge you to kindly convene an early meeting of the Group of Ministers so that a suitable decision could be arrived at. We have given a commitment to the Commonwealth Games Federation to ensure very good connectivity from the Games Village to Games Venues and if we are unable to do so, then it will be a major diplomatic embarrassment for the Govt. of India. Copies of the note have been sent to the DG, Archaeological Survey of India and Ministry of Urban Development.

With regards,

Yours sincerely,

(SHEILA DIKSHIT)

Sh. Arjun Singh
Union Minister for Human Resource Development
Shastri Bhawan, New Delhi-110001

Encl: As above

PHONE : OFF. 23392020, 23392030 • FAX : 23392111

NOTE

IMMEDIATE DECISION NEEDED FOR CONNECTIVITY BETWEEN GAMES VILLAGE AND JLN STÃDIUM FOR CWG 2010

1. There is an urgent need to ensure very good road connectivity between the Games Village and JLN Stadium which is the main venue for Commonwealth Games 2010. There is a commitment given to the Commonwealth Games Federation to ensure smooth connectivity to enable sports persons and their staff to travel to various games venues unhindered. There are important Games Venues near the JLN Stadium namely Tyagaraja Stadium, Siri Fort Sports Complex, Talkatora Stadium and National Stadium. The proposal of government to construct a link road between the Games Village and JLN Stadium has been examined many times before. After the rejection of the proposal to construct the so-called "tunnel road", other options were examined like "depressed carriage way", along the same alignment. Another option was explored to take a road on Barapulla Nalla even though it has no legacy value. This option was tentatively approved by the DUAC. But now the ASI has indicated that since this road would go over the old Barapulla Bridge which is listed as a monument, the road over Barapulla Nalla cannot be allowed to be constructed.

2. We have lost precious time and we are as yet no where near a solution to the problem of providing very good road connectivity between the Games Village and JLN Stadium. The reasons for not being able to do so are the following: -

a) The "tunnel road" was approved by Archeological Survey of India on 8/2/2007 but the permission was later on suspended vide its letter dated 28/2/2007, subject to further clearance. No reason was given for the suspension. Since this tunnel would not damage any monument and would not violate any heritage law, it appears to be the most feasible option. But it has not been possible to go ahead with this option due to the suspension of the approval by Archeological Survey of India. Now it is only possible to make the tunnel road by using "cut and cover" technology by placing box sections on the dug out earth and covering it up. This still appears to be the best option available for the connectivity having huge legacy value.

b) The "depressed corridor" along the same alignment would disturb the two Burj structures along the alignment apart from dividing the Sundar Nursery into two parts and the possibility of high noise levels which would affect the animal hospital run by the Delhi zoo authorities.

c) The construction of a separate corridor on the existing Barapulla Nalla from the Ring Road to JLN Stadium after crossing Mathura road was presented to DUAC on 23rd January 2008 and was technically found feasible by DUAC. In fact DUAC had recommended this option earlier and it was examined by a committee of experts from CEPT Ahmedabad apart from the options at a) and b) above. This option was considered feasible but with no legacy value unless a bridge is built on the river Yamuna as per the view of the experts. Even though it is not the best option but the only option left, it was decided to go ahead with this alignment and approval of Committee of Secretaries was also received vide minutes dated 19/2/2008. However on 28th February the ASI informed its objection to this alignment. Other options along the Barapulla are not at all feasible as they involve large scale demolition of buildings. It is surprising that the ASI did not object to the construction of a large Barapulla Bridge next to the old Barapulla bridge by MCD some years ago. This new bridge has completely eclipsed the old monument and made it useless from the archeological point of view. The old Barapulla bridge is also black topped which appears to be strange since this technology was not available four hundred years ago ! Vendors sell their wares on the bridge at present. ASI is however now insisting that another bridge cannot be built over this bridge even though there are large scale encroachments along the old Barapulla bridge like construction of high tension tower abutting the old bridge, construction of a new bridge merely three meters from the old bridge which has hidden the view of old Barapulla bridge altogether! Water pipelines have been laid right on the bridge, and cement used to strengthen the pillars of the bridge.(enclosed photographs show the current plight of the old Barapulla bridge) ASI has permitted the construction of a wide road abutting a Monument on the approach road turning in from Mathura road to the Nizamuddin Railway station in complete violation of the ASI regulations. It does not stand to reason why in one case there is no objection but in another case which involves the nation's honor and prestige, the ASI is choosing to put conditions in the name of preserving heritage monuments. This is a specious argument even if it is as per the law. Once the law has been broken and it has rendered the monument useless from archeological perspective, it makes no sense to object to a new development near it. In fact the construction of the bridge over it would give an opportunity to restore the architectural glory of the bridge by lighting up the monument and clearing the encroachments, thereby giving tourists an opportunity to view the monument.

3. A number of options are now available:-

a) Allow the construction of the original tunnel road using "cut and cover" section which would not create any vibrations and allow the tunnel to be made through Sundar Nursery. The temporary suspension of permission by ASI, may be withdrawn by ASI and work may be allowed to proceed. (copy of earlier order and subsequent suspension order is enclosed).

b) Allow the road on Barapulla Nalla to be constructed over the old Barapullah bridge in view of the fact that an existing bridge has already blocked the view of the old bridge and the current condition of the bridge does not make it a historical monument. ASI should not object to the construction and allow it to be constructed in view of the existing circumstances.

c) Shift the Games Village site to another location either in Dwarka or some other location from where the commuting commitment given to Commonwealth Games Federation can be fulfilled.

5

3. If nothing is done, there is bound to be traffic chaos and there is bound to be severe international criticism of the inability of the Government of India to keep to its commitment to provide efficient transport system to the athletes and their entourage. We are running out of time as the count down to the Games has begun and any construction would require a minimum period.

A VERY URGENT DECISION ON THIS IS REQUIRED NOW.

xxxxxxxxxxxxxxxxxxxxxxxxxxxxxxxxxxxxxxxxxxxxxxxxxxxxxxx

Documents Annexed :-

1 Minutes of Committee of Secretaries meeting dated 19/2/2008
2 Recommendation of CEPT University dated 5/11/2007
3 NOC from ASI dated 8/2/2007
4 Suspension of NOC by ASI dated 28/2/2007
5 Minutes of DUAC dated 4/2/2008
6 Observation on Barapullah Nallah by ASI dated 28/2/2008

6

डा एम०एस० गिल
Dr. M.S. GILL

युवा कार्यक्रम एवं खेल मंत्री
भारत सरकार
नई दिल्ली-110 115
MINISTER OF YOUTH AFFAIRS & SPORTS
GOVERNMENT OF INDIA
NEW DELHI-110 115

D.O.F.No.70-141/2010-CWG-I

November 29, 2010

Dear Pranab ji,

I am writing to you in respect of a major programme, which had been implemented by this Ministry, for the training and preparation of india teams for the Commonwealth Games. As you are aware, the performance of the Indian contingent at the Commonwealth Games has been quite exceptional, resulting in an unprecedented haul of medals, which were more than double the medals India had won at the last Commonwealth Games held in Melbourne in 2006. India also finished second in the medals tally, ahead of the major sporting nations such as England, Canada, South Africa, etc. This performance has been carried forward in the recently concluded Asian Games in Guangzhou, where India, with a total tally of 64 medals, has won its highest number of medals ever, in any Asian Gamers. This dramatically improved performance by the Indian sports persons, has been a result of the intensive training provided to them over the past two and a half years under the "Scheme for Preparation of Indian Teams for Commonwealth Games". This Scheme had been approved by the Cabinet, in its meeting held on 12.06.2008, with the objective of achieving the highest level of performance for Indian sports persons and maximizing the medals tally in the Commonwealth Games, 2010.

This Scheme had been conceptualized and formulated, with the objective of achieving excellence in multi-disciplinary sporting events. The Scheme had been designed, after intensive consultations with the National Sports Federations and other stakeholders in the field of sports. The shortcomings in the previously conducted training programmes were identified and suitably addressed in the new Scheme.

Further, after 6 months of implementation of the Scheme, the gaps which were identified during the implementation of the Scheme, were further addressed and corrections made with the approval of the Cabinet in December, 2008. This Scheme has thereafter, emerged as a flagship Scheme for preparing Indian teams, for mega multi-disciplinary sporting events. It is our intention to continue this Scheme with appropriate modifications wherever necessary, for preparation of India athletes for Olympic Games and other multi-disciplinary events in the future.

-2-

The expenditure under the Scheme has been around Rs.318 crores against the approved amount of Rs.678 crores. The savings have mainly been on the creation of sports science and medical facilities, at various centers of Sports Authority of India and on certain other items. Even with this level of expenditure under the Scheme, the results have been quite outstanding and the target of medals fixed under the Scheme of 96 to 125 medals had been achieved.

Secretary (Sports), vide her letter No.760-141/2010-CWG-I dated 22nd October, 2010, had requested Finance Secretary, that we may be allowed in the first instance, to extend the Scheme beyond the Commonwealth Games up to 31st March, 2011. In response, we have received a communication from Ministry of Finance, confirming that they have not agreed to the extension of the Scheme up to March, 2011. It has been stated that the expenditure under the Scheme has been low and sufficient funds have already been provided during the current year at RE stage, to enable the Ministry to meet the outstanding liabilities.

You would appreciate that the euphoria created by India's outstanding performance at these Games, has raised the hopes and expectations of the people for greater success in the future. The sporting fraternity in India has also realized that this is the result of the effective implementation of this well-conceived and well-designed Scheme. Abruptly closing the Scheme after the Commonwealth Games, may convey an adverse message to the sporting community and sports lovers of the country. While the provisions at the RE stage would cater to the requirements of the Scheme for the balance period of year, and we would also judiciously make expenditure under the Scheme only on the permissible items, you may kindly agree in-principle that the Scheme may be extended, in the first instance up to 31st March, 2011.

I shall appreciate, if you could fix a time where I could personally explain the details and brief you.

With best wishes,

Yours sincerely,

(M. S. Gill)

Shri Pranab Mukherjee
Union Finance Minister
Government of India
New Delhi.

D.O.NO.40 (4)/PF-II/2008

प्रणब मुखर्जी
PRANAB MUKHERJEE

वित्त मंत्री, भारत
FINANCE MINISTER
INDIA

सत्यमेव जयते

15 DEC 2010
15 DEC 2010

Dear Dr Gill

Please refer to your DO F.No.70-141/2010-CWG-I dated November 29, 2010 regarding extension of an ongoing scheme. I have had the matter re-examined.The scheme in question, viz., "Preparation of Indian Team for the Commonwealth Games 2010", was specific to the Commonwealth Games 2010. I agree that in the long term too the objective of achieving excellence in sporting events of various disciplines should be pursued, but that should happen through the regular activities/schemes of the Ministry of Sports. I trust your Ministry would continue to build upon the experience and strengths of these initiatives to consolidate upon them.

However, as far as the scheme in question is concerned, with both the CWG as well as the Asian Games behind us, it is only logical to wind the scheme up.

With regards,

Yours sincerely,

(Pranab Mukherjee)

Shri M.S. Gill
Minister
Ministry of Youth Affairs & Sports

Office : Room No. 134, North Block, New Delhi-110001 Ph. : 23092810, 23092510 Fax : 23093289
Residence 13, Talkatora Road, New Delhi-110001 Tel. : 23737623, 23323042, 23737658

डॉ० एम०एस० गिल
Dr. M.S. GILL

युवा कार्यक्रम एवं खेल मंत्री
भारत सरकार
नई दिल्ली-110 115
MINISTER OF YOUTH AFFAIRS & SPORTS
GOVERNMENT OF INDIA
NEW DELHI-110 115

No.F.8-53/2010-SP.III

5th January 2011

Dear Pranab ji

Thank you for your reply dated December 16, 2010 regarding extension of the scheme for 'Preparation of Indian team for the Commonwealth Games 2010'.

2. I accept your decision that the Scheme has to be wound up, because it was specifically meant for preparing the Indian team for the Commonwealth Games 2010 (CWG 2010). I am happy, that you have kindly appreciated the need, to make sustained efforts toward promoting sporting excellence, in the long term under the regular activities/schemes of the Ministry.

3. As you are aware, the Indian team has put up its best ever performance at the CWG 2010 held in Delhi, and also improved its ranking to sixth position at the 2010 Asian Games, held in Guangzhou (from eighth position in the previous edition). Apart from doing well in sports like shooting, wrestling, weightlifting and archery, in which we have been traditionally doing well, the performance in athletics, boxing, swimming and gymnastics, which form part of the core sport disciplines, has been highly encouraging and, in a way, marks the watershed in the international sporting performance of India.

4. The generous support of Rs 678 crore, spread over 2½ years, that you gave for the preparation of the Indian team for the CWG 2010 and Asian Games 2010, has been largely responsible for this positive development, as it was possible to train our national athletes, as per international standards in terms of coaching, infrastructure and equipment support, diet and supplements, sports medicine and other scientific support. At this juncture, our next target is 2012 London Olympics, for which we have kept a target of a minimum of 10 medals. It is therefore, absolutely essential, that we maintain the same momentum and intensity of training of our athletes, for the Olympic qualifiers and other major events, and the London Olympics as we did for CWG 2010. In order to ensure that, we would have to maintain, the scales of assistance that are allowed for the various components of preparation of the Indian team under the CWG scheme. We would like to adopt the scales and components of the CWG scheme for training the Indian team, under the existing scheme of "Assistance to National Sports Federations", as suggested by you. Further, we shall do this, within the overall budget allocation made available to us, as per the RE figures communicated by the Ministry of Finance.

5. While we shall be separately formulating a scheme for preparation of the national team, the proposed interim arrangement may be approved, for enabling us to maintain the momentum and intensity of training of the Indian team upto 2012 London Olympics.

With regards

Yours sincerely,

(M S Gill)

Shri Pranab Mukherjee
Union Minister of Finance
North Block, New Delhi

Urgent
PI put up

FM

Dear

Please refer to DO F.No.8-53/2010-SP.III dated January 5, 2011 from your predecessor regarding adoption of the scales and components of the Scheme for Preparation of Indian Team for Commonwealth Games 2010 under the existing Scheme of "Assistance to National Sports Federations".

There has been iterative correspondence between your Ministry and the Ministry of Finance over the earlier proposal regarding the preparation of Indian team. ~~You would notice, that when I had finally communicated this Ministry's disinclination for extending the Scheme for preparation of Indian Teams for the CWG 2010 I had underscored~~ that ~~in~~ the long term the objective of achieving excellence of sporting events of various disciplines should be pursued through the regular activities/schemes of the Ministry of Sports~~. It was expected~~ the Ministry ~~of Sports~~ would continue to build upon the experience and strengths of ~~these~~ initiatives ~~to consolidate upon them.~~

However, if your Ministry proposes to modify the existing scheme, it is suggested that the prescribed procedure for Scheme formulation, appraisal and approval which also governs modifications in existing Plan Schemes should be followed.

(FM)

Shri Ajay Maken
Minister of State (IC) YAS

D.O.F.No.40(4)/PF.II2008(Vol.II)

प्रणब मुखर्जी
PRANAB MUKHERJEE

वित्त मंत्री, भारत
FINANCE MINISTER
INDIA

सत्यमेव जयते

[illegible] .11

Dear Ajay

Please refer to DO F. No. 8-53/2010-SP.III dated January 5, 2011 from your predecessor regarding adoption of the scales and components of the Scheme for preparation of Indian Team for Commonwealth Games 2010 under the existing Scheme for "Assistance to National Sports Federations."

There has been iterative correspondence between your Ministry and Ministry of Finance regarding the proposal for extension of the Scheme for preparation of Indian team for the CWG 2010. The decision that this Scheme should be wound up has also been accepted.

It is expected that the long-term objective of achieving excellence in sporting event of various discipline would be pursued through the regular activities/schemes of Ministry of Sports. In this context, if the Ministry proposes to modify the existing Scheme, it is suggested that the prescribed procedure for scheme formulation, appraisal and approval, which also governs modifications in existing Plan scheme, be followed.

With regards,

Yours sincerely,

(Pranab Mukherjee)

ISSUED

Shri Ajay Maken,
Minister of State for Youth Affairs and Sports,
Room No. 401 'C' wing
Shastri Bhawan,
New Delhi

Office : Room No. 134, North Block, New Delhi-110001 Ph. : 23092810, 23092510 Fax : 23093289
Residence : 13, Talkatora Road, New Delhi-110001 Tel. : 23737623, 23323042, 23737658

सिन्धुश्री खुल्लर
Sindhushree Khullar
सचिव
Secretary
Tel. : 23388623
Telefax : 23388758
E-mail : secy-sports@nic.in

भारत सरकार
युवा कार्यक्रम एवं खेल मंत्रालय
खेल विभाग
शास्त्री भवन, नई दिल्ली–110 015
Government of India
Ministry of Youth Affairs & Sports
Department of Sports
Shastri Bhawan, New Delhi-110 015

D.O.No. F.70-28/2009-CG-I

Dated : July 20th, 2009

Dear Shri Chawla,

I am enclosing for your kind attention letter received from Shri Suresh Kalmadi, Chairman, Organising Committee, Commonwealth Games 2010 regarding some issues pertaining to revenues and expenditure in respect of conduct of the Games, that is under appraisal in your Ministry. I understand that a meeting of Committee for Non-Plan Expenditure has been fixed for 28th July, 2009 to consider all aspects relating to the above mentioned issues.

In this connection, I am enclosing a brief stating the previous correspondence and decisions on the various issues raised in the recent reference received from Chairman, OC. These may kindly be taken on board for discussion in the scheduled CNE meeting.

with regards

Yours sincerely,

(Sindhushree Khullar)

Shri Ashok Chawla,
Finance Secretary,
Ministry of Finance,
North Block,
New Delhi.

Encl. : as above

Government of India
Ministry of Youth Affairs and Sports
Department of Sports

* * * * *

Chairman, Organizing Committee (OC) has requested Minister, Ministry of Youth Affairs and Sports and Secretary (Sports) for necessary assistance in the matter of obtaining exemptions / concessions from payment of Income Tax by OC which has been stated to be necessary for making the OC revised Budget revenue neutral. It has been requested that Department of Sports may recommend the following to Ministry of Finance :

(a) MOF may suitably amend section 2(15) of I.T. Act, 1961, so that OC need not to pay tax on the revenue generated by OC while organizing the CWG-2010.

(b) Necessary notification may be issued by GOI (Department of Revenue, MOF) by exercising powers conferred by clause (39) of section 10 of IT Act, 1961 so that revenue generated by OC from Broadcasting Sponsorship, Ticketing etc. for holding the international event viz. Commonwealth Games -2010, is treated as income which shall not be included in computing taxable income.

(c) Section 80G of IT Act, 1961 may be suitably amended or notification issued under section 80G to provide for the concession to OC which are already available to Indian Olympic Association, who is involved in the sponsorship and development of sports in India, because OC is also engaged in similar activities.

(d) OC may be provided exemption from Service Tax under Section 93 of the Finance Act at par with bodies like UN, International Organizations, Special Economic Zones etc.

(e) Permission may be granted to OC for conducting a nationawide lottery through State Government of Mizoram and Kerala to raise under Section 10 of the Lotteries (Regulation) Act, 1968.

F.No.70-28/2009-CWG-I

Government of India
Ministry of Youth Affairs and Sports
Department of Sports

*****

COMMENTS:

Out of the 5 issues referred by Chairman, OC, the first three were referred to Ministry of Finance. The comments received from MoF were communicated to the OC (copy enclosed). The OC have taken action as suggested by MoF and that it may be reviewed favourably.

02. As regards organization of nationwide Raffle in the name of OC, Ministry of Home Affairs is seized of the matter. At present, 12 States in India allow Raffles / Lotteries. The OC can seek permission from any one state and then run the lottery in these 12 States. No permission / approval of Govt. of India is required. The sharing of revenue of the lottery is a matter between the OC and the State Governments, since initially the revenue is deposited in the State Exchequer. Therefore, the revenue impact of this measure on the OC budget can not be estimated.

03. As regards the request of OC to make it a nationwide lottery/raffle, this, cannot be directed by the GOI (there is apparently a SC Judgment in this regard). The States have to decide individually. A copy of the letter sent by MHA dated 7.7.2009 is enclosed. It is now, therefore a matter on which OC, in its highest decision making body, is to take a decision about going in for the lottery after it has worked out the arrangements and obtained the permission of the concerned States. But it needs to be pointed out that the time available to implement the decision is now short.

04. With regard to Exemption of Service Tax, OC had sent their proposal to MoF and they have been informed through letter of Revenue Secretary dated 29.9.2008 (copy enclosed) that it would not be possible to accede to the request of Exemption of Service Tax. However, this may be reviewed.

F.No.70-28/2009-CWG-I

MOST IMMEDIATE

F.No. V-11019/11/2008-CSR
Ministry of Home Affairs
(CS Division)
*****

New Delhi, dated 7 .7.09

To

Shri Suresh Kalmadi, M.P.,
Chairman, Organising Committee,
Commonwealth Games Delhi 2010,
OLYMPIC BHAWAN, B-29,
Qutub Institutional Area,
New Delhi-110016.
Fax No - 011-24368243

Subject: Conducting of a raffle for raising revenue for Commonwealth Games Delhi, 2010.

I am directed to refer to your letter dated 17.06.09 on the subject mentioned above and to say that your request for issuing directions by the Central Government under Section 10 of the Lotteries (Regulation) Act, 1998 cannot be acceded to. This position was earlier also conveyed to your representative in the course of meeting held by the Additional Secretary, MHA on 22nd May, 2008 in North Block, New Delhi. You are once again advised to directly approach any/all State Governments for conducting any such raffle.

Yours faithfully

Sd/-

(NEERAJ KANSAL)
DIRECTOR (CS)
Tel No. 23092933

17 2009 7:20AM HP LASERJET F

D.O.F.No.356/2/2007-TRU

भारत सरकार
वित्त मंत्रालय
नॉर्थ ब्लाक, नई दिल्ली-११०००१
GOVERNMENT OF INDIA
MINISTRY OF FINANCE
NORTH BLOCK, NEW DELHI-110001

सत्यमेव जयते

राजस्व सचिव
REVENUE SECRETARY

29th September, 2008

Dear Shri Kalmadi,

Please refer to your letter dated 03.09.2008 seeking full exemption from service tax on all taxable services provided for the Organising Committee, Commonwealth Games Delhi 2010.

2. I have had the matter further examined. Service tax is leviable on taxable services provided irrespective of the status of the consumer of service. Moreover, services being intangible in nature, end-use based exemption from levy of service tax is difficult to administer and prone to misuse. The Prime Minister's Economic Advisory Council (EAC), while considering the issue of service tax exemption, has observed that it is an accepted principle of tax reform and administration that first point tax exemption is poor practice and leads to leakage of revenue. Exemption being an indirect subsidy, it is felt that the preferred option is to provide relief, wherever needed, through a direct and transparent budgetary method.

3. In view of the above, we are unable to accede to the request for exemption from service tax in this case.

With regards

Yours sincerely,

(P.V. BHIDE)

Shri Suresh Kalmadi,
Member of Parliament &
Chairman, Organising Committee,
Commonwealth Games Delhi 2010,
Gate No.28A, Jawaharlal Nehru Stadium,
Lodi Raod, New Delhi-110 003.

Phone : 23092653, 23092111 Fax : 23092719 E-mail : rsecy@nic.in

DELHI 2010

Organising Committee
Commonwealth Games Delhi 2010

25th June 2009

Suresh Kalmadi M.P.
Chairman, Organising Committee
President, Indian Olympic Association

Sub: Request for assistance of Sports Ministry for taking up issues concerning OC with Finance Ministry and Home Ministry.

Please accept my sincere thanks for your visit to our office on 24.06.09, which I must admit, has been very inspiring and immensely fruitful. 'Your revised budget of OC' is already in the process of approval by EFC. The revenue neutral aspect of the budget almost entirely hinges upon some key issues, relating to tax exemption / concession to be granted to OC and the permission to conduct a nation wide raffle in the name of Commonwealth Games.

I have already sent letters to the Hon'ble Finance Minster and the Hon'ble Home Minister on the above issues. While taking up the issue on tax exemption / concession, I have also pleaded the case of Indian Olympic Association as well, which is also on the same lines as that of OC. I am sending herewith the copies of my letters addressed to the Hon'ble Finance Minister and the Hon'ble Home Minister of India on the above issues.

I shall be grateful if you would kindly arrange to take up these issues with the respective Ministries for early fructification of the issues concerned.

Encl: As stated

(Suresh Kalmadi)
Chairman

To

Smt. Sindhushree Khullar
Secretary (Sports)
Ministry of Youth Affairs & Sports,
Government of India
Room no. 2, 'C' Wing, Ground Floor
Shastri Bhawan
New Delhi- 110001.

OLYMPIC BHAWAN, B-29, Qutub Institutional Area, New Delhi 110 016. INDIA

DELHI 2010

Organising Committee
Commonwealth Games Delhi 2010

Suresh Kalmadi M.P.
Chairman, Organising Committee
President, Indian Olympic Association

8th June 2009

Sub: Exemptions/Concessions of Tax requested by the Organising Committee Delhi 2010, from the Ministry of Finance

Dear Mr Pranab Mukherjeeji,

Please allow me to extend warm greetings on behalf of the Organising Committee Commonwealth Games Delhi 2010 on your assuming office as the Finance Minister of India. The Organising Committee Commonwealth Games Delhi 2010 is fully geared up for the task ahead and is already on top gear in taking the final phase of preparatory action, as we have less than 500 days to go.

As you may be aware, the Organising Committee is being given loan by Government of India, which is repayable with interest, on conclusion of the games. For this purpose, the Organising Committee has already submitted its revised budget to MoYAS, which is a revenue neutral budget. Organising Committee, Commonwealth Games has set for itself an ambitious target for revenue of Rs. 1876.00 crs, which will certainly be achieved in full. However, Organising Committee, Commonwealth Games Delhi 2010, needs assistance from the Ministry of Finance, in the form of tax exemptions/concessions, in order to ensure that this targeted revenue is met In addition, permission may be granted for raising revenue by conducting a Nationwide Raffle through the governments of Mizoram and Kerala.

I am enclosing a brief on the issues relating to the tax exemptions/tax concessions, which are to be granted by Ministry of Finance, for your benign consideration. I shall be grateful if immediate directives are given to the authorities concerned in the Ministry of Finance to ensure that the request of Organising Committee for tax exemptions/tax concessions are granted immediately.

Suresh Kalmadi
(Chairman)

Encl. as stated

To

Shri Pranab Mukherjee
Hon'ble Finance Minister of India
North Block
New Delhi-110001

HIGH LEVEL COMMITTEE FOR COMMONWEALTH GAMES

On 19th June, 2009, the GOM was reconstituted after obtaining orders of the Prime Minister. A copy of the notification is attached. It is not clear to the High Level Committee as to what powers were delegated to the GOM. In particular, it is noticed that matters which Organising Committee (OC) ought to have decided were put up to the GOM and their approval taken as if GOM was directly supervising the work of OC.

2. Certain powers of sanction were exercised by the GOM to increase the amount for opening and closing ceremonies on two or three occasions. Did the GOM enjoy any financial powers? In this context please see a copy of the Press Note attached, which was issued by the PMO on the re-constitution of the GOM, and which suggests that financial powers were not delegated to the GOM. It should also be pointed out when the GOM was constituted in 2004, a Finance Sub Committee was put in place. However, the GOM decided in January, 2006, that this mechanism would be replaced by the normal EFC system and this decision was duly followed by the Ministry of Youth Affairs & Sports till late 2009, when the GOM started taking financial decisions. An early clarification would be appreciated. We have noted that GOM meetings were regularly attended by officers of Cabinet Secretariat.

CS-2380/...
3/2/11

V.K. Shunglu
(V.K. Shunglu)
Chairman, HLC
03.02.2011

Cabinet Secretary (Shri K.M. Chandrasekhar)
104/ HLC/2010 dated 03.02.2011

The amount agreed to by the GOM (Rs. 300 crore) was with the concurrence of FM. This may kindly be confirmed so that I can reply to the Chairman, HLC

[signature]
3.2.11

Category	DEPARTMENT OF EXPENDITURE
Subject	High Level Committee (HLC) for Commonwealth Games.
Content	Cabinet Secretary has forwarded a note dated 3.02.2011 from Chairman, High Level Committee (HLC) for Commonwealth Games regarding the powers of sanction exercised by the GOM to increase the amount for opening and closing ceremonies to the FM. The Cabinet Secretary has recorded that the amount agreed to by the GOM **(₹ 300 crore)** was with the concurrence of FM. He has sought confirmation of this to enable him to reply to the Chairman, HLC. FM has desired to know the position in this regard from DoE. DoE has stated that the position in this regard is as follows: (i) The Organizing Committee (OC) of CWG 2010 was sanctioned a loan of ₹ 1620 crore for the conduct of CWG 2010. Out of the **₹ 1620 crore** budget of OC, **₹ 106.58 crore** were initially kept for the Opening and Closing ceremonies. (ii) In a CoS meeting to review the progress of works related to the Games held on 4.6.2010 the OC projected an additional requirement over and above the **₹ 1620 crore** sanctioned. It was eventually decided that the OC/MYAS could move for sanction only for the incremental amount for the ceremonies (upto the cap of **₹ 300 crore**). This position was seen by the FM vide notings at page 18/N ante. (iii) In June 2010 Secretary MYAS informed that the GOM had decided that the approved budget under the Ceremonies Functional Area (FA) should be **₹ 300 crore**. She had mentioned that the timelines available for rehearsals and preparations were extremely tight and therefore sought to enable the OC to make commitments and advances subject to the overall cap of **₹ 300 crore** for the ceremonies in anticipation of the approval of the additional amount. The proposal was examined on this file vide notes at page 22/N ante and DoE agreed to the MYAS proposal. (iv) While communicating DoE's approvals permit the OC to go ahead with the RFPs in anticipation of approval of the additional amount, we had advised that "The matter has been considered in the context of increased cost estimates projected by the OC in meetings of the COS as well as GOM." and that "Only in the case of 'Ceremonies' (both Opening and Closing ceremonies taken together) an increase in the cost estimates from the existing **₹ 106 crore** to a maximum of **₹ 300 crore** has been agreed to. Ministry of Sports may permit the OC to go ahead with processing RFPs and make payments in anticipation of this approval only for this. The Ministry of Sports may, as early as possible, move for due sanction of the,

	enhanced amount. In doing so, it may examine the possibility of effecting savings in other heads. The increase, however, should not exceed ₹ **194 crore**. While moving for approval, the Ministry should also bring on board clear reasons for cost over-run and fix responsibility for decisions not taken in time which has led to cost over-runs." (v) Subsequently, DoE received a proposal from MYAS for enhancing the loan budget of the Organizing Committee from ₹ **1620 crore** to ₹ **1813.42 crore** towards the increased expenditure for the Ceremonies from ₹ **106.58 crore** to ₹ **300 crore**. This proposal was put up to the FM at page 33N/ante and it was communicated to MYAS with the approval of FM that this Ministry agrees to enhancing the loan budget of the Organizing Committee from ₹ **1620 crore** to ₹ **1813.42 crore** for the Ceremonies though MYAS should justify the same in the note for GoM/Cabinet and see if some savings are possible.
Action required	For kind information/perusal of Hon'ble FM.

9/2/11

Adviser to FM

9/2/11

Confidential

No.40(7)/PF-II/09
Government of India
Ministry of Finance
Department of Expenditure
Plan Finance-II Division

North Block, New Delhi
Dated: 11. 02.11

Office Memorandum

Subject:- Opening and Closing ceremonies of Commonwealth Games-enhancement of allocation.

The undersigned is directed to refer to the reference from Cabinet Secretary on the above subject and to confirm that the enhanced allocation of Rs. 300 crore by the GM for the opening and closing ceremonies was with the concurrence of the Finance Minister.

Om issued
11/2/11

(Meena Agarwal)
Joint Secretary (PF-II)

To

The Cabinet Secretary
Cabinet Secretariat,
Rashtrapati Bhavan,
New Delhi

Commonwealth Games – D2010 matter

भारत सरकार
युवा कार्यक्रम एवं खेल मंत्रालय
खेल विभाग
शास्त्री भवन, नई दिल्ली–110 115
Government of India
Ministry of Youth Affairs & Sports
Department of Sports
Shastri Bhawan, New Delhi-110 115

सिन्धुश्री खुल्लर
Sindhushree Khullar
सचिव
Secretary
Tel. : 23388623
Telefax : 23388758
E-mail : secy-sports@nic.in

D.O. No.F.70-42/2009-CWG.1(Part.III)
Dated the October 1st, 2010

Please refer to Ministry of Finance (Department of Expenditure) Plan Finance Division II O.M. No.407(&)/PF.II/2009-Vol.II regarding Budget of OC, CWG-2010 Delhi including the personal for re-appropriation of funds within the existing approved budget of OC of Rs.1620 crore from the 'Revenue Generation Functional areas to 'Other Functional areas'.

02. Ministry of Finance have approved the increased expenditure for the Ceremonies from Rs.106.58 crore to Rs.300 crore thus enhancing the budget of OC for the conduct of the Games to Rs.1813.42 crore from the earlier approved budget of Rs.1620 crore. However, Ministry of Finance did not concur with the proposal for re-appropriation of Rs.144 crore from the Head 'Revenue Generation Functional areas' to 'other functional areas'.

03. In this context we would like to invite your attention to the fact that at EFC stage an upper limit had been set for OC's budget at Rs.1620 crore. This also included an amount of Rs.110 crore of the Commonwealth Youth Games, Pune which have been concluded in October, 2008. By not allowing the OC to re-appropriate Rs.144 crore from 'Revenue Generation FA' to 'Other FAs' would effectively mean reduction of the OC's budget from Rs.1620 crore to Rs.1476 crore.

04. Out of the additional approved budget of Rs.1813.42 crore Ministry of Youth Affairs and Sports have released so far Rs.1669.42 crore leaving a balance of Rs.144.00 crore. Now, the OC has submitted an expenditure statement as on 22nd September, 2010 indicating that they have a committed expenditure of Rs.226.86 crore in respect of Functional Areas of Accommodation, Boradcasting, Catering, Office Administration, Technology, Ticketing, TV Rights, Venue Development and Coordination which require more funds immediately. Chairman, OC's letter dated 25th September, 2010 with a detailed statement of commitments is attached. They have requested to release the withheld amount of Rs.144.00 crore out of the sanctioned budget of Rs.1813.42 crore. This would mean that release of the balance amount of Rs.144.00 crore meant for revenue generation to be released for meeting the expenditure in other Functional Areas.

05. In view of the above position, it is requested that Ministry of Finance may reconsider the earlier decision regarding re-appropriation of funds under revenue generation functional area to other functional areas considering the extraordinary funds requirements situation indicated in their letter referred above and permit OC to re-appropriate Rs.144 crore from Revenue Generation FA to other FAs.

Yours sincerely,
Sd./-
(Sindhushree Khullar)

Shri Ashok Chawla,
Finance Secretary,
Ministry of Finance,
North Block, New Delhi.

Copy to :

1. Ms. Meena Agarwal, Joint Secretary (Expenditure), Ministry of Finance, North Block, New Delhi.
2. Shri G.C. Chaturvedi, Spl. Director General, OC, CWG-D2010.

(Sindhushree Khullar)
Secretaru (Sports)
1.10.2010

Original 857/22/18/10

Commonwealth Games – D2010 matter

JS(PF-II) Has se P1e

सिन्धुश्री खुल्लर
Sindhushree Khullar
सचिव
Secretary
Tel. : 23388623
Telefax : 23388758
E-mail : secy-sports@nic.in

4.10

भारत सरकार
युवा कार्यक्रम एवं खेल मंत्रालय
खेल विभाग
शास्त्री भवन, नई दिल्ली–110 115
Government of India
Ministry of Youth Affairs & Sports
Department of Sports
Shastri Bhawan, New Delhi-110 115

D.O. No.F.70-42/2009-CWG.1(Part.III)
Dated the October 1st, 2010

Dear Shri Chawla,

Please refer to Ministry of Finance (Department of Expenditure) Plan Finance Division II O.M. No.407(&)/PF.II/2009-Vol.II regarding Budget of OC, CWG-2010 Delhi including the personal for re-appropriation of funds within the existing approved budget of OC of Rs.1620 crore from the 'Revenue Generation Functional areas to 'Other Functional areas'.

02. Ministry of Finance have approved the increased expenditure for the Ceremonies from Rs.106.58 crore to Rs.300 crore thus enhancing the budget of OC for the conduct of the Games to Rs.1813.42 crore from the earlier approved budget of Rs.1620 crore. However, Ministry of Finance did not concur with the proposal for re-appropriation of Rs.144 crore from the Head 'Revenue Generation Functional areas' to 'other functional areas'.

03. In this context we would like to invite your attention to the fact that at EFC stage an upper limit had been set for OC's budget at Rs.1620 crore. This also included an amount of Rs.110 crore of the Commonwealth Youth Games, Pune which have been concluded in October, 2008. By not allowing the OC to re-appropriate Rs.144 crore from 'Revenue Generation FA' to 'Other FAs' would effectively mean reduction of the OC's budget from Rs.1620 crore to Rs.1476 crore.

04 Out of the additional approved budget of Rs.1813.42 crore Ministry of Youth Affairs and Sports have released so far Rs.1669.42 crore leaving a balance of Rs.144.00 crore. Now, the OC has submitted an expenditure statement as on 22nd September, 2010 indicating that they have a committed expenditure of Rs.226.86 crore in respect of Functional Areas of Accommodation, Boradcasting, Catering, Office Administration, Technology, Ticketing, TV Rights, Venue Development and Coordination which require more funds immediately. Chairman, OC's letter dated 25th September, 2010 with a detailed statement of commitments is attached. They have requested to release the withheld amount of Rs.144.00 crore out of the sanctioned budget of Rs.1813.42 crore. This would mean that release of the balance amount of Rs.144.00 crore meant for revenue generation to be released for meeting the expenditure in other Functional Areas.

05 In view of the above position, it is requested that Ministry of Finance may reconsider the earlier decision regarding re-appropriation of funds under revenue generation functional area to other functional areas considering the extraordinary funds requirements situation indicated in their letter referred above and permit OC to re-appropriate Rs.144 crore from Revenue Generation FA to other FAs.

With regards

Yours sincerely,

(Sindhushree Khullar)

PT put up 7.10.10

Shri Ashok Chawla,
Finance Secretary,
Ministry of Finance,
North Block, New Delhi.

Organising Committee Commonwealth Games 2010 Delhi

DELHI 2010 XIX COMMONWEALTH GAMES

Secretary (Sports) Dy. No. 9557 Date 27/9 M/o Youth Affairs & Sports

3050 29/9/10

25th September 2010

Suresh Kalmadi, M.P
Chairman

Sub: Additional allocation of Funds

Dear Smt Sudhashree Khullar,

Please refer to our discussion held on 21st Sep 2010 regarding additional allocation of funds to OC by the Government.

The Organising Committee had earlier taken up for the consideration of the Government for allocation of additional funds of Rs. 720.52 Cr. However, this proposal is pending for consideration of the Ministry of Sports & Youth Affairs.

In the meantime, we had conducted an exercise to assess critical and urgent requirement of additional funds. We had identified certain Functional Areas like Accommodation, Broadcasting, Catering, Office Administration, Technology, Ticketing, Venue development and Coordination which immediately require more funds.

A list showing the detailed budget allotted, expenditure made as on 22.9.2010 and likely committed expenditure of Rs. 226.86 Cr in respect of the above mentioned Functional Areas is enclosed for better appreciation of the proposal and urgency of funds. It is requested that the amount of Rs. 144.00 Cr, withheld out of the sanctioned budget of Rs. 1620.00 Cr of OC and readily available with the Government, may be released to tide over the immediate financial requirements for the smooth conduct of Games pending the sanction of the proposal. The balance amount of Rs. 82.86 Cr could be released subsequently to discharge the liabilities on account of Rent due to NDMC/Utilities.

I shall be grateful for urgent action in the matter.

Regards

Yours sincerely

(Suresh Kalmadi)

PM(VJ)

To,

842373/FS/10 PRIORITY CWG MATTER
6/9

सिन्धुश्री खुल्लर
Sindhushree Khullar
सचिव
Secretary
Tel. : 23388623
Telefax : 23388758
E-mail : secy-sports@nic.in

भारत सरकार
युवा कार्यक्रम एवं खेल मंत्रालय
खेल विभाग
शास्त्री भवन, नई दिल्ली–110 115
Government of India
Ministry of Youth Affairs & Sports
Department of Sports
Shastri Bhawan, New Delhi-110 115

D.O. No.F.70-42/2009-CWG-I/
Dated : 3rd Sept.. 2010

Dear Shri Chawla

You are aware that a budget of Rs.1620 crores was approved by the Cabinet to the Organizing Committee (OC). Commonwealth Games for the Conduct of the Games. These funds are being provided to the OC as a loan to be repaid from the revenue generation from the Commonwealth Games.

02. In the approved budget of Rs.1620 crores. there is a provision of Rs.106.58 crores for Ceremonies. The OC had presented before Group of Ministers under the Chairmanship of Minister for Urban Development (Dr. Jaipal Reddy) that the scope and content including the innovative features for the Opening and Closing Ceremonies have resulted in an escalation in the cost of the Ceremonies. In the 9th Meeting of the GoM held on 9th December, 2009 it was decided that expenditure on the Ceremonies should be kept at Rs.200 crores. In the 11th Meeting of the GoM held on 29th December, 2010 on the request of the Chairman. Organizing Committee the cost estimates were enhanced from Rs.200 crores to Rs 250 crores. Further. in 22nd Meeting of the GoM held on 2nd June, 2010, Chairman. OC informed that the outer limit of expenditure for Ceremonies may be restricted to Rs.300 crores as stipulated by the Finance Minister. Accordingly, the GoM agreed with this escalation and advised OC to limit their budget to contain their expenditure for Ceremonies within the stipulated limit of Rs.300 crores. Minutes of the GoM are annexed.

03. The stipulation by the Finance Minister of restricting the budget of Ceremonies to Rs.300 crores was followed by your letter D.O. No.40(7)/PG-II/09 dated 12.06.2010 in which it is stated that increase in Cost Estimates from existing provision of Rs.106 crores to a maximum of Rs.300 crores has been agreed to. Now, that the Ceremonies component of the budget has gone up from Rs.106.58 crores to Rs.300 crores the additional amount of Rs.193.42 crores would have to be provided in addition to the Rs.1620 crores of the budget of the OC.

04. The Prime Minister had convened a high level Meeting on 14th August, 2010 to review the preparations for Commonwealth Games. In this meeting, the Group of Ministers headed by Minister, Urban Development was directed to meet immediately, and, frequently, thereafter. The Group of Ministers was also empowered to take all decisions necessary for the smooth Conduct of the Games. It was also decided that the Group of Ministers would refer any matter that may require further consideration to the Finance Minister for a final decision. A copy of the Press Release issued by the Prime Minister's Office is also annexed.

05. In the light of above, we may be advised whether this Ministry may seek the approval of the Group of Ministers for the final approval for enhancing the loan budget of the Organizing Committee from Rs.1620 crores to Rs.1813.42 crores, so that this additional amount which has already been provisioned in the Supplementary Budget of this Ministry can be released to the OC. The matter may then be placed before the Cabinet for information.

: 2 :

06. The other matter on which I seek the comments of the Ministry of Finance is related to re-appropriation of funds within the existing approved budget of OC of Rs.1620 crores from the Head "Revenue Generation Functional Areas" to "Other Functional Areas".

07. The Cabinet while approving the budget of OC of Rs.1620 crores for Conduct of the Games in November, 2009, had stipulated as below:

> **"Flexibility of 25% of re-appropriation between various heads of expenditure of the OC should be retained at that level only. Re-appropriation beyond 25% would require the approval of MYA&S. However, this appropriation would not be permissible on the items of expenditure relating to generation of revenue from sponsorship/broadcasting rights etc."**

08. The OC has now informed that they urgently require funds for Functional Areas that are either under provided, or, have had some cost over runs, or, are not provided at all as they had not been envisaged earlier. They have further informed that none of their Functional Areas, except Revenue Generation Functional Areas, is likely to have savings. Hence, they have requested that Rs.144 crores out of total budget of Rs.218 crores of this Functional Area be re-appropriated for other activities/Functional Areas within the approved overall ceiling of Rs.1620 crores with our approval.

09. In this context, it is noteworthy that the OC has terminated the contract with M/s. Sports Marketing and Management Pvt. Ltd. (SMAM), the firm which had been awarded the contract for mobilizing revenue from sponsorship etc. for the OC. The bulk of the expenditure to be incurred from the "Revenue Generation" was on account of payments to be made to this firm for obtaining sponsorship revenues by marketing the CWG-2010 in India and abroad.

10. We have not been able to approve re-appropriation from the above-mentioned Head to other Functional Areas on account of the decision of the Cabinet. Now, the Games are barely a month away and the OC now has to conclude most of his activities urgently and needs funds. In the light of the above, since the request involves a decision taken at the level of the Cabinet, we may be permitted to allow the OC's request with the approval of the GoM constituted to take all decisions related to the CWG-2010 and inform the Cabinet.

With regards

Yours sincerely

(Sindhushree Khullar)

Shri Ashok Chawla
Finance Secretary
North Block
New Delhi

PRIORITY
CWG MATTER

F.No. 40(7)/PF.II/2009 Vol.II
Government of India
Ministry of Finance
Department of Expenditure
Plan Finance II Division
....

New Delhi, the 14th September, 2010

Office Memorandum

SUBJECT: Budget of Organizing Committee, Commonwealth Games 2010 (OC) Delhi for the conduct of the Games.

Ministry of Youth Affairs and Sports may refer to their DO No. 70-42/2009-CWG.1 dated 3rd September, 2010 wherein MYAS had made two proposals on the captioned subject *viz.*

(i) Enhancing the loan budget of the Organizing Committee from ₹1620 crore to ₹1813.42 crore towards the increased expenditure for the Ceremonies from ₹ 106.58 crore to ₹300 crore; and

(ii) Re-appropriation of funds within the existing approved budget of OC of ₹1620 crore from the Head "Revenue Generation Functional areas" to "Other Functional Areas"

In this regard, the undersigned is directed to state that:

(i) This Ministry agree to enhancing the loan budget of the Organizing Committee from ₹1620 crore to ₹1813.42 crore for the Ceremonies though MYAS should justify the same in the note for GoM/Cabinet and see if some savings are possible.

(ii) However, the re-appropriation of funds within the existing approved budget of OC of ₹1620 crore from the Head "Revenue Generation Functional areas" to "Other Functional Areas" is not acceptable since the said amount and head was meant for revenue generation. It cannot be spent on other activities which would tantamount to an indirect increase in the Organizing Committee's approved budget.

3. This issues with the approval of Finance Minister.

(Piyush Srivastava)
Director(PF.II)
Tel.No. 23092668

Issued
Suman
14/9/2010

Department of Sports,
(Smt. Sindhushree Khullar, Secretary)
Ministry of Youth Affairs and Sports
Shastri Bhawan, New Delhi.

डॉ० एम०एस० गिल
Dr. M.S. GILL

युवा कार्यक्रम एवं खेल मंत्री
भारत सरकार
नई दिल्ली-110 115
MINISTER FOR YOUTH AFFAIRS & SPORTS
GOVERNMENT OF INDIA
NEW DELHI-110 115

30th September, 2010

Dear Shri Pranab ji,

The Government had sanctioned a loan of Rs. 1620 crore to the Organising Committee for the conduct of games. Out of this, Rs. 1476 crore has already been released to the OC. Remaining Rs. 144 crore is withheld as it pertains to revenue generating activities and as per Government decision could not be re-appropriated to other non-revenue generating heads. The Chairman, OC had earlier asked for additional amount of Rs. 720.52 crore for CWG. We were examining the proposal. In the meantime, Chairman OC has sent another letter giving details of additional demand of Rs. 226.96 crore for urgent release for the smooth conduct of games (copy enclosed).

Since, provision of requisite amount through Supplementary Demand would take considerable time, I would be grateful if you could approve the release of Rs. 144 crore, available in the budget to OC for its immediate and urgent requirements. Remaining amount would be considered through Supplementary.

With regards,

Yours sincerely,

(M.S. Gill)

Shri Pranab Mukherjee
Hon'ble Minister of Finance
Government of India
North Block
New Delhi

30-09 2010 23:14 FAX 001

डॉ० एम०एस० गिल
Dr. M.S. GILL

युवा कार्यक्रम एवं खेल मंत्री
भारत सरकार
नई दिल्ली-110 115
MINISTER FOR YOUTH AFFAIRS & SPORTS
GOVERNMENT OF INDIA
NEW DELHI-110 115

30th September, 2010

Dear Shri Pranab ji,

The Government had sanctioned a loan of Rs. 1620 crore to the Organising Committee for the conduct of games. Out of this, Rs. 1476 crore has already been released to the OC. Remaining Rs. 144 crore is withheld as it pertains to revenue generating activities and as per Government decision could not be re-appropriated to other non-revenue generating heads. The Chairman, OC had earlier asked for additional amount of Rs. 720.52 crore for CWG. We were examining the proposal. In the meantime, Chairman OC has sent another letter giving details of additional demand of Rs. 226.96 crore for urgent release for the smooth conduct of games (copy enclosed).

Since, provision of requisite amount through Supplementary Demand would take considerable time, I would be grateful if you could approve the release of Rs. 144 crore, available in the budget to OC for its immediate and urgent requirements. Remaining amount would be considered through Supplementary.

With regards,

Yours sincerely,

(M.S. Gill)

Shri Pranab Mukherjee
Hon'ble Minister of Finance
Government of India
North Block
New Delhi

01-10-2010 00:06 FAX ☒001

23093289 1296

डॉ० एम०एस० गिल
Dr. M.S. GILL

युवा कार्यक्रम एवं खेल मंत्री
भारत सरकार
नई दिल्ली-110 115
MINISTER FOR YOUTH AFFAIRS & SPORTS
GOVERNMENT OF INDIA
NEW DELHI-110 115

30th September, 2010

Dear Shri Pranab ji,

The Government had sanctioned a loan of Rs. 1620 crore to the Organising Committee for the conduct of games. Out of this, Rs. 1476 crore has already been released to the OC. Remaining Rs. 144 crore is withheld as it pertains to revenue generating activities and as per Government decision could not be re-appropriated to other non-revenue generating heads. The Chairman, OC had earlier asked for additional amount of Rs. 720.52 crore for CWG. We were examining the proposal. In the meantime, Chairman OC has sent another letter giving details of additional demand of Rs. 226.96 crore for urgent release for the smooth conduct of games (copy enclosed).

Since, provision of requisite amount through Supplementary Demand would take considerable time, I would be grateful if you could approve the release of Rs. 144 crore, available in the budget to OC for its immediate and urgent requirements. Remaining amount would be considered through Supplementary.

With regards,

Yours sincerely,

(M.S. Gill)

Shri Pranab Mukherjee
Hon'ble Minister of Finance
Government of India
North Block
New Delhi

received on 6/10/10

L-856771/JS(PF-II)/10
1/10/10

D.O. No. 40(7)/PF-II/09

OUT Tel

अशोक चावला
ASHOK CHAWLA

वित्त सचिव
वित्त मंत्रालय
भारत सरकार
नॉर्थ ब्लाक, नई दिल्ली-110001
FINANCE SECRETARY
MINISTRY OF FINANCE
GOVERNMENT OF INDIA
NORTH BLOCK, NEW DELHI-110001
Tel 23092611 Fax 23094075

June 12, 2010

Dear Sindhushree,

Please refer to your DO No. 150/Secy(SP)/10 dated 8th June, 2010 seeking clearance to permit the Organizing Committee to go ahead RFPs in anticipation of approval the additional amount in respect of 'Ceremonies'.

2. The matter has been considered in the context of increased cost estimates projected by the Organizing Committee in meetings of the Committee of Secretaries as well as the Group of Ministers. It is been categorically stated that no further cost increase can be supported. Only in the case of "Ceremonies" (both Opening and Closing ceremonies taken together) an increase in the cost estimate from the existing provision of Rs.106 crore to a maximum of Rs.300 crore has been agreed to. Ministry of Sports may permit the OC to go ahead with processing RFPs and make payments in anticipation of this approval only for this.

3. The Ministry of Sports may, as early as possible, move for due sanction of the enhanced amount. In doing so it may examine the possibility of effecting savings in other heads. **The increase, however, should not exceed Rs. 194 crore.** While moving for approval the Ministry should also bring on board clear reasons for cost over-run and fix responsibility for decisions not taken in time, which has led to cost over-runs.

Regards,

Yours sincerely,

Ashok Chawla

(Ashok Chawla)

Smt. Sindhushree Khullar
Secretary (Sports)
Ministry of Youth Affairs & Sports
Department of Sports
Room No. 2, C-Wing, Shastri Bhawan
New Delhi – 110 115

Issued
Suman
14/6

Rahul Bhatnagar
Joint Secretary

भारत सरकार
युवा कार्यक्रम एवं खेल मंत्रालय
खेल विभाग
शास्त्री भवन, नई दिल्ली-110 115
GOVERNMENT OF INDIA
MINISTRY OF YOUTH AFFAIRS & SPORTS
DEPARTMENT OF SPORTS
SHASTRI BHAWAN, NEW DELHI-110 115

DO No. 1/5/JS(ISD)/2010

Dated the 13th May, 2010

Dear

As you are aware, the Government has approved a budget of Rs. 1620 crores to the Organizing Committee (OC) as a loan for the Conduct of the Games. Out of this approved budget, there is a component of Rs. 106 crores for the Ceremonies which includes the Opening and Closing Ceremonies also. The Concept, Theme and Content related to the Opening and Closing Ceremonies have been discussed in several meetings of the Group of Ministers (GoM) wherein the OC has projected enhanced budgetary requirements for these ceremonies. Keeping in view the various additional features which are now proposed to be included in the Opening and Closing Ceremonies, in the 10th Meeting of the Group of Ministers held on 20th December, 2009, the Group of Ministers accepted the suggestion of the Chairman, OC to enhance the budget of the Ceremonies limiting it to Rs. 250 crores.

In the light of the above, the cost of the Ceremonies may be kept within the limit of Rs. 250 crores and the funds for this purpose may be made available through re-appropriation within the overall budget of the OC for Conduct of the Games and if further any approval of the Government is required in respect of the above re-appropriation, the same may be sought with the details of expenditure on each item of the Ceremonies.

You may kindly take action accordingly.

With regards.

Yours faithfully
Sd/-
(Rahul Bhatnagar)

Shri Jarnail Singh,
CEO, OC
City Centre – Tower II, Opposite Jantar Mantar,
Jai Singh Road,
New Delhi.

Copy to:
(i) Additional Secretary (Expenditure), room no. 143, North Block, New Delhi. Fax: 23092919
(ii) Special DG (Finance), Organizing Committee, NDCC Building, Jai Singh Road, New Delhi.

(Rahul Bhatnagar)

AS(E) - on Leave
ISHPA(I) [illegible] 3/6
[illegible] 4.6 DD/[illegible]

Organising Committee Commonwealth Games 2010 Delhi

DELHI 2010
XIX COMMONWEALTH GAMES

Dated: 3rd June, 2010

Dear Ms. V. Ramachandran,

As you are aware the Commonwealth Games are scheduled to be held between 3rd – 14th October, 2010 at Delhi.

2. One of the main activities associated with successful conduct of Commonwealth Games Delhi 2010 is the management of the ticketing operations. In this context, I am pleased to inform you that we are planning to launch the sale of tickets to public on 4th June, 2010, whereby the tickets for all the 17 sports disciplines of the Commonwealth Games Delhi 2010 would be made available through internet, a dedicated call centre and a few retail outlets. The ticket sales operations are to be carried out by a consortium of firms led by M/s Indian Railways Catering and Tourism Corporation Ltd. (IRCTC), a Public Sector unit under Ministry of Railways. Our official bankers – the Central Bank of India - will also sell tickets from selected branches across the country.

3. It would be my pleasure if you could accept our invitation to grace the occasion of the launch of sale of tickets on 4th June, 2010 at 1000 hrs. The venue for the launch ceremony would be Organising Committee Headquarters, NDCC Towers–II, Opp. Jantar Mantar, Jai Singh Road, New Delhi – 110 001.

With regards,

L-79/049/2010-AS(E)
3/6/2010

Dr. Lalit K. Bhanot

Mrs. V. Ramachandran
Additional Secretary
Ministry of Finance
Govt. of India
North Block,
New Delhi

M. Keep in con OC file
[illegible] 7.6.10

New Delhi City Centre - Tower II, Opposite Jantar Mantar, Jai Singh Road, New Delhi 110001. INDIA
T: +91 11 24500400 F: +91 11 24500451 E: info@cwgdelhi2010.org W: www.cwgdelhi2010.org

सिन्धुश्री खुल्लर
Sindhushree Khullar
सचिव
Secretary
Tel. : 23388623
Telefax : 23388758
E-mail : secy-sports@nic.in

भारत सरकार
युवा कार्यक्रम एवं खेल मंत्रालय
खेल विभाग
शास्त्री भवन, नई दिल्ली—110 115
Government of India
Ministry of Youth Affairs & Sports
Department of Sports
Shastri Bhawan, New Delhi-110 115

D.O. Dy. No.150/Secy.(SP)/10
Dated : June 8th, 2010

Please find enclosed DO No.CEO/E-1/DO-98/2010 dated 7th June, 2010 from Chief Executive Officer, Organizing Committee, Commonwealth Games Delhi 2010, that is self-explanatory.

02. Following the Group of Ministers (GoM) meeting on 2nd June, 2010, wherein it was decided that the approved budget under the Ceremonies Functional Area (FA) should be Rs.300 crores, and, to that extent the allocation of Rs.1620 crores approved for the OC for conduct of the Games should be enhanced. In the CoS meeting held on 4th June, 2010, Ms. Meena Aggarwal, Joint Secretary (Expenditure) stated that it may be possible to consider providing a letter of comfort to permit the OC to go ahead with processing RFPs and make payments in anticipation of the approval of the additional amount in respect of Ceremonies FA.

03. The timelines available for the rehearsals and preparations are extremely tight. It is essential, therefore, to enable the OC to make commitments and advances, if so required, subject to the overall cap of Rs.300 crores for Ceremonies. Therefore, I request that the request be considered favourably.

04. I shall appreciate an early response in this matter.

Yours sincerely,
Sd./-
(Sindhushree Khullar)

Encl. : as above

Shri Ashok Chawla,
Finance Secretary,
Ministry of Finance,
North Block,
New Delhi.

Copy to :

1. Ms. Meena Aggarwal, Jt. Secretary (Exp.), Ministry of Finance, North Block, New Delhi.
2. JS & FA, Ministry of Youth Affairs & Sports, Shastri Bhawan, New Delhi.
3. Jt. Secretary (ISD/CWG).

(Sindhushree Khullar)
08.06.2010

Organising Committee Commonwealth Games 2010 Delhi

DELHI 2010 XIX COMMONWEALTH GAMES

JARNAIL SINGH
Chief Executive Officer

Dated the 7th June, 2010
D.O. No.: CEO/E-1/DO-98/2010

Dear Smt Sindhushree Khullar,

You are aware that the Group of Ministers (GoM) for Commonwealth Games 2010 in its meeting on 2nd June, 2010 had decided that the approved budget for ceremonies should be kept at Rs. 300 crores and we had been approving expenditure commitment under ceremonies only to the extent of Rs. 106 crores.

Since hardly four months are left for the inauguration of games, ceremonies FA has to issue a number of RFPs, finalise them and enter into an agreement with vendors for the execution of works within a short span. In certain cases, ceremonies FA may have to give advances also to the vendors for starting work. Since approved budget is already almost exhausted, it is not possible for Finance & Accounts FA of the Games to agree to proposals over and above Rs. 106 crores. We are already on the job to prepare proposal for additional allocation of Rs. 194 crores for ceremonies on the CNE format. It would take some time to place the proposal before CNE and cabinet thereafter.

In the above situation, I would request you to kindly allow us to make commitment and give advance, if required, to different vendors subject to the the overall cap of Rs. 300 crores for ceremonies. This was discussed in the CoS on 4th June, 2010 and is most essential for smooth conduct of the games.

With regards,

Yours sincerely,

Jarnail Singh

Jarnail Singh

Smt. Sindhushree Khullar
Secretary
Ministry of Youth Affairs and Sports,
Shastri Bhawan
New Delhi-110015

New Delhi City Centre - Tower II, Opposite Jantar Mantar, Jai Singh Road, New Delhi 110001. INDIA
T: +91 11 24500400, 24500574 F: +91 11 24500451 Email : jarnail@nic.in Website : www.cwgdelhi2010.org

19/6
91(PF/II)
Dir PSA
Bajli

Organising Committee Commonwealth Games 2010 Delhi

DELHI 2010™
XIX COMMONWEALTH GAMES

JARNAIL SINGH
Chief Executive Officer

Dated the 8th June, 2010.
D.O.No.: CEO/E-4/DO-18/2010

Dear Smt Sushma Nath,

Smt. Vilasini Ramachandran, Additional Secretary Department of Expenditure, who is a member of the Finance Sub-Committee constituted to consider the proposals exceeding Rs, 6 crore is not able to attend its meeting because of being on leave. 14th (26th & 28th May, 2010), 15th (1st June, 2010) and 16th (07th June, 2010) meetings of the Finance Sub-Committee were held without her presence.

2. Since Finance Sub-Committee has been constituted by the Government to scrutinize the proposals of Organising Committee which involve expenditure exceeding Rs.6 crore, it has a very important role and gives an opportunity to members to go into the details of the proposal at an early stage before they are presented to Executive Board of the Organising Committee. In this situation, you may like to nominate some other senior officer of the Department of Expenditure to be represented in the meeting of the Finance Sub-Committee if Smt. Vilasini Ramachandran is going to be away for a longer period. The meeting of the Finance Sub-Committee is generally held once a week.

With regards,

Yours sincerely,

Jarnail Singh

Jarnail singh

Smt, Sushma Nath,
Secretary,
Department of Expenditure,
Ministry of Finance,
North Block,
New Delhi.

X-7942131SE/10
9/6/10

New Delhi City Centre - Tower II, Opposite Jantar Mantar, Jai Singh Road, New Delhi 110001, INDIA
T: +91 11 24500400, 24500574 F: +91 11 24500451 Email : jarnail@nic.in Website : www.cwgdelhi2010.org

PRIORITY
CONFIDENTIAL

सिन्धुश्री खुल्लर
Sindhushree Khullar
सचिव
Secretary
Tel. : 23388623
Telefax : 23388758
E-mail : secy-sports@nic.in

सत्यमेव जयते

भारत सरकार
युवा कार्यक्रम एवं खेल मंत्रालय
खेल विभाग
शास्त्री भवन, नई दिल्ली–110 115
Government of India
Ministry of Youth Affairs & Sports
Department of Sports
Shastri Bhawan, New Delhi-110 115

D.O. Dy. No.150/Secy.(SP)/10
Dated : June 8th, 2010

Dear Sushma,

As you are aware, the Commonwealth Games – D2010 are now less than 120 days away. The pace of work is now at full speed to make up for all the past delays. Accordingly, the Finance Committee of the Organizing Committee (OCFC) and the Standing Finance Committee (FSC) chaired by Secretary (UD) are meeting frequently, and, at short notice to consider various proposals. The presence of JS&FA (Shri Sanjeev Mittal) is essential in both these Committees. It is not out of place to mention that both the Committees have been constituted with the approval of the Cabinet.

02. Shri Sanjeev Mittal's multifarious duties take him away on tour outside headquarters frequently. It is understood that, since his assignment in this Ministry is in addition to his other charges, his availability to this Ministry is limited by his other onerous duties in his other charges. However, we suggest that until the end of October, 2010, he may be instructed to remain in headquarters, and, moreover, be available to the maximum extent possible for advice on the matters relating to Commonwealth Games to this Ministry. This request is being made in view of the fact that he has been given extension of Central tenure on account of the requirements of the CWG-D2010 with the explicit approval of the Minister for Youth Affairs and Sports (Dr. M.S. Gill).

03. Minister of Youth Affairs and Sports (Dr. M.S. Gill) has discussed this matter and endorses the above.

With warm regards

Yours sincerely.

L-794148/SE/10
9.6.10

(Sindhushree Khullar)

Ms. Sushma Nath,
Secretary (Expenditure),
Ministry of Finance,
North Block, New Delhi.

231

SURESH KALMADI
Member of Parliament, India
Chairman, Organising Committee
Commonwealth Games 2010 Delhi

38
13/1/10

DELHI 2010
XIX COMMONWEALTH GAMES

12th January 2010

Dear Smt Sindushree Khullar ji

Sub: Procedure of repayment of loan released by Govt. of India to OC.

Ref: MoYAS D.O. Letter No. F.70-47/2005-CG (Vol. IV) dated 14.12.09.

Initially, Government was giving funds required for the conduct of the Commonwealth Games Delhi 2010 in the form of an unsecured loan bearing interest of 10% in the form of Ad-hoc grants in aid but after August 2007 the same has been converted into an unsecured loan with an interest of 10%. Till this date the release of advances were made without mentioning any schedule for repayment of the loan. From 7th August 2007 all the letters conveying the sanction of release of funds to OC the following condition is being incorporated.

"The moratorium towards repayment will be upto the end of CW Games (15th October 2010) and repayment of interest along with principal amount will commence from 15th October 2010 and be completed by 31st March 2011".

On 11th October 2007, the Finance Minister has advised that interest on the loan would be payable only from the surplus accruing to OC from the conduct of the Games. Government of India had taken a decision that the repayment schedule, as reproduced below, shall be applicable to the unsecured loan being given to the Organising Committee.

As a part of the efforts taken by OC for raising revenue through selling telecasting rights, sponsorship etc., several contracts with foreign countries have been finalized and several more are in the process of finalization. Arising out of these agreements, OC has already received about Rs. 100 Cr. from various countries / parties as advance receipt in accordance with terms of agreements entered into. This entire revenue receipt has been kept in a separate account with our current banker Andhra Bank.

Now, vide letter No. F.70-47/2005-CG (Vol. IV) dated 14.12.09 MoYAS have amended the provisions relating to the repayment of the loan by OC back to the government, which states that the repayment is required to start now, as OC has started to receive revenue. This stand appears to stem from the original decision of the cabinet approved on 20.03.2007 as follows.

"The repayment of the loan and interest would commence only after the commencement of the revenue generated by the OC".

City Centre-II, (NDCC Towers), Opp. Jantar Mantar, Jai Singh Road, New Delhi - 110001, India
Tel.: +91 11 23438000 Fax: +91 11 23438004 Email: secy.chairman@cwgdelhi2010.org Website: www.cwgdelhi2010.org

However, in as much as this decision has been subsequently revised to the repayment schedule between 15th October 2010 to 31st March 2011, this stand is not tenable. A notable omission in the letter dated 14.12.2009 is that it does not connect the letter issued on 11th October 2007 by the Finance Minister at all.

The change in the original terms of repayment will have the following implication.

The receipts, being only in the form of advance payments in accordance with the terms of agreement, may have to be returned back to the remitters in the event of any failure to provide TV feed or cancellation in part or full of any event(s). Especially, when Government had not agreed to the proposal to take insurance cover against event cancellation, there is a binding obligation on OC to return these advance payments at short notice.

Even though MoYAS were requested not to change the scheme for repayment of loan, which had been approved by Govt. of India after discussing the issue in the GOM, the decision made now on this issue needs a review. Especially, when the revenue receipts received so far, are only in the nature of advance payments made by various countries on account of the sale of telecasting rights and as such are liable to be returned at short notice in the event of any unfortunate failure to fulfill the terms of such agreements.

I would therefore, request you, kindiy to examine this issue de novo and issue suitable directives so that the existing arrangement can continue without any hitch.

Regards

Suresh Kalmadi

To

Smt. Sindhushree Khullar
Secretary (Sports)
Ministry of Youth Affairs & Sports,
Department of Youth Affairs,
Shastri Bhawan,
New Delhi – 110001.

F.No.70-47/2005-CWG-IV

\- 35 -

Reference: Note on pre-page

This case was discussed with JS&FA(YA&S) on 5.1.2010.

This is regarding the terms and conditions for repayment of unsecured loan by the Organizing Committee(OC) to the Government of India(GOI) sanctioned for conducting of the Commonwealth Games 2010.

2. The Cabinet at its meeting held on 20.3.2007 had approved an initial budget of Rs.767±15% crore in favour of OC for conducting the Commonwealth Games 2010. Later on, the Cabinet at its meeting held on 5.11.2009 had approved a revised budget of Rs.1620 crore. Further, recently, the Expenditure Finance Committee(EFC) at its meeting held on 5.1.2010, has recommended an amount of Rs.687.06 crore to be provided to the OC as loan for the purpose of 'overlays' expenditure. Thus, the total loan to the OC, as on date would be worked out to **Rs.2307.06 crore.**

3. The terms and conditions for repayment of loan were worked out when the initial budget was approved in March, 2007. The details in this regard have been mentioned vide the Finance Division's note on pages 25-26/N. **It may be stated that as per the approval of the Cabinet in March, 2007, the repayment of loan and interest would commence only after the commencement of the revenue generation by the OC.** It is also pertinent to mention here that the OC has already started generating the revenues from various channels.

4. Out of Rs.1620.00 crore, the GOI has released an amount of Rs.591.56 crore till 1.1.2010. The year-wise releases are as follows:-

Year	Rs. in crore
2004-05	10.88
2005-06	33.05
2006-07	83.58
2007-08	95.21
2008-09	164.74
2009-10	201.10
Total	591.56

OC has an unspent balance of Rs.97.70 crore with them as on 1.1.2010. They have accrued an interest of Rs.4.65 crore on the releases made by GOI from time to time. Further, as stated above, OC has generated the revenues to the tune of Rs.113.47 crore. A statement showing the Fund Position and details of budget and expenditure under various heads as on 1.1.2010, are placed on file at **Flag-XX and YY** for kind perusal.

5. Secretary(Sports) has convened a meeting on 11.12.2009 with the officers of IS Division and Finance Division and representatives of OC. The issue was also discussed in the meeting of the Finance Sub-Committee held in the last week of December, 2009. It was decided to refer the matter to the Ministry of Finance to re-set the terms and conditions of repayment of loan by the OC to the GOI in view of the revision of loan amount in higher

-36-

from pre-page

scale (Minutes are not available on file). The Department of Sports (IS Division) with the approval of Secretary(Sports) has now referred the file to the Finance Division for onward submission to MOF.

6. In view of the position stated above, the views of the Finance Division in the matter are as follows:-

i) Conversion of past releases into loan was agreed to on the assumption that the revenues would be generated by OC during the Games period. However, the revenues were generated even before the start of the Games and as on date OC has accrued the revenues to the tune of Rs.113.50 crore. The amount has been put into fixed deposits at an annnual interest rate varying 7 to 7.5% in respect of past deposits and 11% in respect of recent deposits. Whereas, OC has to pay an annual interest @ 10% to the GOI. It would, therefore be prudent to start repaying the GOI as this will relieve their burden. By not repaying/postponing, OC has been incurring losses. Further, the possibility of diversion of revenues thus generated for utilization against some of the budget heads over and above the sanctioned provisions cannot be ruled out.

D.S.(F) Dy No. 17 Date 12-1-2010

ii) The repayments thus made would first be accounted against the outstanding principal amount and once the principal amount is cleared, the repayment of interest shall commence.

iii) 10% normal rate of interest will be applicable from the date of conversion of earlier amount into loan, and from the date of sanction of further releases as loan, as the case may be.

iv) Repayment of Principal and interest shall be started immediately and completed not later than 31.3.2011.

Office of JS&FA Diary No. 23 Received on 12/1/10

7. With the above propositions and subject to the approval of JS&FA (YA&S), the file may be referred to the MOF for their consideration/concurrence in the matter please.

D. C. S. Rao
(D.C.S.Rao)
Deputy Secretary(Finance)
11.1.2010

~~JS&FA(YA&S)~~

12/1/2010

15/1 SO(D)

DS(B) 12/1

Ministry of Finance (D/o Economic Affairs Budget Division)
MYA&S ID Note Dy No.16357/09-10 F(Dd) 13/1/10

मानव संसाधन विकास मंत्री
भारत
नई दिल्ली-११० ००१
MINISTER OF
HUMAN RESOURCE DEVELOPMENT
INDIA
NEW DELHI-110 001

अर्जुन सिंह
ARJUN SINGH

D. No. 9/3/05 /M.H.R.D./V.I.P./2005

Dy. No. 1037/VIP/FM/05
14 MAR 2005

March, 2005

Dear Shri Chidambaram,

This is with reference to our discussion regarding budget proposal relating to organization of Commonwealth Games-2010 as submitted by the Chairman, Organizing Committee.

You are aware about the decision taken by the Group of Ministers for co-ordinating the work relating to the organization of the Commonwealth Games-2010 in its meeting held on 29th January, 2005 regarding setting up of a Three Member Sub-committee of the GOM under your Chairmanship to deal with all financial matters; this decision of the GOM was subsequently approved by Hon'ble Prime Minister.

I am enclosing a copy of the budget proposal 2005-06 amounting to [illegible] regarding organization of the Commonwealth Games-2010 as submitted to me by the Chairman, Organizing Committee.

I would like to request you to take further appropriate action.

With regards,

Yours sincerely,

(ARJUN SINGH)

Shri P. Chidambaram
Finance Minister
Government of India
New Delhi

Organising Committee
Commonwealth Games 2010 Delhi

Suresh Kalmadi *M.P.*
Chairman, Organising Committee
Commonwealth Games 2010 Delhi
&
President, Indian Olympic Association
CG 2010/OG

HRM OFFICE
RECEIVED
16 FEB 2005
NEW DELHI

January 31, 2005

Dear Mr Arjun Singhji

Sub: Budget proposal 2005-2006, Organizing Committee
2010 Commonwealth Games

Enclosed please find the Budget for 2005-2006 for the Organizing Committee of the Commonwealth Games 2010.

As would be seen from the details, a sum of Rs. 22 Crores (a sum of Rs. 10.86 Crores already paid by the Ministry of Sports) is towards the License fee of Commonwealth Games Federation and Rs. 47.86 Crores towards the expenses to be incurred by the Organizing Committee.

It is requested that the budget may kindly be approved.

Regards

Yours sincerely,

(Suresh Kalmadi), M.P.

Shri Arjun Singh
Hon'ble Minister for Human Resource & Development,
Government of India,
Shastri Bhawan,
New Delhi.

Encl : As above

Copies to be sent to Minister of Youth Affairs and Sports & FM

Gate No. 23, Jawaharlal Nehru Stadium, Lodhi Road, New Delhi-110003. India.
Tel.: +91-11-24366950, 51, 52. Fax : +91-11-24365395
e-mail : ioa@nde.vsnl.net.in website : www.cwgdelhi2010.com

BUDGET PROPOSAL 2005-2006
ORGANIZING COMMITTEE
2010 COMMONWEALTH GAMES

		Rs. in Crores
1.	Towards License Fee, already paid to Commonwealth Games Federation by Ministry of Youth Affairs and Sport.	10.86
2.	Towards second installment of License fee to be paid to CGF by January 1, 2006.	12
3.	Establishment costs for Organizing Committee office	5
4.	Office equipment including computers, furniture, Telephone , Transport, networking of communication links etc.	2
5.	Travel, Hotel and other expenses for the Key group of officials who would visit Melbourne to study the conduct of Commonwealth Games 2006 (the Key Group would stay at Melbourne for a month at the least) and other related travel.	5
6.	Presentation to the Executive Board and General Assembly of CGF at Melbourne from April 3 to 11, 2005 and Executive Board Meeting in October 2005.	3
7.	Countrywide awareness campaign, publicity and publications.	5
8.	Cultural Troupe & Programmes etc. at the Closing Ceremony of the Commonwealth Games at Melbourne during the handing over of CGF Games flag to India in March 2006 and Presentation to the General Assembly of CGF.	5
9.	Volunteer Identification and Training Programme	2
10.	Hosting and conduct of annual International sporting event leading to Commonwealth Games-Projecting India as a sporting destination	5
11.	Queens Baton Relay passing through Delhi, Mumbai, Kolkata and Bangalore in Sept. 2005.	5
12.	Miscellaneous expenses.	10
	Total	**69.86 Crores**

Secret

भारत सरकार
युवा कार्यक्रम एवं खेल मंत्रालय
नई दिल्ली-110 001
GOVERNMENT OF INDIA
MINISTRY OF YOUTH AFFAIRS & SPORTS
NEW DELHI-110 001

S. KRISHANAN
JOINT SECRETARY
TELEFAX 23384152

No.F.70-28/2004-SP-II

Dated : 28th March, 2005

Dear Shri Gupta

Apropos to our telephonic discussions regarding minutes of the meeting of the Group of Ministers relating to Coordinating the work relating to the organization of the Commonwealth Games, 2010.

2. Please find enclosed herewith a copy No.18 of the minutes of the 3rd meeting of the GOM held on 29th January, 2005 along with the agenda notes of the meeting. A copy of these documents was earlier sent to PS to Finance Minister.

With regards

Yours sincerely,

(S. Krishnan)

Encl : As above

Shri K.M. Gupta,
Director (Plan Finance-II),
Ministry of Finance,
North Block,
New Delhi.

SECRET

No.F.70-28/2004-SP-II
Government of India
Ministry of Youth Affairs and Sports

Copy No. (18)
Shastri Bhavan, New Delhi

Dated: 7th February, 2005

Sub: Decisions taken during the 3rd Meeting of the Core Group of Ministers (GOM) for Coordinating the work relating to the organization of the Commonwealth Games, 2010.

The undersigned is directed to refer the discussions held on 29th January, 2005 at 9.00 PM during 3rd meeting of the Group of Ministers for coordinating the work relating to the organization of the Commonwealth Games 2010. A copy of the note indicating the decisions taken in the above meeting approved by the Chairman of GOM (Human Resource Development Minister) is enclosed for kind information and necessary action.

Sd/-
(S. Krishnan)
Joint Secretary (Sports)
Telefax 23384152

1. Minister of Human Resource Development, Shastri Bhavan, New Delhi.
2. Minister of Parliamentary Affairs and Minister of Urban Development, Nirman Bhavan, New Delhi.
3. Minister of Information and Broadcasting and Minister of Culture, Shastri Bhavan, New Delhi.
4. Minister of Finance, North Block, New Delhi.
5. Minister of External Affairs, South Block, New Delhi
6. Minister of State (Independent Charge) of the Ministry of Non-Resident Indians Affairs, South Block, New Delhi.
7. Minister of State (Independent Charge) of the Ministry Tourism, Transport Bhavan, New Delhi
8. Lt. Governor, Delhi, Raj Niwas, Delhi.
9. Chief Minister, Delhi, Secretariat, Delhi
10. Cabinet Secretary, Cabinet Secretariat, Rashtrapati Bhavan, New Delhi.
11. PS to Minister for Youth Affairs and Sports

Copy to:-

1. Cabinet Secretariat (Shri K.L. Sharma, Deputy Secretary) Cabinet Secretariat, New Delhi for information please.

Sd/-
(S. Krishnan)
Joint Secretary (Sports)
Telefax 23384152

COMMONWEALTH GAMES 2010 : DECISIONS OF THE GROUP OF MINISTERS (GOM)

The Group of Ministers constituted for overseeing the organization and conduct of Commonwealth Games of 2010 met on 29th January 2005 at Shastri Bhavan, New Delhi and took the following decisions:

(a) An Apex Committee headed by the Minister of Sports, Shri Sunil Dutt shall be constituted which will have the over-riding power and responsibility for overseeing and coordinating the Commonwealth Games. The Minutes of all the other Committees related to the conduct of Commonwealth Games 2010 shall be submitted to the Apex Committee periodically for its information. The Chairman of the Apex Committee can also call for such information, which he deems fit and can give such guidance that may be required. The Chairman of the Apex Committee may be kept informed by all the other Committees whenever any major decision is taken.

(b) The organizing Committee shall be headed by the President of the Indian Olympic Association, Shri Suresh Kalmadi and this Committee will conduct the Commonwealth Games

2010. The Organizing Committee will deal with the Government of India through the Ministry of Youth Affairs and Sports and with the Delhi Government. The Executive Board of the Organising Committee will have 15 Members including the Chairman and the Vice Chairman. The members of the Committee will be appointed by the Chairman in consultation with GOM.

(c) A three-member Sub-committee of the GOM, headed by Finance Minister, Shri P. Chidambaram will supervise and deal with all financial matters.

(d) The Lt. Governor of Delhi will have the overall responsibility regarding the games with specific reference to security, law & order and matters coming under DDA.

(e) There will a Sub-Committee headed by CM of Delhi which will look after all other issues that come under the jurisdiction of the Govt. of NCT of Delhi, as per the Constitution.

(f) A Committee of Secretaries (COS) headed by the Cabinet Secretary will be responsible for the implementation of the decisions of the GOM regarding the Commonwealth games. The Sports Department through its Secretary will service this Committee.

(g) All the arrangements worked out above shall apply only to the Commonwealth Games-2010.

Ps. to HRM

MOST IMMEDIATE

Government of National Capital Territory of Delhi

Department for the Welfare of SC/ST/OBC/Minorities

B-Block, 2nd Floor, Vikas Bhawan, I.P. Estate, New Delhi

Website: scst welfare.delhigovt.nic.in Tele Fax No. 23379513

F.No.5(5)/2010-11/DSCST/SCP/ 5397 **Dated the** 6th **August, 2010**

To

The Director (PF-II),
Ministry of Finance,
Department of Expenditure,
(Plan Finance II Division),
New Delhi.

Sub: **Notice of Short Duration Discussion under Rule 193.**

Sir,

With reference to your Office Memorandum No.40(7)/PF-II/2009(Part) dated 05.08.2010 on the subject noted above. I am enclosing herewith the note on utilization of funds under Scheduled Caste Sub Plan (SCSP) by Government of NCT of Delhi.

This is for your kind information and necessary action.

Yours faithfully,

(K.LAL NGHINGLOVA)
Spl. Secretary (SC/ST/OBC/Min

Encl: As above.

F.No.5(5)/2010-11/DSCST/SCP/ **Dated the** 6th **August, 2010**

Copy to:-

1. The Secretary to Minister of SC/ST Welfare, Government of NCT of Delhi, Delhi Sectt., I.P. Estate, New Delhi.
2. The Special Officer to Chief Secretary, Government of NCT of Delhi, Delhi Sectt., I.P. Estate, New Delhi.
3. The P.S. to Pr. Secretary to Chief Minister, O/o the Chief Minster, Government of NCT of Delhi, Delhi Sectt., I.P. Estate, New Delhi.

(K.LAL NGHINGLOVA)
Spl. Secretary (SC/ST/OBC/Min

Dir (PF-II)

6.8.10

2227 6/8/2010

827855

Recived today at 3 PM

9.8.10

NOTE ON UTILIZATION OF SCHDULED CASTE SUB PLAN (SCSP) FUNDS BY GOVT. OF NCT OF DELHI

As per guidelines of the Planning Commission, Govt. of NCT of Delhi should ensure its contribution to SCSP equal to size of Scheduled Caste population. SC population of total population of Delhi is about 16.9% as per Census 2001 as such about 16.9% of the total outlay of Delhi Govt. is earmarked as flow to SCSP.

In NCT of Delhi the situation is entirely different from other States the composition of population of Delhi is cosmopolitan in nature. This is because of the facts that urbanization in NCT of Delhi is much faster in comparison to the other cities located on the peripherals of Delhi. The difficulties in preparing SCSP document in NCT of Delhi has been described in the Annual Plan document of 2010-11, which has been submitted to the Planning Commission (Annexure-1). Following strategies have been adopted while preparing the SCSP document:-

Out of the outlay of each scheme identified for SCSP, flow to SCSP has been marked in two heads- (1) Divisible and (2) Indivisible.

Divisible : The funds under category of divisible are earmarked in the Finance Deptt. (demand code 789). This fund directly goes to the welfare of SC and once this fund is earmarked, it has to be spent and cannot be diverted or lapsed without the consent of SC/ST Deptt. An Office Memorandum to the effect dated 17/3/2008 has been issued to ensure this arrangement (Annexure-2). During the last 3 years no Govt. Deptt. has requested for diversion of funds earmarked from SCSP nor has the SC/ST Deptt. granted any such permission. It is, therefore,

Contd...2/

=2=

clear that there has been no diversion of funds meant for SCSP for any other purpose including Commonwealth Games. During the last 4 years funds earmarked under divisible category (Code 789) have been almost fully utilized (details at Annexure-3). Some of the major achievements in respect of schemes taken under this category by the department of Welfare of SC/ST/OBC/Minorities during the period from April 2005-March 2009 is annexed (Annexure-4)

Indivisible : The amount could be spent for the welfare of SCs which is not marked as SCSP in the demand book, has been taken under this head, presuming that the benefit under the scheme is flowing to SC

In Delhi the SC/ST population is not residing in any particular locality except for a few bastis. Therefore, they are also benefited from various infrastructure projects being taken up by the Govt. Therefore, it is presumed that any infrastructure projects viz. hospitals, schools, widening of roads, drainage improvement, modernization of street lights, construction of flyovers, foot over bridges, under bridges, construction of stadiums, development of bus terminal depots etc. which benefit the entire community and are not targeted at a particular section of society also benefit the SC population in the ratio of their population to the total. This amount comes under indivisible funds under SCSP.

Prior to the commencement of the games the SCSP was treated as integral part of the infrastructure development plan of the city. This is an accepted practice all over the country. The various plans submitted

-3-

to the Planning Commission indicate this division between divisible and indivisible components.

The conduct of the Commonwealth Games envisages improvement of the city infrastructure as well as creating a legacy for the city by development of such infrastructure. The city development plan therefore in the last 3 years focused on building of infrastructure. Progress of such development is periodically monitored by the Organizing Committee and Commonwealth Games Federation. To highlight the efforts of the State Govt. for development of infrastructure a large number of projects which are routinely implemented for the improvement of city infrastructure were included under the template of Commonwealth Games projects. This was also necessary to obtain funds from the Planning Commission for some of these projects.

The total expenditure made under 'indivisible category of SCSP' during the 2006-2011 is of the order of Rs. 7128.21 crores.

In response to your query raised under RTI Act by Ms. Shivani Chaudhry, the PIO of the department has given the following reply in the tabular form (without any narrative):

[Rs. In lakh]

ANNUAL PLAN	TOTAL OUTLAY	TOTAL EXPEND.	FLOW OF EXPEND. UNDER SCSP	% FLOW OF EXPEN. UNDER SCSP	AMONT SPENT IN CWG
2	3	4	5	6	7
2006-07	520000	508370.26	88458.95	17.40	197.12
2007-08	900000	874316.51	146872.24	16.79	1557.63
2008-09	1000000	962498.80	172,500.46	17.92	21472.70
2009-10	1000000	1109000.00	209,430.02	18.88	28844.00
2010-11	1120000		190155.74	16.98	22364.00
				Total	74435.45

-4-

In this statement the amount shown to have been spent for Commonwealth Games Projects under column no. 7 are in fact the expenditure under in-divisible category, which forms part of the total expenditure incurred under SCSP as shown in column no. 5 of the above table. It has been wrongly interpreted by certain persons that this amount has been diverted out of SCSP.

Perusal of Details of Infrastructure Development Projects covered under SCSP relating to this amount of Rs.744.35 crores, total of column clearly establishes that the expenditure relates to infrastructure development projects, which will have the long term benefits for all the citizens of Delhi. Details of Infrastructure Development Projects are as below:

Details of Infrastructure Development Projects covered under SCSP

(Rs. In Lakh)

Year	Sector	Expenditure
2006-07	**Transport**	
	1) MCD (Constructions & Improvement of Roads & Bridges)	34.94
	Urban Development	
	1) Commonwealth Games (To cover any new project)	162.18
	Total (2006-07)	**197.12**
2007-08	**Transport**	
	1) PWD (Constructions & Improvement of Roads & Bridges)	389.05
	2) NDMC (Park & Ride and holding facilities at Safdarjung Airport/Street Scaping and Beautification of Roads/Installation of Road signages/Construction of Foot Over Bridge)	59.52
	3) MCD (Constructions & Improvement of Roads & Bridges)	137.00
	Sports & Youth Services-	
	Dte of Education/NDMC	
	1) Commonwealth Games (Strengthening of existing Sports Infrastructure)	971.33

-5-

	Water Supply & Sanitation	
	Delhi Jal Board *	
	1) Commonwealth Games (Water treatment Plan at Commonwealth Games Village)	0.73
	Total (2007-08)	1557.63
2008-09	**Transport**	
	1) DTC-Dev. Of Bus Terminals/Depots	1308.85
	2) PWD (Construction & Improvement of Roads & Bridges)	16001.83
	3) DTTDC-Roads/Flyovers	255.00
	4) NDMC (Park & Ride and holding facilities at Safdarjung Airport/Street Scaping and Beautification of Roads/Installation of Road sign ages/ Construction of Foot Over Bridge)	119.00
	5) MCD (Construction & Improvement of Roads & Bridges)	1266.29
	Sports & Youth Services-	
	Dte. of Education/NDMC	
	1) Commonwealth Games (Strengthening of existing Sports Infrastructure)	2520.11
	Water Supply & Sanitation	
	Delhi Jal Board *	
	1) Commonwealth Games (Water treatment Plan at Commonwealth Games Village)	1.62
	Total (2008-09)	21472.70
2009-10	**Transport**	
	1) DTC-Dev. Of Bus Terminals/Depots	1020.00
	2) PWD (Construction & Improvement of Roads & Bridges)	17850.00
	3) NDMC (Park & Ride and holding facilities at Safdarjung Airport/Street Scaping and Beautification of Roads/Installation of Road signages/Construction of Foot Over Bridge)	459.00
	4) MCD (Construction & Improvement of Roads & Bridges)	4624.00
	Sports & Youth Services-	
	Dte of Education/NDMC	
	1) Commonwealth Games (Strengthening of existing Sports Infrastructure)	4500.00
	Water Supply & Sanitation	
	Delhi Jal Board *	
	1) Commonwealth Games (Water treatment Plan at Commonwealth Games Village)	340.00
	Urban Development	
	1) Commonwealth Games (To cover any new project)	51.00

-6-

	Total (2009-10)	28844.00
2010-11	**Transport**	
	1) DTC-Dev. Of Bus Terminals/Depots	969.00
	2) PWD (Construction & Improvement of Roads & Bridges)	11169.00
	3) PWD CWG (Widening & improvements)	3400.00
	4) DTTDC-Roads/Flyovers	3145.00
	5) NDMC (Park & Ride and holding facilities at Safdarjung Airport/Street Scaping and Beautification of Roads/Installation of Road signage/Construction of Foot Over Bridge)	255.00
	6) MCD (Construction & Improvement of Roads & Bridges)	2550.00
	Sports & Youth Services-	
	Dte of Education/NDMC	
	1) Commonwealth Games (Strengthening & Sports Infrastructure)	740.00
	Water Supply & Sanitation	
	Delhi Jal Board *	
	1) Commonwealth Games (Water treatment Plan at Commonwealth Games Village)	119.00
	Urban Development	
	1) Commonwealth Games (To cover any new project)	17.00
	Total (2010-11)	22364.00
	Grand Total (2006 to 2011)	**74435.45**

*DDA to reimburse the cost of plant and therefore these projects will be deleted from SCSP during 2011-12.

The details of the development projects indicated about clearly establish that they are part of the indivisible expenditure under SCSP scheme and have in no way different from similar projects which have been indicated under SCSP Sub-Plan in the past.

To ensure full and effective implementation of the SCSP nodal officers have been designated in all the implementing departments at senior levels, Orders in this regard have been issued and are at Annexure-5.

Annexure- 1

Difficulties in implementing SCSP in NCT of Delhi

Every metropolitan city like Delhi, has its own priorities and requirements and accordingly, while preparing Development Plans the special needs and requirements have to be kept in view. The Delhi is not only the metropolitan city but a historical as well as capital city of India. Therefore, to maintain the heritage and special security needs of Delhi, highest priorities have to be accorded. Further, the land management, law and orders are under the control of Government of India. In spite of all these constraints, Government of Delhi is committed to maintain and to develop proper infrastructure in all sectors of development.

The situation of Delhi is entirely different from other states. The composition of population of National Capital Territory of Delhi is cosmopolitan in nature. This is because of the fact that urbanization process in NCT of Delhi is much faster in comparison to the cities and the subcities located on the peripherals of Delhi i.e. the area covered under National Capital Region.

The service sector's contribution in the economy of NCT of Delhi is much larger than the contribution of other sectors as a result of large scale urbanization process. This has attracted a large number of skilled, semi skilled and unskilled workers from all corners of India. The above mentioned factors are responsible for mixture for all castes/ religion including SCs, OBCs and Minorities. through out the habitation in NCT of Delhi. This has not only resulted in large scale urbanization but development of JJR Colonies, Un-authorized Colonies & JJ Clusters.

In other states a large number of SCSP schemes with huge SCSP outlays stand included in the sector "Agriculture & Allied Services". But in Delhi due to very fast process of urbanization and acquisition of land for Social Development Programmes, the land of agriculture purposes and allied activities, has almost become extinct. Consequently, only very small outlay is provided in the Annual Plans of Delhi for this sector as a whole, whereas in other states it is a pre-dominant sector having the maximum outlay. Consequently, the scope of activities in its sub sector like Animal Husbandry, Fisheries, Bee Keeping, Food Processing etc. is also depleting fast in Delhi resulting in very low outlay for this sector as a whole and consequently under SCSP also.

Due to the same reason of urbanization, the schemes like IRDP, Indira Vikas Yojana, National Rural Employment Programme are not being implemented in NCT of Delhi.

While in other states there is huge concentration exclusively of SC & ST in particular pockets or areas, this is not the case in Delhi. Mostly SCs/STs in Delhi live along with other population and therefore a special scheme exclusively for them have a limited scope. Since the SC population in Delhi is not residing in clusters, as is the position in other states, it is not possible to adopt cluster approach and formulate specific schemes for the welfare of SCs, adopted in the State of Maharashtra.

In the circumstances explained above specific schemes for social and economic development of SCs are not feasible. As such the flow of outlay under SCSP remains on the lower side in the earlier years.

The matter of formulation of SCSP was also discussed by the Working Group, constituted by Government of NCT of Delhi for preparing 11th Five Year Plan.

Annexure-2

Government of National Capital Territory of Delhi
Finance & Planning Department, 4th Level,'A' & B" Wing, Delhi Secretariat, IP Estate, New Delhi110113

No. F. 13(22)/Plg/2006-07- 2502-2611 Dated: 17.3.2008

Office Memorandum

Subject: Guidelines regarding Scheduled Caste Sub Plan (SC Sub-Plan)

The Scheduled Caste Sub Plan for focused development of Scheduled Castes has been prepared in accordance with the guidelines of the Planning Commission and has been circulated to all departments by the Department of Welfare of SC/ST/OBC & Minorities.

2 It may be noted that provisions have been made under 61 separate budgetary heads/sub-heads in the various demands for grants in the demand book of Govt. of Delhi so that the allocation to the schemes/programmes under Scheduled Caste Sub-Plan (SC Sub-Plan) is specific and is non- divertible.

3 The Secretary of the Department for Welfare of Scheduled Castes is the Nodal Officer in respect of SC Sub-Plan who will monitor the financial and physical targets. Further he is the competent authority for considering proposals for re-prioritisation or re-appropriation within the schemes covered under SC Sub-Plan.

4 All the Heads of Departments are requested to take note of the above and to furnish periodical reports to Secretary, Department for Welfare of SCs, for facilitating the coordinated implementation of SC Sub Plan.

Diary No. 9136 DSC-I
Date 25/3/08

13.3.08
(V.V.BHAT)
Pr. Secretary (Fin/Plg)

To

All Pr. Secretaries/Secretaries & HoDs of Govt. of N.C.T. of Delhi

71. Secretary,
Welfare of SC/ST Department
Government of NCT of Delhi
Vikas Bhawan I.P. Estate New Delhi.

Annexure-3

Flow to SSCP out of Annual Plan Size (Rs. in Crores)

S. No.	Year	Divisible	In-Divisible	Total
1.	2006-07			
	i) Approved outlay	129.74	835.88	965.62
	ii) Expenditure	109.30	775.28	884.58
2.	2007-08			
	i) Approved outlay	187.36	1346.70	1534.06
	ii) Expenditure	187.28	1281.44	1468.72
3.	2008-09			
	i) Approved outlay	231.55	1599.12	1830.67
	ii) Expenditure	210.55	1514.45	1725.00
4.	2009-10			
	i) Approved outlay	217.02	1567.38	1784.40
	ii) Expenditure	220.98	1873.32	2094.30
5.	2010-11			
	i) Approved outlay	217.83	1683.72	1901.55
	ii) Expenditure			
	2006-11			
	i) Approved outlay	983.50	7032.80	8016.30
	ii) Expenditure	945.94	7128.21	8074.15

Annexure-L

Major achievements in respect of the schemes being implemented by the Department for the Welfare of SC/ST/OBC/Min during the period from April, 2005 to March, 2009.

1 Dr. Ambedkar State Award for toppers amongst SC /ST/OBC/Min. students.

Period	Approved Outlay	RE	Expenditure (Rs. in lakhs)	% with RE	Physical Achievement (in numbers)
April 04 to March 05	3.00	2.00	0.28	14.00	04
April 05 to March 06	3.00	0.50	0.42	84.00	6
April 06 to March 2007	4.00	1.00	1.00	100.00	13
April 07 to March, 2008	5.00	5.00	1.28	25.60	32
April 08 to March 2009	5.00	4.00	2.72	68.00	34
April 09 to March 2010	4.00	6.00	0.72	12.00	09
April 10 to March 2011	7.00				36 (Target)

2. Improvement of SC Basties.

Period	Approved Outlay	RE	Expenditure (Rs. in lakhs)	% with RE	Physical Achievement (in numbers)
April 04 to March 05	2200.00	2200.00	1126.11	51.19	61
April 05 to March 06	2200.00	2163.00	66.85	3.09	–
April 06 to March 2007	2200.00	1600.00	1578.34	98.65	80
April 07 to March 08	2200.00	2380.00	2376.85	99.87	50 (Including 2 Chaupals)
April 08 to March 2009	2200.00	2890.00	2887.58	99.92	Basties=45 Chaupal=06
April 09 to March 2010	2400.00	1800.00	1506.59	83.70	Bastioes=23 Chaupal=36
April 10 to March 2011	2350.00				Basties & Chaupal=60 (Target)

3. Hostel for SC/ST/OBC/Min. boys at Dilshad Garden.

Period	Approved Outlay	RE	Expenditure (Rs. in lakhs)	% with RE	Physical Achievement (in numbers)
April 04 to March 05	40.00	44.00	35.28	80.18	101
April 05 to March 06	47.00	44.00	36.10	82.05	96
April 06 to March 2007	48.00	43.00	42.94	99.86	100
April 07 to March 08	50.00	50.00	48.03	96.06	93
April 08 to March 2009	51.00	56.00	50.91	90.91	96
April 09 to March 2010	100.00	62.00	47.70	76.94	99
April 10 to March 2011	85.00				100 (Target)

4. **Hostel for SC/ST/OBC/Min. Girls at Dilshad Garden.**

Period	Approved Outlay	RE	Expenditure (Rs. in lakhs)	% with RE	Physical Achievement (in numbers)
April 04 to March 05	10.00	7.50	3.66	48.80	32
April 05 to March 06	8.00	6.00	4.68	78.00	28
April 06 to March 2007	8.00	8.00	7.06	88.25	35
April 07 to March 08	10.00	8.00	5.84	73.00	25
April 08 to March 2009	10.00	10.00	9.24	92.40	33
April 09 to March 2010	10.00	11.0	9.61	87.36	55
April 10 to March 2011	13.00				70 (Target)

5. **Free supply of stationery to SC/ST/OBC/Min. students.**

Period	Approved Outlay	RE	Expenditure (Rs. in lakhs)	% with RE	Physical Achievement (in numbers)
April 04 to March 05	480.00	480.00	232.52	48.44	49361
April 05 to March 06	480.00	470.50	469.59	99.81	88313
April 06 to March 2007	533.00	555.00	554.94	99.99	85000
April 07 to March 08	580.00	1100.00	1099.98	99.99	193058
April 08 to March 2009	1100.00	767.00	762.14 (Rs. 760.00 released to Edu. Deptt.)	99.37	386 (Edu. Deptt awaited)
April 09 to March 2010	695.00	698.00	692.88	99.27	652 (do)
April 10 to March 2011	695.00				115750

6. **Merit Scholarship to SC/ST/OBC/Min. (Class VI to VIII).**

Period	Approved Outlay	RE	Expenditure (Rs. in lakhs)	% with RE	Physical Achievement (in numbers)
April 04 to March 05	30.00	30.00	27.86	92.87	7814
April 2005 to March 06	35.00	67.00	61.31	91.51	14558
April 2006 to March 2007	45.00	95.00	90.51	95.27	16315
April 07 to March 08	--	--	Scheme merged with VIth to XIIth	--	

7. **Merit Scholarship to SC/ST/OBC/Min. (Class VIth to XII).**

Period	Approved Outlay	RE	Expenditure (Rs. in lakhs)	% with RE	Physical Achievement (in numbers)
April 04 to March 05	100.0	59.00	56.42	95.63	4046
April 2005 to March 06	100.00	92.00	90.98	98.89	6474
April 2006 to March 2007	110.00	155.00	149.91	96.72	9248
April 07 to March 2008	290.00	442.00	441.92	99.98	44259 (Including class VIth to VIIIth)
April 08 to March 2009	430.00	689.00	683.91 (Rs. 670.00 released to Edu. Deptt)	99.26	646 (Edu. Deptt) Awaited
April 09 to March 2010	695.00	700.00	693.22 (Rs.675.00 released)	99.03	12.85 (Edu. Deptt. awaited)
April 10 to March 2011	695.00				69500 (Target)

8. **Merit Scholarship for college & professional institutions students belonging to SC/ST/OBC/Min.**

Period	Approved Outlay	RE	Expenditure (Rs. in lakhs)	% with RE	Physical Achievement (in numbers)
April 04 to March 05	40.00	40.00	30.55	76.38	403
April 2005 to March 06	50.00	60.00	59.91	99.18	931
April 2006 to March 2007	55.00	80.00	79.80	99.75	724
April 07 to March, 2008	85.00	153.00	151.19	98.82	2081
April 08 to March 2009	160.00	160.00	146.80	91.75	1984
April 09 to March 2010	170.00	210.00	172.66	82.22	2750
April 10 to March 2011	245.00				45 (Target)

9. **Reimbursement of tution fee for SC/ST/OBC/Min. students in public schools.**

Period	Approved Outlay	RE	Expenditure (Rs. in lakhs)	% with RE	Physical Achievement (in numbers)
April 04 to March 05	25.00	25.00	14.24	56.96	254
April 2005 to March 06	125.00	20.00	17.33	86.65	372
April 2006 to March 2007	76.00	30.00	21.25	70.83	433
April 07 to March, 2008	40.00	40.00	32.62	81.55	378 (Includes OBC & Min.)
April 08 to March 2009	40.00	83.00	65.19	78.54	1122 (-do)
April 09 to March 2010	89.00	222.00	192.53	86.73	2477 (do)
April 10 to March 2011	175.00				6000 (Target)

10. **Vocational & Technical Education Scholarship**

Period	Approved Outlay	RE	Expenditure (Rs. in lakhs)	% with RE	Physical Achievement (in numbers)
April 04 to March 05	50.00	17.00	17.00	100.00	Awaited
April 2005 to March 06	20.00	20.00	20.00	100.00	–
April 2006 to March 2007	35.00	35.00	–		–
April 07 to March, 2008	40.00	6.00	–		Scheme being imple. By TTE
April 08 to March 2009	40.00	40.00	40.00	100.00	Awaited (-do)
April 09 to March 2010	40.00	40.00	40.00	100.00	-do-
April 10 to March 2011	40.00				3000 (Target)

11. **Vocational Training through ATDC & NSIC.**

Period	Approved Outlay	RE	Expenditure (Rs. in lakhs)	% with RE	Physical Achievement (in numbers)
April 04 to March 05	–	–	–	–	–
April 05 to March 06			–		–
April 06 to March 2007	–	–	08.06	–	122
April 07 to March, 2008	–	40.00	30.00	75.00	–
April 08 to March 2009	–	–	8.58	–	611
April 09 to March 2010	–	–	–	–	318
April 10 to March 2011	–				500 (Target)

12. **Financial assistance to SC/ST/OBC/Min. 386 for LCV/DLY Taxi, TATA-470, Tempo by DSFDC.**

Period	Approved Outlay	RE	Expenditure (Rs. in lakhs)	% with RE	Physical Achievement (in numbers)
April 05 to March 06			--		--
April 06 to March 2007			--		--
April 07 to Mar.08			--		--
April 08 to March 2009			262.88		119
April 09 to March 2010	--	--	62.06	--	28
April 10 to March 2011	--	--	--	--	77 (Target)

13. **Loan for technical education to SC/ST/OBC/Min. students by DSFDC.**

Period	Approved Outlay	RE	Expenditure (Rs. in lakhs)	% with RE	Physical Achievement (in numbers)
April 05 to March 06			--		--
April 06 to March 2007			0.28		03
April 07 to March, 2008			1.47		02
April 08 to March 2009			2.01		02
April 09 to March 2010			0.97		01
April 10 to March 2011	--				55 (Target)

14. **Composite Loan Schemes for SC/ST/OBC/Min./PH. through DSFDC.**

Period	Approved Outlay	RE	Expenditure (Rs. in lakhs)	% with RE	Physical Achievement (in numbers)
April 05 to March 06			130.39		291
April 06 to March 2007			43.09		91
April 07 to Mar.08			276.64		450
April 08 to March 2009			303.12		325
April 09 to March 2010			225.78		245
April 10 to March 2011					470 (Target)

15. **Big Loan to SC/ST/OBC/Min. for Economic Upliftment through DSCFDC.**

Period	Approved Outlay	RE	Expenditure (Rs. in lakhs)	% with RE	Physical Achievement (in numbers)
April 05 to March 06					
April 06 to March 2007					
April 07 to Mar.08					
April 08 to March 2009			2.70		01
April 09 to March 2010	--	--	--	--	--
April 10 to March 2011					27 (Target)

16. **Financial Assistance to DSCFDC**

Period	Approved Outlay	RE	Expenditure (Rs. in lakhs)	% with RE	Physical Achievement (in numbers)
April 05 to March 06					
April 06 to March 2007					
April 07 to Mar.08	900.00	700.00	700.00	100.00	
April 08 to March 2009	70.00	102.00	99.76	97.80	
April 09 to March 2010	50.00	655.00	650.00	99.24	
April 10 to March 2011	55.00				

Major Achiev of Schemes

Annexure– 5

Government of NCT of Delhi
Department for the Welfare of SC/ST/OBC/Minorities
B-Block, 2nd Floor, Vikas Bhawan, I.P. Estate, New Delhi
E-Mail: ddscstdel@hub.nic.in Website: scst welfare.delhigovt.nic.in
Tele Fax No. 23379513

CIRCULAR

This department vide letter No. 5(5)/08-09/DSCST/5057-5121 dated 07.09.2009 circulated the relevant potion of Scheduled Caste Sub Plan 2009-10, among all the concerned departments/ organizations with the request to furnish regular progress made on quarterly basis under SCSP separately for divisible and indivisible heads.

You are requested to designate a Nodal Officer from your department exclusively dealing with SCSP and convey to us. The nodal officer should be senior officer preferably of the level of second senior most in the Department/ Directorate/ Organization.

It may kindly be ensured that outlay earmarked under divisible head is not diverted and has to be utilized in full during the current financial year and also in the subsequent financial years.

17.11.09

(B.V. SELVARAJ)
Ppl. Secretary (SC/ST/OBC/Min.)

F.No. 5(8)/09-10/DSC(ST)/SCP/7829-7897 Dated: 17/11/09

Copy forwarded to:-

1. The Principal Secretary/ Secretary of all SCSP implementing departments/ organizations, Government of NCT of Delhi/ New Delhi with the request to take necessary action in the matter and intimate the action taken immediately, preferably, within a month.
2. The Principal Secretary to 'the Hon'ble Chief Minister, New Delhi.
3. The Secretary to the Hon'ble Minister for Welfare of SC/ST, New Delhi.

17.11.09

(B.V. SELVARAJ)
Ppl. Secretary (SC/ST/OBC/Min.)

826120/FS/10
4/8

MOST IMMEDIATE

LOK SABHA SECRETARIAT
(Legislative Branch-I)

Urgent
F.S. 4/8/2010

JS(AF-II)
5/8/2010.

Let us seek inputs urgently
5/8
DD/G

SUBJECT: Notices of Short Duration Discussion under rule 193 regarding alleged diversion of funds meant for the welfare of the scheduled castes/scheduled tribes to the Commonwealth Games projects.

......

Notices of Short Duration Discussion under rule 193 on the above subject have been received from Sarvashri Shailendra Kumar and Dara Singh Chauhan, MPs.

A copy each of the above notice is being forwarded herewith.

2. The Ministry is requested that a note (both in English and Hindi versions and **a floppy/CD of the English version**) indicating the factual position with regard to the matter raised in the notices may please be furnished to this Secretariat immediately to decide the admissibility of the notices.

3. While sending the factual note, it may please be indicated whether there would be any objection to the copy thereof being given to the members concerned.

3/8/2010
(AJAY KUMAR SOOD)
UNDER SECRETARY
Tel. 23034721
Fax. 23012862

(1) Ministry of Youth Affairs & Sports (Ms. Sindhushree Khullar, Secretary), 'C' Wing, Shastri Bhawan, New Delhi.
(2) Ministry of Finance (Shri Ashok Chawla, Secretary), North Block, New Delhi

L.S.S. U.O. No. 18/4(14)/2010/L-I, dated: 3.8.2010

Parliament Matter
Most Immediate
Out Today

No. 40(7)/PF-II/2009(Part)
Ministry of Finance
Department of Expenditure
(Plan Finance-II Division)
*****

New Delhi, dated the 5.08.2010

OFFICE MEMORANDUM

Subject: Notice of Short Duration Discussion under rule 193 regarding alleged diversion of fund meant for the welfare of the scheduled castes/scheduled tribes to the Commonwealth Games projects.

The undersigned is directed to enclose herewith the Notice received from Lok Sabha Secretariat on the subject mentioned above. It is requested that a self contained note in the matter may please be sent to this Department urgently.

Piyush Srivastava

(Piyush Srivastava)
Director (PF-II)

Shri Rahul Bhatnagar, Joint Secretary(ISD), Ministry of Youth Affairs & Sports, Pragati Vihar Hostel, Lodhi Road Complex, New Delhi. Sh. Manoj, P.A.

2. Shri Vishwapati Trivedi, AS&FA (Home), North Block, New Delhi.

3. Shri Shaktikant Das, Joint Secretary (Budget), Deptt. of Economic Affairs, North Block, New Delhi.

✓4. Shri Rakesh Mehta, Chief Secretary, Govt. of Delhi, Delhi Sectt., I.P. Estate, New Delhi. Sh. Manohar, P.A.

Issued
Suman
5/8/010

D.O. No. 10093/FM/IMP/05
वित्त मंत्री
भारत
नई दिल्ली-110001
FINANCE MINISTER
INDIA
NEW DELHI - 110001

November 12, 2005

Dear Shri Chauhan,

The Finance Sub-Committee of GoM for Commonwealth Games, 2010, held its first meeting under my chairmanship on June 3, 2005 and stressed that all proposals for release of funds to various implementing agencies, including the Organising Committee (OC), would need to be backed by a detailed project document and would also require approval of EFC/Cabinet in case the projected expenditure was Rs.100 crore or more. The estimates presented by the Organising Committee at this meeting were sketchy and were required to be elaborated through a detailed and self-contained proposal. The Finance Sub-Committee also took the view that the organisation structure of the Organising Committee should be lean, IT enabled and efficient and should not replicate the hierarchical structure of a typical government office. Subsequently, a decision was taken to release Rs.10 crore to the Organising Committee as a special case to enable them to incur urgent expenditure, pending approval of EFC/Cabinet. Even though considerable time has elapsed since then, no detailed proposal or project document has been placed before the Finance Sub-Committee so far.

As per the procedure agreed to between Finance Ministry and Ministry of Youth Affairs & Sports, the OC, DDA and Sports Authority of India are required to submit proposals to MYAS. The proposals are required to be backed by a self-contained project document and should confirm to the EFC format. MYAS is required to examine the proposals in consultation with Planning Commission and forward the proposals with comments to the Member-Secretary of the Finance Sub-Committee of the GoM. Thereafter, the proposals will be considered by the Finance Sub-Committee, which will make appropriate recommendations to the GoM. MYAS is required to obtain approval of Cabinet, thereafter, based on the recommendations of the GoM.

I understand that a proposal has been recently forwarded by the Organising Committee to MYAS in the EFC format, projecting an expenditure of Rs.802.23 crore till 2010-11. This is expected to be backed by a revenue stream of Rs.900 crore. I would suggest that the OC proposal be examined expeditiously by MYAS and recommendations forwarded for consideration by the Finance Sub-Committee of GoM. The Member-Secretary of the Finance Sub-Committee may be associated with this examination by MYAS as required. Similar action may be taken on receipt of proposals from SAI and DDA.

....2

वित्त मंत्री
भारत
नई दिल्ली-110001
FINANCE MINISTER
INDIA
NEW DELHI - 110001

-2-

I am sure you will appreciate that it will not be possible to release any further funds to these agencies without due diligence by MYAS as well as by the Finance Sub-Committee.

I also find that agenda papers and notices for meetings of the GoM are only being sent to my office and not to the offices of Secretary(Expenditure) and Member Secretary, Finance Sub Committee. This is resulting in avoidable communication gaps within Ministry of Finance. In future, I would request that copies of the agenda papers and meeting notices may also be endorsed to Secretary(Expenditure) and Member-Secretary of the Finance Sub-Committee of GoM.

I am afraid, if the required coordination and understanding between OC, MYAS and the F.S.C. regarding the procedure to be followed are not effected soon, we might have to face a situation in which entire efforts at faster decision making come to be stalled creating disappointment all over.

I would, therefore, strongly urge upon you to please have necessary instructions issued to all functionaries concerned to work in a coordinated fashion in accordance with the procedure agreed upon.

With regards,

Yours sincerely,

(P. Chidambaram)

ISSUED

Shri Prithvi Raj Chauhan,
Minister of State for Youth Affairs & Sports,
Shastri Bhavan,
New Delhi.

वित्त मंत्री
भारत
नई दिल्ली-110001
FINANCE MINISTER
INDIA
NEW DELHI - 110001

सत्यमेव जयते

For kind personal attention

December 19, 2005

Dear Shri Fernandes,

On the matters related to the Commonwealth Games, I am writing further to my letter of November 12, 2005 to which a response from your Ministry is awaited. Though considerable time has elapsed since the first meeting of the Finance Sub-Committee held under my chairmanship on June 3, 2005, detailed expenditure proposals, which were expected to be available for consideration by the Finance Sub-Committee of GoM, **are yet to be received**. Plan schemes of OC, DDA and Sports Authority of India, after obtaining in-principle approval of the Planning Commission, **are yet to be circulated by MYAS** for consideration by the Finance Sub-Committee.

The Games operating expenses were supposed to be revenue-neutral; hence, the expenditure proposals were to be firmly supported by realistic revenue estimates. In absence of any revenue estimates conducted in the Indian scenario, the constantly burgeoning expenditure estimates is worrisome. Meanwhile, I understand that posts are being created and filled up by the Organizing Committee, even though there appears to be **no formal approval of Government for the organization structure of OC**. The issues raised on the Memorandum of Association have also not been addressed.

At the first meeting of the Finance Sub-Committee, it was emphasized that the organization structure of OC should be lean, IT enabled and efficient and should not replicate the hierarchical structure of a typical government office. A strategy for outsourcing important functions was to be developed to enable OC to function as a lean body. In order that the Government is not presented with a top heavy and cost intensive organization structure for the OC as a fait accompli, it is necessary that the envisaged organization structure for the OC be examined on priority, alongwith the financial implications.

Since time is passing, I would request you to please look into these issues **urgently** so that the proposals for release of funds are not presented to the Finance Sub-Committee at the last moment, as fait accompli. This would cause embarrassment both to the Government as well as the Organizing Committee.

With regards,

Yours sincerely

(P. Chidambaram)

Shri Oscar Fernandes
Minister of State (IC)
Ministry of Youth Affairs & Sports
Shastri Bhavan,
New Delhi

Organising Committee
Commonwealth Games 2010 Delhi

Suresh Kalmadi *M.P.*
Chairman, Organising Committee
Commonwealth Games 2010 Delhi
&
President, Indian Olympic Association

Urgent

796/AS(E)/06
31/5

May 30, 2006

Dear Mr Adarsh Kishoreji

The EFC Meeting to finalize the Budget of the Organizing Committee has been scheduled at 1600 hrs on 30.5.2006. We have already forwarded the EFC Memo of the Organizing Committee's indicating the anticipated expenditure and anticipated revenue streams vide our letter No.OCCWG/MoYS/2005 dt.30.11.2005. My officers have also had two/three rounds of discussions with officers of the Ministry of Sports at the level of Secretary, Jt. Secretary in MoYAS as also with Mr Vivek Rae, Jt. Secretary(Plan Finance-II), Ministry of Finance, Department of Expenditure.

Further to this, I would like to place certain areas of concern of the Organizing Committee on record:-

1. The Budget of the Organizing Committee has been firmed up keeping in mind the requirements of CGF and parameters of the Host City Contractual clauses. We have been given Operating Advances by MoYAS to tide over initial setting up expenditures, participation in M 2006, and commitments to the Commonwealth Games Federation(CGF) as fees. It may be pointed out that the delays caused in our depositing the second installment to the CGF led to adverse criticism in the General Assembly as we faulted on the time schedule of an international commitment.
2. The various disciplines in the Commonwealth Games numbering 15 and the 3 additional games proposed, namely, Billiards & Snookers, Tennis and Archery, need to be put on the Priority List by the Sports Ministry and the necessary support for training venue infrastructure, technical equipments, coaches, etc need to be provided unstintingly so that we equip ourselves to be in a better position in 2010 Commonwealth Games as we are the Host Nation. We were ranked 4th in the Manchester Games in 2002 as well as in Melbourne 2006 wherein we collected 50 medals.

The spin offs of hosting Commonwealth Games by way of enhanced tourism, inflow of foreign exchange, building up of homogenous and healthy Society, up-gradation of our various venue infrastructures etc, are certain. We also need to ensure that we set up the Dope Lab of such standards that we get accreditation

Gate No. 28A, Jawaharlal Nehru Stadium, Lodhi Road, New Delhi-110003. India.
Tel.: +91-11-24367928 / 7929 / 7930. Fax : +91-11-24367931
e-mail : cwg2010@bol.net.in

Organising Committee
Commonwealth Games 2010 Delhi

Suresh Kalmadi *M.P.*
Chairman, Organising Committee
Commonwealth Games 2010 Delhi
&
President, Indian Olympic Association

the World Anti Doping Agency(WADA), Montreal Canada. This will not only enable our athletes being certified correctly but also bring revenues by way of other Countries sending samples to us for testing.

It is essential that the revenue budget as projected to the tune of Rs.896.01 crores is approved in the EFC and sanction of CCEA obtained for the same for release of funds as per year-wise projections of the Organizing Committee. The revenue receipts should not be linked with the release of funds as the revenues can be actually realized only after our Marketing Agents for sponsorship and Commercial Rights & National and International Broadcasting Rights respectively are appointed and the various entities who come forward for sponsorship etc are selected and contracts concluded with them. Therefore linking release of funds on the basis of revenue collections would only lead to 'tap-on' 'tap-off' approach, which especially when the Games are nearing will hamper our activities severely and seriously curtail our operational efficiency. The revenue collections in the M 2006 shows that while the Games were held in March 2006, the accrual of revenues in 2004 was 1% in sponsorship and 31% in Broadcasting and in the year 2005, 15% in sponsorship, 1% in ticketing, 13% in Broadcasting and others 1%. The most relevant point to be highlighted is collection of revenue in 2006 till December when the Games were held in March 2006 is anticipated to be 84% in sponsorship, 99% in ticketing, 56% Broadcasting and others 99%. An e-mail to this effect received from Ms Brenda LaPorte, General Manager, Project Planning, Risk and Strategy, M 2006 is placed at annexure A..

5. It is therefore essential that the Budgetary Allocations are accepted in the EFC and approved by the Cabinet for inclusion in the Demands for Grants of the Ministry of Sports taking into account the projections given by the Organizing Committee, which already has a laid down budgetary process to be followed as per the Financial Bye Laws. Therefore, BE & RE requirements will be projected by the Organizing Committee as per the laid down schedules and Ministry of Sports may allocate funds without linking them with the revenue generation as accruals of revenue will be based on various contractual obligations entered into by the Organizing Committee with the help of the Marketing Agent and in consultation with other stake holders like venue owners, Host City, IOA etc and the flow of revenues will be only towards and after the end of the Games as per norms in Sports Events sponsorships.

Gate No. 28A, Jawaharlal Nehru Stadium, Lodhi Road, New Delhi-110003. India.
Tel.: +91-11-24367928 / 7929 / 7930. Fax : +91-11-24367931
e-mail : cwg2010@bol.net.in

Organising Committee
Commonwealth Games 2010 Delhi

Suresh Kalmadi *M.P.*
Chairman, Organising Committee
Commonwealth Games 2010 Delhi
&
President, Indian Olympic Association

6. The Organizing Committee has already formulated and adopted the Administrative and Financial Bye Laws which have also been approved by the Executive Board in their meeting held on 3.3.2006 and these were forwarded to MoYAS on 6.3.2006. The projections of the staff numbers are favorably comparable with the actual numbers in Melbourne to the extent that they are only 282 viz a viz 1120. Therefore, the Organizing Committee which has been working with a meager staff strength has now to start the activities with augmented strength and carry on its activities to reach up to the conduct of the Games in a focused manner and therefore the Budgetary Allocations are an immediate requirement. We have taken note of Finance Minister's directions regarding putting in place a lean and I.T. enabled set up.
7. The institutional arrangements made for the conduct of the Games entail that Organizing Committee Commonwealth Games 2010 Delhi is the pivotal body which has been entrusted with the conduct of the Games, with the support of Government of India, Host City, stake holders. . The Organizing Committee has been registered as an autonomous Society under the Societies Registration Act, 1860 with the Executive Board as its apex decision making body. The Executive Board of the Organizing Committee consists of Members from the Government of India and Govt of NCT of Delhi and others and therefore re-submitting the decisions already taken by the Executive Board to other institutions/committees would only lead to delays. Thus, the organization of Games revolves around the fulcrum which is the Organizing Committee Commonwealth Games, 2010 Delhi. All other institutional arrangements have been put in place to facilitate the Organizing Committee to carry out its functions smoothly
8. In conclusion, it is requested that the Budget of the Organizing Committee as proposed to the tune of Rs.896.01 crores is approved by the EFC. The revenue neutrality as directed by the Finance Minister will be possible to be ensured by the Organizing Committee as the M 2006 have achieved their revenue targets. The Beijing Olympics 2008 is expected to generate 30% more revenue than the previous Olympics which were held in Athens. All the mega Sports events are proving to be revenue surplus. Apart from revenue earnings, various other spin offs and multiplier effect which the conduct of an event of such magnitude is likely to have on Indian Economy has been compiled and is enclosed in the form of a study titled 'Socio Economic Impact on Host City & Country on hosting of International Games.'

Gate No. 28A, Jawaharlal Nehru Stadium, Lodhi Road, New Delhi-110003. India.
Tel.: +91-11-24367928 / 7929 / 7930. Fax : +91-11-24367931
e-mail : cwg2010@bol.net.in

Organising Committee
Commonwealth Games 2010 Delhi

Suresh Kalmadi *M.P.*
Chairman, Organising Committee
Commonwealth Games 2010 Delhi
&
President, Indian Olympic Association

A copy of the Administrative and Financial Bye Laws passed in the Executive Board is also enclosed (Annexure B) . It can be seen that the Financial Bye Laws is a prudential mix of Generally Accepted Accounting Standards, Commonwealth Games Federation Rules and conditions in the Host City Contract. It encompasses overall financial management, management of accounts and inventory management related to conduct of the Games. We propose to have a transparent accounting and financial systems and are in the process of appointing a Financial Consultant of international repute who would also help us in risk assessment, risk management and advise on strategies to cover any gaps in revenue. This would ensure that the financial and accounting edifice in the Organizing Committee is maintained in a professional manner. The process to appoint the Consultant is in an advanced stage. Therefore, any monitoring mechanism over and above the institutional arrangements already in place if proposed by the Ministry of Sports may be superfluous.

Regards

Yours sincerely,

Suresh Kalmadi

(SURESH KALMADI), M.P.
Chairman, Organising Committee
Commonwealth Games Delhi 2010

Dr Adarsh Kishore
Finance Secretary
Ministry of Finance
North Block,
NewDelhi

Gate No. 28A, Jawaharlal Nehru Stadium, Lodhi Road, New Delhi-110003. India.
Tel.: +91-11-24367928 / 7929 / 7930. Fax : +91-11-24367931
e-mail : cwg2010@bol.net.in

2010 COMMONWEALTH GAMES DELHI

Organising Committee
Commonwealth Games 2010 Delhi

Secretary Dy. No. 2792 Dated 1/6 (Youth & Sports)

ANNEX. II

JS (SPORTS) Dy. No. 3410 Date (F) 5/6/06 (S)

Suresh Kalmadi, M.P
Chairman

CWG/2010/GoM/Minutes 01.06.2006

Dear Shri Quraishi Ji,

In the 9th meeting of the GoM held on 4th January, 2006 under the Chairmanship of Shri Arjun Singh, Minister for Human Resource Development I made a presentation on the Final report on the Sports infrastructure (Competition venues & Training venues) and the Games Village which has been approved as presented. But in the minutes of the meeting mention was made only about the Competition Venues. I would request you kindly to add the **Training Venues** also as per the enclosed list as it is mandatory item.

The following omissions may also be added to the minutes:

1. Appointment of an International consultant to guide in developing the International standard infrastructure keeping in view of India's bid for 2014 Asian Games and our proposal for bidding for 2016 Olympic Games.

2. To add to Item 3 (a)... in consultation with the Infrastructure Coordination Committee of 2010 OC as the approval of the CGF is required.

3. The infrastructure should be handed over to OC 2010 soon after their completion latest by 31-8-2009 which will remain with it till the Games are over.

4. As regards the Games village for 2010 CWG if it is developed under the Public and Private Partnership model as proposed by DDA, I said that an under taking should be taken from the developers of the Games village that the accommodation created for 2010 CWG would be made available to the Organizing Committee of the 2014 Asian Games if the Games are allotted to Delhi for accommodating the contingents of the Asian countries. The GoM has agreed to it. This point may be added to Item 4 of the minutes.

Cont...2

Page 18 of 59

No. 28A, Jawaharlal Nehru Stadium, Lodhi Road, New Delhi-110003. India.
Tel.: +91-11-24367928 / 7929 / 7930. Fax : +91-11-24367931
e-mail : cwg2010@bol.net.in

#2#

Revised minutes of the 9th meeting of the GoM may please be issued attaching a copy of the final report on the infrastructure presented by OC 2010 and the four points mentioned in this letter.

Regards

Yours sincerely,

Suresh Kalmadi, M.P.

Dr. S.Y. Quraishi,
Secretary,
Ministry of Youth Affaires and Sports,
Shastri Bhavan,
New Delhi.

Page 19 of 59

F-20-38/2004-SP-II Secret

C.No. 5064/07
6/3

Annex II

MOST IMMEDIATE

पुलिस आयुक्त
दिल्ली
COMMISSIONER OF POLICE
DELHI
PHONES: 23319661, 23490201
FAX: 23722052

सत्यमेव जयते

C.No. 5064/CA.V
7-3-07

अर्ध सरकारी पत्र संख्या
D. O. No. 615 .P.Sec
Delhi dt 6-3-07

Dr. K. K. Paul
I.P.S

Dear Sir,

As you are kindly aware, the planning process for the ensuing Commonwealth Games is at an advanced stage. In this context intensive exercises for security, law and order as well as management of traffic have already been undertaken by Delhi Police. Nehru Stadium will be the main venue for the games with inaugural and Closing ceremonies besides the events for athletics being held there at the stadium. The initial planning was undertaken alongwith the organizers and Department of Sports keeping in view the past experience of handling events at the Nehru Stadium including the Asian Games, for which the stadium was initially constructed.

A few months ago we were informed that the northern flank of the stadium facing the CGO complex was being assigned for an event called 'Lawn Bowles'. This came as a surprise as the vacant space on the northern flank was originally earmarked as a pedestrian holding area as also for evacuation drills in case of any emergent situation or a disaster. As the enclosed map would indicate almost the entire northern flank has now been taken away, leaving virtually no space for these two important provisions for management of crowds. The location of the proposed underground Metro Station is in between the Pragati Vihar Hostel and CGO complex, resulting in the entire movement of pedestrian traffic heading for the Stadium from that very side. In the absence of any vacant space to act as a holding or a spill over area the crowd would only be milling around the road net work obstructing the smooth flow of traffic and creating other problems in the absence of any cushion hampering the smooth discharge and flow from the Metro Station.

We had taken up this matter with Secretary, Sports, Government of India, so as to shift the venue from this location,but that has not been possible. I shall be grateful if this matter is immediately taken up in the meeting of Secretaries so that all the pros and cons of having this event very close to the main location can be discussed and a final decision is arrived at.

With kind regards

Yours sincerely,

(DR.K.K.PAUL)
6/3

Shri Vijai Sharma,
Additional Secretary,
Cabinet Secretariat,
R.P. Bhawan,
New Delhi.

Encls: Map of Nehru Stadium

Page 9 9 15

वित्त मंत्री
भारत
नई दिल्ली-110001
FINANCE MINISTER
INDIA
NEW DELHI - 110001

सत्यमेव जयते

For kind personal attention

December 19, 2005

Dear Shri Fernandes,

On the matters related to the Commonwealth Games, I am writing further to my letter of November 12, 2005 to which a response from your Ministry is awaited. Though considerable time has elapsed since the first meeting of the Finance Sub-Committee held under my chairmanship on June 3, 2005, detailed expenditure proposals, which were expected to be available for consideration by the Finance Sub-Committee of GoM, **are yet to be received.** Plan schemes of OC, DDA and Sports Authority of India, after obtaining in-principle approval of the Planning Commission, **are yet to be circulated by MYAS** for consideration by the Finance Sub-Committee.

The Games operating expenses were supposed to be revenue-neutral; hence, the expenditure proposals were to be firmly supported by realistic revenue estimates. In absence of any revenue estimates conducted in the Indian scenario, the constantly burgeoning expenditure estimates is worrisome. Meanwhile, I understand that posts are being created and filled up by the Organizing Committee, even though there appears to be **no formal approval of Government for the organization structure of OC.** The issues raised on the Memorandum of Association have also not been addressed.

At the first meeting of the Finance Sub-Committee, it was emphasized that the organization structure of OC should be lean, IT enabled and efficient and should not replicate the hierarchical structure of a typical government office. A strategy for outsourcing important functions was to be developed to enable OC to function as a lean body. In order that the Government is not presented with a top heavy and cost intensive organization structure for the OC as a fait accompli, it is necessary that the envisaged organization structure for the OC be examined on priority, alongwith the financial implications.

Since time is passing, I would request you to please look into these issues **urgently** so that the proposals for release of funds are not presented to the Finance Sub-Committee at the last moment, as fait accompli. This would cause embarrassment both to the Government as well as the Organizing Committee.

With regards,

Yours sincerely

(P. Chidambaram)

Pl. keep in on com file K.C. 9.1.05

Shri Oscar Fernandes
Minister of State (IC)
Ministry of Youth Affairs & Sports
Shastri Bhavan,
New Delhi

Commonwealth file

Smt. Kah

Annexure - I

Madhukar Gupta

गृह सचिव
HOME SECRETARY
भारत सरकार
GOVERNMENT OF INDIA

सत्यमेव जयते

North Block,
New Delhi.

D.O. No.VI-23014/78/2009-VS

6 May 2009

This refers to the discussions in the meeting held today regarding various aspects pertaining to funding in respect of security related equipments, etc. in the context of Commonwealth Games-2010. It had been mentioned by you in the meeting that a proposal has been submitted for consideration of the Cabinet in respect of the estimates pertaining to the Commonwealth Games venues under the charge of the Sports Authority of India, on which comments of the Ministry of Home Affairs had been sought.

2. I am enclosing herewith a summary record of discussions in the meeting held today. In view of the position brought out therein, it would be appropriate that, insofar as the proposal pertaining to the capital cost of the Sports Authority of India venues is concerned, it may be brought to the notice of the Cabinet that the security related components of the proposal which, in any case, would be a very small percentage of the overall costs, are tentative and subject to possible escalation/revision.

Yours sincerely,

(Madhukar Gupta)

Ms. Sindhushree Khullar,
Secretary (Sports),
Ministry of Youth Affairs & Sports,
Room No.1, C-Wing,
Shastri Bhawan
New Delhi.

"Please visit our website at.http://mha.nic.in"

A-T(1)

The issue of provision of funds for security requirements in respect of the Commonwealth Games was discussed today in a meeting with the Secretary (Sports) in which officers of the Delhi Police were also present. It was noted that the Ministry of Sports has put up a Cabinet Note regarding the Capital Costs in respect of the Commonwealth Games venues owned by the Sports Authority of India. It was also noted that the Capital Cost estimates in respect of these venues include a component for CCTV camera systems, which has been provided on the basis of rough initial estimations, and also that only those elements related to security have been included which had a direct relationship with the civil and electrical engineering design and construction aspects.

2. In the course of time, a view has been taken in the High-level Empowered Security Committee under the chairmanship of the Union Home Secretary and the Lt. Governor of Delhi that ECIL, who are currently implementing a project for CCTV surveillance and monitoring systems for the Delhi Police on a turn-key basis, may also be given a turn-key assignment for the design and installation of security related surveillance and monitoring systems in respect of the Commonwealth Games. It was also noted that a proposal to give the ECIL a turn-key contract for this purpose for all the venues related to Commonwealth Games is also included in the proposal submitted to the Cabinet.

3. In the last meeting of the High-level Empowered Security Committee on 24 April 2009, it had, inter alia, been decided that coverage of CCTV and other monitoring, surveillance and access control systems should not be confined only to the games venues but should also cover other important venues like the Media Centre/IBC, Central Warehouse, OCs Headquarters, etc., and certain other venues such as parking lots which would be set up exclusively in the context of the Commonwealth Games. Not all of these may require CCTV coverage, in which case separate security schemes would be prepared for such locations by the Delhi Police.

4. The ECIL is in the process of firming up the designs and the Bill of Materials, etc., in respect of the Games related venues and the first presentation in this regard is to be made by them before the High-level Empowered Security Committee on 15 May 2009. In the meanwhile, all these aspects are being monitored and reviewed by a Committee set up

A-I (2)

by the Lt. Governor under the Chairmanship of the Special Adviser, GNCTD, for the Commonwealth Games.

5. In the above background it would not be possible, at this stage, to precisely estimate the costs to be incurred on CCTV and other security related equipments to be installed in the various venues related to the Commonwealth Games. Further, it was noted that some of the CCTV systems, etc., which may be installed at different locations may not be required for each of those venues on a permanent basis. The possibility of diverting some such equipments towards the main project of the Delhi Police, which is separately under the execution of the ECIL would also be there. Once the details about the locational coverage of the work to be done by ECIL, and the nature of equipments to be provided at different venues, becomes clearer, it would be possible to determine what element of the costs would need to be included in the capital cost of various venues, what can be done by way of overlays and what is the scope for equipments to be taken over by the Delhi Police or any other agency thereby making costs attributable to that agency.

- - - - -

Organising Committee
Commonwealth Games Delhi 2010

Suresh Kalmadi M.P.
Chairman, Organising Committee
President, Indian Olympic Association

Nov 21, 2007

Dear Shri Chidambaram ji

Subject: Organising Committee Budget

Reference is made to our meeting on 15 November 2007 in which you may kindly recall that I had brought to your kind attention the need for total flexibility to reallocate funds among budget heads within the approved budget similar to CWG Melbourne 2006 (M-2006) instead of ±25% flexibility accorded now to OC, CWG D 2010.

The Commonwealth Games Federation in their review has also indicated that "It is noted that the terms of the loan from the Government do not provide the OC with total flexibility to reallocate budget funds. M2006 were able to manage their budget across the entire organization with significant flexibility – major variations being subject to the OC Finance Committee approval. The flexibility resulted in M2006 senior management being able to manage expenditure across the organization as a whole and redirect funds easily to areas of most need and is the primary reason the Games were delivered under budget."

I would be grateful if suitable instructions are issued in this regard ensuring total flexibility in reallocation of funds among budget heads within the overall ceiling.

Regards

Yours sincerely,

Suresh Kalmadi, M.P.

Dy. No 2403/VIP/FM/07
26/11/07

Shri P. Chidambaram
Hon'ble Finance Minister
Government of India
North Block
New Delhi

US(E.III) 27.11.07

26/11/07

Gate No. 28A, Jawaharlal Nehru Stadium, Lodhi Road, New Delhi-110003, India.
Tel.: +91-11-24307000, 24367928 / 29 / 30, Fax: +91-11-24307040
e-mail: suresh.kalmadi@cwgdelhi2010.com

D.O. No. 4937 min, (YAS&S) 07

मणि शंकर अय्यर
MANI SHANKAR AIYAR

मंत्री
पंचायती राज, युवा कार्यक्रम एवं खेल और
उत्तर-पूर्वी क्षेत्र विकास
भारत सरकार
नई दिल्ली-110001
Minister
Panchayati Raj, Youth Affairs & Sports and
Development of the North Eastern Region
Government of India
New Delhi-110 001

D.O.No.F.70-47/2005-SP.II(Vol.III) 5 December 2007

Dear PC

Please refer to your letter of the 16th November, 2007 addressed to Shri Suresh Kalmadi, MP, Chairman, Organizing Committee of Commonwealth Games, which has been communicated to us through Ministry of Finance O.M. No.40(1)/PF-11/2007 dated the 21st November, 2007.

2. In the 12th Meeting of the Group of Ministers (GOM) of Commonwealth Games, the issue of release of funds to OC was discussed at length. I and my Ministry officials flagged four issues for decision. We sought the guidance of the Group of Ministers on whether the further release of funds to OC should be contingent on the following or not:-

i) Submission of Utilization Certificates as per GFR;

ii) Submission of cash flow statements of income & expenditure to enable the Government to satisfy itself that the releases are as per their requirements and should not lead to the parking of funds by OC;

iii) Approval of the revalidation exercise of the income & expenditure budget of OC, as stipulated by the EFC/Cabinet;

iv) Decision on institutional arrangements to give adequate and effective representation to the Government of India in the Executive Board and Important Committees of the Organizing Committee to ensure public financial accountability and reasonableness of expenditure to minimize financial commitments of Government emanating from its guarantee to fully meet the revenue deficit of the OC budget.

3. The Group of Ministers decided to constitute a Sub-Committee of the Hon. HRM and yourself to give guidance on these four issues. Thank you for the guidance given on the first two issues. First, you have instructed the OC to submit Utilization Certificates, if any are pending, for further releases. And secondly, you have laid down the principle of staggered releases to avoid the parking of funds by OC. However, it is not clear from the instructions in your letter whether to avoid the parking of funds the release of each of the five monthly installments is contingent upon the actual incurring of expenditure from previous releases or not (as distinct from submission of Utilization Certificates). This may please be clarified.

4. As far as the remaining two issues are concerned, they still need to be addressed.

May kindly see before the matter is processed ...2

401-सी, शास्त्री भवन, नई दिल्ली-110001 दूरभाष : 011-23386520, 23384183 फैक्स: 011-23381898
401-C, Shastri Bhawan, New Delhi-110001 Tele :011-2338 6520, 2338 4183, Fax : 2338 1898

:: 2 ::

5. As I had mentioned during the last meeting of the Group of Ministers, the role of our Ministry seems to be funnel funds to the Organizing Committee. The Chairman, Organizing Committee continuously highlights the fact that the Government is merely giving a loan to the Organizing Committee, which they are obliged to return with interest. And, therefore, Chairman, OC insists that the funds should be released to him as per the annual phasing approved by the Cabinet with no further questions asked. Even now, we rarely get any information sought from the Organizing Committee. For instance, our letter of the 23rd October, 2007 asked for some requirements remains unanswered. But the Chairman, OC seems to have given some information to you directly on their funds requirement which has led you to advise us to release the balance of Rs. 70.21 crores in five monthly installments during the remaining part of the financial year. The Ministry of Finance letter of 21st November, 2007 also does not enlighten us on the basis of these monthly releases.

6. It seems our following the GFRs and other financial prudence norms is leading to acrimony and making our position rather invidious. After all, as Chairman, OC puts it, it is a loan to OC, repayable with interest. The quantum is Rs. 767.00 crores and the OC is an asset-less organization!

7. I would, therefore, request you to kindly consider the possibility of relieving my Ministry of the responsibility of releasing the balance of the loan amount, which is under the Non-Plan category and instead consider the alternative of the Ministry of Finance directly releasing the rest of the loan to the Organizing Committee. The Ministry of Finance is much better placed than we are to monitor compliance with GFRs and other financial prudence norms.

With all good wishes.

Yours sincerely,

Shri P. Chidambaram
Minister of Finance
North Block
New Delhi

SECRET

95.2]
25.2
75.2]

No.F.70-19/2002-SP-II/CG (pt)
Government of India
Ministry of Youth Affairs and Sports

Gate No.19, J.N. Stadium
Lodi Road, New Delhi

Dated : 9th April, 2007

To,

The Secretary General,
Organizing Committee Commonwealth Games, 2010,
J.N. Stadium,
New Delhi.

Sub: Holding of the XIX Commonwealth Games at New Delhi in the year 2010 –

Sir,

I am directed to say that Government has approved the expenditure budget of Organising Committee Commonwealth Games, 2010 for conduct of the Games in the following manner:-

"Non-Plan Expenditure budget of Rs.767.00 crores of Organizing Committee Commonwealth Games, 2010 towards conduct of the Games and Government funding to this extent (to be recouped on the basis of revenue neutrality) with flexibility to sanction escalation upto 15% by the Ministry of Youth & Sports without reference to the Expenditure Finance Committee. The Organizing Committee Commonwealth Games, 2010 will be allowed reappropriation of funds upto ± 25% across various heads, within the overall approved ceiling. Re-appropriation beyond ± 25% will be done with the approval of Ministry of Youth Affairs and Sports. The funds will be provided to OC as an unsecured Loan at the Government rate of interest prevailing at the time of release. The repayment of the loan and interest would commence only after the commencement of the revenue generation by the OC. The schedule and other details including moratorium etc. in this regard would be worked out in consultation with the Ministry of Finance."

--2/-

-2-

2. The following is year-wise phasing of requirement of the funds:-

Rs. In crores

2004-05	2005-06	2006-07	2007-08	2008-09	2009-10	2010-11	Total
10.88	33.05	83.58	95.21	132.74	164.42	247.13	767.01

3. Accordingly, OC is requested to take further necessary action in the matter.

Yours faithfully,

(P.K. Ahuja)
Under Secretary to the Government of India
Telefax 24368708

2010 COMMONWEALTH GAMES DELHI

1689

02 AUG 2007

Organising Committee
Commonwealth Games Delhi 2010

Suresh Kalmadi M.P.
Chairman, Organising Committee
Commonwealth Games Delhi 2010
&
President, Indian Olympic Association

July 23, 2007

Dear Shri Chidambaramji

Re: Commonwealth Games Delhi 2010 Organising Committee's Budget

The Government has approved the Expenditure Budget of the Organising Committee, Commonwealth Games Delhi 2010, under the Non-Plan Expenditure amounting to Rs 767.01 crores. The funds have been provided to the Organising Committee as an unsecured loan at the Government rate of interest prevailing at the time of release of the funds (copy of the sanction enclosed).

Considering the fact that this is a revenue neutral budget and that the Government of India has given a guarantee to bridge the gap between revenue and expenditure, it is requested that the interest clause may be deleted. This would reduce the burden of re-payment by the Organising Committee.

This has reference to my discussions with you on 14th July, 2007.

I seek your kind help in the matter.

Have you received a proposal? Se (Exp)

Regards

Yours sincerely,

Suresh Kalmadi

SURESH KALMADI, M.P.

Shri P. Chidambaram,
Hon'ble Finance Minister,
Govt. of India,
North Block,
New Delhi

Encl.: As above

Gate No. 28A, Jawaharlal Nehru Stadium, Lodhi Road, New Delhi-110003, India.
Tel.: +91-11-24367928 / 7929 / 7930 Fax : +91-11-24367931
e-mail: cwg2010@bol.net.in

No. F.70-19/2002 CWG
Government of India
Ministry of Youth Affairs & Sports
******

Gate No.19, JN Stadium,
Lodhi Road, New Delhi 110003

Dated the 28th August ,2007

OFFICE MEMORANDUM

Sub: VIP letter dated 23rd July, 2007 from MP & Chairman, Organising Committee (Shri Suresh Kalmadi) addressed to Finance Minister regarding the expenditure budget of Organising Committee, Commonwealth Games,2010 for the conduct of the Games.

The undersigned is directed to refer to Ministry of Finance, Department of Expenditure's OM No.40(1)/PFII/2007 dated 7.8.2007 on the subject mentioned above.

2. In this context, it is informed that in the EFC meeting held on 13.9.2006 to consider the budget of the Organising Committee(OC) for 'Conduct of the Games', the EFC recommended the approval for budget of Rs.767 crore. The EFC, however, had not made any recommendation with respect to the release of funds as loan with interest to OC. Based on the recommendations of the EFC, the Ministry prepared a draft Cabinet Note, which was sent to all the concerned Ministries for comments. On the draft Cabinet Note, Ministry of Finance had conveyed among other observations, that the budgetary support to OC should be provided as loan at the Government rate of interest prevailing at the time of release. A meeting was held under the Chairmanship of Secretary, YAS to consider the comments, as above, of the Ministry of Finance. This meeting was attended by representatives of OC also. While the representatives of the OC were of the opinion that the loan should be interest free, after extensive discussion, it was felt that, taking into consideration the fact that the Government was funding the entire expenditure to be incurred on the creation and up gradation of sports infrastructure (including all competition and training venues) and the budget of the OC was being funded on a revenue neutral

basis in terms of their own assurances regarding revenue generation, there appeared to be no justification for providing the loan to the OC on interest free basis. It was also noted in the meeting that since the revenue stream of the OC would only commence closer to the Games, the exercise on 'Validation of Budget' and 'Risk Assessment and Mitigation Strategies' of OC was underway, which indicated that a degree of uncertainty would be there, the payment schedule could be worked out with suitable provisions for moratorium etc. Accordingly, the Ministry supported the views of Ministry of Finance to provide funds as loan with interest to OC and incorporated the same in the Cabinet Note for consideration of the Cabinet. The Cabinet in its meeting held on 15.3.2007 approved the budget of OC amounting to Rs.767 crore as loan under Non-Plan at the Government rate of interest prevailing at the time of release. Accordingly, the decision was communicated to the OC.

3. Thereafter, in consultation with the IFD of this Ministry, the terms of repayment of loan to OC have been determined. For releases made earlier, the said amounts have been converted to the interest bearing loan from the date of issue of the order of conversion i.e., 7.8.2007. For subsequent releases, the date of release of loan will also be the date from which the interest to the loan will accrue. The repayment of the principal and the interest will commence only after the Games are over i.e., from 15th October, 2010 to 31st March, 2011. In other words, it has been taken into account that the repayment of principal and interest would commence well after the revenue generation of the OC has started.

4. Article 37 of the Host City Contract, to which the Commonwealth Games Federation (CGF), the OC, the Government of NCT and the Government of India are signatories, reads as under:

> "The OC will ensure that any surplus resulting from the celebration of the Games which remain after all financial commitments and other obligations to the CGF as provided in the Games Documents are discharged, will be paid to the CGF and the IOA for use in legacy programmes to operate Games Venues"

It is clear from the above that any surplus resulting from the Games after meeting the obligations of the CGF would be paid to the CGF and the IOA for use in legacy programmes for the Games venues. In the case of India/Delhi, the National Olympic Committee i.e., the IOA is not the venue owning agency for any of the disciplines. The IOA would therefore not have any siginificant role in legacy programmes related to the Games Venues after the Games are over. The Games Venues are mostly owned by Government agencies such as Sports Authority of India(SAI), Government of NCT of Delhi, DDA, NDMC etc. The responsibility for the maintenance and upkeep of the stadia would primarily vest with the Government agencies while the surplus of the Games would be shared between CGF and IOA as per the Host City Contract. Since the surplus from the Games would not come to the Government there appears no justification for the loan to be interest free.

5. The Government of India has also committed to underwrite any shortfall in the revenue and expenditure of the OC. This commitment would in no way be undermined since the repayment of interest and principal would commence only after the Games have been concluded by which time, the quantum of revenue generation by OC from the Games would be amply clear.

6. In the light of the above, this Ministry is still of the opinion that the loan to the OC for the conduct of the Games should be interest bearing loan, which should be repaid to the Government through the revenues generated by the OC.

28/08/07
(S.S. Chhabra)
Director(ISD)
Tele/Fax 24368706

Ministry of Finance
Department of Expenditure
(Mrs. Reema Prakash, Director, PF II)
North Block,
New Delhi

Copy for information to FA, YAS

D.O. No. 40 (1)/PF.II/2007

सत्यमेव जयते

वित्त मंत्री
भारत
नई दिल्ली-110001
FINANCE MINISTER
INDIA
NEW DELHI - 110001

October 11, 2007

Dear Shri Kalmadi,

Kindly refer to your D.O. dated 23rd July, 2007 regarding the deletion of the interest clause on the unsecured loan of Rs.767.01 crore to the Organizing Committee, Commonwealth Games, 2010.

The matter has been examined in consultation with the Ministry of Youth Affairs & Sports. You would appreciate that the budget of the Organizing Committee (OC) is being funded on a revenue neutral basis in view of the significant scope for revenue generation to the OC from the conduct of the Games. Further, the funding of the entire expenditure to be incurred on the creation, upgradation and the maintenance of sports infrastructure connected with the Games will be borne by the Government or its agencies with no liability on the IOA. Since the surplus from the Games would not accrue to the Government, there appears to be little justification for the loan to be interest free.

While Government would insist on the repayment of the principal amount of the unsecured loan to the OC, we would be willing to agree that the interest on the loan may be paid only from the **surplus** accruing to the OC from the conduct of the Games. The commitment of the Government of India to underwrite any shortfall in expenditure over the revenue generated by the OC is reiterated. In view of this, the deletion of the interest clause at this juncture appears quite unnecessary.

With regards,

Yours sincerely,

(P. Chidambaram)

Shri Suresh Kalmadi,
Chairman, Organizing Committee,
Commonwealth Games, Delhi, 2010,
Jawaharlal Nehru Stadium
New Delhi.

जारी किया
ISSUED

Dy. No. 2342/VIP/FM/07

वित्त मंत्री
भारत
नई दिल्ली - 110001
FINANCE MINISTER
INDIA
NEW DELHI-110001

November 16, 2007

Dear Shri Kalmadi,

Please refer to your letter dated 15.11.2007 on release of funds to the Organizing Committee for 2007-08.

Ministry of Finance, Department of Expenditure has advised Department of Youth Affairs and Sports to release the balance of Rs.70.21 crore in a phased manner over the next 4½ months.

Meanwhile, may I advise you to furnish Utilisation Certificates, if any are pending in respect of the sums of money released in the years 2004-05, 2005-06 and 2006-07. Furnishing Utilisation Certificates will expedite the release of money by Department of Youth Affairs and Sports.

With regards,

Yours sincerely

(P. Chidambaram)

ISSUED
19/11/07

Shri Suresh Kalmadi, MP
Chairman
Organizing Committee of the
Commonwealth Games
Jawaharlal Nehru Stadium
Lodhi Road, New Delhi

Letters issued. Papers are returned for record pl

19/11/07

L-2211 JS (PF-II)/08
Date 20.XI.07

For action pl. file has been sent to you

AS(E)
JS(PF-II)
Dir (RP) 20/11
DD(...)

Pl. place on relevant file
19/XI/07

O.M.No.40(1)/PF-II/2007
Government of India
Ministry of Finance
Department of Expenditure
New Delhi, dated 21st November, 2007

OFFICE MEMORANDUM

Subject:-Release of funds to Organising Committee, CW 2010

Reference is invited to the Group of Minister's meeting on Arrangement of Commonwealth Games held on 12.11.2007 under the Chairmanship of Minister of Human Resources Development.

2. Regarding the issue of utilization certificates, the Finance Minister has advised Chairman Organising Committee, Commonwealth Games, 2010 to furnish the pending utilization certificates for the years 2004-05, 2005-06 and 2006-07. Copy of the Finance Minister's letter is enclosed.

3. Regarding the expenditure issues raised in the meeting, Ministry of Youth Affairs and Sports is advised to release the balance of Rs. 70.21 crores out of the total of Rs.95.21 crores for the year 2007-08 as per the given schedule to the Organizing Committee of Common Wealth Games 2010.

By November 30, 2007	Rs.20.00 crore
By December 31, 2007	Rs. 20.00 crore
By January 31, 2008	Rs.10.00 crore
By February 29, 2008	Rs. 10.00 crore
By March 31, 2008	Rs. 10.21 crore
Total	Rs. 70.21 crore

This issues with the approval of Finance Minister.

(Reema Prakash)
Director (PF-II)

Ministry of Youth Affairs and Sports,
(Shri Sanjeev Mittal, JS&FA)
Shastri Bhavan, New Delhi.

Organising Committee
Commonwealth Games Delhi 2010

Suresh Kalmadi M.P.
Chairman Organising Committee
President, Indian Olympic Association

15 November 2007

Dear Shri Chidambaram ji.

Sub : Release of funds to OC for the financial year 2007-08

In the 12th meeting of the Core Group of Ministers held on 12 November 2007, the issue of release of funds to OC for the financial year 2007-08 came up for discussion in the light of the fact that despite the approval by the Cabinet of item wise annual budget of OC of Rs. 95.21 Cr for the year 2007-08, the Sports Ministry had released only Rs. 25 Cr till date when almost ¾ of the year was over.

Dy. No 2342/VIP/FM/07 15/11/07

Responding to the issue raised, Secretary (MoYAS) informed that as per Government decision, the balance of Rs. 70.21 Cr for the year 2007-08 can be released to OC only when it (i) provides details of cash flow management and (ii) completes budget revalidation exercise. Accordingly, he sought GoM's approval for relaxation in this regard. In your absence, GoM felt that this matter should be discussed with Finance Minister separately.

In this regard, I would like to bring it to your kind notice that the above stand of Secretary (Sports) is contrary to following -

a) the decision of the 11th meeting of GoM wherein you had observed that the Ministry of Sports should ensure that the current year budgetary allocation of Rs. 95.21 Cr be released to the OC at the earliest. On Secretary (Sports) pointing out in the meeting that MoYAS was awaiting budgetary allocation under 'Non-Plan head' under which only Rs. 25 Cr were available, you had instructed that within the approved budgetary allocation of the OC, Sports Ministry must release Rs. 25 Cr available with it to the OC immediately,

b) at no point of time, the Cabinet decision of approving the budget for OC and linking the release of funds with budget revalidation exercise by OC was ever communicated to us, and

Gate No. 28A, Jawaharlal Nehru Stadium, Lodhi Road, New Delhi-110003, India.
Tel.: +91-11-24367928/29/30, 24307000 Fax: +91-11-24367931
email: cwg2010@bol.net.in

Organising Committee
Commonwealth Games Delhi 2010

Suresh Kalmadi M.P.
Chairman Organising Committee
President, Indian Olympic Association

c) the terms and conditions of the loan, as communicated to OC vide Government order dated 7 August 2007 only referred to submission of utilization certificate by OC .

Therefore, it can be seen that the Ministry of Sports is going beyond the prescribed procedure in blocking release of funds to the OC.

I would also like to mention that the uncertainty about the release of funds by MoYAS, despite year wise, item wise sanction of budget by the Union Cabinet as loan to OC has brought all decision making to halt. In the absence of release of total annual loan amount, OC is not able to make any financial commitment to operationalise its various Functional Areas. This may result in cost overruns in the future.

In view of the above, I shall request you to issue necessary directions to MoYAS to release OC's sanctioned budget for the year 2007-08 immediately.

Regards Yours sincerely

Suresh Kalmadi

Suresh Kalmadi,(M.P.)

Shri P Chidambaram
Minister for Finance
North Block, New Delhi

Gate No. 28A, Jawaharlal Nehru Stadium, Lodhi Road, New Delhi-110003, India.
Tel.: +91-11-24367928/29/30, 24307000 Fax: +91-11-24367931
email: cwg2010@bol.net.in

सत्यमेव जयते

B. K. CHATURVEDI

Secret/Most Immediate

मंत्रिमंडल सचिव
CABINET SECRETARY
NEW DELHI

No.781/2/1/2004-Cab.

September 3, 2004

Dear Minister,

Prime Minister has approved the constitution of a Core Group of Ministers under your chairmanship for coordinating the work relating to the organization of the Commonwealth Games to be held in Delhi in 2010. A copy of order issued in this regard is enclosed.

2. The Prime Minister has desired that the first meeting of this Core Group of Ministers may be chaired by him. Subsequent meetings as per the constitution of the GOM will be under your Chairmanship. The first meeting of the GOM is proposed to be arranged on 8th September, 2004.

3. PMO has also indicated that the following items, may be considered for inclusion in the agenda for the first meeting of the GOM apart from others.

(i) Strengthening of the Ministry of Sports in the form of a Division headed by a Joint Secretary for the Commonwealth Games Village; and

(ii) Setting up of an Empowered Committee under the Chairmanship of LG. Delhi, which could include representatives from various concerned central Ministries/agencies, State Governments and other organizations like DDA, MCD, NDMC, National Airports Authority, DMRC etc.

4. A copy of the order constituting the Group is being separately forwarded to Secretary, Ministry of Youth Afftairs & Sports, who will provide the Secretariat to GOM, for further follow up action.

Yours sincerely,

Sd/-

(B.K. Chaturvedi)

Shri Arjun Singh,
Minister of Human Resource Development,
New Delhi.

Copy to Secretary, Ministry of Youth Affairs & Sports.

(P.I. Suvrathan)
Additional Secretary

Copy of the order not enclosed with this letter

ANNEXURE

ESSENTIAL POINTS TO BE KEPT IN VIEW BY THE MINISTRY/DEPARTMENT WHILE SERVICING THE MEETINGS OF GROUP OF MINISTERS (GOM).

1) The GOM should be chaired by the first named Minister in terms of the constitution of the GOM and the meetings of the GOM may be convened after ascertaining his convenience. The minutes may also be got approved by him before issue. The minutes should, inter alia, indicate the list of participants, date, time and venue of the meeting.

2) Notes constituting the agenda for the meeting may be prepared in accordance with the existing instructions governing the preparation of notes for the Cabinet and its Committees, spelt out in the Cabinet Sectt. d.o. letter No.1/16/1/2000-Cab., dated 15.4.2002 (also available in Cabinet Secretariat web-site "http://cabsec.nic.in").

3) Only senior officers shall be in attendance in the meetings of the GOM. In case any other Minister or a special invitee including officers of PSU or autonomous organisations are to be invited to the meetings of the GOM, prior permission of the Minister chairing the GOM may be obtained.

4) Invitation for the meetings of the GOM may be extended to Cabinet Secretary who may attend these meetings or depute his representative to be present in the meetings. A copy of the minutes of the meeting shall also be endorsed to Cabinet Secretary for his information.

SKB

मंत्री
युवा कायक्रम एवं खेल
भारत सरकार
नई दिल्ली-110 001

सुनील दत्त
SUNIL DUTT

Minister
Youth Affairs and Sports
Government of India
New Delhi-110 001

D.O. letter No.F.70-10/2004-SP-II

11 November, 2004

Dear Shri Arjun Singh Ji

I take this opportunity to draw your attention on the letter dated 28th October, 2004 by Hon'ble Prime Minister to Shri Suresh Kalmadi, Member of Parliament and President, Indian Olympic Association in response to his letter dated 26th October, 2004 regarding Commonwealth Games, 2010. The Prime Minister has asked both of us to examine the issues raised by Shri Suresh Kalmadi in his above mentioned letter by endorsing the copies to both of us. I have gone through the letters of Shri Suresh Kalmadi and got the issues referred therein examined.

2. There are certain points raised by Shri Suresh Kalmadi, President, Indian Olympic Association, which would require clarification on record.

3. Firstly, the Society known later as Special Organising Committee for Asian Games, 1982 did not have any founding member, who was an office bearer of IOA. Shri V.C. Shukla and later Shri Buta Singh were Chairpersons of the Society in their capacities as Ministers of the Union Government (**Annexure-I**). In fact Shri Buta Singh, while resigning as Chairperson of the Special Organising Committee had submitted his resignation to the Hon. Prime Minister of India. Even the website of Indian Olympic Association mentions that Shri Buta Singh, India's Sports Minister, was the Chairman of SOC of the Games. (**Annexure-II**).

4. It has been asserted in the letter of Shri Kalmadi that IOA as the apex organization had successfully bid for Commonwealth Games, 2010 with Government's support. A reading of Protocol 1.1 (Games Management Protocol) of Commonwealth Games Federation stipulates "The Commonwealth Games (the Games) are awarded to a country through its Commonwealth Games Association (CGA), which shall nominate the city to host it".

5. Moreover, recapitulation of the events also indicates the primal role of Government of India in getting the Commonwealth Games, 2010 allotted to India. As indicated in a detailed note at **Annexure-III** it is only with the Government of India's written support, the Games were allotted to Delhi.

मंत्री
युवा कार्यक्रम एवं खेल
भारत सरकार
नई दिल्ली-110 001

सत्यमेव जयते

Minister
Youth Affairs and Sports
Government of India
New Delhi-110 001

सुनील दत्त
SUNIL DUTT

6. Therefore the contention of the IOA that the Games solely belong to IOA appears to be misconceived both in terms of Commonwealth Games Charter and also in the above mentioned sequence of events.

7. It is also pertinent to add that the original bid document (May, 2003) on the basis of which games have been allotted to India clearly mentioned that the Organizing Committee will be a "non-profit Government owned registered society" and Chairperson of the Executive Board of the Organizing Committee would a "Government Appointee" (**Annexure-IV**). This must have been incorporated keeping in view the fact the organizing Commonwealth Games involve large financial commitments on the part of Government of India.

8. A subsequent revised bid document received in the Ministry on 17th September, 2004 which has been prepared after the allotment of the Games to India in November, 2003 has made significant changes with major structural and financial implications. Surprisingly, there was no consultation/approval of the Ministry of Youth Affairs and Sports for making these changes. These changes relates to :-

a) Structure of Organizing Committee:-
   i) Constitution of non-profit Government owned registered society into non-profit non-Government registered society.
   ii) Deletion of word "Government Appointee" as Chairperson of the Executive Board of the Organizing Committee.

b) Non-Structural issues:-
   i) Providing travel grant and accommodation to participants.
   ii) Revised competition schedule and opening of Games Village for 25 days.
   iii) Training grant to 72 participating countries
   iv) Additional Venues
   v) Games Village to be constructed at No Cost to Organizing Committee.
   vi) Construction of training sites.
   vii) Free trip of all participants to Agra to visit Taj Mahal.

मंत्री
युवा कार्यक्रम एवं खेल
भारत सरकार
नई दिल्ली-110 001

Minister
Youth Affairs and Sports
Government of India
New Delhi-110 001

सुनील दत्त
SUNIL DUTT

9. Incidentally, I would like to mention here that the Minister for Youth Affairs was the Chairperson of the Organising Committee constituted for the First Afro Asian Games which were to be held at New Delhi in November, 2001.

10. I had the opportunity to meet you today in your office and we could discuss some of the issues raised in Shri Kalmadi's letter to Hon'ble Prime Minister and referred to us by the Prime Minister.

With Regards.

Yours sincerely,

Sunil Dutt

(SUNIL DUTT)

Shri Arjun Singh,
Minister for Human Resource Development,
Government of India,
Shastri Bhavan,
New Delhi.

मंत्री
युवा कार्यक्रम एवं खेल
भारत सरकार
नई दिल्ली-110 001

Minister
Youth Affairs and Sports
Government of India
New Delhi-110 001

सुनील दत्त
SUNIL DUTT

CONFIDENTIAL
14th November, 2004

Dear Dr. ManMohan Singh Ji

This is to acknowledge with thanks your gracious gesture in permitting me to go to USA and Canada on a mission to support the cause of cancer. You will be happy to know that I have been able to collect large voluntary donations. Meanwhile, I have been closely following your success in the international fora in projecting our case against terrorism as well as in handling domestic issues.

I take this opportunity to refer to the Group of Ministers (GOM) meeting chaired by you on 25th October, 2004 which discussed the plan of action related to allotment and hosting of Commonwealth Games 2010 in New Delhi. After the meeting, the media persons were also briefed about the gist of discussions and decisions taken under your able leadership and Government's strategy for a successful conduct of the Games was highlighted. Thereafter, I went abroad. During my stay abroad, I was surprised to see newspaper reports about a resolution passed by Indian Olympic Association (IOA) regarding appointment of President, IOA as Chairman of the Organising Committee which is at variance with the decisions taken in the GOM meeting. The letter of President, IOA dated 28th October, 2004 addressed to you (a copy of which has been received in my office from PMO) clearly shows that President, IOA was aware of the decision of the GOM appointing Minister, Youth Affairs & Sports as Chairman of the Organising Committee for preparation and conduct of Commonwealth Games, 2010. Notwithstanding a serious sense of disquiet, I waited for the formal minutes of the GOM meeting which reached my office on 10th November, 2004. The minutes, as issued by the Cabinet Secretariat, do not reflect the decisions taken in the meeting of 25th October,2004 regarding various aspects of composition of Organising Committee. It seems the word 'Apex', instead of the word 'Organising' has been used inadvertantly in para

Page 1 of 2

8(ii) of the minutes. Moreover, the decision regarding constitution of Executive Board under my Chairmanship has not been recorded. I may add that 'Empowered Committee on Infrastructure' under the Chairmanship of LG, Delhi was also to report to the Organising Committee as per the decision taken in the GOM. You may kindly consider issuing directions to amend the minutes accordingly.

In view of the above facts, I seek your indulgence for withholding the circulation of the minutes of the GOM meeting of 25th October, 2004 till a final view is taken by you on the above issues.

I request you to grant me an early audience so as to enable me to brief you on the facts and recent developments on the issue of hosting of Commonwealth Games, 2010.

With kind regards and happy Diwali and EID MUBARAK

Yours Sincerely,

Sunil Dutt

(Sunil Dutt)

To,
Dr. Manmohan Singh,
Hon'ble Prime Minister of India,
South Block,
New Delhi

MOST IMMEDIATE

PRIME MINISTER'S OFFICE

New Delhi – 110011.

Prime Minister had earlier approved the constitution of a Group of Ministers (GoM) headed by Shri Arjun Singh, Minister of HRD, for overseeing the organisation and conduct of Commonwealth Games of 2010 in New Delhi. The first meeting of the GoM for coordinating the work relating to the organisation of the Games was held on 25.10.2004 under the Chairmanship of the Prime Minister. Subsequently, President, IOA, had also written to the Prime Minister for associating IOA in organizing the Games.

2. Based on the views expressed at the GoM, communications received from Minister of Youth Affairs & Sports and President, IOA, the following institutional arrangements have been evolved for the conduct of the Commonwealth Games.:

(a) The Group of Ministers headed by Shri Arjun Singh, Minister of HRD, to monitor and oversee the preparation for the Games.

(b) An Empowered Committee to look after the construction of stadia and any other infrastructure facilities required for the Games. This Committee may be chaired by the Minister of Youth Affairs & Sports and would comprise of three Vice Chairmen, viz. Lt. Governor, Delhi, Chief Minister. Delhi and Chairman of the Organising Committee. The composition of the Empowered Committee, other than the three Vice Chairmen, may be decided by the GoM or by the Prime Minister, on the suggestions of the Minister of Youth Affairs and Sports in his capacity as its Chairman.

An Organising Committee and Executive Board responsible for the conduct of the Games and formulation of Sub-Committees to be chaired by Shri Suresh Kalmadi, President of IOA. The Organising Committee will deal with the Government of India through the Ministry of Youth Affairs & Sports and with the Delhi Administration. The composition of the Organising Committee may be decided by the GoM or by the Prime Minister taking into account the suggestions of its Chairman.

(d) A Committee of Secretaries (CoS) headed by the Cabinet Secretary for the implementation of the decisions of the GoM regarding the Commonwealth Games. The CoS will be responsible for implementation of the decisions of the GoM which do not fall within the purview of the Empowered Committee and the Organising Committee.

2. The Prime Minister has directed that the institutional arrangements mentioned above may be sent to Shri Arjun Singh, Minister of HRD, who heads the GoM on the Commonwealth Games, for consideration in the next meeting of the GoM.

[Rohit Khera]
Officer on Special Duty
Tele : 23015655
Fax : 23016857

Cabinet Secretary

PMO I.D. No. 570/50/C/1/04-ES.II dated 06.12.2004

✓Copy to PS to Minister of HRD for kind information of Hon'ble Minister.

[Rohit Khera]
Officer on Special Duty

Secret

ANNEX. II

Organising Committee
Commonwealth Games 2010 Delhi

Suresh Kalmadi, M.P
Chairman

CWG/2010/GoM/Minutes

01.06.2006

Dear Shri Quraishi Ji,

In the 9th meeting of the GoM held on 4th January, 2006 under the Chairmanship of Shri Arjun Singh, Minister for Human Resource Development I made a presentation on the Final report on the Sports infrastructure (Competition venues & Training venues) and the Games Village which has been approved as presented. But in the minutes of the meeting mention was made only about the Competition Venues. I would request you kindly to add the **Training Venues** also as per the enclosed list as it is mandatory item.

The following omissions may also be added to the minutes:

1. Appointment of an International consultant to guide in developing the International standard infrastructure keeping in view of India's bid for 2014 Asian Games and our proposal for bidding for 2016 Olympic Games.

2. To add to Item 3 (a)... in consultation with the Infrastructure Coordination Committee of 2010 OC as the approval of the CGF is required.

3. The infrastructure should be handed over to OC 2010 soon after their completion latest by 31-8-2009 which will remain with it till the Games are over.

4. As regards the Games village for 2010 CWG if it is developed under the Public and Private Partnership model as proposed by DDA, I said that an under taking should be taken from the developers of the Games village that the accommodation created for 2010 CWG would be made available to the Organizing Committee of the 2014 Asian Games if the Games are allotted to Delhi for accommodating the contingents of the Asian countries. The GoM has agreed to it. This point may be added to Item 4 of the minutes.

Cont...2

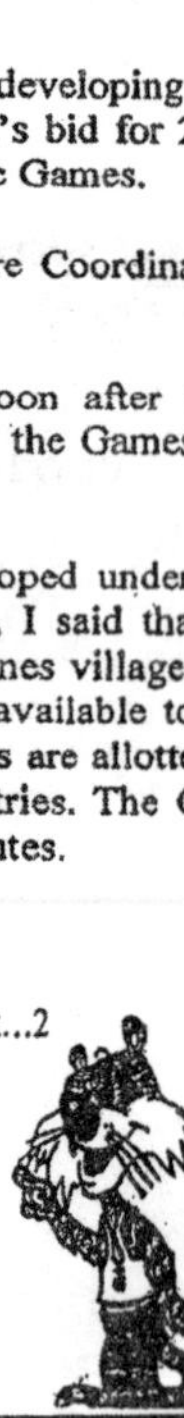

No. 28A, Jawaharlal Nehru Stadium, Lodhi Road, New Delhi-110003. India.
l.: +91-11-24367928 / 7929 / 7930. Fax : +91-11-24367931
e-mail : cwg2010@bol.net.in

Secret

#2#

Revised minutes of the 9th meeting of the GoM may please be issued attaching a copy of the final report on the infrastructure presented by OC 2010 and the four points mentioned in this letter.

Regards

Yours sincerely,

Suresh Kalmadi, M.P.

Dr. S.Y. Quraishi,
Secretary,
Ministry of Youth Affaires and Sports,
Shastri Bhavan,
New Delhi.

-291-

D.O 4661/MYAS/07
14/c

मणि शंकर अय्यर
MANI SHANKAR AIYAR

मंत्री
पंचायती राज, युवा कार्यक्रम एवं खेल और
उत्तर-पूर्वी क्षेत्र विकास
भारत सरकार
नई दिल्ली-110001
Minister
Panchayati Raj, Youth Affairs & Sports and
Development of the North Eastern Region
Government of India
New Delhi-110 001

Secret

23 October 2007

Dear Pulok,

At 5.00 pm day-after-tomorrow, Thursday, 25 October, the Prime Minister has convened a meeting to review the arrangements for the Commonwealth Games. This is the first review at his level after a lapse of over a year.

2. My officers have done all they can to alert Government, specifically the Cabinet Secretariat and PMO, to a number of our extremely serious concerns which have only been mounting over the past year. I fear that if these concerns are not met in the meeting day- after-tomorrow, we may find ourselves irretrievably damaged.

3. My primary concern is that, in sharp distinction to the structure of the Special Organising Committee for the Asian Games, 1982, which was chaired by the Minister of State for Sports, Sardar Buta Singh, and packed with Government Ministers, MPs and Government officials, the Executive Committee for the Commonwealth Games 2010, chaired by Suresh Kalmadi, has no Government Ministers, just one back-bench MP and only two Government Secretaries, and they too lack veto powers; almost all decisions are taken in the committees of the Executive Board that do not include these Government officials; and the Executive Board does not report the decisions of these committees to the Ministry of Youths Affairs and Sports. In consequence, money is being squandered, such as appointing Mike Hooper of the Commonwealth Games Federation as an international consultant with *monthly* first-class air passages for him, and sometimes his wife, between London and Delhi and a farm house in Delhi to live in with scores of air-conditioners, at a total estimated cost of some Rs. 2 crore! Other international consultants have been appointed at a cost of up to $ 5,000 *per day*.

4. Also, unlike the Special Organising Committee of the Asian Games, 1982 which had a large number of distinguished and powerful public-minded representatives, including Shri Rajiv Gandhi, then a back-bench MP, to guide the Executive Board, the present Organising Committee is packed with yes-men (and a few yes-women) and has no one with any influence on the Executive Board or its Committees to press an alternative opinion, leaving the Chairman with virtually dictatorial powers. Without a drastic overhaul of both the Executive Board and Organising Committee for the Commonwealth Games, I fear it will prove to be practically impossible for the Government to significantly address the excesses of Chairman Suresh Kalmadi and his cohorts.

401-सी, शास्त्री भवन, नई दिल्ली-110001 दूरभाष : 011-23386520, 23384183 फैक्स: 011-23381898
401-C, Shastri Bhawan, New Delhi-110001 Tele :011-2338 6520, 2338,4183, Fax : 2338 1898

:2:

5. Moreover, the direct and indirect costs of CWG have already soared to over Rs. 20,000 crore! The total expenditure on the Asian Games 1982 was of the order of Rs. 55 crore. *O tempora! O mores!*

6. My Ministry has suggested three alternatives of dealing with the situation, any one of which could retrieve the situation even at this juncture:

(a) Since Chairman Kalmadi insistently maintains that Commonwealth Games revenues will substantially exceed expenditures by the Organising Committee, he may be invited to take his 'bankable' propositions to financial institutions or commercial banks and raise the required finances from the market, thus releasing the Government of any expenditure on the Organising Committee and any responsibility to Parliament for the antics of its Executive Board.

Or :

(b) A Minister of State for International Sporting Events may be appointed Chairman of the Organising Committee with an adequate number of Government nominees on the Executive Board, including influential sports-minded back-bench MPs, with the power of veto over inappropriate decisions taken by the Board or any of its committees. And:

(c) Recasting the Organising Committee and the Executive Board for the Commonwealth Games to conform to the pattern that was so successfully evolved for the Asian Games 1982.

6. If at all possible, I would appreciate an opportunity to meet Madam on Thursday, 25 October in the forenoon to discuss with her the line I should be taking in the Prime Minister's meeting in the afternoon of the same day.

With all good wishes,

Yours sincerely,

Shri Pulok Chatterji
Additional Secretary
Prime Minister's Office
South Block
New Delhi

४५AS/10/C.0./09

डॉ॰एम॰एस॰ गिल
Dr. M.S. GILL

युवा कार्यक्रम एवं खेल मंत्री
भारत सरकार
नई दिल्ली-110 115
MINISTER FOR YOUTH AFFAIRS & SPORTS
GOVERNMENT OF INDIA
NEW DELHI-110 115

सत्यमेव जयते

CONFIDENTIAL

26th September 2009

Subject : Commonwealth Games – October 2010, and Fennell letter.

Dear Prime Minister,

You are aware of the controversies and concerns, that have come up on the Fennell letter, which points to serious doubts, about the capacity of the 500 member Organising Committee, under Shri Suresh Kalmadi, to deliver the conduct of the Games, from the 3rd of October 2010 to the 16th, when they all finally depart.

The 1982 Asian Games in Delhi, held 28 years ago, on a much smaller scale, than any current games, were a great success. The main reason was that, as in all Games anywhere, then and now, the preparation and conduct was entirely in government's hands. Shri Rajiv Gandhi was a unique point of authority, able to break any inter-ministerial or other road blocks. The actual work was given to the then Home Minister Shri Buta Singh, and a selected group of twenty odd officials. The Games were a great success, and are admired. Today the Asian Games, after such a long interval, are very much bigger, and more complex. The Commonwealth Games of course, are in the big league.

The then Government of India and the Government of Delhi, alongwith the IOA, signed the agreement, taking the Games, in 2003 The original signed document had a government Chairman, but later somehow that was changed. The basic design of these games, requires that nine major stadiums, are funded and built by the Government through the Central PWD. Some lesser stadiums are being built by the DDA, and other Delhi Government authorities, through the State PWD. The Athletes village, unfortunately, across the river, is being built by a Dubai Company under the DDA. The Delhi Government and Chief Minister, are undertaking a major infrastructure improvement effort, for the city of Delhi. All the work of Delhi authorities, is funded through, and linked to the Urban Development Ministry. The security is the responsibility of the Home Ministry and the Lt Governor, Delhi. The Nine Government Stadiums, are being built with all the energy, at our command. Though I have to point out that work was slow, till I took over on 6th April 2008.

The Shooting, Cycling and Swimming Stadiums had not even been started, due to internal arguments. Nor had the bridge, to bring the athletes across the river from the village, to the Stadium. These were immediately got started, and under constant supervision, will be got ready, in time. The time lost in the past cannot be recovered. The Delhi Chief Minister is also pushing all the infrastructure in every possible way. We would like to see you, to discuss all this, and at that time, will make a presentation on this work, if permitted.

Contd on page 2.

96

-2-

But the most vital part, that of the conduct of the Games, from 3rd to 16th October 2010, is the sole responsibility of the Organising Committee of 500, and such staff as they appoint – currently about 400, and said to come up to even 1200. The Ministry of Sports, ensures that the funds as necessary, are promptly provided. At the time of the Agreement, they were to be about 200 crores, are now something less than 800 crores, and we are coming to Cabinet soon, for something above 1600 crores.

The Organising Committee has an Executive Committee of 15 Members, with three from the Commonwealth Games Federation, include one Mr Hooper, looked after by the Organising Committee, and based in Delhi, since long, the Chairman Shri Kalmadi with four other colleagues from the IOA and five Government Officers, namely Secretary (Sports), Secretary (Urban Development), Chief Secretary (Delhi), Principal Secretary to CM, Delhi, and Additional Secretary (Finance) Govt of India. In the past, the Committee rarely met and generally endorsed post-facto decisions, taken in a highly centralised system. When I came in on 6th April 2008, I pushed with my Secretary, to get some order, insisting on regular meetings, with minutes, advanced agenda etc. Finance Committees too, were set up for greater financial control, and concurrent audit was brought in. Some order has been restored.

But the question raised by Fennell is, about the ability and the capability of the Organising Committee and its higher staff, to deliver the Games, to the quality expected. They are expected to lookafter 17000 sports persons and officials, from the time, they leave they countries, their travel cost, unfortunately being our burden, to the 16th of October, when they depart. Every aspect of their living in Delhi, and their competitions are to be organized with clock work precision. The OC have 23 Sub Committees, which have rarely met, or performed in the situation described above. Yesterday 25th September 2009, the Chairmen of all these Committees were called by the OC Chairman, I suppose in view of the current controversy, and given an exhortation, in the hope that they will buckle down to the job. The competence of the Committees, and the decentralization, necessary for them, to function effectively, is yet to be seen.

In this background, I have had intensive meetings with Shri Kalmadi and Shri Randhir Singh the Secretary General, and with the Delhi Chief Minister, the Cabinet Secretary, and Shri T K Nair. We have devised a line of action, to strengthen the management, inside the Organising Committee, immediately. The structure cannot be changed, but this is the essential minimum now, with no time to lose. The Cabinet Secretary has identified individuals, and I agree with him. This first step needs to be taken without delay, and then we will go on, from there. I may also mention that I had asked for a detailed written report from Shri Kalmadi, on the Fennell letter, and he has now put in a formal request to my

Contd on page 3.

-3-

Secretary, asking for senior staff injection, into the OC. It will be necessary that the persons asked to undertake this fire fighting job, are fully backed by the Minister of Sports, and Yourself, in order to be effective and do the job to the country's satisfaction.

I would request an early meeting, alongwith the Delhi Chief Minister, with the Cabinet Secretary and Shri Nair, being present. We will also make a presentation on the progress of the construction, if allowed.

With regards

Yours sincerely,

(M S Gill)

Dr Manmohan Singh
Hon'ble Prime Minister of India
7, Race Course Road
New Delhi

Annexure III

BBP

Bharatbala Productions P. Ltd

October 16, 2009

Mrs. Sindhushree Khullar
Secretary (Sports)
Ministry of Youth Affairs & Sports, Govt. of India
Room No. 1, C-Wing, Gate No. 6
Shastri Bhawan,
New Delhi 110001

Dear Mrs. Khullar,

Please find enclosed my letter to Mr. Suresh Kalmadi, Chairman – Organising Committee Commonwealth Games Delhi 2010 with regards to engaging the Internanonal experts for the opening and closing ceremonies.

Further to my conversation with you last evening it is my request that your office takes urgent steps to engage the services of Mark Fisher, Production Designer & Entertainment Architect Stufish

Only on engaging his services can we begin to meet the deadlines for providing all the engineering designs for CPWD.

I look forward to your support in achieving this objective.

Thanks & best regards,

Bharatbala

Creative Director,
Opening & Closing Ceremonies,
Commonwealth Games Delhi 2010

BBP

BharatBala *Productions* P. Ltd

October 16, 2009

Mr. Suresh Kalmadi
Chairman
Organising Committee Commonwealth Games Delhi 2010
City Centre-II, (NDCC Towers)
Opp Jantar Mantar, Jai Singh Road
New Delhi 110001

Dear Mr Kalmadi,

As you are aware, we had a very successful Production Planning Workshop last week for the Opening & Closing ceremonies of the Delhi Commonwealth Games. After our successful presentations to you and the GOM based on outcomes of the workshop, we had a productive meeting with SAI/CPWD officials where they agreed to accommodate the construction of a trench/tunnel and foundation for a bandstand into their plans for the JN Stadium. However, since they are under extreme time pressure already to deliver the finished stadium to the OC on time, and as this adds further complexity to their plans, they've asked for final engineering drawings for the trench and the bandstand foundation from our International experts by 20th October. While we try to find out what is the earliest that the international experts can deliver the engineering drawings, it is imperative that we formally engage them as we won't be able to proceed on this without this first step.

In this context, it is important to bear in mind that with the exception of Rio Birch, who is in the process of being appointed as the overall international consultant for the CWG ceremonies, we do not have any official arrangement with any other specialist international experts (production design & architecture, technical direction, lighting, sound, communication systems, video screens & lasers, pyrotechnics, aerial rigging, etc.). We will definitely need these capabilities, which are currently not available in India and for which there are only a handful of global experts, for a world-class live show of the vision and scale that we have planned.

Specifically, we need to immediately engage a team of experts, led by Mark Fisher & Piers Sheppard, for the design & construction of the trench & bandstand, both of which are critical for our show. Mark is a Production Designer & Entertainment Architect, while Piers is a Technical Director. Mark & Piers have already committed a large amount of time and effort on this project, without any official contract or payment. Mark has already attended our Ideation Workshop in Mumbai and our Production Planning Workshop in Delhi, in both of which he made significant contributions, apart from creating and supervising the design of the Bandstand. Piers has helped create a preliminary design for the trench that has been shared with CPWD. They are currently

BBP

engaged with a set of designers in creating the final designs and architectural/engineering drawings that we need to provide CPWD and use to construct the bandstand. They have been kind enough to share their professional expertise and go ahead with a lot of work in good faith, assuming that they will be officially engaged and suitably compensated. For them to work further, we need to approve their proposal for phase 1 of the work - design & engineering drawings - and clear their invoice for immediate advance payment. I am attaching the invoice they sent to the OC a couple of days back, and request the OC to arrange for immediate clearance and payment. This is critical to our meeting our delivery schedules for the Ceremonies.

On the 10th October 2009 presentation to the GoM, both the GoM and OC had given assurance to the international experts that fast track clearance will be made this week in order to kick start this mammoth work that needs to be accomplished.

I am hoping that we will be able to give the confirmation to the international experts before October 23rd 2009.

Thank you, and best regards,

Bharatbala

Creative Director,
Opening & Closing Ceremonies,
Commonwealth Games Delhi 2010

SECRET

F.No.70-16/2010-eWG-I
GOVERNMENT OF INDIA
MINISTRY OF YOUTH AFFAIRS AND SPORTS
(DEPARTMENT OF SPORTS)
*****

SECRET Page____of_____

Annexure-6

D.O. No 40(7)/PF-II/09

ASHOK CHAWLA

FINANCE SECRETARY
MINISTRY OF FINANCE
GOVERNMENT OF INDIA
NORTH BLOCK, NEW DELHI-110001
Tel : 23092611 Fax: 23094075

June 12, 2010

Dear Sindhushree,

Please refer to your DO No. 150/Secy(SP)/10 dated 8th June, 2010 seeking clearance to permit the Organizing Committee to go a ahead RFPs in anticipation of approval the additional amount in respect of Ceremonies.

2. The matter has been considered in the context of increased cost estimates projected by the Organizing Committee in meetings of the Committee of Secretaries as well as the Group of Ministers, It is been categorically stated that no further cost increase can be supported, Only in the Case of "Ceremonies"(both Opening and Closing ceremonies taken together) an increase in the cost estimate from the existing provision of Rs. 106 crore to a maximum of Rs. 300 crore has been agreed to, Ministry of Sports may permit the OC to go ahead with processing RFPs and make payments in anticipation of this approval only for this.

3. The Ministry of Sports may, as early as possible, move for due sanction of the enhanced amount. In doing so it may examine the possibility of effecting savings on other heads. **The increase, however, should not exceed Rs. 194 crore.** While moving for approval the Ministry should also bring on board clear reasons for cost over-run and fix responsibility for decisions not taken in time, which has led to cost over-runs.

Yours sincerely
Sd/-
(Ashok Chawla)

Smt. Sindhushree Khullar
Secretary-(Sports)
Ministry of Youth Affairs & Sports
Room No. 2, C-Wing, Shastri Bhawan
New Delhi- 110001

F.No.70-16/2010-CWG-I **SECRET**
GOVERNMENT OF INDIA
MINISTRY OF YOUTH AFFAIRS AND SPORTS
(DEPARTMENT OF SPORTS)
....

Annexure-7

New Delhi, the 14th September, 2010

Office Memorandum

SUBJECT: Budget of Organization Committee, Commonwealth Games 2010 (OC) Delhi for the conduct of the Games.

Ministry of Youth Affairs and Sports may refer to their DO No. 70-42/2009-CWG.1 dated 3rd September,2010 wherein MYAS had made two proposals on the captioned subject *viz.*

(i) Enhancing the loan budget of the Organizing Committee from Rs. 1620 crore to Rs. 1813.42 crore towards the increased expenditure for the Ceremonies Rs. 106.58 crore to Rs. 300 crore; and

(ii) Re- appropriation of funds within the existing approved budget of OC of Rs. 1620 crore from the Head "Revenue Generation Functional areas" to "Other Functional Areas"

In this regard, the undersigned is directed to state that:

(i) This Ministry agrees to enhancing the loan budget of the Organizing Committee from Rs. 1620 crore to Rs. 1813.42 crore for the Ceremonies though MYAS should justify the same in the note for GoM/Cabinet and see if some saving are possible.

(ii) However, the re-appropriation of funds within the existing approved budget of OC of Rs. 1620 crore from the Head "Revenue Generation Functional areas" to Other Functional Areas" is not acceptable since the said amount and head was meant for revenue generation. It cannot be spent on their activities which would tantamount to an indirect increase in the Organizing Committee's approved budget.

4. This issue with the approval of Finance Minister.

Sd/-
(Piyush Srivastava)
Director (PF II)
Tel.No. 23092668

Department of Sports,
(Smt. Sindhushree Khullar, Secretary)
Ministry of Youth Affairs & Sports
Shastri Bhawan, New Delhi

SECRET

SECRET

No.F.70-19/2002-SP-II Vol.IV
Government of India
Ministry of Youth Affairs and Sports

R.B 9968296672

Copy No. 76

New Delhi, the 6th March, 2007

NOTE FOR THE CABINET

Sub: Holding of the XIX Commonwealth Games at New Delhi in the year 2010.

1. Background

1.1 On a proposal of Indian Olympic Association (IOA) for holding of the XIX Commonwealth Games at New Delhi in the year 2010, the following approvals had been sought vide Cabinet Note of even number dated 20th May, 2003.

i) To allow the IOA to bid for the XIX Commonwealth Games, 2010

ii) To approve, in principle, holding of the XIX Commonwealth Games, 2010 in Delhi in case the IOA is successful in its bid.

iii) To allow the Ministry of Finance and Company Affairs and the Ministry of Youth Affairs and Sports (MYAS) to settle between themselves the financial arrangements for an estimated expenditure of Rs.1,61,53,600/- towards the bidding process for the Games.

iv) To allow this Ministry to issue the following guarantees:-

a) Undertaking to support the bid of Delhi to host the Games;

b) free entry for all accredited athletes and delegations of all participating countries; and

SECRET

No.F.70-19/2002-SP-II Vol.IV
Government of India
Ministry of Youth Affairs and Sports

-----

c) that the Games will be organized in accordance with the Constitution and Protocols & Regulations of the Commonwealth Games Federation (CGF)

1.2 In the above Cabinet Note an expenditure of Rs.295.50 crores was indicated towards upgradation of sports infrastructure and conduct of the Games (**Annex-I**). The expenditure on Security and on the Games Village was proposed to be incurred by the respective agencies, i.e. Government and DDA. The IOA had indicated sponsorship revenue of US$ 100 million.

1.3 Since time was short, approval of the Hon. Prime Minister was sought under Rule 12 of the Government of India (Transaction of Business) Rules, 1961 for the proposal indicated in para 1.1 above. The Cabinet Secretariat vide their U.O. No.781/2/1/203-Cab. dated 24.05.2003 conveyed the approval of the Hon. Prime Minister, and desired that the MYAS should seek ex-post facto approval of the Cabinet in the matter.

1.4 The MYAS vide Cabinet Note of even number dated 10th September, 2003 while seeking ex-post facto approval as above, sought the following further approvals:-

a) Agree to and enter into the Host City Contract as provided by CGF;

b) Underwrite any shortfall between revenue and expenditure of the Organising Committee (OC);

SECRET

No.F.70-19/2002-SP-II Vol.IV
Government of India
Ministry of Youth Affairs and Sports

-----

c) Approve, in principle the proposal of the Lt. Governor of Delhi to set up the Games Village, in the form of hostel type accommodation, at a site off NH-24, next to the Akshardham Temple, at a preliminary estimated cost of Rs.186 crores, to be met by the Ministry of Human Resource Development (MHRD) and handing over the same to the University of Delhi after the Games are over.

d) Approve, in principle, the proposal of the Lt. Governor of Delhi for construction of indoor and outdoor stadia in the Yamuna Sports Complex, and upgradation of existing infrastructure of the DDA, at an estimated cost of Rs.32.50 crores.

1.4.1 Apart from the additional expenditure on the Games Village and construction/upgradation of sports infrastructure by DDA, the Cabinet Note also brought out that the IOA had also revised their budget estimates from Rs.295.50 crores to Rs.399.05 crores (**Annex-II**).

1.4.2 The Cabinet Secretariat vide communication No.26/CM/2003(i) dated 17th September, 2003 and 1st October, 2003 communicated the approval of the Cabinet in its meeting held on 11th September, 2003 to proposals contained in para 1.1. and 1.4 above with the modification that the manner of funding and post games utilization of the Games Village would be decided later.

SECRET

No.F.70-19/2002-SP-II Vol.IV
Government of India
Ministry of Youth Affairs and Sports

1.5 Thereafter, the Games were allotted to Delhi on 13th November, 2003 by the CGF, and are scheduled to be held from 3rd to 14th October, 2010.

2. The purpose of this note is to apprise the Cabinet of the various actions taken after the allotment of the Games to Delhi, and the status of the preparations for the Games, and to seek approval for the budgetary estimates which have been considered by the Expenditure Finance Committee (EFC) so far in respect of this Ministry.

3. Vide Cabinet Secretariat letter No.781/2/1/2004-Cab dated 3rd September, 2004 it was indicated that the Hon. Prime Minister had decided to constitute a core Group of Ministers (GoM) under the Chairmanship of Minister of Human Resource Development (**Annex-III**) and also that the first meeting would be chaired by Hon'ble Prime Minister. Accordingly, the meeting was held under the Chairmanship of Hon'ble Prime Minister on 25/10/2004. Interalia, it was brought out during this meeting that the estimated expenditure as per the revised bid document presented by the IOA to the CGF had been now projected at US $ 384 Million. It was mentioned that the estimates of the revenue receipts had been revised upwards from US $ 100 million to US $ 186 million and that the preparations and organization of the games would require Government support of approximately Rs.1200 to Rs.1400 crores.

4. The GoM in its initial meetings decided to establish various institutional mechanisms for overseeing and coordination in respect of various aspects for preparation

SECRET

No.F.70-19/2002-SP-II Vol.IV
Government of India
Ministry of Youth Affairs and Sports

-----

and organization of the Games. A copy of the decision taken in this regard is at **Annex-IV.**

5. In the 4th meeting of the GoM, on a proposal of the Organising Committee (OC) to have a reappraisal of the venues proposed for the Games conducted through a Consultant, M/s Event Knowledge Services (EKS), it was decided that the same may be undertaken, and expenses for it would be borne by the Delhi Development Authority (DDA). Also the GOM while considering the additional commitments from by the IOA (which were not part of the original bid document) observed that detailed proposals along with financial implications be placed before the Cabinet for approval with the recommendation of the GOM. These additional commitments now from part of the budget of the OC of Rs.767.00 crores which has been recommended by the EFC.

6. In the 9th meeting of the GoM, on the basis of a presentation of the OC, the venues for the different events were approved. It was also decided that the respective agencies should proceed with the process of concept and design on the basis of global tendering and that the Plans & Designs be finalized in consultation with the OC to ensure that the technical requirements for various disciplines are taken care of, and that the infrastructure is completed in all respects and with required quality well in advance, before Commonwealth Games, 2010.

SECRET

No.F.70-19/2002-SP-II Vol.IV
Government of India
Ministry of Youth Affairs and Sports

-----

7. It may be mentioned here that, initially, 15 disciplines were proposed for the Games, but keeping in view the country's medal prospects, 3 more disciplines, namely Cue Sports, Archery and Tennis were proposed to be included. However, the CGF has approved inclusion of only 2 more disciplines i.e. Archery and Tennis. Hence there are now a total of 17 disciplines for the Commonwealth Games, 2010. A list indicating these disciplines, the venues and the implementing agencies is at **Annex-V**.

8. The various options submitted by DDA, for development of the Games Village were considered in the 9th meeting of GoM, and it was decided to develop the Games Village on a Public Private Participation (PPP) model, involving Government funding for development works and temporary overlays and private funding for development of residential accommodation.

9. The GoM also decided that the budget allocations would be made through the EFC route by the respective Ministries as indicated below:-

(a) MYAS shall be responsible for preparing the EFC Memo related to requirements of Sports Authority of India (SAI), Budget for Conduct of Games submitted by OC and requirements for preparation of Indian sportspersons for Commonwealth Games 2010.

(b) DDA, for its requirements related to Venue Infrastructure to be developed by them and the Games Village, shall seek capital grant on Plan Account and

SECRET

No.F.70-19/2002-SP-II Vol.IV
Government of India
Ministry of Youth Affairs and Sports

Ministry of Urban Development (MoUD) shall move the EFC Memo for that purpose.

(c) The requirement of Delhi University for Venue Infrastructure was to be handled through MHRD.

(d) Delhi Government shall include all its requirements covering civic infrastructure and venue infrastructure in its proposal submitted to the Planning Commission.

(e) MYAS shall be invited for all the EFC meetings dealing with Commonwealth Games matters.

10. Hon. Prime Minister had chaired a meeting to review the preparation for the Commonwealth Games, 2010 on 7th August, 2006. It had been decided in the meeting that after the requisite EFC/Planning Commission/Ministry of Finance approvals a consolidated proposal for the Cabinet would be put up. This Note is being put up accordingly. With regard to other issues highlighted, the Committees in respect of clearances have been set up as has been summarized in the subsequent paragraphs. The OC has provided detailed item-wise expenditure estimates of its budget alongwith year-wise phasing which have been incorporated in the Note. In respect of residential accommodation for officers on deputation to the OC, a Note has been moved for the Cabinet Committee on Accommodation. The OC has now included Secretary, Urban Development as Member and Vice Chairman, Delhi Development Authority and Commissioner of Police as Special Invitees on the Executive Board of OC. Time lines in respect of the Competition Venues have been provided by the various agencies. Time

SECRET

No.F.70-19/2002-SP-II Vol.IV
Government of India
Ministry of Youth Affairs and Sports

-----

lines in respect of other projects are being established. The work in respect of these would commence by mid 2007 and be completed by end of 2009. A Web-based monitoring system is being prepared in consultation with the Department of Information Technology and the Software Technology Parks of India (STPI) which is likely to be in place shortly. The progress in respect of other issues highlighted in the meeting have been brought out in the subsequent paragraphs.

11. **Budget**

11.1 The budget proposals in respect of various stakeholders have been discussed at various levels from time to time. However, in order to meet the immediate requirements, pending approval of the Cabinet/CCEA, this Ministry, with the approval of Ministry of Finance, has released Rs.112.51 crores to the OC for meeting international commitments and other requirements of expenditure, and Rs.12.50 crores to SAI for appointment of consultants for the preparation of designs, etc. in respect of the infrastructure to be developed by them.

11.2 The EFC has since considered the proposals of the MYAS in respect of the budget of the OC for conduct of the Games, and SAI for development of Venue Infrastructure; and, the proposals of MoUD regarding Venue Infrastructure and the Games Village to be established by the DDA. The EFC has made the following recommendations in respect of the proposals for allocation of budget to the OC and SAI.

SECRET

No.F.70-19/2002-SP-II Vol.IV
Government of India
Ministry of Youth Affairs and Sports

11.3 Organizing Committee for Commonwealth Games (OC): The EFC in its meeting held on 13th September, 2006 after detailed deliberations recommended the OC's budget for consideration of Cabinet, subject to the following observations:-

i) Given the nature of the OC Budget, funds may be provided under Non-Plan instead of Plan, as suggested by Planning Commission (However, there would be no need to hold a separate meeting of the Committee on Non-Plan Expenditure to approve the OC Budget).

ii) In view of the scope for economy in expenditure, the OC budget may be fixed at Rs.767 crores on a revenue netural basis, with flexibility to sanction escalation upto 15% by the MYAS without reference to the EFC.

iii) In view of the need for flexibility, the OC may be given flexibility of ± 25% for re-appropriation of funds across various heads, within the overall approved ceiling. Re-appropriation beyond ± 25% may be done with the approval of MYAS.

iv) The items for reduction in the OC Budget from Rs.896.00 crores to Rs.767.00 crore cover catering, transport, games technical conduct, opening & closing ceremonies, Commonwealth Youth Games and contingencies. Details may be worked out by the MYAS and incorporated in the Draft Note for Cabinet.

v) Provision for furniture and fixtures for the Games Village may continue to be made in the OC Budget for the time being.

SECRET

No.F.70-19/2002-SP-II Vol.IV
Government of India
Ministry of Youth Affairs and Sports

-----

vi) Concurrent audit by C&AG may be put in place from 1st April,. 2008 and specific items identified for pre-audit. An appropriate system for internal audit may also be worked out by the OC with approval of MYAS till March, 2008.

vii) Year-wise phasing of expenditure may be worked out and incorporated in the draft Note for Cabinet.

viii) A risk analysis of the projected revenue stream may be undertaken expeditiously and incorporated in the Draft Note for Cabinet to validate the assumption regarding revenue neutrality of the OC budget.

11.4 The minutes of the EFC held on 13.9.2006 and the Action Taken Report (ATR) thereon are placed at <u>Annex-VI & VII</u> respectively and the itemwise proposed budget of the OC is at <u>Annex - VIII</u>.

11.5 <u>Sports Authority of India (SAI)</u>: The EFC held on 20th September, 2006 after detailed deliberations recommended the proposal for sanction of Rs.1000.00 crores to SAI subject to following observations:-

i) The scope for variation in total is only 10%. Variation beyond 10% will require further approval and sanction of EFC.

ii) The provision of 1200 hostel rooms appears to be very high and should be reduced to 700 rooms.

iii) The tunnel and extra turf being provided at MDC National Stadium should be deleted.

SECRET

No.F.70-19/2002-SP-II Vol.IV
Government of India
Ministry of Youth Affairs and Sports

-----

iv) The modern technology that is being sought to be introduced in India should be tested and should not be sub-optimal.

v) All the tenders should be on a turn key basis on global competitive bidding.

vi) In the preparation of DPR, legacy aspect may also be incorporated which should clearly bring out the revenue generation potential which will go a long way in taking care of the maintenance of the Stadia and will result in reduction of central budgetary support over the years.

vii) The possibility of utilizing the infrastructure of ITPO for some of the events should be examined, and if found feasible, the proposal approved by EFC would stand amended to the extent of the next monitised value of the new facilities now proposed.

viii) Ballpark figures of revenue generation would be specified.

ix) All India Tennis Association (AITA) proposal will be moved separately by MYAS.

11.6 The minutes of the EFC held on 20.9.2006 and ATR thereon are placed at **Annex- IX & X** respectively and the itemwise proposed budget of SAI is at **Annex-XI**.

11.7 As per the suggestion of the Department of Expenditure, the proposal of All India Tennis Association (AITA) in respect of the Venue for Tennis was considered by Departmental EFC on 15.2.2007. The Departmental EFC has recommended Rs.30.00 crores for the project with variation of ± 15%. This has been approved by the Hon. Minister for Youth Affairs and Sports.

SECRET

No.F.70-19/2002-SP-II Vol.IV
Government of India
Ministry of Youth Affairs and Sports

11.8 The tentative year-wise phasing of the requirements of funds by the OC, SAI and AITA, have been placed at **Annex-XII.**

11.9 The financial/budget proposals described in the foregoing paragraphs cover all the competition venues except Rugby 7's regarding which it has now been decided to develop and use the main ground of Delhi University. There could be some issues requiring further detailing in respect of the venues of Archery which are under discussion with the OC. Apart from the competition venues, after detailed discussions with all stake holders, the locations of various training venues have also been firmed up and the cost estimates in respect of most of these are already included in the earlier mentioned estimates of various agencies. The residual issues pertaining to competition and training venues as mentioned above would also have some financial implications but these are not likely to be very significant.

11.10 Apart from the Competition & Training Venues there will be some non-competition venues in the form of the International Broadcasting Centre (IBC) and Main Press Centre (MPC) which would be established primarily through temporary overlays. After considerable discussions and looking at various options it has been decided at the level of Committee of Secretaries (COS) that this may be set up in the premises of Indian Trade Promotion Organization (ITPO) at Pragati Maidan. A Committee has been set up in the Ministry of Information and Broadcasting to work out the details regarding the establishment and operations of IBC/MPC including the likely expenditure. Further consideration, as may be required with reference to the budgetary implication would be taken up after receipt of report of the Committee.

SECRET

No.F.70-19/2002-SP-II Vol.IV
Government of India
Ministry of Youth Affairs and Sports

11.11 With regard to preparation of Indian teams, it had been initially projected that an expenditure of Rs.300 crores would be incurred for the same. Subsequently, significantly higher estimates of Rs.1500 crores had been submitted by the IOA. After extensive discussions with all stakeholders the view has emerged that expenditure on preparation of teams should be subsumed to the extent possible within the existing schemes of the Ministry related to Assistance to National Sports Federations and Talent Search and Training and through the Scheme pertaining to the National Sports Development Fund (NSDF). The norms and entitlements under the former two Schemes are proposed to be appropriately modified and the corpus available under the NSDF is proposed to be enhanced both through private/corporate contributions and the budget. Necessary EFC proposals in this respect are under preparation.

11.12 Apart from the expenditure on establishment of the various venues, there would be an important issue of temporary overlays required at various venues in the operational phase of the Games and the Games Village and other temporary arrangements that may be required at different places (including IBC/MPC) for the conduct of the Games. Some provisions in this regard have been made in the budget of the OC. They have been advised to look into this matter in details in the context of their ongoing exercise of Risk Assessment and Validation of Budget.

11.13 The Commonwealth Youth Games, 2008, are proposed to be organized as a sub-event of the Commonwealth Games, 2010. It was found that it would not be possible to hold these Games in Delhi, since most of the sports infrastructure would be under development/up-gradation in the context of the main Games. Three possible locations, viz., Bangalore, Hyderabad and Pune had been identified and it was decided by the CGF, that the Games may be held in Pune. The Government of Maharashtra had submitted

SECRET

No.F.70-19/2002-SP-II Vol.IV
Government of India
Ministry of Youth Affairs and Sports

-----

proposals to the Planning Commission for an amount of Rs.626.00 crores for up-gradation of civic infrastructure in the city of Pune and Rs.192.00 crores (revised to Rs.285.00 crores) for the creation/up-gradation of sports infrastructure.

11.13.1 The Planning Commission deputed a team of officials to Pune and, after examination, has agreed to provide an amount of Rs.110.00 crores over a two year period i.e. Rs.50 crores in 2007-08 and Rs.60 crores in 2008-09 for sports infrastructure as special central assistance to the Government Maharashtra. The Government of Maharastra has, however, requested for a higher allocation in the light of its revised proposal. As regards civic infrastructure, the Planning Commission has indicated specific projects related to civic infrastructure to be taken up under the Jawaharlal Nehru National Urban Renewal Mission (JNNURM) under the Ministry of Urban Development (MoUD). Further action is being taken by MoUD in respect of the proposals regarding civic infrastructure.

12. <u>Other Related Issues</u>

12.1 <u>Delhi Development Authority (DDA)</u>: The proposals of the MoUD projecting an estimated budget of Rs. 474 crores, for the construction of venue infrastructure and the establishment of the Games Village by DDA were considered by the EFC, which has approved/recommended an amount of Rs.325.00 crores to be provided to DDA with a flexibility of 25% within which the Ministry could give the

SECRET

No.F.70-19/2002-SP-II Vol.IV
Government of India
Ministry of Youth Affairs and Sports

-----

necessary approvals. The MoUD is seeking approval of Cabinet/CCEA in this regard separately.

12.2 Ministry of Home Affairs - Security related arrangements for the Commwealth Games, 2010. The Delhi Police has submitted a proposal to the Ministry of Home Affairs (MHA) for strengthening/up-gradation of security related arrangements, including, enhancement of manpower, vehicles and equipments, etc. involving an estimated expenditure of Rs.264.00 crores. The proposal is under consideration of MHA, who have to move the proposal for consideration by the EFC and thereafter seek the approval of the Cabinet/CCEA.

12.3 The Ministry of Culture have indicated a requirement of funds for conservation, restoration and upgradation of certain historical monuments in Delhi as a measure of beautification of Delhi in the context of the Commonwealth Games, 2010. The Planning Commission has been requested to consider their proposal as part of the plans for up gradation of infrastructure and beautification of Delhi.

12.4 The Ministry of Civil Aviation have also indicated requirement of funds for the Bureau of Civil Aviation Security (BCAS) and Hotel Corporation of India in respect of increased tourist inflow during Commonwealth Games, 2010. They had been advised to place their proposal through the EFC route before the Ministry of Finance. The Ministry of Civil Aviation vide their O.M. No.F.38/1/2006-C&W(Vol.II) dated 16.01.2007 have

SECRET

No.F.70-19/2002-SP-II Vol.IV
Government of India
Ministry of Youth Affairs and Sports

-----

expenditure budget are underway.

			Rs. In crores	
	(i)	SAI for Sports Infrastructure	Rs.1000.00	± 10%
(V)	~~(ii)~~	DDA for International Zone, etc. Games Village and Sports Infrastructure	Rs.325.00	± 25%
(ii)	~~(iii)~~	Venue for Tennis (AITA)	Rs.30.00	± 15%
VIII	~~(iv)~~	Sports Infrastructure for Commonwealth Youth Games, 2008	Rs.110.00	
(III)	~~(v)~~	OC for Conduct of the Games	Rs.767.00	± 15%
(IV)	~~(vi)~~	Preparation of Teams	Rs.300.00	
VI	~~(vii)~~	NCTD of Delhi for civic Infrastructure	Rs.770.00	
VII	(viii)	Security through MHA	Rs.264.00	
		Total	***Rs.3566.00 crores*** ± Rs.300 crores	

13. **Status of Preparedness**

13.1 The proposals which have already been considered by the EFC and the Planning Commission cover most of the critical areas pertaining to the preparation for the Games in respect of establishing the required basic infrastructure. It is expected that the designs and estimates pertaining to the various sports infrastructure works will be finalized in the near future, and after calling for tenders the process of awarding works would be commenced by the middle of 2007, and the projects completed by the end of 2009. Specific time lines are being established in respect of each project together with a system of monitoring so that timely completion of all works can be closely monitored and ensured. Detailed discussions with various stakeholders viz. IOA, National Sports Federations (NSFs) and SAI are also underway with regard to preparation of teams for

SECRET

No.F.70-19/2002-SP-II Vol.IV
Government of India
Ministry of Youth Affairs and Sports

-----

the Commonwealth Games, 2010 with a view to preparing specific plans to enhance the performance levels and medal prospects in the Games.

13.2 An Empowered Committee has also been set up under the Chief Secretary, Government of NCT of Delhi, with representatives of all the agencies/authorities concerned to facilitate speedy and time bound clearances in respect of games related projects. Another Committee has been set up, with the MYAS as convenor, to deal with clearances pertaining to the Delhi Urban Arts Commission (DUAC) and other central agencies, as may be required.

13.3 Government has also constituted a Task Force in the Ministry of Tourism for coordination and follow up action with all agencies concerned for creation of additional tourist accommodation including Bed and Breakfast facilities, in the context of Commonwealth Games, 2010.

14. Following the consideration and recommendations by the EFC, consolidated proposals, were to be put up for consideration and approval of the Cabinet. However, since finalization of budget proposals for different components would be a continuing process, it was decided after deliberations in the Committee of Secretaries (COS) that proposals which had already been considered by the EFC should be put up for consideration of the Cabinet immediately in order that the provisions could be suitably

SECRET

No.F.70-19/2002-SP-II Vol.IV
Government of India
Ministry of Youth Affairs and Sports

-----

incorporated in the budget for 2007-08 and subsequent years. Action is being taken accordingly.

15. ***Comments of Ministry/Department received on the draft Cabinet Note and observation of this Minister thereon***

Comments of Ministry of Finance, Department of Expenditure, Planning Commission and Ministry of Civil Aviation on the draft Cabinet have been received. The comments and response of this Ministry thereon is placed at **Annex XIII.** Approval of the Cabinet is being sought accordingly.

16. **Present Proposal**

16.1 In the light of the foregoing and with a view to expediting the execution of the projects, approval of the Cabinet is solicited for the following:-

16.2 Ex-post approval for release of Rs.112.51 crores to the Organising Committee for the Commonwealth Games, 2010 and Rs.12.50 crores to Sports Authority of India.

16.3 Expenditure budget of Rs.767.00 crores of Organizing Committee Commonwealth Games, 2010 towards conduct of the Games and Government funding to this extent (to be recouped on the basis of revenue neutrality) with flexibility to sanction escalation upto 15% by the Ministry of Youth & Sports without reference to the Expenditure Finance Committee. The Organizing Committee Commonwealth Games, 2010 may be allowed reappropriation of funds upto ± 25% across various heads, within

SECRET

No.F.70-19/2002-SP-II Vol.IV
Government of India
Ministry of Youth Affairs and Sports

-----

the overall approved ceiling. Re-appropriation beyond ± 25% may be done with the approval of Ministry of Youth Affairs and Sports. A decision may also be taken whether the budget of Organizing Committee Commonwealth Games, 2010 is to be provided as Non-Plan expenditure as recommended by Expenditure Finance Committee or as Plan expenditure. The funds will be provided to OC as an unsecured Loan at the Government rate of interest prevailing at the time of release. The repayment of the loan and interest would commence only after the commencement of the revenue generation by the OC. The schedule and other details including moratorium etc. in this regard would be worked out in consultation with the Ministry of Finance.

16.4 Expenditure budget of Rs.1000.00 crores of Sports Authority of India towards venue infrastructure to be developed by it and Government funding to this extent. This may be approved with provision for variation upto ± 10% as Plan expenditure. Variation beyond 10% would require further approval of the Expenditure Finance Committee.

16.5 Expenditure budget of Rs.30.00 crores of All India Tennis Association towards tennis venues infrastructure to be up gradated by it and Government fund to this extent. This may be approved with provision for variation upto ± 15% as Plan expenditure. Variation beyond 15% would required further approval of Departmental Expenditure Finance Committee.

SECRET

No.F.70-19/2002-SP-II Vol.IV
Government of India
Ministry of Youth Affairs and Sports

-----

17. A statement of Implementation Schedule on the above proposals has been given in Appendix to the note.

18. This Cabinet Note has been seen and approved by Minister of Youth Affairs and Sports.

(Rahul Bhatnagar)
Joint Secretary to the Government of India
Telephone No.24368705

SECRET

No.F.70-19/2002-SP-II Vol.IV
Government of India
Ministry of Youth Affairs and Sports

New Delhi, the 6th March, 2007

STATEMENT OF IMPLEMENTAION SCHEDULE

Sub: Holding of the XIX Commonwealth Games at New Delhi in the year 2010.

Gist of decision required	Project benefits/results	Time-frame and manner of implementation/ Reporting got the Cabinet Secretariat
(1) Ex-post approval for release of Rs.112.51 crores to the Organising Committee Commonwealth Games, 2010 and Rs.12.50 crores to Sports Authority of India. (2) Expenditure budget of Rs.767.00 crores of Organizing Committee Commonwealth Games, 2010 towards conduct of the Games and Government funding to this extent (to be recouped on the basis of revenue neutrality) with flexibility to sanction escalation upto 15% by the Ministry of Youth & Sports without reference to the Expenditure Finance Committee. The Organizing Committee Commonwealth Games, 2010 may be allowed reappropiration of funds upto ± 25% across various heads, within the overall approved ceiling. Re-appropriation beyond ± 25%	The Games will be held in accordance with the international commitments made by Indian Olympic Association and to be honoured now by Organising Committee Commonwealth Games, 2010. This will facilitate smooth preparation for the Games till the revenue starts flowing to Organising Committee Commonwealth Games, 2010. as per projections	The Commonwealth Games will be held in New Delhi in October, 2010.

SECRET

No.F.70-19/2002-SP-II Vol.IV
Government of India
Ministry of Youth Affairs and Sports

-----

may be done with the approval of Ministry of Youth Affairs and Sports. A decision may also be taken whether the budget of Organising Committee Commonwealth Games, 2010 is to be provided as Non-Plan expenditure as recommended by Expenditure Finance Committee or as Plan expenditure. The funds will be provided to OC as an unsecured Loan at the Government rate of interest prevailing at the time of release. The repayment of the loan and interest would commence only after the commencement of the revenue generation by the OC. The details of this would be worked out with the Ministry of Finance. (3) Expenditure budget of Rs.1000.00 crores of Sports Authority of India towards venue infrastructure to be developed by it and Government funding to this extent. This may be approved with provision for variation upto 10% as Plan expenditure. Variation beyond 10% would require further approval of the Expenditure Finance Committee. (4) Expenditure budget of Rs.30.00 crores of All India Tennis Association towards tennis venues infrastructure to		

SECRET

No.F.70-19/2002-SP-II Vol.IV
Government of India
Ministry of Youth Affairs and Sports

-----

be up gradated by it and Government funding to this extent. This may be approved with provision for variation upto ± 15% as Plan expenditure. Variation beyond 15% would required further approval of Departmental Expenditure Finance Committee.		

(Rahul Bhatnagar)
Joint Secretary to the Government of India
Telephone No.24368705

****

MOST IMMEDIATE
SECRET

No.F.70-19/2002-SP-II (Vol.IV)
Government of India
Ministry of Youth Affairs and Sports

Gate No.19, J.N. Stadium,
Lodi Road, New Delhi-110003

Dated : 26th December, 2006

OFFICE MEMORANDUM Copy No. 2

Sub: Holding of the XIX Commonwealth Games at New Delhi in the year 2010 – Draft Cabinet Note thereon

The undersigned is directed to enclose herewith a draft Note for the Cabinet on the above mentioned subject. The draft Note has been prepared on the recommendations of the Expenditure Finance Committee held on 13th September, 2006 and 20th September, 2006 wherein the budget proposals of two components related to Commonwealth Games, viz conduct of the Games and Sports Authority of India's sports infrastructure were discussed.

2 In view of the above, the Ministries/Departments concerned are requested to offer their comments on the draft note for the Cabinet on the above subject.

26/12/06
(S. S. Chhabra)
Deputy Secretary to the Government of India
Telefax 24368706

1. Secretary (Shri V.K. Duggal), Ministry of Home Affairs North Block, New Delhi.
2. Secretary (Shri Sanjeev Mishra), Department of Expenditure, Ministry of Finance, North Block, New Delhi.
3. Secretary, (Shri Ajay Prasad) Ministry of Civil Aviation, Rajiv Gandhi Bhavan, New Delhi
4. Secretary (Shri B.K. Das), Ministry of Culture, Shastri Bhavan, New Delhi.
5. Prime Minister's Office (Shri Sanjay Mitra, Joint Secretary), South Block, New Delhi.
6. Adviser Education (Dr. C. Chandramohan) Planning Commission, Yojana Bhavan, New Delhi
7. Adviser (PAMD) (Dr, Nagesh Singh), Planning Commission, Yojana Bhavan, New Delhi.

SECRET

No.F.70-19/2002-SP-II Vol.IV
Government of India
Ministry of Youth Affairs and Sports

Copy No. 2

New Delhi, the December, 2006

DRAFT NOTE FOR THE CABINET

Sub: Holding of the XIX Commonwealth Games at New Delhi in the year 2010.

1. **Background**

1.1 On a proposal of Indian Olympic Association (IOA) for holding of the XIX Commonwealth Games at New Delhi in the year 2010, the following approvals had been sought vide Cabinet Note of even number dated 20th May, 2003.

i) To allow the IOA to bid for the XIX Commonwealth Games, 2010

ii) To approve, in principle, holding of the XIX Commonwealth Games, 2010 in Delhi in case the IOA is successful in its bid.

iii) To allow the Ministry of Finance and Company Affairs and the Ministry of Youth Affairs and Sports (MYAS) to settle between themselves the financial arrangements for an estimated

SECRET

No.F.70-19/2002-SP-II Vol.IV
Government of India
Ministry of Youth Affairs and Sports

-----

expenditure of Rs.1,61,53,600/- towards the bidding process for the Games.

iv) To allow this Ministry to issue the following guarantees:-

a) Undertaking to support the bid of Delhi to host the Games;

b) free entry for all accredited athletes and delegations of all participating countries; and

c) that the Games will be organized in accordance with the Constitution and Protocols & Regulations of the Commonwealth Games Federation (CGF)

1.2 In the above Cabinet Note an expenditure of Rs.295.50 crores was indicated towards upgradation of sports infrastructure and conduct of the Games (**Annex-I**). The expenditure on Security and on the Games Village was proposed to be incurred by the respective agencies, i.e. Government and DDA. The IOA had indicated sponsorship revenue of US$ 100 million.

1.3 Since time was short, approval of the Hon. Prime Minister was sought under Rule 12 of the Government of India (Transaction of Business) Rules,

SECRET

No.F.70-19/2002-SP-II Vol.IV
Government of India
Ministry of Youth Affairs and Sports

1961 for para 1.1 above. The Cabinet Secretariat vide their U.O. No.781/2/1/203-Cab. dated 24.05.2003 conveyed the approval of the Hon. Prime Minister, and desired that the MYAS should seek ex-post facto approval of the Cabinet in the matter.

1.4 The MYAS vide Cabinet Note of even number dated 10th September, 2003 while seeking ex-post facto approval as above, sought the following further approvals:-

a) Agree to and enter into the Host City Contract as provided by CGF;

b) Underwrite any shortfall between revenue and expenditure of the Organising Committee (OC);

c) Approve, in principle the proposal of the Lt. Governor of Delhi to set up the Games Village, in the form of hostel type accommodation, at a site off NH-24, next to the Akshardham Temple, at a preliminary estimated cost of Rs.186 crores, to be met by the Ministry of Human Resource Development

SECRET

No.F.70-19/2002-SP-II Vol.IV
Government of India
Ministry of Youth Affairs and Sports

(MHRD) and handing over the same to the University of Delhi after the Games are over.

d) Approve, in principle, the proposal of the Lt. Governor of Delhi the cost of construction of indoor and outdoor stadia in the Yamuna Sports Complex, and upgradation of existing infrastructure of the DDA, at an estimated cost of Rs.32.50 crores.

1.4.1 Apart from the additional expenditure on the Games Village and construction/upgradation of sports infrastructure by DDA, the Cabinet Note also brought out that the IOA had also revised their budget estimates from Rs.295.50 crores to Rs.399.05 crores (**Annex-II**).

1.4.2 The Cabinet Secretariat vide communication No.26/CM/2003(i) dated 17th September, 2003 and 1st October, 2003 communicated the approval of the Cabinet in its meeting held on 11th September, 2003 to proposals contained in para 1.1. and 2 above with the modification that the manner of funding and post games utilization of the Games Village would be decided later.

SECRET

No.F.70-19/2002-SP-II Vol.IV
Government of India
Ministry of Youth Affairs and Sports

1.5 Thereafter, the Games were allotted to Delhi on 13th November, 2003 by the CGF, and are scheduled to be held from 3rd to 14th October, 2010.

2. The purpose of this note is to apprise the Cabinet of the various actions taken after the allotment of the Games to Delhi, and the status of the preparations for the Games, and to seek approval for the budgetary estimates which have been considered by the Expenditure Finance Committee (EFC) so far in respect of this Ministry.

3. Vide Cabinet Secretariat letter No.781/2/1/2004-Cab dated 3rd September, 2004 it was indicated that the Hon. Prime Minister had decided to constitute a core Group of Ministers (GoM) under the Chairmanship of Minister of Human Resource Development (**Annex-III**) and also that the first meeting would be chaired by Hon'ble Prime Minister. Accordingly, the meeting was held under the Chairmanship of Hon'ble Prime Minister on 25/10/2004. Interalia, it was brought out during this meeting that the estimated expenditure as per the revised bid document presented by the IOA to the CGF had been now projected at US $ 384 Million. It was mentioned

SECRET

No.F.70-19/2002-SP-II Vol.IV
Government of India
Ministry of Youth Affairs and Sports

-----

that the estimates of the revenue receipts had been revised upwards from US $ 100 million to US $ 186 million and that the preparations and organization of the games would require Government support of approximately Rs.1200 to Rs.1400 crores.

4. The GoM in its initial meetings decided to establish various institutional mechanisms for overseeing and coordination in respect of various aspects for preparation and organization of the Games. A copy of the decision taken in this regard is at **Annex-IV.**

5. In the 4th meeting of the GoM, on a proposal of the Organising Committee (OC) to have a reappraisal of the venues proposed for the Games conducted through a Consultant, M/s Event Knowledge Services (EKS), it was decided that the same may be undertaken, and expenses for it would be borne by the Delhi Development Authority (DDA). In the 9th meeting of the GoM, on the basis of a presentation of the OC, the venues for the different events were approved. It was also decided that the respective agencies should proceed with the process of concept and design on the basis of global tendering and that the Plans & Designs be finalized in consultation

SECRET

No.F.70-19/2002-SP-II Vol.IV
Government of India
Ministry of Youth Affairs and Sports

-----

with the OC to ensure that the technical requirements for various disciplines are taken care of, and that the infrastructure is completed in all respects and with required quality well in advance, before Commonwealth Games, 2010.

6. It may be mentioned here that, initially, 15 disciplines were proposed for the Games, but keeping in view the country's medal prospects, 3 more disciplines, namely Cue Sports, Archery and Tennis were proposed to be included. However, the CGF has approved inclusion of only 2 more disciplines i.e. Archery and Tennis. Hence there are now a total of 17 disciplines for the Commonwealth Games, 2010. A list indicating these disciplines, the venues and the implementing agencies is at **Annex-V**.

7. The various options submitted by DDA, for development of the Games Village were considered in the 9th meeting of GoM, and it was decided to develop the Games Village on a Public Private Participation (PPP) model, involving Government funding for development works and temporary overlays and private funding for development of residential accommodation.

SECRET

No.F.70-19/2002-SP-II Vol.IV
Government of India
Ministry of Youth Affairs and Sports

-----

8. The GoM also decided that the budget allocations would be made through the EFC route by the respective Ministries as indicated below:-

(a) MYAS shall be responsible for preparing the EFC Memo related to requirements of Sports Authority of India (SAI), Budget for Conduct of Games submitted by OC and requirements for preparation of Indian sportspersons for Commonwealth Games 2010.

(b) DDA, for its requirements related to Venue Infrastructure to be developed by them and the Games Village, shall seek capital grant on Plan Account and Ministry of Urban Development (MoUD) shall move the EFC Memo for that purpose.

(c) The requirement of Delhi University for Venue Infrastructure was to be handled through MHRD.

(d) Delhi Government shall include all its requirements covering civic infrastructure and venue infrastructure in its proposal submitted to the Planning Commission.

(e) MYAS shall be invited for all the EFC meetings dealing with Commonwealth Games matters.

SECRET

No.F.70-19/2002-SP-II Vol.IV
Government of India
Ministry of Youth Affairs and Sports

-----

9. Budget

9.1 The budget proposals of various stakeholders have been discussed at various levels from time to time. However, in order to meet the immediate requirements, pending approval of the Cabinet/CCEA, this Ministry, with the approval of Ministry of Finance, has released Rs.112.51 crores to the OC for meeting international commitments and other requirements of expenditure, and Rs.12.50 crores to SAI for appointment of consultants for the preparation of designs, etc. in respect of the infrastructure to be developed by them.

9.2 The EFC has since considered the proposals of the MYAS in respect of the budget of the OC for conduct of the Games, and SAI for development of Venue Infrastructure; and, the proposals of MoUD regarding Venue Infrastructure and the Games Village to be established by the DDA. The EFC has made the following recommendations in respect of the proposals for allocation of budget to the OC and SAI.

SECRET

No.F.70-19/2002-SP-II Vol.IV
Government of India
Ministry of Youth Affairs and Sports

9.3 Organizing Committee for Commonwealth Games (OC): The EFC held on 13th September, 2006 after detailed deliberations recommended the OC's budget for consideration of Cabinet, subject to the following observations:-

i) Given the nature of the OC Budget, funds may be provided under Non-Plan instead of Plan, as suggested by Planning Commission. (However, there would be no need to hold a separate meeting of the Committee on Non-Plan Expenditure to approve the OC Budget).

ii) In view of the scope for economy in expenditure, the OC budget may be fixed at Rs.767 crores on a revenue netural basis, with flexibility to sanction escalation upto 15% by the MYAS without reference to the EFC.

iii) In view of the need for flexibility, the OC may be given flexibility of ± 25% for re-appropriation of funds across various heads, within the overall approved ceiling. Re-appropriation beyond ± 25% may be done with the approval of MYAS.

SECRET

No.F.70-19/2002-SP-II Vol.IV
Government of India
Ministry of Youth Affairs and Sports

-----

iv) The items for reduction in the OC Budget from Rs.896.00 crores to Rs.767.00 crore cover catering, transport, games technical conduct, opening & closing ceremonies, Commonwealth Youth Games and contingencies. Details may be worked out by the MYAS and incorporated in the Draft Note for Cabinet.

v) Provision for furniture and fixtures for the Games Village may continue to be made in the OC Budget for the time being.

vi) Concurrent audit by C&AG may be put in place from 1st April,. 2008 and specific items identified for pre-audit. An appropriate system for internal audit may also be worked out by the OC with approval of MYAS till March, 2008.

vii) Year-wise phasing of expenditure may be worked out and incorporated in the draft Note for Cabinet.

viii) A risk analysis of the projected revenue stream may be undertaken expeditiously and incorporated in the Draft Note for Cabinet to validate the assumption regarding revenue neutrality of the OC budget.

SECRET

No.F.70-19/2002-SP-II Vol.IV
Government of India
Ministry of Youth Affairs and Sports

9.4 The minutes of the EFC held on 13.9.2006 and the Action Taken Report (ATR) thereon are placed at **Annex-VI & VII** respectively and the itemwise proposed budget of the OC is at **Annex - VIII**.

9.5 Sports Authority of India (SAI): The EFC held on 20th September, 2006 after detailed deliberations recommended the proposal for sanction of Rs.1000.00 crores to SAI subject to following observations:-

i) The scope for variation in total is only 10%. Variation beyond 10% will require further approval and sanction of EFC.

ii) The provision of 1200 hostel rooms appears to be very high and should be reduced to 700 rooms.

iii) The tunnel and extra turf being provided at MDC National Stadium should be deleted.

iv) The modern technology that is being sought to be introduced in India should be tested and should not be sub-optimal.

v) All the tenders should be on a turn key basis on global competitive bidding.

vi) In the preparation of DPR, legacy aspect may also be incorporated which should clearly bring out the revenue generation potential which will go a long way in taking care of

SECRET

No.F.70-19/2002-SP-II Vol.IV
Government of India
Ministry of Youth Affairs and Sports

-----

the maintenance of the Stadia and will result in reduction of central budgetary support over the years.

vii) The possibility of utilizing the infrastructure of ITPO for some of the events should be examined, and if found feasible, the proposal approved by EFC would stand amended to the extent of the next monitised value of the new facilities now proposed.

viii) Ballpark figures of revenue generation would be specified.

ix) All India Tennis Association (AITA) proposal will be moved separately by MYAS.

9.6 The minutes of the EFC held on 20.9.2006 and ATR thereon are placed at **Annex- IX & X** respectively and the itemwise proposed budget of SAI is at **Annex-XI**.

9.7 Year wise phasing of the requirement of funds have been submitted by OC & SAI and the same are under discussion and finalization in the context of the Annual Plan and the XIth Five Year Plan.

9.8 Proposals in respect of the venues for Tennis and Rugby 7s have not yet been finalized. Tennis has only recently been included among the disciplines for the Commonwealth Games, 2010 and in respect of Rugby 7 s some issues were raised in the 10th meeting of GoM regarding the location of

SECRET

No.F.70-19/2002-SP-II Vol.IV
Government of India
Ministry of Youth Affairs and Sports

-----

venue. Discussions are underway with the concerned stakeholders and as indicated in Annexure-X these will be finalized soon. However, this is not likely to affect the schedule because the quantum of work will not be very time consuming.

9.9 Proposals of a large number of training venues are already included in the estimates of various agencies. Discussions are underway with the concerned stakeholders for the identification of the other training venues and these would be finalized in the near future.

9.10 As far as the International Broadcasting Centre (IBC) and the Main Press Centre (MPC) are concerned these would be established primarily through temporary overlays and expenditure on these and other overlays would be a part of the budget of the OC and other agencies.

9.11 With regard to preparation of Indian teams, it had been initially projected that an expenditure of Rs.300 crores would be incurred for the same. Subsequently, significantly higher estimates of Rs.1500 crores had been submitted by the IOA. After extensive discussions with all stakeholders it was decided that expenditure on preparation of teams should be subsumed within the existing schemes of the Ministry related to talent search, training, competition, etc. with suitable modifications and

SECRET

No.F.70-19/2002-SP-II Vol.IV
Government of India
Ministry of Youth Affairs and Sports

-----

enhancements. These Schemes are already being reviewed in the context of the XIth Plan. Other requirements over and above these would be placed before the EFC for consideration.

9.12. The Commonwealth Youth Games, 2008, are proposed to be organized as a sub-event of the Commonwealth Games, 2010. It was found that it would not be possible to hold these Games in Delhi, since most of the sports infrastructure would be under development/up-gradation in the context of the main Games. Three possible locations, viz., Bangalore, Hyderabad and Pune had been identified and it was decided by the CGF, that the Games may be held in Pune. The Government of Maharashtra had submitted proposals to the Planning Commission for an amount of Rs.626.00 crores for up-gradation of civic infrastructure in the city of Pune and Rs.192.00 crores for the creation/up-gradation of sports infrastructure.

9.12.1 The Planning Commission deputed a team of officials to Pune and, after examination, had recommended that an amount of Rs.100.00 crores may be provided in the budget of MYAS for sports infrastructure, and has indicated specific projects related to civic infrastructure to be taken up

SECRET

No.F.70-19/2002-SP-II Vol.IV
Government of India
Ministry of Youth Affairs and Sports

-----

under the Jawaharlal Nehru National Urban Renewal Mission (JNNURM) under MoUD. Further action is being taken by the MYAS, to put up a proposal for consideration of the EFC regarding the sports infrastructure, and by MoUD in respect of the proposals regarding civic infrastructure.

10. **Other Related Issues**

10.1 Delhi Development Authority (DDA): The proposals of the MoUD projecting an estimated budget of Rs. 474 crores, for the construction of venue infrastructure and the establishment of the Games Village by DDA were considered by the EFC, which has approved/recommended an amount of Rs.325.00 crores to be provided to DDA with a flexibility of 25% within which the Ministry could give the necessary approvals. The MoUD is seeking approval of Cabinet/CCEA in this regard separately.

10.2 Ministry of Home Affairs - Security related arrangements for the Commwealth Games, 2010. The Delhi Police has submitted a proposal to the Ministry of Home Affairs (MHA) for strengthening/up-gradation of security related arrangements, including, enhancement of manpower,

SECRET

No.F.70-19/2002-SP-II Vol.IV
Government of India
Ministry of Youth Affairs and Sports

-----

vehicles and equipments, etc. involving an estimated expenditure of Rs.264.00 crores. The proposal is under consideration of MHA, who have to move the proposal for consideration by the EFC and thereafter seek the approval of the Cabinet/CCEA.

10.3 The Ministry of Culture have indicated a requirement of funds for conservation, restoration and upgradation of certain historical monuments in Delhi as a measure of beautification of Delhi in the context of the Commonwealth Games, 2010. The Planning Commission has been requested to consider their proposal as part of the plans for up gradation of infrastructure and beautification of Delhi.

10.4 The Ministry of Civil Aviation have also indicated requirement of funds for the Bureau of Civil Aviation Security (BCAS) and Hotel Corporation of India in respect of increased tourist inflow during Commonwealth Games, 2010. They are being advised to place their proposal through the EFC route before the Ministry of Finance.

SECRET

No.F.70-19/2002-SP-II Vol.IV
Government of India
Ministry of Youth Affairs and Sports

10.5 Government of NCT of Delhi had initially approached the Planning Commission with a budget of Rs.1314.00 crores in respect of upgradation of infrastructure of Delhi in preparation for the Commonwealth Games 2010. Based on a decision to revisit the budget estimates, Government of NCT of Delhi had submitted its proposal of Rs.770.00 crores comprising the following agency-wise elements:-

Transport	:	Rs. 270.00 crores
PWD	:	Rs. 165.00 crores
MCD	:	Rs. 75.55 crores
Health & Family Welfare	:	Rs. 45.70 crores
Delhi Jal Board	:	Rs. 40.00 crores
UP/PWD	:	Rs. 100.00 crores
NDMC	:	Rs. 33.75 crores
Dte. of Education (Sports)	:	Rs. 40.00 crores
Total	:	**Rs.770.00 crores**

10.5.1 These proposals have been considered, and approved in principle, by the Planning Commission.

10.6 In view of the above as per present estimates the total expenditure of the Games would be around Rs.3563.45 as indicated below. There are likely to be variations in these figures. As mentioned in the relevant paragraphs of the Cabinet Note these estimates could be subject to variations

SECRET

No.F.70-19/2002-SP-II Vol.IV
Government of India
Ministry of Youth Affairs and Sports

-----

as brought out in them. This can be particularly so in the case of the OC where the exercise for risk assessment with respect to revenue projections and validation with reference to expenditure budget are underway.

		Rs. In crores	
(i)	SAI for Sports Infrastructure	Rs.1000.00	± 10%
(ii)	DDA for International Zone, etc. Games Village and Sports Infrastructure	Rs.325.00	± 25%
(iii)	Venue for Tennis (AITA)	Rs.37.45	
(iv)	Sports Infrastructure for Commonwealth Youth Games, 2008	Rs.100.00	
(v)	OC for Conduct of the Games	Rs.767.00	± 15%
(vi)	Preparation of Teams	Rs.300.00	
(vii)	NCTD of Delhi for civic Infrastructure	Rs.770.00	
(viii)	Security through MHA	Rs.264.00	
	Total	**Rs.3563.45 crores**	

11. **Status of Preparedness**

11.1 The proposals which have already been considered by the EFC and the Planning Commission cover most of the critical areas pertaining to the preparation for the Games in respect of establishing the required basic infrastructure. It is expected that the designs and estimates pertaining to the various sports infrastructure works will be finalized in the near future, and

SECRET

No.F.70-19/2002-SP-II Vol.IV
Government of India
Ministry of Youth Affairs and Sports

-----

after calling for tenders the process of awarding works would be commenced by the middle of 2007, and the projects completed by the end of 2009. Specific time lines are being established in respect of each project together with a system of monitoring so that timely completion of all works can be closely monitored and ensured. Detailed discussions with various stakeholders viz. IOA, National Sports Federations (NSFs) and SAI are also underway with regard to preparation of teams for the Commonwealth Games, 2010 with a view to enhancing the performance levels and medal prospects in the Games.

11.2 An Empowered Committee has also been set up under the Chief Secretary, Government of NCT of Delhi, with representatives of all the agencies/authorities concerned to facilitate speedy and time bound clearances in respect of games related projects. Another Committee has been set up, with the MYAS as convenor, to deal with clearances pertaining to the Delhi Urban Arts Commission (DUAC) and other central agencies, as may be required.

SECRET

No.F.70-19/2002-SP-II Vol.IV
Government of India
Ministry of Youth Affairs and Sports

11.3 Government has also constituted a Task Force for coordination and follow up action with all agencies concerned for creation of additional tourist accommodation including Bed and Breakfast facilities, in the context of Commonwealth Games, 2010.

12. Following the consideration and recommendations by the EFC, consolidated proposals, were to be put up for consideration and approval of the Cabinet. However, since finalization of budget proposals for different components would be a continuing process, it was decided after deliberations in the Committee of Secretaries (COS) that proposals which had already been considered by the EFC should be put up for consideration of the Cabinet immediately in order that the provisions could be suitably incorporated in the budget for 2007-08 and subsequent years. Action is being taken accordingly.

SECRET

No.F.70-19/2002-SP-II Vol.IV
Government of India
Ministry of Youth Affairs and Sports

-----

13. **Present Proposal**

13.1 In the light of the foregoing and with a view to expediting the execution of the projects, approval of the Cabinet is solicited for the following:-

13.2 Ex-post approval for release of Rs.112.51 crores to the Organising Committee Commonwealth Games, 2010 and Rs.12.50 crores to Sports Authority of India.

13.3 Expenditure budget of Rs.767.00 crores of Organizing Committee Commonwealth Games, 2010 towards conduct of the Games and Government funding to this extent (to be recouped on the basis of revenue neutrality) with flexibility to sanction escalation upto 15% by the Ministry of Youth & Sports without reference to the Expenditure Finance Committee. The Organizing Committee Commonwealth Games, 2010 may be allowed reappropiration of funds upto ± 25% across various heads, within the overall approved ceiling. Re-appropriation beyond ± 25% may be done with the approval of Ministry of Youth Affairs and Sports. A decision may also

SECRET

No.F.70-19/2002-SP-II Vol.IV
Government of India
Ministry of Youth Affairs and Sports

-----

be taken whether the budget of Organising Committee Commonwealth Games, 2010 is to be provided as Non-Plan expenditure as recommended by Expenditure Finance Committee or as Plan expenditure.

13.4 Expenditure budget of Rs.1000.00 crores of Sports Authority of India towards venue infrastructure to be developed by it and Government funding to this extent. This may be approved with provision for variation upto 10% as Plan expenditure. Variation beyond 10% would require further approval of the Expenditure Finance Commtitee.

14. A statement of Implementation Schedule on the above proposals has been given in Appendix to the note.

15. This **draft** Cabinet Note has been seen and approved by Minister of Youth Affairs and Sports.

(Rahul Bhatnagar)
Joint Secretary to the Government of India
Telephone No.24368705

SECRET

No.F.70-19/2002-SP-II Vol.IV
Government of India
Ministry of Youth Affairs and Sports

New Delhi, the December, 2006

STATEMENT OF IMPLEMENTAION SCHEDULE

Sub: Holding of the XIX Commonwealth Games at New Delhi in the year 2010.

Gist of decision required	Project benefits/results	Time-frame and manner of implementation/ Reporting got the Cabinet Secretariat
1. Ex-post approval for release of Rs.112.51 crores to the Organising Committee Commonwealth Games, 2010 and Rs.12.50 crores to Sports Authority of India. 2. Expenditure budget of Rs.767.00 crores of Organizing Committee Commonwealth Games, 2010 towards conduct of the Games and Government funding to this extent (to be recouped on the basis of revenue neutrality) with flexibility to sanction escalation upto 15% by the Ministry of Youth &	The Games will be held in accordance with the international commitments made by Indian Olympic Association and to be honoured now by Organising Committee Commonwealth Games, 2010. This will facilitate smooth preparation for the Games till the revenue starts flowing to Organising Committee Commonwealth Games, 2010. as per projections	The Commonwealth Games will be held in New Delhi in October, 2010.

SECRET

No.F.70-19/2002-SP-II Vol.IV
Government of India
Ministry of Youth Affairs and Sports

Sports without reference to the Expenditure Finance Committee. The Organizing Committee Commonwealth Games, 2010 may be allowed reappropiration of funds upto ± 25% across various heads, within the overall approved ceiling. Re-appropriation beyond ± 25% may be done with the approval of Ministry of Youth Affairs and Sports. A decision may also be taken whether the budget of Organising Committee Commonwealth Games, 2010 is to be provided as Non-Plan expenditure as recommended by Expenditure Finance Committee or as Plan expenditure. 3. Expenditure budget of Rs.1000.00 crores of Sports Authority of India towards venue infrastructure to be developed by it and Government funding to this extent. This may be approved with provision		

SECRET

No.F.70-19/2002-SP-II Vol.IV
Government of India
Ministry of Youth Affairs and Sports

-----

for variation upto 10% as Plan expenditure. Variation beyond 10% would require further approval of the Expenditure Finance Committee.		

(Rahul Bhatnagar)
Joint Secretary to the Government of India
Telephone No.24368705

****

SECRET

No.F.70-85/2007-CWG
Government of India
Ministry of Youth Affairs and Sports

MINUTES OF THE 13TH MEETING OF GROUP OF MINISTERS (GOM) FOR COORDINATING THE WORK RELATING TO THE ORGANISATION OF THE COMMONWEALTH GAMES 2010 HELD ON 10TH MARCH 2008 AT 1630 HRS IN THE OFFICE CHAMBER OF HRM

The 13th meeting of the Group of Ministers for coordinating the work relating to the organization of the Commonwealth Games 2010 was held on 10th March, 2008 at 1630 hrs under the Chairmanship of the Union Minister for Human Resource Development. A list of participants in the meeting is at Annexure.

2. Minister, HRD at the outset stated that there is growing concern that there would be a shortage of hotel rooms in Delhi for the Commonwealth Games and that effective steps should be taken in this regard.

3. Lieutenant Governor, Delhi stated that DDA had been set a target of 6600 rooms in the context of the Commonwealth Games. Out of these 5500 were confirmed and there were few more sites to be auctioned for additional rooms. He however felt that in order to increase the stock of hotel rooms there was a need to permit a higher FAR for new as well as for existing hotels with the condition that this benefit would only accrue to them if the hotels are functional by 30th June 2010. He informed that a proposal in this regard had been submitted to Ministry of Urban Development.

4. With regard to the Opening and Closing Ceremonies, Chief Minister, Delhi stated that these two major functions of the Commonwealth Games should be planned much in advance and organized professionally, while smaller cultural functions in the city and at various venues, during the Games period, could be organized by Delhi Government.

SECRET

No.F.70-85/2007-CWG
Government of India
Ministry of Youth Affairs and Sports

----

5. Agenda Item No.1

Confirmation of Minutes of the 12th meeting of the GOM held on 12th November 2007.

(i) Secretary, YAS informed that the Minutes of the 12th meeting of GOM had been circulated, no comments had been received, hence the Minutes may be confirmed by the GOM. Minister, HRD indicated that he had received some comments from Chairman, OC regarding the Minutes.

(ii) Chairman, OC stated that the Agenda Notes for the meeting had been received late and that there were number of holidays immediately preceding the meeting. While referring to the Minutes of the previous meeting he said that it had been desired from all agencies related to Commonwealth Games to function in a manner that the Games are conducted efficiently and smoothly and not from the OC only as had been incorrectly recorded. He also mentioned that the statement made by the Secy, YAS in the last meeting that the international consultants will be paid $5000 per day by the OC as remuneration was incorrect. He did, however accept that remuneration could go upto $4000 per day for a special category of international consultants, although none of this category had been appointed so far by the OC. Minister of Parliamentary Affairs also desired that the Agenda Papers be sent well in advance to have a meaningful discussion in the meeting.

6. Cabinet Secretary requested that the discussions should first focus on key issues and areas of concern, viz. Availability of Hotel Accommodation, Clearance/NOC for the Tennis Venue at R.K. Khanna Tennis Stadium, Financial Releases to the Organizing Committee, Accommodation for National Sports Federations, Clearances/approvals related to the Scheme for Preparation of Teams for Commonwealth Games and provision of overlays and their synchronization with the construction /upgradation of the stadia and issues related to road connectivity of Govt. of NCT Delhi.

SECRET

No.F.70-85/2007-CWG
Government of India
Ministry of Youth Affairs and Sports

----

7. <u>Item No.6:</u> **Grant of NOC by Land & Development Officer (Ministry Of Urban Development) for development of Tennis Venue at R K Khanna Stadium.**

Minister, Urban Development informed that the issue has now been settled and NOC has been issued.

8. <u>Item No. 10</u>: **Availability of Hotel Rooms**

(i) Minister, Tourism & Culture stated that there were three sites which were to be transferred to ITDC by Ministry of Urban Development for creation of budget hotels. Minister, UD informed that since auction was the mode by which the plots for hotels were allotted, builders were not inclined to create budget hotels. He, however, suggested that there was an option to organize auction of smaller plots of around 2000 Sq. Mtrs. on which budget hotels could come up.

(ii) LG, Delhi suggested that the FAR should be increased even for the existing hotels so that more rooms could come up and a mechanism of incentives could be evolved so that they become functional by 30/06/2010.

(iii) Secretary, Tourism, suggested that Akbar Hotel which was being presently used by MEA should be reverted to ITDC to be run as a hotel after the Ministry of External Affairs shifts to its new premises so that 250 more rooms would become available. The proposal was found agreeable and further necessary action could be taken.

SECRET

No.F.70-85/2007-CWG
Government of India
Ministry of Youth Affairs and Sports

(iv) The option of converting the Eastern and Western Courts into heritage hotels was also discussed. Minister, Urban Development while agreeing with the proposal felt that the matter could be taken up further.

(v) Chief Minister, Delhi indicated that after completion of the new MCD office, the possibility of converting the old MCD office into a heritage hotel could be explored.

(vi) Chairman, OC stated that the CGF too was concerned about the shortage of hotel rooms in Delhi.

9. Item No.14: O.C. related issues

(ii) Provision of alternative accommodation for offices of National Sports Federations

Chairman, OC stated that the matter related to the accommodation for National Sports Federations was still to be resolved. Secretary, YA&S informed that the space at the IG Stadium Complex which was being requested for, by the Federations was a playing area and was currently being used for training for Gymnastics and Boxing and once the construction activity picked up this area would get blocked with heavy equipment and machinery and would be unsafe for use as offices. He further stated that the Director General, Sports Authority of India had assessed the availability of space in the administrative block where the offices of SAI were to shift and informed that there was not enough space there to accommodate the Federations also. The representative of the OC stated that it was necessary for the National Federations of the 17 Sports disciplines of the Commonwealth Games to be located together and to the extent possible near the OC since they would be closely involved in the preparations for the technical conduct of the Games. He said that he had visited the IG Stadium as part of the team to

SECRET

No.F.70-85/2007-CWG
Government of India
Ministry of Youth Affairs and Sports

----

assess the availability of space and felt that the Federations could either be accommodated in the playing area or on the first floor of the administrative block in which SAI was going to shift. It was decided that Chairman OC would meet and separately discuss the matter with Minister, YA&S to resolve the issue.

(iii) Financial Releases to OC

Chairman, OC stated that in spite of the fact that there were no UCs pending with the OC, MYAS has not released funds to the OC as per the schedule provided by the Ministry of Finance. He stated that the OC was as much concerned about proper use of the loan amount since they were responsible for its repayment. Minister, YA&S stated that following release of funds, UCs become due only after certain period of time and that for further releases during that period, as clarified by the Ministry of Finance, the Administrative Ministry had to be reasonably satisfied that the funds released were being utilized for the purpose toward which they were intended and for which periodical progress of expenditure could be sought by the Administrative Ministry. Hon'ble Minister, YAS informed that till date as per their own statement , OC had unspent balance of roughly 20% (amounting to approx. 35 crores) and stated that since public funds were involved, the Ministry had to exercise due diligence to see that the provisions of the GFRs regarding release of funds were being followed. He sought the advice of Addl. Secretary (Expenditure) in the matter of release of balance funds to OC in the circumstances. Addl. Secretary (Expenditure) clarified that if unspent balance related to committed expenditure, then balance of funds could be released to OC, where after it was agreed that the balance of funds for the current year would be released to OC since OC had stated that these were required to meet various commitments and obligations.

SECRET

No.F.70-85/2007-CWG
Government of India
Ministry of Youth Affairs and Sports

It was also decided that from the year 2008-09 the release of funds by MYAS to the OC would be quarterly based on quarterly Statement of Expenditure and Projection of Expenditure.

10. Item No.17 : **Status regarding Scheme of 'Preparation of Indian Team/s for Commonwealth Games, 2010**

Secretary, YAS informed that the EFC note for a Scheme of Rs. 802 crores for preparation of Indian Teams for Commonwealth Games had been prepared and circulated for comments. Addl. Secretary (Expenditure) informed that the comments of Ministry of Finance had been sent. Cabinet Secretary requested the Planning Commission to expedite their comments.

11. Minister, Parliamentary Affairs, desired that there should be a cell for monitoring of all the projects of the Commonwealth Games. Minister, Tourism & Culture also reiterated the need for close monitoring. Cabinet Secretary suggested that since Ministry of YA&S was the nodal Ministry a dedicated cell should be created in MYAS for this purpose. Hon'ble Minister, UD however felt that the dedicated cell for monitoring should be located in the Cabinet Secretariat since it would be more effective in dealing with various Departments/Agencies. Hon'ble Minister, YAS informed the GOM that the progress on all sports infrastructure was on track and would be completed well in time for the Games. He also stated that the OC had informed, that the CGF had appreciated the progress in the preparation of the Games at the CGF, General Assembly meeting in Colombo. While informing that under the guidance of the GOM he had set up an Apex Committee for the CWG in March, 2006, the same had been dormant for the last year and a half due to resistance from the OC. Minister, YAS felt that the MYAS being the nodal ministry could take up the responsibility of monitoring of all projects if it was adequately strengthened. Cabinet Secretary suggested that a senior level officer of the rank of Addl. Secretary/ Special Secretary could be positioned in

SECRET

No.F.70-85/2007-CWG
Government of India
Ministry of Youth Affairs and Sports

----

the MYAS exclusively for this purpose. Minister, YAS while agreeing with this suggestion felt that care should be taken to post an officer, who could continue on that post upto the end of the Games i.e. March, 2011.

12. The other items on the Agenda could not be discussed due to paucity of time.

13. The meeting ended with a vote of thanks to the Chair.

SECRET

No.F.70-85/2007-CWG
Government of India
Ministry of Youth Affairs and Sports

Annexure

LIST OF PARTICIPANTS OF THE 13th MEETING OF GROUP OF MINISTERS (GOM) FOR COORDINATING THE WORK RELATING TO THE ORGANISATION OF THE COMMONWEALTH GAMES 2010 HELD ON 10.03.2008 AT 1630 HRS IN THE OFFICE CHAMBER OF MINISTER OF HUMAN RESOURCE DEVELOPMENT

1. Shri Arjun Singh, Minister of Human Resource Development.
2. Shri Shivraj Patil, Minister of Home Affairs.
3. Shri S. Jaipal Reddy, Minister of Urban Development.
4. Shri Priyaranjan Dasmunshi, Minister of Parliamentary Affairs and Minister of Information & Broadcasting.
5. Shri Mani Shankar Aiyar, Minister of Panchayati Raj, Youth Affairs & Sports & Development of North Eastern Region.
6. Smt. Ambika Soni, Minister of Tourism and Minister of Culture.

Special Invitees

7. Shri Tejinder Khanna, Lt. Governor, Delhi.
8. Smt. Shiela Dikshit, Chief Minister, Delhi.
9. Shri Suresh Kalmadi, Chairman, Organizing Committee, CWG 2010.
10. Shri K.M. Chandrasekhar, Cabinet Secretary.

Shri Anwarul Hoda, Member, Planning Commission

In attendance

1. Shri S.K. Arora, Secretary, Ministry of Youth Affairs & Sports.
2. Shri Sujit Banerjee, Secretary & Chairperson National Authority for Chemical Weapons Convention, Cabinet Secretariat.
3. Shri S. Banerjee, Secretary Ministry of Tourism.
4. Smt. Rita Menon, Additional Secretary (Expenditure), Ministry of Finance.
5. Shri U. K. Varma, Additional Secretary, Ministry of I & B.
6. Shri Rakesh Mehta, Chief Secretary, Govt. of NCT of Delhi.

Page 8 of 9

SECRET

No.F.70-85/2007-CWG
Government of India
Ministry of Youth Affairs and Sports

----

7. Shri Sanjay Kothari, Additional Director General, Ministry of Tourism.
8. Shri Rahul Bhatnagar, JS (ISD), Ministry of Youth Affairs & Sports.
9. Shri S.S. Chhabra, Director (ISD), Ministry of Youth Affairs & Sports.
10. Shri V. K. Sadhu, Principal Commissioner, Delhi Development Authority.
11. Shri Lalit Bhanot, Secretary General, OC CWG 2010
12. Shri V. K. Gautam, Chief Operating Officer, OC CWG
13. Shri A. S. V. Prasad, Additional Director General, OC, CWG 2010.
14. Shri R.K. Sacheti, Additional Director General (Coord.), OC, CWG

****

विजय शुंगलू
अध्य
V.K. Shunglu
Chairman
Tel. : 23063318
23063319

CS-3267/11
15/2/11

राष्ट्रमंडल खेल, 2010
उच्च स्तरीय समिति
विज्ञान भवन एनेक्सी,
नई दिल्ली-110 011
High Level Committee
for Commonwealth Games, 2010
Vigyan Bhavan Annexe
New Delhi-110 011

Dy. No.113(HLC)/CSM/2011

Dated : 15th February, 2011

My dear Cabinet Secretary,

Group of Ministers (GOM) was reconstituted in June / July, 2009. On the assumption that it was empowered to take all decisions as mentioned in your Note No.294/2/1/2011-CA.V dated 11.02.2011, it would follow that financial sanctions sought in relation to Commonwealth Games Delhi 2010 could now also be secured from the GOM. It is observed that the following cases were posed to the Cabinet thereafter :

i) Modernization of traffic and communication network (Note for CCA dated 23.03.2009);
ii) Revised cost estimates for Delhi University (Note for Cabinet from MYA&S dated 25.09.2009);
iii) Revised cost estimates for DDA (MYA&S Note for Cabinet dated 09.10.2009);
iv) Integrated Security System (Note for Cabinet MHA dated 14.10.2009);
v) Revised budget estimates of Organizing Committee (MYA&S Note dated 19.10.2009);
vi) Telecom service provider for CWG (Note for Cabinet dated 12.02.2010);
vii) Budget of OC (MYA&S Note for Cabinet dated 04.03.2010).

02. It seems that all matters with financial implications were being posed to the Cabinet / CCEA. Before doing so, consultation with Ministry of Finance is obligated by the Transaction of Business Rules but such consultation / consent does not substitute approval by the competent authority for financial sanctions. The GOM action in September, 2010 seems to be an aberration because .

i) After agreement of Ministry of Finance it took nearly three months to approach the GOM; and
ii) In an emergent situation, as the flavor of the GOM Note shows, procedure prescribed in Rule of 12 of the Transaction of Business Rules could have been followed.

03. High Level Committee is unclear on what to make of all these facts.

With regards,

Yours sincerely,

(V.K. Shunglu)

Shri K.M. Chandrasekhar,
Cabinet Secretary,
Cabinet Secretariat,
Rashtrapati Bhawan,
New Delhi.

Print

Press Information Bureau
Government of India
Prime Minister's Office

14-August-2010 18:47 IST

PM Reviews Preparations for the Commonwealth Games

The Prime Minister, Dr. Manmohan Singh today convened a high-level meeting to review the preparations for the Commonwealth Games scheduled to begin on 3rd October. The meeting was attended by Shri S. Jaipal Reddy, Minister of Urban Development; Dr. M.S. Gill, Minister of Youth Affairs and Sports; Shri Tejendra Khanna, Lt. Governor of Delhi; Smt. Sheila Dikshit, Chief Minister of Delhi; Shri T.K.A. Nair, Principal Secretary to Prime Minister; Shri K.M. Chandrasekhar, Cabinet Secretary; Shri Suresh Kalmadi, Chairman, Organizing Committee, CWG and other senior officials.

The Prime Minister was briefed by the Ministry of Sports, the Ministry of Urban Development, the Government of Delhi and the Organising Committee on the progress of Commonwealth Games preparatory works assigned to them. The Prime Minister observed that there had been slippages in the time schedules of some of the construction works and deficiencies had also been observed in some of the works. He said that, in the run up to the Games, it was important to gain public confidence by instilling order and carrying out effective supervision of the preparation works.

The Prime Minister directed the Ministries concerned, the Government of the National Capital Region and the Organizing Committee to complete all pending works expeditiously through time-bound action plans and carry out a quality audit of the completed facilities. All the facilities must meet international standards.

The Group of Ministers set up for the Commonwealth Games headed by the Minister of Urban Development Shri S. Jaipal Reddy was directed to meet immediately and frequently thereafter. The Group was empowered to take all decisions necessary for the smooth conduct of the Games. The Group of Ministers will refer any matter that may require further consideration to the Finance Minister for a final decision.

The Cabinet Secretary was directed to liaise closely with the Group of Ministers to ensure effective coordination among all the concerned authorities. The Committee of Secretaries headed by the Cabinet Secretary will continue to review implementation and it will have the status of an Empowered Committee. It will have jurisdiction over matters relating to the Organising Committee and a Secretary level officer of the Cabinet Secretariat will liaise with the Organising Committee on a daily basis.

The Organizing Committee would take appropriate steps urgently to conclude all pending preparations. The Senior Management Committee of the Organising Committee would meet daily and be chaired by the CEO in the absence of the Chairman or Vice-Chairman, Organising Committee. Additional senior and experienced officers from the Government of India would be deputed as required.

The Prime Minister further directed the concerned Ministries to conduct thorough investigations into all the complaints that have been received of procedural and other irregularities. He said that those found guilty should face severe and exemplary punishment.

The Cabinet will be briefed on the state of preparations on a weekly basis.

The public has a right to know the facts and the Group of Ministers will ensure that timely and authentic information on the state of preparations and in particular on the remaining tasks at hand is released to the public. The promotional campaign of the various events should be stepped up to generate enthusiasm among sports lovers in the largest sporting event the country has held in many years.

The Prime Minister has decided to visit selected venues of the Commonwealth Games in the last week of August.

The Prime Minister said that the eyes of the world were on the country as we conduct this prestigious event. The Commonwealth Games was an occasion not only to celebrate sporting excellence but also the spirit of kinship and camaraderie among the Commonwealth fraternity. India will have an opportunity to present its culture, its achievements, its warm hospitality and its organizational capabilities to the world.

The Prime Minister emphasized that it was very important that as a country, the people should work together to give our honoured guests a warm welcome and a memorable experience of all that our nation has to offer. Our athletes and sportsmen are training hard and need the full support and encouragement of their fellow Indians. He urged all concerned to work single-mindedly so that the Games could be held in a manner the nation could be justifiably proud of.

At the conclusion of the meeting, the Prime Minister expressed confidence that the ongoing preparations supervised directly by the Group of Ministers would enable the Games to be conducted smoothly and in a befitting manner.

***

HS/SKS

RASHTRAPATI BHAVAN
NEW DELHI
January 14, 1961.

Pausa 24, 1882(S)

ORDER

THE GOVERNMENT OF INDIA (TRANSACTION OF BUSINESS) RULES

In exercise of the powers conferred by clause (3) of article 77 of the Constitution and in supersession of all previous rules and orders on the subject, the President hereby makes the following rules for the more convenient transaction of the business of the Government of India: -

1. Short Title.- These rules may be called the Government of India (Transaction of Business) Rules, 1961.

2. Definition.- In these rules, "department" means any of the Ministries, Departments, Secretariats and Offices specified in the First Schedule to the Government of India (Allocation of Business) Rules, 1961.

3. Disposal of Business by Ministries.- Subject to the provisions of these Rules in regard to consultation with other departments and submission of cases to the Prime Minister, the Cabinet and its Committees and the President, all business allotted to a department under the Government of India (Allocation of Business) Rules, 1961, shall be disposed of by, or under the general or special directions of, the Minister-in-charge.

4. Inter-Departmental Consultations.- (1) When the subject of a case concerns more than one department, no decision be taken or order issued until all such departments have concurred, or, failing such concurrence, a decision thereon has been taken by or under the authority of the Cabinet.

Explanation- Every case in which a decision, if taken in one Department, is likely to affect the transaction of business allotted to another department, shall be deemed to be a case the subject of which concerns more than one department.

(2) Unless the case is fully covered by powers to sanction expenditure or to appropriate or re-appropriate funds, conferred by any general or special orders made by the Ministry of Finance, no department shall, without the previous concurrence of the Ministry of Finance, issue any orders which may-

(a) involve any abandonment of revenue or involve any expenditure for which no provision has been made in the appropriation act;

(b) involve any grant of land or assignment of revenue or concession, grant, lease or licence of mineral or forest rights or a right to water power or any easement or privilege in respect of such concession;

(c) relate to the number or grade of posts, or to the strength of a service, or to the pay or allowances of Government servants or to any other conditions of their service having financial implications; or

(d) otherwise have a financial bearing whether involving expenditure or not;

2

Provided that no orders of the nature specified in clause (c) shall be issued in respect of the Ministry of Finance without the previous concurrence of the Department of Personnel and Training.

(3) The Ministry of Law shall be consulted on-

(a) proposals for legislation;

(b) the making of rules and orders of a general character in the exercise of a statutory power conferred on the Government; and

(c) the preparation of important contracts to be entered into by the Government.

(4) Unless the case is fully covered by a decision or advice previously given by the Department of Personnel and Training that Department shall be consulted on all matters involving-

(a) the determination of the methods of recruitment and conditions of service of general application to Government servants in civil employment; and

(b) the interpretation of the existing orders of general application relating to such recruitment or conditions of service.

(5) Unless the case is fully covered by the instructions issued or advice given by that Ministry, the Ministry of External Affairs shall be consulted on all matters affecting India's external relations.

5. Requests for Papers.- (1) The Prime Minister may call for papers from any Department.

(2) The Finance Minister may call for papers from any Department in which financial consideration is involved.

(3) Any Minister may ask to see papers in any other Department if they are related to or required for the consideration of any case before him.

6. Committees of the Cabinet.-

(1) There shall be Standing Committees of the Cabinet as set out in the First Schedule to these Rules with the functions specified therein. The Prime Minister may from time to time amend the Schedule by adding to or reducing the numbers of such Committees or by modifying the functions assigned to them.

(2) Each Standing Committee shall consist of such Ministers as the Prime Minister may from time to time specify.

(3) Subject to the provisions of rule 7, each Standing Committee shall have the power to consider and take decisions on matters referred to it by order of the Minister concerned or by the Cabinet.

(4) Ad hoc Committees of Ministers including Group of Ministers may be appointed by the Cabinet, the Standing Committees of the Cabinet or by the Prime Minister for investigating and reporting to the Cabinet on such matters as may be specified, and, if so authorised by the Cabinet, Standing Committees of the Cabinet or the Prime Minister, for taking decisions on such matters.

3

(5) To the extent, there is a commonality between the cases enumerated in the Second Schedule and the cases set out in the First Schedule, the Standing Committees of the Cabinet, shall be competent to take a final decision in the matter except in cases where the relevant entries in the First Schedule or the Second Schedule, preclude the Committees from taking such decisions.

(6) Any decision taken by a Standing or Ad hoc Committee may be reviewed by the Cabinet.

(7) No case which concerns more than one Department shall be brought before a Standing or Ad hoc Committee of the Cabinet until all the Departments concerned have been consulted.

7. Submission of Cases to the Cabinet.- (i) all cases specified in the Second Schedule to these Rules except cases covered by sub-rule(5) of rule 6, shall be brought before the Cabinet :

Provided that no case which concerns more than one Department shall, save in cases of urgency, be brought before the Cabinet until all the Departments concerned have been consulted.

Provided further that no case which falls under entry (h) of the Second Schedule and where specific powers have been delegated to Ministries/ Departments or Public Sector Undertakings under a decision of the Cabinet or a Standing Committee of the Cabinet and duly notified by the concerned Department, shall be brought before the Cabinet .

Provided also that cases pertaining to the implementation of the nuclear doctrine and handling/deployment of the strategic assets, including matters relating to staffing and creation of the assets, shall be brought before the Political Council of the Nuclear Command Authority, headed by the Prime Minister.

(ii) The Prime Minister may from time to time amend the Second Schedule by adding to or reducing the number or class of cases required to be placed before the Cabinet.

8. Submission of Cases to the Prime Minister and the President.- All cases of the nature specified in the Third Schedule to these Rules shall, before the issue of orders thereon, be submitted to the Prime Minister or to the President or to the Prime Minister and the President, as indicated in that Schedule.

9. Submission of Periodical Returns to the Cabinet.- Each department shall submit to the Cabinet a monthly summary of its principal activities and such other periodical returns as the Cabinet or the Prime Minister may from time to time require.

10. Submission of Certain Papers to the President.- The periodical reports and other papers specified in the Fourth Schedule to these Rules shall be submitted to the President for information as early as possible.

11. Responsibility of Departmental Secretaries.- In each department, the Secretary (which term includes the Special Secretary or Additional Secretary or Joint Secretary in independent charge) shall be the administrative head thereof, and shall be responsible for the proper transaction of business and the careful observance of these rules in that department.

12. Departure from Rules.- The Prime Minister may, in any case or classes of cases permit or condone a departure from these rules, to the extent he deems necessary.

RAJENDRA PRASAD,
President.

No. F.70-50/2005 SP-II
Government of India
Ministry of Youth Affairs & Sports

Secret

MINUTES OF THE 8TH MEETING OF THE CORE GROUP OF MINISTERS FOR CO-ORDINATING THE WORK RELATED TO THE ORGANISATION OF THE COMMONWEALTH GAMES 2010, HELD ON 7TH NOVEMBER, 2005 AT 1700 HOURS

List of those who attended the meeting is placed at **Annexure-I**

ITEM NO. 1 CONFIRMATION OF MINUTES OF THE 7TH MEETING OF THE GROUP OF MINISTERS HELD ON 27.9.2005

Comments had not been received from those who attended the last meeting. Approved.

ITEM NO. 2 ACTION TAKEN REPORT ON THE DECISIONS IN THE MEETINGS HELD ON 29TH JANUARY 2005, 17TH MARCH 2005, 8TH SEPTEMBER 2005 AND 27TH SEPTEMBER 2005

Action Taken Report was noted.

ITEM NO. 3 PROPOSAL FOR IDENTIFICATION AND DEVELOPMENT OF VENUE INFRASTRUCTURE FOR COMMONWEALTH GAMES 2010

The agenda note that was circulated by the Ministry of Youth Affairs & Sports comprising of the presentation of M/s Event Knowledge Services and the proposal of the Ministry on the above subject were not taken up for discussion.

OTHER ITEMS WITH THE PERMISSION OF CHAIRPERSON

ITEM NO. 4 DRAFT REPORT OF CHAIRMAN, ORGANISING COMMITTEE ON GAMES VILLAGE AND VENUES FOR 15 DISCIPLINES WAS CIRCULATED IN THE MEETING

A presentation on the item was also made. MOS(PMO) pointed out the following issues –

Page 3 of 7

No. F.70-50/2005 SP-II
Government of India
Ministry of Youth Affairs & Sports

Secret

(i) As per the minutes of the Seventh Meeting of GOM, the Organising Committee was expected to complete its consultation process on the Games Village and Venues by 15th October, 2005 after discussion with stake holders and submit their views to the Ministry for placing before the GOM for their consideration. This had not been done. The Ministry was therefore not in a position to give their comments.

(ii) The Cabinet Note for seeking approval of Commonwealth Games of September 2003 had indicated an estimate of Rs.150 crores for repair and upgradation and construction of existing infrastrueture. The EKS report has given projection in the range of Rs.1950 crores. The draft proposal of OC with its emphasis on new construction of venues and site for Athletics and Swimming would prima-facie push the infrastructure costs to about Rs.2500 crores. There is also a new provision for five disciplines in which people with disabilities would also participate. MOS(PMO) felt that there were significant cost escalations, which were not projected earlier.

Regarding the Games Village, Vice Chairman, DDA indicated that with proper adoption of technology and other adjustments the original proposal would be a cost effective option.

Lt. Governor Delhi stated that the alternate plot of 175 hectares suggested by OC would not be feasible in view of the lead time required for clearances and objections from environment activists.

Chairman, OC indicated that due to a number of intervening holidays, the draft report could not be submitted to Ministry of Youth Affairs & Sports; and that the report was therefore given in draft format to elicit the comments of members of the GOM and also facilitate discussion with the Ministry of Youth Affairs & Sports.

Page 4 of 7

No. F.70-50/2005 SP-II
Government of India
Ministry of Youth Affairs & Sports

Secret

It was decided that after further consultation Chairman, OC would send the draft after further modification, if required, to the Ministry of Youth Affairs & Sports by 17th November morning. Accordingly, Chairman of the GOM fixed 21st November (afternoon) for the meeting. MOS(PMO) indicated that only if the draft is received in Ministry by 17th November morning it would be possible to put up comments of Ministry of Youth Affairs & Sports at the time of next meeting of GOM on 21.11.2005. It was also decided to re-submit the proposal of EKS and that of Ministry as at Item No. 3 along with the final draft report of OC to give a comprehensive picture.

ITEM NO. 5 PRESENTATION BY MINISTRY OF TOURISM

The presentation of Ministry of Tourism was on projecting Delhi and its environs as a multi faceted tourist destination. Finance Minister observed that the requirement of various categories of hotel sites was about 75, but the Games Village and master plan together offer only about 25 sites. It was therefore decided that DDA and Ministry of Tourism would hold discussions so as to arrive at the optimum number of hotel sites for the Commonwealth Games, 2010.

No. F.70-50/2005 SP-II
Government of India
Ministry of Youth Affairs & Sports

Secret

Annexure-I

LIST OF MEMBERS AND SPECIAL INVITEES PRESENT DURING THE EIGHTH MEETING OF THE GROUP OF MINISTERS FOR COORDINATIING THE WORK RELATING TO THE ORGANISATION OF THE COMMONWEALTH GAMES, 2010 HELD ON 7TH NOVEMBER, 2005 AT 1700 HRS.

1. Shri Arjun Singh - In Chair
   Minister of Human Resource Development
2. Shri P. Chidambaram
   Minister of Finance
3. Shri Priyaranjan Dasmunsi
   Minister of Water Resources
4. Shri Natwar Singh
   Minister of External Affairs
5. Smt. Renuka Chowdhury
   Minister of State (Independent Charge)
   Ministry of Tourism
6. Shri Prithviraj Chavan
   Minister of State (PMO)
7. Shri B.L. Joshi
   Lt. Governor, Delhi
8. Smt. Sheila Dixit
   Chief Minister, Delhi
9. Shri Suresh Kalmadi
   Chairman, Commonwealth Games
   Organising Committee 2010

Officers in Attendance

1. Shri B.K. Chaturvedi
   Cabinet Secretary

No. F.70-50/2005 SP-II
Government of India
Ministry of Youth Affairs & Sports

Secret

2. Smt. Meenaxi Anand Chaudhry
   Secretary
   Ministry of Youth Affairs & Sports
3. Shri Dinesh Rai
   Vice Chairman, DDA
4. Shri D. Sarkar
   Director (Sports), DDA
5. Shri Atul Chaturvedi
   Joint Secretary, Ministry of Tourism
6. Shri Amitabh Kant
   Joint Secretary, Ministry of Tourism
7. Shri O.P. Kelkar
   Principal Secretary (UD)
   Govt. of NCT Delhi
8. Smt. Alka Diwan
   Additional Secretary to Chief Minister, Delhi
9. Shri S. Krishnan
   Joint Secretary
   Ministry of Youth Affairs & Sports
10. Shri A. Chakraborty
    Addl. DG
    CPWD
11. Dr. Lalit Bhanot
    Secretary General
    Organising Committee
    Commonwealth Games, 2010
12. Smt. Vijaylakshmi Gupta
13. Shri A.S.V. Prasad
14. Shri R.K. Sacheti

(12–14) } Organising Committee Commonwealth Games, 2010

Page 7 of 7

No. F.70-28/2004-SP.II
Government of India
Ministry of Youth Affairs and Sports

Copy No._____

Shastri Bahvan, New Delhi

Dated: 8 th October, 2004

NOTE FOR THE GROUP OF MINISTERS

Subject: Preparations for Commonwealth Games 2010 at New Delhi

1. **Introduction**

With the approval of the Prime Minister, a core Group of Ministers (GOM) has been constituted for coordinating the work relating to the organization of the Commonwealth Games to be held in Delhi in 2010. The same has been notified vide Cabinet Secretariat No. 781/2/1/2004-Cab. on 3 September, 2004. A copy of the same is at **Annexure I.**

2. **Background**

2.1. On the proposal of the Indian Olympic Association (IOA), Government of India on 2 July, 2002 conveyed its no objection to making a bid presentation at the Manchester Commonwealth Games, 2002 for the XIX Commonwealth Games, 2010.

3. Subsequently, Government of India approved the following:-

Allowing the Ministry of Youth Affairs & Sports, Government of NCT, Delhi and IOA to bid for the XIX Commonwealth Games, 2010.

No. F.70-28/2004-SP.II
Government of India
Ministry of Youth Affairs and Sports

In principle approving holding of the XIX Commonwealth Games, 2010 in case the bid to host the Games at New Delhi was successful.

3.1 It was also decided to issue the following guarantees:-

i) Undertaking to support the bid of Delhi to host the Games;

ii) Guaranteeing free entry for all accredited athletes and delegations of all participating countries, and

iii) Guaranteeing that the Games will be organized in accordance with the Constitution and Protocols & Regulations of the Commonwealth Games Federation (CGF).

4. Accordingly, a delegation led by the then Minister of Youth Affairs and Sports, Shri Vikram Verma, the then President AICS, Shri V K Malhotra, the then Lt. Governor (LG) of Delhi, Shri Vijai Kapoor, President IOA, Shri Suresh Kalmadi and Shri Randhir Singh, Secretary-General IOA, presented a formal bid before the Commonwealth Games Federation in London on 30 May, 2003.

5. Following the formal bidding a Strategic Committee under the Chairmanship of the Minister of Youth Affairs and Sports was formed with President, AICS, Minister of State (Youth Affairs & Sports), LG-Delhi, Secretary (Sports) GOI, Director General, Sports Authority of India, Secretary (Urban Development), President (IOA) and Secretary General, IOA. The Evaluation Commission of the Commonwealth Games Federation visited New Delhi on 3-8 August 2003 to inspect available infrastructure and hold formal discussions with

No. F.70-28/2004-SP.II
Government of India
Ministry of Youth Affairs and Sports

various agencies likely to be involved in the staging of the Games. India made a forceful presentation during this visit.

6. With the approval of the Cabinet in its meeting on 11 September 2003, Government further approved the following:-

i) To agree to and enter into the host city contact as provided by the CGF.

ii) To underwrite any shortfall between revenue and expenditure of the Organizing Committee.

iii) In principle, the proposal of the Lt. Governor of Delhi to set up the Games village on the bank of the Yamuna near the Akshardham Temple. (The L.G. had proposed that the Games Village be set up with hostel type construction so that after the Games, the same could be handed over to the University of Delhi for meeting its unmet need for hostel accommodation). However, the Cabinet deferred a decision on the manner of funding and utilization of the Games Village.

iv) In principle, to meet the cost of construction of the indoor and outdoor stadium in the Yamuna Sports Complex and that of up gradation of existing infrastructure.

7. Delegates from various Commonwealth Countries (about 50), on our invitation, visited India during the First Afro Asian Games held at Hyderabad

No. F.70-28/2004-SP.II
Government of India
Ministry of Youth Affairs and Sports

from 24 October 2003 to 1 November 2003. The delegates also visited Delhi to oversee the existing infrastructure and assess its preparedness for hosting the Commonwealth Games, 2010.

8. A high powered delegation from India headed by the then Minister of Youth Affairs and Sports and comprising the Lt. Governor of Delhi, Members of the IOA and a few eminent sportspersons made a presentation before the General Assembly of the Commonwealth Games Federation held at Montego Bay, Jamaica. Delhi and Hamilton (Canada) were the two candidates for hosting the Commonwealth Games, 2010.

9. On 13 October 2003, voting through a secret ballot, the Commonwealth Games Federation, by a majority vote of 46 to 22 in favour of Delhi allotted hosting of the 2010 Commonwealth Games in its favour.

10. The Commonwealth Games 2010 are scheduled to be held over a period of 11 days while the competitions will take place over 12 days in 12 individual sports and 3 team sports as under:-

Aquatics, Athletics, Badminton, Boxing, Cycling, Gymnastics, Hockey, Lawn Bowls, Net Ball, Rugby 7"s, Shooting, Squash, Table-Tennis, Weightlifting and Wrestling.

No. F.70-28/2004-SP.II
Government of India
Ministry of Youth Affairs and Sports

10.1 The Indian Olympic Association in their bid documents have suggested the inclusion of Cricket and Basketball subject to approval of the respective international federation and the Commonwealth Games Federation. This matter would be decided by the proposed Organising Committee.

11 **Budget for the Games**

11.1 Based on the revenue forecast made by Sports & Marketing Management, an UK-based agency commissioned by the IOA, an estimated revenue projection of 100 million US Dollar (Rs.490 crores at the relevant time) was made before the Cabinet. As against this an expenditure projection of Rs.399.05 crores was made towards conduct of the Games. This included an amount of Rs.150.00 crores towards upgradation of existing infrastructure, Rs.55.00 crores as CGF Licence fee and Rs.48.00 crores towards travel grant to the participants. However an amount of Rs.186.00 crores towards construction of the Games village and Rs.32.50 crores towards construction of an outdoor and an indoor stadium in the Yamuna Sports Complex were not included in the amount of Rs.399.05 crores but shown separately. Considering that the estimates on revenue and expenditure were prepared in a hurry, there is a need to have a fresh look at the projections.

No. F.70-28/2004-SP.II
Government of India
Ministry of Youth Affairs and Sports

12. Organization of the Games

As per the bid documents submitted by the Indian Olympic Association for conduct of the Games, an Organising Committee (OC) – a non-profit Government owned Registered Society – is to be constituted. Its draft constitution was to be finalized by the second half of 2004. The OC was to have an Executive Board, which will be headed by a Chairman who will be a Government nominee. The President of the IOA would be its Vice-Chairman. It would have 3 members from the Commonwealth Games Federation, 2 IOA appointees, 2 State Government nominees and 4 nominees from the National Sports Federations. It is proposed that Organizing Committee and Executive Board be constituted with Minister, Youth Affairs and Sports as Chairperson.

13. Action taken after the allotment of the Games

13.1 Payment of the CGF Fee

13.1.1 Subsequent to the allotment of the Games, as per the Host City Contract, the first instalment of the license fee amounting to 1.3 million Pound Sterling (Rs.10,88,16,350/-) was to be paid by the Organizing Committee for the Commonwealth Games to CGF by 13th May, 2004. However, since the Organizing Committee could not be formed in time, Government of India had per force to release the said amount to the Indian Olympic Association for onward transmission to the CGF with the condition that this would be a liability of the OC to be discharged in due course. As per the Host City Contract,

No. F.70-28/2004-SP.II
Government of India
Ministry of Youth Affairs and Sports

further instalments of 1.5 million pound sterling are to be paid in January, 2006, 2007, 2008 and 2009.

13.1.2 At the time of the final presentation of the bid at Montego Bay, the President of the IOA had also made a commitment of paying US $ 1 lakh each to the 72 member countries through the CGF towards endowment and preparation of the sportspersons after the Commonwealth Games 2006.

13.2 **Constitution of the Organising Committee**

13.2.1 As per the Host City Contract, the Organizing Committee was to be formed within 6 months from date of signing of the Contract. However, in the last meeting of the CGF General Assembly at Athens on 17 August, 2004 the request of the IOA for extension of the deadline to 31 December, 2004 has been approved.

13.2.2 In this connection, it may be noted that for the 1982 Asian Games in Delhi, the Special Organizing Committee (SOC) was registered as a Society under the Societies Registration Act. It had an Executive Board with 39 members plus 6 special invitees. It also had a Secretariat headed by a Secretary General. In addition, the SOC had 27 functional committees.

13.2.3. For the 1st Afro-Asian Games held at Hyderabad between 24 October -1 November, 2003, an Organizing Committee was set up and registered under the Societies Registration Act. It had an Executive Board and

No. F.70-28/2004-SP.II
Government of India
Ministry of Youth Affairs and Sports

a Secretariat. An Empowered Committee was also constituted to take administrative and financial decisions of urgent nature on behalf of the Executive Board. In addition, 22 subject matter committees were also set up for successful conduct of the Games.

13.3 **Creation/up gradation of infrastructure**

13.3.1 As stated earlier, a Games Village is to be constructed next to the Akshardham Temple off the new Nizamuddin Bridge. However, it has been brought to the notice of the Government subsequently that a small portion of the proposed land belongs to the Government of U.P. The Government of NCT of Delhi are required to acquire this land from the State Government of U.P.

13.3.2. In a meeting taken by the Minister of Youth Affairs & Sports on 16 March, 2004, the DDA had stated that in view of structural constraints, the Squash Courts in the Siri Fort Sports Complex may have to be constructed anew. DDA were to submit fresh estimates in this regard as well as for augmenting the seating capacity of the existing badminton court in the same complex, so that approval of the Cabinet could be sought in the matter.

13.3.3 In August, 2004, a meeting was taken by the Minister, Youth Affairs and Sports with L.G. Delhi, Chief Minister, Delhi and President, IOA for setting up of Organizing Committee and related issues. Various aspects of organizing the Commonwealth Games were informally discussed. It was decided to defer the final decision till completion of Athens Olympic Games.

No. F.70-28/2004-SP.II
Government of India
Ministry of Youth Affairs and Sports

14. Strengthening of the Ministry of Youth Affairs and Sports

14.1. With a view to coping with the additional workload that will be generated in connection with the preparations for the Commonwealth Games including the setting up of the Games Village in particular, it is considered necessary to strengthen the Ministry in the form of a new Division to be headed by a Joint Secretary with the following complement of officers and staff:-

1. Two Directors/Deputy Secretaries
2. Two Under Secretaries
3. Two Section Officers (two Sections)
4. Four Assistants (two Assistants for each of the Sections)
5. Four LDC/UDCs (two for each of the Sections)
6. Two Private Secretaries (one each for JS & Director)
7. One Personal Assistant for DS
8. Two Grade "D" Stenographers (one for each Under Secretaries)
9. Seven Peons.

Further strengthening of the Divison may be considered with subsequent increase in the workload.

14.2. As per laid down procedure, approval of the Department of Personnel and Training and the Department of Expenditure are to be obtained for creation/sanction of posts as outlined above. However, since the time is short and the Prime Minister's Office has desired that the matter may be placed

No. F.70-28/2004-SP.II
Government of India
Ministry of Youth Affairs and Sports

before the GOM as an agenda item in its first meeting, Ministry of Finance are requested to indicate their comments/approval at the earliest. A copy of this Note has been sent to the Department of Personnel and Training with a request to convey their approval at the earliest and the same will be placed before the GOM.

15. **Setting up of an Empowered Committee**

The Prime Minister's Office has further directed that the proposal for setting up of an Empowered Committee under the Chairmanship of LG, Delhi with representatives from various concerned Central Ministries/Agencies, State Governments and other organizations like DDA, MCD, NDMC, National Airports Authority, and DMRC, etc., be also placed before the GOM. Accordingly, it is proposed to set up an Empowered Committee to take all administrative and financial decisions in connection with the preparations for the Commonwealth Games Village. The proposed composition of the Empowered Committee is at **Annexure-II**.

16. **Matters for decisions of the GOM:-**

16.1 In the light of the foregoing, approval/decisions of the GOM are solicited on the following:-

(a) Constitution of an Organising Committee in the form of a Registered Society with Minister, Youth Affairs & Sports as Chairperson.

No. F.70-28/2004-SP.II
Government of India
Ministry of Youth Affairs and Sports

(b) Constitution of an Executive Board, as indicated under para 12 of the Note for the GOM with Minister Youth Affairs & Sports as Chairperson.

(c) Setting up of an Empowered Committee, as indicated under para 15 of the Note for the GOM, under the Chairmanship of L.G. Delhi.

(d) Proposal for strengthening the Ministry of Youth Affairs and Sports in the form of a Division headed by a Joint Secretary as indicated under para 14 of the Note for the GOM.

(e) Constitution of a few Committees, to begin with, to deal with matters of finance, infrastructure and marketing.

(f) Commissioning of a study to reassess the forecast regarding revenue and expenditure projections.

(g) Manner of funding and utilization of the Games Village.

17. **A statement of Implementation schedule is appended to this Note.**

18. **Approval of the Minister, YA & S** .

The Note for the GOM has been seen and approved by the Minister (YA & S)

(R.K. Mishra)
Joint Secretary to the Government of India
Tel: 23384152

1

फार्म नं. 1

प्रथम सूचना प्रतिवेदन (धारा 154 द. प्रक्रिया संहिता के अन्तर्गत) वि.पु.स्था.सी.-II

FIRST INFORMATION REPORT (Under Sec. 154 Cr.P.C.) S.P.E.C.-II

बुक नं. Book No. 606 क्रम सं. Serial No. 04

1. जिला : District New Delhi थाना : PS: CBI ACB New Delhi वर्ष : Year 2011 प्र.सू.प्र.क्र. FIR No. RG-DAI-2011-A-0001 दिनांक : Date 5.1.2011

2. (1) विधान : Act IPC धाराएं : Sections 120 B r/w 420

(2) विधान : Act PC Act 1988 धाराएं : Sections 13(2) r/w 13(1)(d)

(3) विधान : Act धाराएं : Sections

(4) अन्य विधान एवं धाराएं : Other Acts & Sections

3. (क) प्रतीत अपराध : (a) Suspected Offence Criminal Conspiracy, Cheating and abuse of official position

(ख) दिन : (b) Day दिनांक Date समय Time
From 2009 onward

(ग) थाने पर सूचना प्राप्त होने का (c) Information received at PS दिनांक Date

कायमी अपराध : Entry No. 04 दिनांक Date 5.1.2011 समय Time 10:30 A.M.

4. सूचना का प्रकार : Type of Information लिखित/मौखिक Written/Oral oral

5. घटना का स्थान Place of Occurrence New Delhi

(क) थाने से दिशा व दूरी : (a) Direction & Distance from PS about six K.M. South West

बीट नं. / Beat No.

2

(ख) पता:
(b) Address Office of Organising Committee, CWG 2010, Jai Singh Road, New Delhi.

(ग) घटनास्थल अन्य थाना क्षेत्राधिकार में है तो थाना -
(c) In case, outside the limit of this Police Station, then

पुलिस थाना का नाम
Name of PS

जिला
District

6. अभियोगी / सूचनाकर्ता :
Complainant / Informant Source

(क) नाम
(a) Name

(ख) पिता / पति का नाम
(b) Father's / Husband's Name

(ग) जन्म तिथि
(c) Date of Birth

(घ) राष्ट्रीयता :
(d) Nationality

(ङ) पासपोर्ट नं. .... जारी दिनांक .... जारी होने का स्थान ....
(e) Passport No Date of Issue Place of Issue

(च) व्यवसाय
(f) Profession

(छ) पता -
(g) Address

7. ज्ञात / संदेही / अज्ञात / आरोपी का पूर्ण विवरण :
Details of known / suspected / unknown accused with full particulars
(यदि आवश्यक हो तो अलग से पन्ना संलग्न करें)
(Attached separate sheet, if necessary)

(1) Separate Sheet enclosed.

(2)

(3)

List of Accused in RC-DAI-2011-A-0001

1. Sh. V.K. Verma, D.G., Organising Committee, CWG 2010, New Delhi.
2. Sh. Binu Nanu, Managing Director of M/s Meroform India Pvt. Ltd./ Ms GL Events Pvt. Ltd.
3. M/s PICO Deepali Overlays Consortium, Delhi.
4. M/s Nussli (Switzerland) Ltd., Switzerland.
5. M/s ESAJV:D Art: Indo Consortium, New Delhi.
6. M/s G L Events- Meroform, France.
7. And others.

~~~~~~~~~~~~
~~~~~~~~~~~~

3

8. अभियोगी / सूचनाकर्ता द्वारा सूचना दिए जाने में विलंब का कारण :
Reasons for delay in reporting by the complainant / informant

9. अपहृत / सम्बद्ध सम्पत्ति का पूर्ण विवरण : (यदि आवश्यक हो तो अलग से पन्ना संलग्न करें)
Particulars of properties Stolen (Attach separate sheet, if necessary)

10. अपहृत / सम्बद्ध सम्पत्ति का कुल मूल्य :
Total value of property stolen

11. मर्ग / अकाल मृत्यु सूचना क्रमांक :
Inquest Report / U.D. case No. if any

12. प्रथम सूचना विवरण :- (यदि आवश्यक हो तो अलग से पन्ना संलग्न करें)
First Information contents (Attach separate sheet, if required)

A reliable source information has been received to the effect that during 2009-2010, Shri V K Verma, Director General, Organizing Committee (OC), Commonwealth Games 2010 and other officials of OC entered into a criminal conspiracy with Shri Binu Nanu, Managing Director of M/s Meroform India Pvt Ltd / M/s GL Events Pvt Ltd; and others to cause undue benefit to M/s GL Events - Meroform, France; M/s PICO Deepali Overlays Consortium, Delhi; M/s Nussli (Switzerland) Ltd., Switzerland and M/s ESAJV:D Art: Indo Consortium, New Delhi in the award of contracts for overlays for different venues of Commonwealth Games 2010, Delhi at exorbitant rates. The accused public servants by abusing their official positions thereby cheated and caused undue loss to the Govt of India and corresponding gain to the said four companies and themselves.

Overlays are temporary structures that are required only for the duration of the games and removed after the games e.g. Marquees, Tents, Porta Cabins, Portable WC, Containers, Video Screens, Video Boards, Looks and Images, Furniture and Fixture, Diesel Generator sets, UPS, Cables, Air-conditioners, Grandstands etc.

The overlays work required Global tendering, however, in furtherance of the criminal conspiracy wide publicity was not given. Against the norms of GFR for inviting global tenders, the tender notice was not publicised in Indian Trade Journal and was also not sent to Indian Embassies as well as Foreign Embassies in India to tap potential Bidders. The tender notice was also not endorsed to specialised firms dealing in the subject. The EOI were only publicised on the website of the OC and Indian Newspaper between 5th and 7th of December 2009.To further restrict the participation, highly restrictive conditions were put in the Expression of Interest (EOI), which resulted in only ten firms participating in the tender. The ten Bids for EOI were opened on 6th Jan 2010.

Information further exists that out of the ten Bidders who participated in EOI, six were recommended by EOI Evaluation Committee, on 14.01.2010, for issuance of Request For Proposal (RFP). However, on 15.01.2010, Shri V K Verma, DG, OC, in furtherance of the above criminal conspiracy, arbitrarily selected only the favourite four Bidders namely M/s PICO Deepali Overlays Consortium, Delhi; M/s Nussli (Switzerland) Ltd, Switzerland; M/s GL Events - Meroform, France; and M/s ESAJV:D Art: Indo Consortium, New Delhi for issuance of RFPs after rejecting the Bids of remaining two companies for shortcomings which were also present in the Bids of the selected four companies.

Information further exists that after issuance of RFPs, the aforesaid four companies submitted their Technical, Commercial and Sponsorship Bids. The Technical Bids were opened on 15.02.2010. The Technical Bids Evaluation Committee (TEC), on 19.02.2010, observed that the requisite Solvency Certificate of M/s PICO Deepali Overlays Consortium, Delhi was not in order as the Solvency Certificate issued by HSBC was for M/s PICO Far East Holdings Ltd and not in the name of PICO Hongkong Ltd, the lead member of the applicant company. TEC also observed that no Solvency Certificate was available for M/s Nussli (Switzerland) Ltd. TEC accordingly recommended that clarification with regard to solvency certificate may be sought from the Bidders. However, Sh V K Verma, DG in furtherance of the above criminal conspiracy overruled the recommendations of the TEC on these discrepancies and thereby fraudulently allowed the Bids of these four firms to be considered for next stage of tender process.

Information further exists that the Commercial Bid / Sponsorship Bid of the above four Bidders were opened on 26.2.2010. The Commercial Bid Evaluation Committee of OC while evaluating the Bids, on 09.03.2010, observed that the rates quoted were very high and that the rates quoted by the same Bidders for the same items varies widely from one cluster to other. The Committee also recommended for negotiations to reduce rates.

Information further exists that the First Negotiation Committee, negotiated with the four Bidders between 26th to 29th of March 2010 and vide a report dated 6.04.2010 observed that the rental prices of the Bidders were very high. The committee recommended for further negotiations by a higher level committee for reducing the rates. It further recommended to alternatively re-invite quick and short dated tender after relaxing the stipulated condition of eligibility of having participated in organising Asian Games, Commonwealth Games or Olympics Games in last 5 years to attract more overlays suppliers so that they don't have to deal with only four suppliers who have shown unwillingness to reduce rates to expected levels. However, in furtherance of the above conspiracy, Shri V K Verma deliberately rejected the recommendations of the first Negotiation Committee.

Information further exists that further negotiations were held by Second Negotiation Committee with the four Bidders. With option of re-tendering already refused by the competent authority and the four Bidders not reducing their rates to a reasonable level, the Second Negotiation Committee was left with no option but to recommend award of the work at the rates dictated by the aforesaid firms. The same was finally awarded to the above named four Bidders on 02.06.2010 on the following rates:-

Cluster no	Lowest bidder (L-1)	Agreement no & date	Contract price (Rs.) excluding service tax	Contract Price including service tax (Rs.)
I	M/s PICO Deepali Overlays Consortium, Delhi	OCCWG/OVL/100-PICO/2010 dt 2.06.10	1239597128	136.73 Crores
II	M/s Nussli (Switzerland) Ltd., Switzerland	OCCWG/OVL/099-Nussli/2010 dt 2.06.10	574777574	63.40 Crores

III	M/s GL Events - Meroform, France	OCCWG/OVL/098-GL/2010 dt 2.06.10	776310843	85.63 Crores
IV	M/s Nussli (Switzerland) Ltd., Switzerland	OCCWG/OVL/099-Nussli/2010 dt 2.06.10	704221779	77.68 Crores
V	M/s ESAJV:D Art: Indo Consortium, New Delhi	OCCWG/OVL/097-ESAJV/2010 dt 2.06.10	842586312	92.94 Crores
VI	M/s PICO Deepali Overlays Consortium, Delhi	OCCWG/OVL/100-PICO/2010 dt 2.06.10	852455662	94.03 Crores
VII	M/s GL Events - Meroform, France	OCCWG/OVL/098-GL/2010 dt 2.06.10	723649986	79.82 Crores
	Total		5713599284	630.23 Crores

Due to Collusive bidding, unrealistically high rates were quoted by the bidders and the accused public servants deliberately refrained from ascertaining the reasonable rates of these overlays. The accused officials of OC in collusion with the accused Bidders also curtailed the competition and thereby facilitated award of these contracts at exorbitant rates causing huge financial loss to the govt. For example, the "Surge Protector" has been awarded at rates ranging between Rs. 616/- to 31,551/-. Rates for demolition of walls have been awarded ranging from Rs. 98/- to Rs. 13,368/- per cubic mtr. Garbage solid waste bags have been ordered at Rs.4 per unit to Rs. 3068/- per unit. Tissue rolls are awarded at Rs. 22/- to Rs. 3751/- per unit. The rental charge for award of air conditioning at Rs. 1,32,759/- per ton were much higher than the purchase cost of AC at Rs. 10000-15000/- per ton. The rental charge for refrigerators at Rs. 17,407/- to Rs. 38,261/- was much higher than its purchase price between Rs. 9500/- to Rs. 12889/-. Information further reveals that the rental charges for Marquees, tents and pre fabricated structure at Rs. 24,500/-, Rs. 35,623/- and Rs. 55,852/- per sq. mtr respectively were even more than construction cost of permanent structure. Water dispensers were ordered at rates as high as Rs. 32,986/- per unit and the same were not even used as water bottles were supplied by the OC.

Information further exists out of Rs.687 crores approved for overlays, Rs. 419.19 crores was to be spent on acquiring overlays on rental basis while assets were to be created for rest of Rs. 267.85 crores. However, in the tenders for all seven clusters, the scope was completely changed to rental basis without any asset creation.

Information also exists that for the Public Display System, total nineteen screens were ordered by OC from four vendors. These screens have been installed by M/s

MIC Electronics Ltd, Hyderabad which executed the work on behalf of all the four vendors for Rs. 8.56 Crores against which the four vendors have charged a huge amount of Rs. 29.40 Crores. The collusion amongst the suppliers is further manifested in the fact that M/s PICO Deepali ordered for installation of all the 19 screens on behalf of all the vendors.

Information further exists that Shri Binu Nanu, Managing Director of M/s Meroform India Pvt Ltd / M/s GL Events Pvt Ltd, had allegedly made illegal payments to the tune of 15% of the contract amount to the accused public servants for obtaining the contracts for overlays for the consortium of M/s GL Litmus, France and M/s Meroform India at exorbitant prices. Information further exists that the other companies which were awarded the work of overlays also paid huge kick-backs to the accused public servants for obtaining the said contracts at exorbitant rates.

The above facts and circumstances prima facie disclose commission of offences u/s 120B r/w 420 IPC and u/s 13(2) r/w 13(i)(d)of PC Act 1988 on the part of Shri V K Verma, Director General, Organising Committee and other officials of OC; Shri Binu Nanu; M/s PICO Deepali Overlays Consortium, Delhi; M/s Nussli (Switzerland) Ltd., Switzerland, M/s ESAJV:D Art: Indo Consortium, New Delhi, M/s GL Events - Meroform, France and others in the award of contracts for overlays at different venues for Commonwealth Games 2010, Delhi at exorbitant rates. A Regular Case is therefore registered and entrusted to Shri Raj Singh, DSP, CBI, ACB, New Delhi for investigation.

4

13. कार्यवाही जो की गई : चूँकि उपरोक्त विवरण क्रमांक 2 में उल्लिखित धारा(ओं) के अंतर्गत घटने वाले अपराध को उद्घाटित करता है
Action taken : Since the above information reveals commission of offence(s) u/s as mentioned at Item No. 2

(1) मामला पंजीकृत किया गया एवं जांच प्रारंभ हुआ अथवा
Registered the case and took up the investigation or

R.C. registered.

(2) निर्देशित (जांच अधिकारी का नाम) Directed (Name of IO)	रैंक Rank	नं. No.	जांच हेतु लिया गया Took up for investigation
Sh. Raj Singh	DSP, CBI, ACB, New Delhi.		

(3) कारण से जांच के नामंजूर
Refused investigation due to — अथवा or

(4) पुलिस थाना को स्थानांतरित किया गया — जिला — क्षेत्राधिकार के आधार पर
Transferred to PS — District — on point of jurisdiction

अभियोगी / सूचनाकर्त्ता को प्र.सू. पत्र पढ़ाकर / पढ़कर सुनाया गया, जिन्होंने सही-सही अभिलिखित होना स्वीकार किया। इसकी एक प्रति अभियोगी / सूचनाकर्त्ता को नि:शुल्क प्रदान की गई।
FIR read over to the complainant/informant, admitted to be correctly recorded and a copy given to the complainant/informant, free of cost.

पढ़ कर सुनाया व सही स्वीकृत होना पाया।
R.O.A.C.

14. अभियोगी / सूचनाकर्त्ता के हस्ताक्षर
Signature/Thumb impression of the complainant/informant

थाना अधिकारी के हस्ताक्षर
Signature of Officer in-charge Police Station
नाम / Name (Samit Sharan)
(पद)/Rank Supdt. of Police, CBI ACB New Delhi.

15. न्यायालय को भेजने का दिनांक एवं समय
Date and time of despatch to the court

(प्रभारी अधिकारी के हस्ताक्षर तारीख सहित)
Signature of recording Officer with date

1

फार्म नं. 1

प्रथम सूचना प्रतिवेदन (धारा 154 द. प्रक्रिया संहिता के अन्तर्गत) वि.पु.स्था.सी.-II

FIRST INFORMATION REPORT (Under Sec. 154 Cr.P.C.) S.P.E.C.-II

बुक नं.
Book No. **606**

क्रम सं.
Serial No. **02**

1. जिला : District	थाना : PS:	वर्ष : Year	प्र.सू.प्र.क्र. FIR No.	दिनांक : Date
New Delhi	CBI ACB New Delhi	2010	RC-DAI-2010-A-0044	29.11.2010

2. (1) विधान : Act IPC — धाराएं : Sections : 120-B r/w 420

(2) विधान : Act PC Act,1988 — धाराएं : Sections : 13(2) r/w 13(1)(d)

(3) विधान : Act — धाराएं : Sections

(4) अन्य विधान एवं धाराएं :
Other Acts & Sections

3. (क) प्रतीत अपराध :
(a) Suspected Offence — Criminal conspiracy, cheating and abuse of official position

(ख) दिन : (b) Day — दिनांक Date: 2009-2010 — समय Time

(ग) थाने पर सूचना प्राप्त होने का
(c) Information received at PS — दिनांक Date

कायमी अपराध :
Entry No. : 06 — दिनांक Date 29.11.2010 — समय Time 11.[illegible] Hrs.

4. सूचना का प्रकार :
Type of Information : Source — लिखित/मौखिक Written/Oral

5. घटना का स्थान
Place of Occurrence : Delhi

(क) थाने से दिशा व दूरी :
(a) Direction & Distance from PS

बीट नं. / Beat No.

2

(ख) पता:
(b) Address

(ग) घटनास्थल अन्य थाना क्षेत्राधिकार में है तो थाना –
(c) In case, outside the limit of this Police Station, then

पुलिस थाना का नाम
Name of PS

जिला
District

6. अभियोगी / सूचनाकर्ता :
Complainant / Informant Source Information

(क) नाम
(a) Name

(ख) पिता / पति का नाम
(b) Father's / Husband's Name

(ग) जन्म तिथि
(c) Date of Birth

(घ) राष्ट्रीयता :
(d) Nationality

(ङ) पासपोर्ट नं. .... जारी दिनांक .... जारी होने का स्थान ....
(e) Passport No Date of Issue Place of Issue

(च) व्यवसाय
(f) Profession

(छ) पता –
(g) Address

7. ज्ञात / संदेही / अज्ञात / आरोपी का पूर्ण विवरण :
Details of known / suspected / unknown accused with full particulars
(यदि आवश्यक हो तो अलग से पन्ना संलग्न करें)
(Attached separate sheet, if necessary)

1. (1) Shri V.K. Verma, Director General, Organising Committee, Commonwealth Games, Delhi, 2010.
(2)

2. (3) Shri Lalit Kumar Bhanot, Secretary General, Organising Committee, Commonwealth Games, Delhi, 2010.

3. M/s. Swiss Timing Limited, Switzerland and other Unknown persons

3

8. अभियोगी / सूचनाकर्ता द्वारा सूचना दिए जाने में विलंब का कारण :
Reasons for delay in reporting by the complainant / informant

9. अपहृत / सम्बद्ध सम्पत्ति का पूर्ण विवरण : (यदि आवश्यक हो तो अलग से पन्ना संलग्न करें)
Particulars of properties Stolen (Attach separate sheet, if necessary)

10. अपहृत / सम्बद्ध सम्पत्ति का कुल मूल्य :
Total value of property stolen

11. मर्ग / अकाल मृत्यु सूचना क्रमांक :
Inquest Report / U.D. case No. if any

12. प्रथम सूचना विवरण :- (यदि आवश्यक हो तो अलग से पन्ना संलग्न करें)
First Information contents (Attach separate sheet, if required)

Source information has been received that Sh. V. K Verma and Sh. Lalit Kumar Bhanot, while functioning in the capacity of Director General and Secretary General respectively of the Organizing Committee, Commonwealth Games, Delhi – 2010 abused their official position and entered into criminal conspiracy with M/s. Swiss Timing Ltd., Swtizerland and other unknown persons to cheat the Government of India in the matter of awarding contract for timing, scoring and result system to be acquired for the CWG Delhi – 2010.

The Expression of Interest (EOI) dated 23.03.2009 was issued in the Hindustan Times newspaper & Other dailes by Lalit Kumar Bhanot. In the EOI it was mentioned that "This is for the information of manufacturers and suppliers of Multi Sports Electronic Timing, Scoring and Results (TSR) systems for 16 sports events (other then shooting) to be held during Commonwealth Games in Delhi 2010". It was also mentioned therein that indication on eligibility and qualification criteria of suppliers/brands is available on the website of the Organizing Committee (www.cgwdelhi2010.org). The names of brands which have been considered as meeting the laid down criteria have also been listed therein. On the website of CWG it is mentioned that "only Swiss Timing- Omega meets out above all criteria".

The Organizing Committee (OC) of the Commonwealth Games (CWG)-2010 Delhi, issued a request for proposal (RFP), on 1.10.2009 to obtain bids from reputed and experienced companies for providing Timing, Scoring and Results (TSR) system through an open tender process. The bid was to be submitted in three parts viz. pre qualifying, technical and commercial. The RFP conditions were so framed as to further restrict competition in favour of M/s Swiss Timing Ltd., Switzerland.

In furtherance of the aforesaid criminal conspiracy with a view to preclude any other company except M/s. Swiss Timing Ltd.. Switzerland to clear the pre-qualification stage, further alterations were made in the RFP conditions in non-transparent manner on 04.10.2009 on the written directions of Sh. V.K. Verma through his note dated 3.10.2009 subsequent to the publishing of the RFP on 01.10.2009.

In response to the RFP, 2 TSR bids, one from M/s. Swiss Timing Ltd., Switzerland and the other from M/s. MSL, Spain, were received. However, due to the conspiracy to limit competition and in furtherance of the illegal and surreptitious alterations made in the RFP, M/s MSL, Spain was wrongfully eliminated, thereby causing pecuniary benefit to the only bidder left in the fray viz. M/s.Swiss Timing Ltd., Switzerland to which contract was awarded at exorbitant rate of Rs.107 crores. In the process, it is learnt that huge undue loss has been caused to the Govt of India.

The above facts prima-facie disclose the commission of offences punishable under section 120B r/w Section 420 IPC and Section 13(2) r/w 13(1) (d) of PC Act, 1988 and substantive offences thereof on the part of S/Sh. Lalit Kumar Bhanot, Secretary General, OC, V.K. Verma, the then DG, OC, CWG Delhi 2010, M/s Swiss Timing Ltd., Switzerland and other unknown persons. A Regular Case is therefore registered and entrusted to Shri Girish Bhardwaj, Inspector, CBI, ACB, Delhi for investigation.

3

4

13. कार्यवाही जो की गईं : चूँकि उपरोक्त विवरण क्रमांक 2 में उल्लिखित धारा(ओं) के अंतर्गत घटने वाले अपराध को उद्घाटित करता है
Action taken : Since the above information reveals commission of offence(s) u/s as mentioned at Item No. 2

(1) मामला पंजीकृत किया गया एवं जांच प्रारंभ हुआ अथवा
Registered the case and took up the investigation or

RC Registered

(2) निर्देशित (जांच अधिकारी का नाम) Directed (Name of IO)	रैंक Rank	नं. No.	जांच हेतु लिया गया Took up for investigation

Shri Girish Bhardwaj, Inspector of Police, CBI, ACB, New Delhi.

(3) कारण से जांच के नामंजूर अथवा
Refused investigation due to or

(4) पुलिस थाना को स्थानांतरित किया गया Transferred to PS	जिला District	क्षेत्राधिकार के आधार पर on point of jurisdiction

अभियोगी / सूचनाकर्त्ता को प्र.सू. पत्र पढ़ाकर / पढ़कर सुनाया गया, जिन्होंने सही-सही अभिलिखित होना स्वीकार किया। इसकी एक प्रति अभियोगी / सूचनाकर्त्ता को निःशुल्क प्रदान की गई।
FIR read over to the complainant/informant, admitted to be correctly recorded and a copy given to the complainant/informant, free of cost.

पढ़ कर सुनाया व सही स्वीकृत होना पाया।
R.O.A.C.

14. **अभियोगी / सूचनाकर्त्ता के हस्ताक्षर**
Signature/Thumb impression of the complainant/informant

थाना अधिकारी के हस्ताक्षर
Signature of Officer in-charge Police Station
29/11/10

नाम / Name Superintendent of Police
(पद) / Rank CBI ACB New Delhi **No.**

15. न्यायालय को भेजने का दिनांक एवं समय
Date and time of despatch to the court

(प्रभारी अधिकारी के हस्ताक्षर तारीख सहित)
Signature of recording Officer with date

Confidential/By Name

Endst.No. RC-DAI-2010-A-0044/17048 to 17053 Dated 29.11.2010

Copy to :-

1. The Spl Judge, Patiala House Court, New Delhi.
2. The Joint Director, Delhi, CBI, ACB, New Delhi.
3. The DIG, CBI, ACB, New Delhi.
4. The Secretary CVC, Satarkata Bhawan, GPO Complex, INA, New Delhi.
5. The Chief Vigilance Officer, Organising Committee, Delhi Common Wealth Games-2010, NDCC-II, Jai Singh Road, Opp. Jantar Mantar, New Delhi.
6. The I.O.

29/11/10

Superintendent of Police,
CBI, ACB, New Delhi.

FIR Book

1

फार्म नं. 1

प्रथम सूचना प्रतिवेदन (धारा 154 द. प्रक्रिया संहिता के अन्तर्गत) वि.पु.स्था.सी.-II

FIRST INFORMATION REPORT (Under Sec. 154 Cr.P.C.) S.P.E.C.-II

बुक नं. Book No. **1361** क्रम सं. Serial No. **20**

1. जिला : District | थाना : PS: | वर्ष : Year | प्र.सू.प्र.क्र. FIR No. | दिनांक : Date

New Delhi CBI ACB New Delhi 2010 RC-DAI-2010-A-0042 14.11.2010

2. (1) विधान : Act IPC धाराएं : Sections : 120-B, 420, 468, 471

(2) विधान : Act PC Act, 1988 धाराएं : Sections : 13(2) r/w 13(1)(d)

(3) विधान : Act धाराएं : Sections

(4) अन्य विधान एवं धाराएं : Other Acts & Sections

3. (क) प्रतीत अपराध :
(a) Suspected Offence Criminal conspiracy, cheating, forgery for the purpose of cheating using the forged documentsxx as genuine, abuse of official position.

(ख) दिन : (b) Day Date समय Time

During the years 2009-2010

(ग) थाने पर सूचना प्राप्त होने का (c) Information received at PS दिनांक Date

कायमी अपराध : Entry No. : 04 दिनांक Date 14.11.2010 समय Time : 1330 Hrs.

4. सूचना का प्रकार : Type of Information : Source लिखित/मौखिक Written/Oral

5. घटना का स्थान Place of Occurrence : Delhi, London & other places

(क) थाने से दिशा व दूरी : (a) Direction & Distance from PS

बीट नं. / Beat No.

2

(ख) पता:
(b) Address

(ग) घटनास्थल अन्य थाना क्षेत्राधिकार में है तो थाना -
(c) In case, outside the limit of this Police Station, then

पुलिस थाना का नाम
Name of PS

जिला
District

अभियोगी / सूचनाकर्ता :
Complainant / Informant : Source Information

(क) नाम
(a) Name

(ख) पिता / पति का नाम
(b) Father's / Husband's Name

(ग) जन्म तिथि
(c) Date of Birth

(घ) राष्ट्रीयता :
(d) Nationality

(ङ) पासपोर्ट नं. .... जारी दिनांक .... जारी होने का स्थान ....
(e) Passport No Date of Issue Place of Issue

(च) व्यवसाय
(f) Profession

(छ) पता -
(g) Address

7. ज्ञात / संदेही / अज्ञात / आरोपी का पूर्ण विवरण :
Details of known / suspected / unknown accused with full particulars
(यदि आवश्यक हो तो अलग से पन्ना संलग्न करें)
(Attached separate sheet, if necessary)

(1)

(2) - Separate sheet attached -

(3)

List of Accused Persons in Case RC-DAI-2010-A-0042

1. Sh. T.S. Darbari, Joint Director General, Revenue Marketing and Chairmen Secretariat (RM & CS), Organising Committee, Delhi Common Wealth Games 2010, R/o D-I/40, Bharti Nagar, New Delhi.

2. Dr. Sanjay Mohindroo, Deputy Director General, (Marketing), Organising Committee, Delhi Common Wealth Games 2010, R/o 650, Sector 10 A, Gurgaon, Haryana

3. Sh. Ashish Patel, Director, M/s AM Films UK Limited, London, UK.

4. M/s AM Films UK Limited, London, UK through its Director Sh. Ashish Patel.

5. Other Unknown Persons.

3

8. अभियोगी / सूचनाकर्ता द्वारा सूचना दिए जाने में विलंब का कारण :
Reasons for delay in reporting by the complainant / informant

9. अपहृत / सम्बद्ध सम्पत्ति का पूर्ण विवरण : (यदि आवश्यक हो तो अलग से पन्ना संलग्न करें)
Particulars of properties Stolen (Attach separate sheet, if necessary)

10. अपहृत / सम्बद्ध सम्पत्ति का कुल मूल्य :
Total value of property stolen

11. मर्ग / अकाल मृत्यु सूचना क्रमांक :
Inquest Report / U.D. case No if any

12. प्रथम सूचना विवरण :- (यदि आवश्यक हों तो अलग से पन्ना संलग्न करें)
First Information contents (Attach separate sheet, if required)

- As enclosed -

INFORMATION

A reliable source information has been received that the Commonwealth Games Organizing Committee (OC) was created in February 2005, as a registered society vested with the responsibility of organizing the Delhi Commonwealth Games 2010 The Queens Baton Relay (QBR) was organized by the Organizing Committee (OC) of Delhi Commonwealth Games 2010 (CWG) at London on 29.10.2009. Sh. T.S. Darbari was Jt. DG Revenue, Marketing & Chairman Secretariat (RM&CS) of the OC, CWG, a senior officer assigned with the task of coordinating various activities for the Launch event being overall incharge of the conduct of the ceremony. Dr. Sanjay Mohindroo was Dy.DG (Marketing), OC, CWG. Both the said officials visited London in August 2009 and also in Sept.-Oct.2009 to oversee the work related to the QBR and finalization of allotment of work to various parties.

It is alleged that Shri T.S. Darbari, Joint DG (RM&CS),OC,CWG, overall Incharge of the conduct of the QBR Ceremony & Dr. Sanjay Mohindroo, Dy. DG (Marketing), OC, CWG entered into criminal conspiracy with Sh. Ashish Patel of M/s AM Films UK Ltd., London, UK and awarded the work for providing video screens to M/s AM Films UK Ltd.,London, UK at highly exorbitant rates without following the stipulated tendering procedure.

It is alleged that for the work of installation of three video screens at the venue, fake quotations purportedly received from M/s. A.M. Films UK Ltd., London, UK, M/s. 3Dots Vision Ltd., UK and M/s. Movietech Ltd., UK were placed in record. The alleged fake quotations are neither signed by the person who purportedly submitted these quotations, nor have been initialed by the person who received the same. It is clear that Shri T.S. Darbari, Joint DG (RM&CS) and Dr. Sanjay Mohindroo were acting in conspiracy with each other and M/s. A.M. Films UK Ltd., London, UK and did not open any file for award of this work. No committee was formed to scrutinize the tenders, quotations so received and prepare a comparative chart to come to a conclusion regarding the party which is L-1. The work was awarded to M/s. A.M. Films UK Ltd., London, UK which is a small company without any expertise or experience. This is further corroborated by the fact that M/s. A.M. Films UK Ltd., London, UK itself did not execute the work relating to installation of the screens. The same was got executed through another firm, namely, M/s.Creative Technologies. The work was got executed even without issuance of work order.

It is further alleged that the work to be awarded was above Rs.50 lakh and as per the procedure it should have been referred to the Finance Committee of the OC, CWG for approval. However, this was not done deliberately. Although there was ample time to follow the standard procedure and refer the same to the Finance Committee of the OC, the quotations received from three parties by 5th October, 2009 were not processed to create artificial emergency and obviate the standard procedure.

It is further alleged that the entire process of award of work/contract related to QBR has been done in a fashion which shows complete disregard to the rule and procedure by Sh. T.S. Darbari and Dr. Sanjay Mohindroo without raising a formal work order, justification for rates at which the work was to be executed and huge payment were made to the said firm Dr. Sanjay Mohindroo put up a note on 24.10.09 on the writing pad of Hotel Crowne Plaza, mentioning that GBP 146868 had to be cleared immediately for paying the same to M/s. A.M. Films UK Ltd., London, UK on the basis of invoice received from the firm and the same was approved by the Chairman OC and the payment was accordingly made to M/s AM Films. It is alleged that both Dr. Sanjay Mohindroo and Shri T.S. Darbari, Joint DG (RM&CS), were acting in conspiracy with Shri Ashish Patel, Director, M/s. A.M. Films UK Ltd., London, UK, to cheat Govt. of India and by abuse of their official position made payments at exorbitant rates, thereby causing huge wrongful loss to Govt. of India and corresponding wrongful gain to M/s.AM Films UK Ltd., London, UK.

The aforesaid facts and circumstances prima facie reveals offences punishable u/s.120B IPC r/w Section 420 IPC and Section 13(2) r/w 13(i)(d) of PC Act, 1988 and substantive offences thereof against Shri T.S. Darbari, Joint DG (RM&CS); Dr. Sanjay Mohindroo, Dy.DG, OC , Shri Ashish Patel, Director, M/s. AM Films UK Ltd., London, UK and M/s. AM Films UK Ltd., London, UK through its director. Hence, a regular case is registered against Shri T.S. Darbari, Joint DG (RM&CS), Dr. Sanjay Mohindroo, Dy.DG, OC and Shri Ashish Patel, Director, M/s.AM Films UK Ltd., London, UK and M/s. AM Films UK Ltd., London, UK through its director for aforesaid offences and is entrusted for investigation to Sh.M.R. Kadole, Addl. SP, CBI, ACB, New Delhi.

4

13. कार्यवाही जो की गई : चूँकि उपरोक्त विवरण क्रमांक 2 में उल्लिखित धारा(ओं) के अंतर्गत घटने वाले अपराध को उद्घाटित करता है
Action taken : Since the above information reveals commission of offence(s) u/s as mentioned at Item No. 2

(1) मामला पंजीकृत किया गया एवं जांच प्रारंभ हुआ अथवा
Registered the case and took up the investigation or

RC Registered

(2) निर्देशित (जांच अधिकारी का नाम) | रैंक | नं. | जांच हेतु लिया गया
Directed (Name of IO) | Rank | No. | Took up for investigation

Shri M.R. Kadole, Addl. Supdt. of Police, CBI, ACB, New Delhi

(3) कारण से जांच के नामंजूर अथवा
Refused investigation due to or

(4) पुलिस थाना को स्थानांतरित किया गया | जिला | क्षेत्राधिकार के आधार पर
Transferred to PS | District | on point of jurisdiction

अभियोगी / सूचनाकर्त्ता को प्र.सू. पत्र पढ़ाकर / पढ़कर सुनाया गया, जिन्होंने सही सही अभिलिखित होना स्वीकार किया। इसकी एक प्रति अभियोगी / सूचनाकर्त्ता को निःशुल्क प्रदान की गई।
FIR read over to the complainant/informant, admitted to be correctly recorded and a copy given to the complainant/informant, free of cost.

पढ़ कर सुनाया व सही स्वीकृत होना पाया।
R.O.A.C.

14. अभियोगी / सूचनाकर्त्ता के हस्ताक्षर
Signature/Thumb impression of the complainant/informant

थाना अधिकारी के हस्ताक्षर
Signature of Officer in-charge Police Station
14/11/10
नाम / Name (SUMIT SHARAN)
(पद) / Rank Superintendent of Police No.
CBI; ACB; New Delhi.

15. न्यायालय को भेजने का दिनांक एवं समय
Date and time of despatch to the court

(प्रभारी अधिकारी के हस्ताक्षर तारीख सहित)
Signature of recording Officer with date

Confidential/By Name

Endst.No. RC-DAI-2010-A-0042/ 16322-333 Dated 14.11.2010

Copy to :-

1. The Spl Judge, Patiala House Court, New Delhi.
2. The Joint Director, Delhi, CBI, ACB, New Delhi.
3. The DIG, CBI, ACB, New Delhi.
4. The Secretary CVC, Satarkata Bhawan, GPO Complex, INA, New Delhi.
5. The Chief Vigilance Officer, Organising Committee, Delhi Common Wealth Games-2010, NDCC-2, Jai Singh Road, Opp. Jantar Mantar, New Delhi.
6. The I.O.

14/11/10

Superintendent of Police,
CBI, ACB, New Delhi.

फार्म नं. 1

प्रथम सूचना प्रतिवेदन (धारा 154 द. प्रक्रिया संहिता के अन्तर्गत) वि.पु.स्था.सी.-II

FIRST INFORMATION REPORT (Under Sec. 154 Cr.P.C.) S.P.E.C.-II

बुक नं. Book No. **1361**

क्रम सं. Serial No. **19**

जिला : District	थाना : PS:	वर्ष : Year	प्र.सू.प्र.क्र. FIR No.	दिनांक : Date
New Delhi	CBI ACB New Delhi	2010	RC-DAI-2010-A-0041	14.11.2010

(1) विधान : Act IPC धाराएं : Sections : 120-B, 420, 468, 471

(2) विधान : Act PC Act, 1988 धाराएं : Sections : 13(2) r/w 13(1)(d)

(3) विधान : Act धाराएं : Sections

(4) अन्य विधान एवं धाराएं : Other Acts & Sections

(क) (a) प्रतीत अपराध : Suspected Offence Criminal conspiracy, cheating, forgery for the purpose of cheating using the forged documents as genuine, abuse of official position.

(ख) (b) दिन : Day दिनांक Date समय Time

During the years 2009-2010

(ग) (c) थाने पर सूचना प्राप्त होने का Information received at PS दिनांक Date

कायमी अपराध : Entry No : 03 दिनांक Date 14.11.2010 समय Time 1300 hrs.

4. सूचना का प्रकार : Type of Information Source लिखित/मौखिक Written/Oral

5. घटना का स्थान Place of Occurrence : Delhi, London & other places.

(क) थाने से दिशा व दूरी : (a) Direction & Distance from PS

बीट नं. / Beat No.

2

(ख) पता:
(b) Address

—

(ग) घटनास्थल अन्य थाना क्षेत्राधिकार में है तो थाना –
(c) In case, outside the limit of this Police Station, then

पुलिस थाना का नाम
Name of PS

जिला
District

6. अभियोगी / सूचनाकर्ता :
Complainant / Informant : Source Information

(क) नाम
(a) Name

(ख) पिता / पति का नाम
(b) Father's / Husband's Name

(ग) जन्म तिथि
(c) Date of Birth

(घ) राष्ट्रीयता :
(d) Nationality

(ङ) पासपोर्ट नं. .... जारी दिनांक .... जारी होने का स्थान ....
(e) Passport No Date of Issue Place of Issue

(च) व्यवसाय
(f) Profession

(छ) पता –
(g) Address

7. ज्ञात / संदेही / अज्ञात / आरोपी का पूर्ण विवरण :
Details of known / suspected / unknown accused with full particulars
(यदि आवश्यक हो तो अलग से पन्ना संलग्न करें)
(Attached separate sheet, if necessary)

(1)

(2) – Separate sheet attached –

(3)

List of Accused Persons in Case RC-DAI-2010-A-0041

1. Sh. T.S. Darbari, Joint Director General, Revenue Marketing and Chairmen Secretariat (RM & CS), Organising Committee, Delhi Common Wealth Games 2010, R/o D-I/40, Bharti Nagar, New Delhi.

2. Dr. Sanjay Mohindroo, Deputy Director General, (Marketing), Organising Committee, Delhi Common Wealth Games 2010, R/o 650, Sector 10 A, Gurgaon, Haryana

3. Sh. Raj Singh, Director, Organising Committee, Delhi Common Wealth Games 2010, R/o 19/998, Lodhi Colony, New Delhi.

4. Sh. Ashish Patel, Director, M/s AM Car & Van Hire Ltd., London, UK.

5. M/s AM Car & Van Hire Ltd., London, UK through Its Director Sh. Ashish Patel.

6. Other Unknown Persons.

3

8. अभियोगी / सूचनाकर्ता द्वारा सूचना दिए जाने में विलंब का कारण :
Reasons for delay in reporting by the complainant / informant

9. अपहृत / सम्बद्ध सम्पत्ति का पूर्ण विवरण : (यदि आवश्यक हो तो अलग से पन्ना संलग्न करें)
Particulars of properties Stolen (Attach separate sheet, if necessary)

10. अपहृत / सम्बद्ध सम्पत्ति का कुल मूल्य :
Total value of property stolen

11. मर्ग / अकाल मृत्यु सूचना क्रमांक :
Inquest Report / U.D. case No. if any

12. प्रथम सूचना विवरण :- (यदि आवश्यक हो तो अलग से पन्ना संलग्न करें)
First Information contents (Attach separate sheet, if required)

- As enclosed -

INFORMATION

A reliable source information has been received to the effect that the Commonwealth Games Organizing Committee (OC) was created in February 2005, as a registered society vested with the responsibility of organising the Games. The Queens Baton Relay (QBR) was organized by the Organizing Committee (OC) of Delhi Commonwealth Games 2010 at London on 29.10.2009. Sh. T.S. Darbari was Jt. DG Revenue, Marketing & Chairman Secretariat (RM&CS) of the OC, CWG was a senior officer assigned with the task of co-ordinating various activities for the Launch event being overall incharge of the conduct of the ceremony. Dr. Sanjay Mohindroo was Dy.DG (Marketing), OC, CWG. Both the said officials visited London in August 2009 and also in Sept.-Oct.2009 to oversee the work related to the QBR and finalization of allotment of work to various parties.

It is alleged that in relation to the Queens Baton Relay (QBR) held on 29.10.2009 the OC awarded the work of transportation to the company namely M/s AM Car and Van Hire Ltd., owned by one Sh. Ashish Patel, at exorbitantly high rates. It is alleged that the officials of OC namely, Sh. T.S. Darbari, Joint Director General, Dr. Sanjay Mohindroo, Dy. Director General and Sh. Raj Singh, Director conspired with Sh. Ashish Patel, Director of M/s AM Car and Van Hire Ltd. to cause undue favour to M/s AM Car and Van Hire Ltd. in the allotment of the said contract. It is alleged that the work of hiring of transportation was awarded to M/s AM Car and Van Hire Ltd. without ascertaining the credentials/ work experience of the said company.

It is alleged that the work was awarded to M/s AM Car and Van Hire Ltd. without following the standard tender process. The work was awarded to this company on the false premise that it was on the panel of the Indian High Commission, London.

It is further alleged that two e-mails were forged for justifying selection of M/s A M Car & Van Hire Ltd. by the officials of the OC. One of the e-mails was shown to be received from the Indian High Commission in the mail box of Sh. Raj Singh Director, OC, CWG from Sh. Raju Sebstian of Indian High Commission in UK on 16.09.2010 and the same was also dealt by Dr. Sanjay Mohindroo, Dy. DG, OC and Sh. T.S. Darbari, Joint DG, OC. In this e-mail M/s AM Car & Van Hire Ltd was shown to be an approved vendor for transport for Indian High Commission, London.

The other e-mail was shown to have been received from the Indian High Commission in this connection to justify higher rates for hiring the Cars. The e-mail reflected the rates of £ 375 per day for hiring the S-Class Mercedes cars. This e-mail was also allegedly received in the mail box of Sh. Raj Singh, Director, OC, CWG from Sh. Raju Sebstian of Indian High Commission in UK on 16.09.2010 and the same was also dealt by Dr. Sanjay Mohindroo, Dy. DG, OC, CWG and Sh. T.S. Darbari, Joint DG, OC, CWG.

In furtherance of the said criminal conspiracy, Sh. T.S. Darbari and Dr. Sanjay Mohindroo fraudulently obtained approval for payment @ £ 375 per day for hiring the cars for the Queens Baton Relay (QBR) held on 29.10.2009 enclosing the said forged e-mails. It is further alleged that approvals for agreement had already been signed by Dr. Sanjay Mohindroo with M/s AM Car and Van Hire Ltd. on 22.8.2009 for hiring the cars @ £ 325 per day for the function to be held in Oct. 2009. This agreement was addressed to Sh. T.S. Darbari/Sanjay Mohindroo. Sh. T.S. Darbari and Dr. Mohindroo conspired to conceal this agreement from other officials of the OC, CWG to subsequently justify engagement at still higher rates in Oct. 2009 against the prevailing rates approved by High Commission of India, London at GBP 200 per day for the same class of vehicles.

S/Sh. T.S. Darbari, Joint Director General, OC, Sanjay Mohindroo, Dy. Director General, OC, Raj Singh, Director, OC have thus entered into a criminal conspiracy with Sh. Ashish Patel of M/s AM Car and Van Hire Ltd. and cheated the Govt. of India and by abuse of official position caused wrongful loss to the Govt. Of India and corresponding wrongful gain to M/s AM Car and Van Hire Ltd.

The aforesaid facts and circumstances prima facie reveal commission of offences punishable U/s 120-B IPC r/w 420, 468 & 471 IPC and 13 (2) r/w 13 (i)(d) of PC Act 1988 and substantive offence thereof by the officials of OC, CWG namely, S/Sh. T.S. Darbari, Joint Director General, OC, CWG Dr. Sanjay Mohindroo, Dy. Director General, OC, CWG, Raj Singh, Director, OC, CWG, Ashish Patel, Director, M/s AM Car and Van Hire Ltd, UK and M/s AM Car and Van Hire Ltd, UK and others. Hence, a regular case is registered against Shri T.S. Darbari, Joint DG (RM&CS); Dr. Sanjay Mohindroo, Dy.DG, OC, Sh. Raj Singh, Director, OC, CWG and Shri Ashish Patel, Director, M/s AM Car and Van Hire Ltd, UK and M/s AM Car and Van Hire Ltd, UK and others for aforesaid offences and is entrusted for investigation to Sh. M R Kadole, Addl SP, CBI, ACB, New Delhi.

4

13. कार्यवाही जो की गई : चूँकि उपरोक्त विवरण क्रमांक 2 में उल्लिखित धारा(ओं) के अंतर्गत घटने वाले अपराध को उद्घाटित करता है
Action taken : Since the above information reveals commission of offence(s) u/s as mentioned at Item No. 2

(1) मामला पंजीकृत किया गया एवं जांच प्रारंभ हुआ अथवा
Registered the case and took up the investigation or

RC Registered

(2) निर्देशित (जांच अधिकारी का नाम) रैंक नं. जांच हेतु लिया गया
Directed (Name of IO) Rank No. Took up for investigation

Shri M.R. Kadole, Addl. Supdt. of Police, CBI, ACB, New Delhi

(3) कारण से जांच के नामंजूर अथवा
Refused investigation due to or

(4) पुलिस थाना को स्थानांतरित किया गया जिला क्षेत्राधिकार के आधार पर
Transferred to PS District on point of jurisdiction

अभियोगी / सूचनाकर्त्ता को प्र.सू. पत्र पढ़ाकर / पढ़कर सुनाया गया, जिन्होंने सही-सही अभिलिखित होना स्वीकार किया। इसकी एक प्रति अभियोगी / सूचनाकर्त्ता को नि:शुल्क प्रदान की गई।
FIR read over to the complainant/informant, admitted to be correctly recorded and a copy given to the complainant/informant, free of cost.

पढ़ कर सुनाया व सही स्वीकृत होना पाया।
R.O.A.C.

14. अभियोगी / सूचनाकर्त्ता के हस्ताक्षर
Signature/Thumb impression of the complainant/informant

थाना अधिकारी के हस्ताक्षर
Signature of Officer in-charge Police Station 14/11/10
नाम / Name (SUMIT SHARAN)
(पद) / Rank Superintendent of Police
CBI: ACB: New Delhi

15. न्यायालय को भेजने का दिनांक एवं समय
Date and time of despatch to the court

(प्रभारी अधिकारी के हस्ताक्षर तारीख सहित)
Signature of recording Officer with date

Confidential/By Name

Endst.No. RC-DAI-2010-A-0041/ 16322 -327 Dated 14.11.2010

Copy to :-

1. The Spl Judge, Patiala House Court, New Delhi.
2. The Joint Director, Delhi, CBI, ACB, New Delhi.
3. The DIG, CBI, ACB, New Delhi.
4. The Secretary CVC, Satarkata Bhawan, GPO Complex, INA, New Delhi.
5. The Chief Vigilance Officer, Organising Committee, Delhi Common Wealth Games-2010, NDCC-II, Jai Singh Road, Opp. Jantar Mantar, New Delhi.
6. The I.O.

14/11/10

Superintendent of Police,
CBI, ACB, New Delhi.

HR Bosh

ANNEXURE – "A"

1

फार्म नं. 1

प्रथम सूचना प्रतिवेदन (धारा 154 द. प्रक्रिया संहिता के अन्तर्गत) वि.पु.स्था.सी.-II

FIRST INFORMATION REPORT (Under Sec. 154 Cr.P.C.) S.P.E.C.-II

बुक नं. Book No. **1361** क्रम सं. Serial No. **04**

1. जिला : District — New Delhi; थाना : PS: — CBI ACB New Delhi; वर्ष : Year — 2010; प्र.सू.प्र.क्र. FIR No. — RC-DAI-2010-A-0026; दिनांक : Date — 16.06.2010

2. (1) विधान : Act IPC धाराएं : Sections : 120-B, 420, 468, 471

   (2) विधान : Act : PC Act,1988 धाराएं : Sections : 13(2) r/w 13(1)(d)

   (3) विधान : Act धाराएं : Sections

   (4) अन्य विधान एवं धाराएं : Other Acts & Sections : XXX

3. (क) प्रतीत अपराध : (a) Suspected Offence Criminal conspiracy, cheating, forgery

   (ख) दिन : (b) Day दिनांक Date समय Time

   2006 onwards

   (ग) थाने पर सूचना प्राप्त होने का (c) Information received at PS दिनांक Date

   कायमी अपराध : Entry No. : 12 दिनांक Date 16.06.2010 समय Time : 05:00 PM

4. सूचना का प्रकार : Type of Information लिखित/मौखिक Written/Oral : Written

5. घटना का स्थान Place of Occurrence : Delhi

   (क) थाने से दिशा व दूरी : (a) Direction & Distance from PS

बीट नं. / Beat No.

2

(ख) पता:
(b) Address --

(ग) घटनास्थल अन्य थाना क्षेत्राधिकार में है तो थाना -
(c) In case, outside the limit of this Police Station, then

--

पुलिस थाना का नाम
Name of PS --

जिला
District

6. अभियोगी / सूचनाकर्ता :
Complainant / Informant

(क) नाम
(a) Name : Ms. Mamta Upadhyay Lal, Director, Central Vigilance Commission, Satarkta Bhawan, INA, Block-A, New Delhi.

(ख) पिता / पति का नाम
(b) Father's / Husband's Name

(ग) जन्म तिथि
(c) Date of Birth

(घ) राष्ट्रीयता :
(d) Nationality

(ड़) पासपोर्ट नं. .... जारी दिनांक .... जारी होने का स्थान ....
(e) Passport No Date of Issue Place of Issue

(च) व्यवसाय
(f) Profession

(छ) पता -
(g) Address

7. ज्ञात / संदेही / अज्ञात / आरोपी का पूर्ण विवरण :
Details of known / suspected / unknown accused with full particulars
(यदि आवश्यक हो तो अलग से पन्ना संलग्न करें)
(Attached separate sheet, if necessary)

(1)

- Separate sheet attached -

(2)

(3)

3

8. अभियोगी / सूचनाकर्ता द्वारा सूचना दिए जाने में विलंब का कारण :
Reasons for delay in reporting by the complainant / informant

---

9. अपहृत / सम्बद्ध सम्पत्ति का पूर्ण विवरण : (यदि आवश्यक हो तो अलग से पन्ना संलग्न करें)
Particulars of properties Stolen (Attach separate sheet, if necessary)

---

10. अपहृत / सम्बद्ध सम्पत्ति का कुल मूल्य :
Total value of property stolen

---

11. मर्ग / अकाल मृत्यु सूचना क्रमांक :
Inquest Report / U.D. case No. if any

---

12. प्रथम सूचना विवरण :- (यदि आवश्यक हो तो अलग से पन्ना संलग्न करें)
First Information contents (Attach separate sheet, if required)

A letter bearing No. 010/MCD/023-74225 dated 10.02.2010 of Ms. Mamta Upadhyay Lal, Director, Central Vigilance Commission, Satarkta Bhawan, GPO Complex, Block-A, INA, New Delhi, a copy of which is enclosed in the annexed sheets.

010/MCD/023-74225
सं. / No.

CONFIDENTIAL (14)
BY SPL. MESSENGER

भारत सरकार
केन्द्रीय सतर्कता आयोग
GOVERNMENT OF INDIA
CENTRAL VIGILANCE COMMISSION

सतर्कता भवन, जी.पी.ओ. कॉम्पलेक्स,
ब्लॉक-ए, आई.एन.ए., नई दिल्ली-110023
Satarkta Bhawan, G.P.O. Complex,
Block A, INA, New Delhi 110023

दिनांक / Dated 10.02.2010

OFFICE MEMORANDUM

Subject: Intensive examination of 'Upgradation of street lighting on roads in Delhi under jurisdiction of MCD, Phase-I' – regarding.

During the Intensive Examination of the above work was carried out by a team of this Commission during October, 2009, it has been strongly suspected that the bid of L1 firm i.e. consortium of M/s Sweka Engineering Works Pvt. Ltd. has been tampered, after opening of bids, in order to increase the quoted amount to avail the difference between the next higher quoted amount without changing the overall status.

2. After examining the said I/E report, the Commission has desired that CBI may undertake an investigation in the irregularities noticed in manipulation of the tender documents. A copy of the Intensive Examination report is enclosed herewith. CBI may investigate the issues raised in para 3.2 of the I/E report and furnish investigation report in the matter to the Commission at the earliest. Following documents in original, as collected from CVO, MCD, are being forwarded herewith for undertaking requisite investigation in the matter:-

(i) Original Tender Documents to M/s Sweka Power-Tech Engineer (pages 1 to 171).

(ii) Original Tender Document of M/s Spaceage Switch Gears Pvt. Ltd. (pages 1 to 163).

(iii) Original Tender opening register (pages 1 to 229).

3 Receipt of this OM may be acknowledged.

(Mamta Upadhyay Lal)
Director

Central Bureau of Investigation,
[Shri Alok Kumar Pateria, JD (Policy)],
North Block,
New Delhi.

Enclosure : As above.

List of Accused Persons in case RC-DAI-2010-A-0026

1. Shri D K Sugan, SE(E)(II), MCD, Ambedkar Stadium, Delhi Gate, Delhi
2. Shri O.P. Mahla, EE(E) (V) (now SE), MCD, Ambedkar Stadium, Delhi Gate, Delhi
3. Shri Pradeep Rawat, Accountant, MCD, Ambedkar Stadium, Delhi Gate, Delhi
4. Shri Raju V., Accountant, MCD, Delhi Gate, Delhi,
5. Shri Gurucharan Singh, UDC (Tender Clerk), MCD, Ambedkar Stadium, Delhi Gate, Delhi
6. Shri Bharat Singh, AE(E) (under suspension)
7. M/s Sweka Engineering Works Pvt Ltd., 254, Vardhman Plaza-II, J-Block, Community Center, Rajouri Garden, New Delhi through its Managing Director Sh. T.P.Singh.
8. Unknown others

~~~~~~~~
~~~~~~~~

Ms.Mamta Upadhyay Lal, Director, Central Vigilance Commission, Satarkata Bhawan, INA, New Delhi vide letter No.010/MCD/023/74225 dated 10.02.2010 has intimated that CVC has conducted Intensive Examination of 'Upgradation of street lighting on roads in Delhi under jurisdiction of MCD, Phase-1. The information revealed that (1) Shri D K Sugan, SE(E)(II), MCD, Ambedkar Stadium, Delhi Gate, Delhi (2) Shri O.P. Mahla,EE(E) (V) (now SE), MCD, Ambedkar Stadium, Delhi Gate, Delhi (3) Shri Pradeep Rawat, Accountant, MCD, Ambedkar Stadium, Delhi Gate, Delhi (4) Shri Raju V., Accountant, MCD, Delhi Gate, Delhi, (5) Shri Gurucharan Singh, UDC (Tender Clerk), MCD, Ambedkar Stadium, Delhi, Gate, Delhi (6) Shri Bharat Singh, AE(E), (7) M/s Sweka Engineering Works Pvt Ltd and unknown others have entered into a criminal conspiracy in the matter of award of contract worth Rs.34,53,68,925/- regarding upgradation of Street lighting of 101.56 Kms roads in Delhi under MCD jurisdiction (phase-I) during the year 2008. The above mentioned accused persons by manipulating the tender document of M/s.Sweka Engineering Works Pvt. Ltd. (L-1) caused undue pecuniary loss of Rs.3.62 crores to the Govt. and corresponding undue pecuniary advantage to the accused firm.

Information further revealed that MCD has 960 Kms of various types of roads in Delhi. In view of the forthcoming Common Wealth Games in Delhi, it was decided to upgrade the street lighting to International Level. It was further decided that in the Phase-1, street lighting of 101.56 Kms roads would be taken up. The Expression of Interest was advertised in National and Local daily vide NIT dated 14.09.2007. In response to this, 3 firms submitted their bids, however, some of the firms could not submit their bids and requested for extending the dates for submission of Expression of Interest documents. Considering the request, second call of Expression of Interest was advertised on 07.12.2007 and date for submission of Expression of Interest documents were kept as 01.01.2008. In response to that following 5 firms submitted their bids:-

1. M/s Crompton Greaves Ltd.
2. M/s Keselac Schreder Pvt Ltd. BP Projects Pvt Ltd, Sevka Engineering Works Pvt Ltd.
3. M/s Bajaj Electrical Ltd. TRILUX-LENZE GmbH + Co KG, POLYCAB cabies Pvt Ltd. Behat Hortivision Pvt Ltd.
4. M/s Space Age, GE India Industrial Pvt. Ltd.

5. M/s SPML (Subhash projects and Marketing Ltd.) Philips India Ltd.

The Technical Committee under the chairmanship of Chief Engineer (Electrical) scrutinized the Expression of Interest documents and selected following 4 firms as qualified:-

1. M/s Keselac Schreder Pvt Ltd. BP Projects Pvt Ltd, Sevka Engineering Works Pvt Ltd.
2. M/s Bajaj Electrical Ltd. TRILUX-LENZE GmbH + Co KG, POLYCAB cabies Pvt Ltd. Behat Hortivision Pvt Ltd.
3. M/s Space Age, GE India Industrial Pvt. Ltd.
4. M/s SPML (Subhash projects and Marketing Ltd.) Philips India Ltd.

The 4 pre-qualified firms were given tender documents and were asked to submit their technical bids and price bids. Both the bids were of single go, i.e. both technical bids and price bids were to be opened simultaneously. In response to this, only two firms submitted their bids which are as follows:-

1. M/s Sweka Engineering Works Pvt Ltd.
2. M/s Space Age, GE India Industrial Pvt. Ltd.

Information further revealed that the work order vide contract agreement No.07/EEE/-V dated 01.07.2008 was issued to M/s Sweka Engineer (Consortium) being L-1 after justification of market rates. However, it has been further learnt that there has been cuttings and overwriting on the following items of tender document of L-1:

(i) Rate of item no. 1 on page no. 439 has been changed from 32149 to 42149. Here the numeral 3 has been changed as 4 and word "three" has been changed as "four".

(ii) In the page no. 438, the rate of item no. 3 has been changed from 23974 to 28974. The 3 appears to have altered to 8. The word "three" has been cut and it has been mentioned as "eight".

(iii) At Page No. 435 in item no. 21(A), the rate has been changed from 215 to 315. The numeral 2 has been changed to 3 and the word "two" has been altered as "three". At the same page in item no. 22, the rate 185 has been changed as 285. The numeral 1 has been changed as 2 and letter "one" has been changed as "two".

(iv) At page no. 433, it is mentioned that if their payment will be released within 10 days after submission of bill then we are ready to give discount of Nil % on the total amount of work. The conditional discount of 1% offered by the agency has been subsequently changed to Nil by prefixing Ni

It is very clear that there is no discount as Nil %. It was mentioned that 1 % of discount would be given which was subsequently change as Nil %. This is further corroborated by letter dated 5.6.2008 addressed to EE, MCD that they withdraw the payment conditions in their tender document with immediate effect. The issue of withdrawing Nil % discount does not have any meaning.

It has been further revealed that the Technical Committee of CVC found that Measurement Books were not maintained properly as the provisions of CPWD Account Code Part 10.2.8(g). The Technical Committee further found that the structure of the post along with its base, bolts and foundations are not technically sound, apparently it can not withstand the load with the said design and can not be declared safe. Similarly, electrical installation has not been checked as per the provisions of Indian Electrical Rules. All these have been done to cut corners to save money and in complete disregard to the public safety. The Intensive Examination Report have also brought forth a number of technical shortcomings in the design and execution of street lighting project.

Thus, it is clear that the officers of MCD who were part of the committee which opened the tender and processed the matter further and Asstt. Engineer Shri Bharat Singh who was supposed to fill in the MB Books, have abused their official position in the matter of award of contract. The accused officials of MCD, M/s.Sweka Engineering Works Pvt Ltd and unknown others in criminal conspiracy with each other manipulated the tender document of L-1 and thereby caused undue pecuniary loss of Rs.3.62 crores to the Govt. and corresponding undue pecuniary advantage to the accused firm. In view of this, a Regular Case against (1) Shri D K Sugan, SE(E)(II), MCD, Ambedkar Stadium, Delhi Gate, Delhi (2) Shri O.P. Mahla,

EE(E) (V) (now SE), MCD, Ambedkar Stadium, Delhi Gate, Delhi (3) Shri Pradeep Rawat, Accountant, MCD, Ambedkar Stadium, Delhi Gate, Delhi (4) Shri Raju V., Accountant, MCD, Delhi Gate, Delhi, (5) Shri Gurucharan Singh, UDC (Tender Clerk), MCD, Ambedkar Stadium, Delhi, Gate, Delhi (6) Shri Bharat Singh, AE(E) (under suspension), (7) M/s Sweka Engineering Works Pvt Ltd and unknown others u/s 120 B IPC, r/w 420, 468, 471 IPC and section 13(2) r/w 13(1) (d) of PC Act 1988 is registered and entrusted to Shri Anand Sarup, Inspector, CBI, ACB, New Delhi for investigation.

4

13. कार्यवाही जो की गई : चूँकि उपरोक्त विवरण क्रमांक 2 में उल्लिखित धारा(ओं) के अंतर्गत घटने वाले अपराध को उद्घाटित करता है
Action taken : Since the above information reveals commission of offence(s) u/s as mentioned at Item No. 2

(1) मामला पंजीकृत किया गया एवं जांच प्रारंभ हुआ अथवा
Registered the case and took up the investigation or

RC Registered

(2) निर्देशित (जांच अधिकारी का नाम) रैंक नं. जांच हेतु लिया गया
Directed (Name of IO) Rank No. Took up for investigation

Shri Anand Sarup, Inspector of Police, CBI, ACB, New Delhi.

(3) कारण से जांच के नामंजूर अथवा
Refused investigation due to or

(4) पुलिस थाना को स्थानांतरित किया गया जिला क्षेत्राधिकार के आधार पर
Transferred to PS District on point of jurisdiction

अभियोगी / सूचनाकर्त्ता को प्र.सू. पत्र पढ़ाकर / पढ़कर सुनाया गया, जिन्होंने सही-सही अभिलिखित होना स्वीकार किया। इसकी एक प्रति अभियोगी / सूचनाकर्त्ता को नि:शुल्क प्रदान की गई।
FIR read over to the complainant/informant, admitted to be correctly recorded and a copy given to the complainant/informant, free of cost.

पढ़ कर सुनाया व सही स्वीकृत होना पाया।
R.O.A.C.

14. अभियोगी / सूचनाकर्त्ता के हस्ताक्षर
Signature/Thumb impression of the complainant/informant

थाना अधिकारी के हस्ताक्षर
Signature of Officer in-charge Police Station 16/6/10
नाम / Name (SUMIT SHARAN)
(पद) / Rank Superintendent of Police
No. CBI: ACB: New Delhi

15. न्यायालय को भेजने का दिनांक एवं समय
Date and time of despatch to the court

(प्रभारी अधिकारी के हस्ताक्षर तारीख सहित)
Signature of recording Officer with date